Meet the Men and Women
We Call

Heroes

Edited by
Ann Spangler
and
Charles Turner

Servant Publications
Ann Arbor, Michigan

Vine Books is an imprint of Servant Publications especially designed to serve Evangelical Christians.

Part I of this book was previously published under the title of *Bright Legacy* © 1983. Part II of this book was previously published under the title of *Chosen Vessels* © 1985.

Published by Servant Publications
P.O. Box 8617
Ann Arbor, Michigan 48107

Cover design by Michael Andaloro

90 91 92 93 94 10 9 8 7 6 5 4 3 2 1

Printed in the United States of America
ISBN-0-89283-703-9

Library of Congress Cataloging-in-Publication Data

Heroes / edited by Ann Spangler and Charles Turner.
p. cm.
Contents: 1. Portraits of ten outstanding Christian women—pt. 2. Portraits of ten outstanding Christian men.
Pt. 1 previously published as: Bright legacy. 1983; pt. 2. previously published as: Chosen vessels. 1985.
ISBN 0-89283-703-9 :
1. Christian biography. I. Spangler, Ann. II. Turner, Charles. III. Bright legacy. 1990. IV. Chosen vessels. 1990.
BR1700.2.H45 1990
209'.2'2—dc20 90-48196
[B]

Contents

PART II:
Portraits of Ten Outstanding Christian Men

ACKNOWLEDGMENTS

Excerpts from the following books are gratefully acknowledged. They have been used by permission of the publisher.

The Helper, copyright © 1978 by Catherine Marshall. Published by Chosen Books, Lincoln, Virginia 22078.

Meeting God at Every Turn, copyright © 1980 by Catherine Marshall LeSourd. Published by Chosen Books, Lincoln, Virginia 22078.

To Live Again, copyright © 1957 by Catherine Marshall. Published by Chosen Books, Lincoln, Virginia 22078.

The poems of Wilma Burton are reprinted with permission of her estate.

The poems of Elizabeth Rooney are copyright © Elizabeth Rooney and reprinted here with permission.

Quotations from the works of Amy Carmichael are taken from copyrighted material and used by permission of the Christian Literature Crusade, Fort Washington, Pennsylvania 19034.

A portion of the material in chapter nine is excerpted from *The Summer of the Great Grandmother*, copyright © 1974 by Crosswicks, Ltd., published by Farrar, Straus, Giroux, New York, and from *The Irrational Season*, copyright © 1977 by Crosswicks, Ltd., published by Seabury Press, New York.

Contributors

Harry Blamires started writing in the late 1940s at the encouragement of his friend C.S. Lewis, his tutor at Oxford. His best-known books include *The Christian Mind* and *On Christian Truth.* He is also the author of three novels, *The Devil's Hunting-Grounds, Cold War in Hell,* and *Highway to Heaven.*

Robert E. Coleman is Director of the School of World Evangelism at Trinity Evangelical Divinity School. His books include *The Master Plan of Evangelism, The Mind of the Master, Songs of Heaven,* and *The New Covenant.*

Charles Colson holds degrees from Brown University and George Washington University. From 1969 to 1973 he served as Special Counsel to President Richard M. Nixon. Colson is president and founder of Prison Fellowship. His books include *Loving God, Born Again, Life Sentence,* and *Against the Night.* Mr. Colson's associate Ellen Santilli Vaughn collaborated on his chapter in *Heroes.*

Elisabeth Elliot is the author of *A Path through Suffering, Through Gates of Splendor, Let Me Be a Woman, Love Has a Price Tag, The Savage My Kinsman,* and many other books. Her first husband, Jim Elliot, along with four other missionaries, was speared to death by Auca Indians in Ecuador. She currently resides with her husband Lars Gren in Massachusetts.

Thomas Howard is author of several books, including *Evangelical is Not Enough, The Novels of Charles Williams,* and *The Achievement of C.S. Lewis.*

Gladys Hunt is the author of *Honey for a Child's Heart, Ms. Means Myself,* and several Fisherman Bible Study Guides. She and her husband Keith are associated with Inter-Varsity Christian Fellowship.

W. Phillip Keller is best known for his devotional commentaries. In addition to *A Shepherd Looks at Psalm 23*, he has written *A Layman Looks at the Lord's Prayer*, *A Shepherd Looks at the Good Shepherd*, and *As a Tree Grows*.

Kathryn Koob was one of two women held hostage in Iran during the U.S. Embassy takeover from November 1979 to January 1981. Awarded a Medal of Valor from the United States Government, she tells her story in *Guest of the Revolution*.

Madeleine L'Engle is a prolific author. Her best-known books include *A Wrinkle in Time*, *A Wind in the Door*, *A Swiftly Tilting Planet*, and *The Summer of the Great Grandmother*.

Karen Burton Mains is the author of *Open Heart, Open Home: The Key to a Loving Heart*, *Karen! Karen!* and *The Fragile Curtain*. The mother of four children, she frequently joins her husband David on radio broadcasts of Chapel of the Air.

Kitty Muggeridge collaborated on a life of her aunt, the celebrated Beatrice Webb. She has translated *La Fontaine's Fables* from the French as well as *The Sacrament of the Present Moment* by Jean Pierre de Caussade. She is the wife of Malcolm Muggeridge, well-known on both sides of the Atlantic as one of the most perceptive social critics of our time.

Malcolm Muggeridge was the former editor of *Punch* and the author of several books, including *Something Beautiful for God*, *Christ and the Media*, *Jesus Rediscovered*, and *Chronicles of Wasted Time*.

J.I. Packer is the author of *Knowing God*, *Evangelism and the Sovereignty of God*, *Knowing Man*, and *Keep in Step with the Spirit*, as well as several other books. He was an editor of the *New Bible Dictionary* and *The Bible Almanac*. He is currently Professor of Systematic and Historic Theology at Regent College, in Vancouver, British Columbia.

Rebecca Manley Pippert is the author of *Out of the Saltshaker: Evangelism as a Way of Life.* and *Hope Has Its Reasons.*

Luci Shaw is the author of *The Sighting, Colossians: Focus on Christ, Listen to the Green,* and *God in the Dark.*

Elizabeth Sherrill has co-authored over a dozen bestsellers, including *The Hiding Place, The Cross and the Switchblade,* and *God's Smuggler.* Her most recent book is *A Journey into Rest.* She is an editor of Chosen Books and *Guideposts* magazine.

R.C. Sproul is president of Ligonier Valley Study Center and Professor of Systematic Theology and Apologetics at Reformed Theological Seminary. His books include *Reason to Believe, In Search of Dignity, Who Is Jesus?* and a novel, *Johnny Come Home.*

Ingrid Trobisch is the author of *On Our Way Rejoicing* and co-author with her late husband Walter, of *My Beautiful Feeling: Letters to Ilona.* Her best known book is *The Joy of Being a Woman.*

Charles Turner has published short stories in a number of magazines in the United States and Europe. He is the author of *The Celebrant,* a historical novel.

Philip Yancey is editor-at-large for *Christianity Today.* His books include *Where Is God When It Hurts?,* and *Disappointment with God.* He is co-author, with Paul Brand, of *Fearfully and Wonderfully Made* and *In His Image.*

Preface

EACH PERSON ENTERS LIFE with an inheritance, a legacy, if you will. Listen to the family's remarks when a baby comes home from the hospital. His dimpled chin looks just like Uncle Harold's. Her delicate fingers are exactly like her sister Ellen's. Once a child was fondly dubbed "Winston Churchill" by loving parents and friends. The child's stubby nose, wrinkled brow, and serious face lacked only a cigar to complete the resemblance.

In truth, each of us arrives in this world with certain characteristics inherited from our parents and their parents before them. This inheritance profoundly shapes our life and identity. And in these things we have no choice.

But there is another inheritance that does come to us by choice. It is the Christian inheritance that becomes ours when we give our lives to Christ and are called by his name. Even so, it is an inheritance which comes to us now only in part. It is a promise not fully realized until the life to come. Meanwhile, as Paul says in Philippians, we "press on toward the goal for the prize of the upward call of God in Christ Jesus."

Part of this striving, this pressing on toward the goal, involves the struggle to become better persons, to penetrate the darkness that threatens to envelop the world around us. It will help us in this struggle to look for real people, fellow Christians who though flawed in heart and mind have nonetheless given their all to God and emerged as individuals who can light the way ahead. It is simply good sense to learn from other Christians about the perils that face us and the rewards that await us. It can be tremendously encouraging to realize from their examples that we can succeed—and succeed gloriously—despite the obstacles.

With this in mind we posed the following question to each of the contributors to this book: "Would you write about someone you particularly admire, a person remarkable for his or her Christian heroism?" The response was enthusiastic—and varied. The contributors have written chapters about missionaries, authors, doctors, mothers, social activists, and ministers. As varied as the circumstances of these men and women were, their lives of courage, love, and faithfulness speak powerfully of the One they followed.

This is not to imply that they were perfect people. On the contrary, each of these men and women had to contend against external and internal obstacles—their own pride, stubbornness, discouragement, and doubts. But through it all God has made them better persons, stronger Christians, heroes to be followed.

Dwight Moody said, "Character is what you are in the dark." Certainly many of these people faced the darkest circumstances, and the contributors have not tried to hide the dark or to magnify the light in the lives of those they write about. Their goal was only to tell the truth. As a result, we learn not only about the men and women whose stories they tell but also about the authors themselves—their hopes, struggles, and deepest ideals. As Rebecca Pippert puts it, "The underlying assumption of this book is that in addition to needing heroes and role-models we must be ones for others."

This, then, is the inheritance we share and, through the grace of God, pass on to others.

THE EDITORS

Part One

Portraits of Ten Outstanding Christian Women

ONE

Mother Teresa of Calcutta

by Kitty Muggeridge

SHE WAS TINY and her white sari, edged with blue, framed a shrewd face with a mischievous smile and serious grey eyes. She spoke of love and suffering in the slums of Calcutta and of meeting Jesus there. When she was not speaking herself, she listened humbly, her head bent, her hands folded, her eyes closed as though in prayer. It was 1967 and Mother Teresa was being interviewed on BBC television by my husband Malcolm.

At first, he said, the tape was considered unimpressive and disappointing. However, when it was shown on a Sunday evening, the response was immediate and enthusiastic. "It was greater than I have ever known to any comparable programme," he wrote later on. "Both in mail and in contributions of money for Mother Teresa's work; from young and old, rich and poor, educated and uneducated. All of them said approximately the same thing: 'This woman spoke to me as no one ever has and I feel I must help her.'" Mother Teresa had captivated her audience. "She has no exceptional gift of eloquence or charisma," Malcolm explained. "It might indeed be said that her ordinariness itself was a kind of rare beauty, as her homilies are, in their simplicity and sincerity, a kind of rare eloquence."

Although this was her first public appearance in the West, she had been known for some years in India for her work among the poor of Calcutta. The success of this first television appearance in England led to the BBC arranging for the television producer, Peter Chafer, to go to Calcutta with Malcolm to make a film of her work there. "We will do something beautiful for God," she said, thus providing the title. The temple of Kali, the Hindu Goddess, renamed the House of the Dying, where Mother Teresa and her sisters brought the sick and dying in off the streets, was so dark that the cameraman, Ken MacMillan, insisted that there could be no question of filming there. However, he was persuaded to have a try, taking, as a precaution, shots of some of the sick people lying outside the temple. When the film was processed, the shots in the temple were bathed in a beautiful soft light and the shots outside appeared blurred and unuseable. No one could account for it. Ken, a sceptic, could not believe his eyes. As often with Mother Teresa, God had done something beautiful for her. A miracle had happened. Later, the book *Something Beautiful for God* was published. The author cannot remember taking any part in writing it except that he held the pen. The words were Mother Teresa's. But she herself says that she is only "a little pencil in God's hands," which must be the reason why this slender volume has been translated into many foreign languages and has continued to earn money for her work. Since then, many miracles have happened.

Mother Teresa was born in 1910 in Yugoslavia and christened Gonxha. She had one sister, Aga, born in 1905, and one brother, Lazar, two years younger then herself and now her only living, close relative. Her parents, Nicola and Dronda Bojaxhui, were Albanians who settled in Skopije, a town in a part of Albania annexed by Yugoslavia in 1909. Her father was a merchant builder and an Albanian nationalist, active in the prevailing political strife, fighting on the side dedicated to restoring independence for his country. Her mother was a pious Catholic at a time when the majority of the population was Moslem; the rest were Greek Orthodox except for a tiny Catholic minority. She brought up her family in strict accord with Catholic principles. And together they took part in the various activities of their church.

The Bojaxhuis were a happy, prosperous family, full of love and joy until one day in 1919. Nicola Bojaxhui, then forty-six years old, came home one evening from work in acute pain. He was rushed to a hospital, but nothing could be done and he died a few hours later. His son believes that he was poisoned by his political enemies.

After that, the family's fortune changed radically and Dronda was left with the task of bringing up her young family alone and of making financial provision for them and for herself. She soon started a business, with the help of her children after school hours, which dealt in rugs, embroideries, and all manner of handicrafts.

From then on the family became even more involved in their church, and little Gonxha spent every spare moment at the Jesuit headquarters in the parish. This is how her brother describes his young sister at age nine: "She was plump, round, tidy, sensible, and a little too serious for her age. Of the three of us, she alone did not steal jam." She and her sister Aga were both very musical and enjoyed singing in the choir. But what Gonxha loved most was to listen to the missionaries from India recounting stories of their work in the field.

It was about the time of her twelfth birthday that she first felt called to become a missionary. She said nothing about this at the time and continued studying until she completed high school. Then, at eighteen she confided in her mother. Despite her dismay at the thought of losing her daughter, Dronda Bojaxhui agreed that she could not object if it was truly God's will. But her brother, by now a lieutenant in the Albanian army, was shocked to hear that his pretty, lively, mischievous sister had decided to become a nun. "How could you?" he wrote. "A little girl like you become a nun? Do you realise you are burying yourself?"

Her answer shocked him even more. "You think you are so important as an officer serving a king of two million subjects. Well, I am serving the king of the whole world. Which one of us is right?" To others she said simply: "I could never face God if I didn't do this work."

The parish priest, whose order was related to the Loreto sisters, was impressed by this devout young girl's resolve to become a nun, and it was through him that Gonxha was admitted to the

Congregation of Loreto Nuns in Bengal. First she was sent to the Loreto Abbey in Rathfarnham, near Dublin, where she arrived January 29, 1928. She stayed there for barely two months to learn English before going on to Bengal. She found herself in austere surroundings, unable to understand a word of English. Life at the abbey was far different than the life she had led in her native Yugoslavia. Mother Teresa admits that the only thing she remembers of her stay in Rathfarnham was the dining room. Some of the nuns who were her contemporaries remember the small, shy postulant who had trouble making herself understood. One nun recalls that the only remarkable thing about her was that she was so ordinary.

On January 29 Gonxha reached India to begin her novitiate with the Loreto sisters in Darjeeling, sometimes known as the City of Lightning. Here the well-to-do would come with their families to escape the stifling heat of a summer in the plains. The convent was a magnificent building, located at the foot of Kanchenjunga, far removed from the poverty the young nun had expected to find. Here she spent two years as a novice until, on May 24, 1931, she took her first vows, choosing the name Teresa, after the "little one not the big one" she insists, meaning Thérèse of Lisieux not Teresa of Avila.

Having completed her novitiate, Sister Teresa was sent to the Loreto Convent in Calcutta, another fine building, surrounded by beautiful grounds in the select district of Entally. Here she taught history and geography for seventeen years in St. Mary's School. This school was run by the nuns and catered to the daughters of the moneyed families. On May 17, 1937, she took her final vows. Eventually, she became the principal of the school as well as head of the Daughters of St. Anne, a congregation of Indian nuns who taught in a Bengali school for girls.

Sister Teresa's room overlooked the slums of Motijeel, and from her window she would often gaze down into the crowded streets. One day in August 1946, she descended into those dark alleys. Standing amid the squalor, poverty, and suffering, she realized that her role lay not as a teacher in the select school for English-speaking girls but here in the slums to live among the poorest of the poor. "I knew where I belonged," she says, "but I didn't know how to reach it."

And then the day came when Sister Teresa heard a second call from God. On September 10, 1946, a day now celebrated by the Missionaries of Charity as "Inspiration Day," Sister Teresa was on her way to Darjeeling, when she heard what she describes as a "call within a call." She was being called to another form of service. "I was to leave Loreto and help the poor while living among them. It was an order. To fail would have been to break faith." She has admitted since "that it was much more difficult to leave Loreto than to leave my family. Loreto, my work, my spiritual training meant everything to me."

Realizing that some medical experience would be essential in her new role, she went off to Patna to take a short course in nursing and dispensary under the direction of the medical missionaries there. Her intention was to start a congregation of sisters who would live like the poorest of the poor, on a diet of rice and salt. They would be allowed to eat what was necessary—nothing more.

Before she was allowed to leave Loreto, permission had to be obtained from the Archbishop of Calcutta for her to live outside the convent and create a new order. Such a request was unlikely to meet with success at any time, but now, on the eve of Indian independence, there were doubts as to whether a European Christian nun working in the slums would be accepted by the Bengal authorities. She had to wait for two years before permission was granted in 1948.

Mother Teresa, founder of the Congregation of the Missionaries of Charity, was thirty-eight years old when she set out alone from the Loreto convent, wearing the now famous white cotton sari, edged with blue and designed by herself, to begin her new work. Thousands of refugees from Pakistan had been driven into Calcutta as a result of the partition of India which took place when the British left in 1947. It was not easy to launch out alone on this challenging new venture into the crowded, poverty-stricken slums. Trudging for miles in search of a home for herself and her sisters to be, Mother Teresa was tempted to abandon her resolve by thoughts of the comfortable life she had left behind. But she never looked back. It was God's will—she must obey.

While continuing her search for a home, she lodged with the Little Sisters of the Poor. Anxious to begin her new work, she rented a hovel in a deserted garden in the slums of Motijeel for five rupees a month and opened a school. Here she taught reading and writing to the children who came in off the streets. With no equipment of any kind, kneeling on the bare ground, she traced out words with a stick. When lessons were over, she made off to the poverty-stricken districts to tend the sick and comfort the dying. At length, through the generosity of Michael Gomes, a Catholic friend, she was lent the use of rooms in his large house in Creek Lane, where she received her first postulant, Sister Agnes, a former student at Loreto. Soon after, ten more followed, all of them former pupils.

In 1950 the Pope approved of the constitution of the Missionaries of Charity, drawn up by Mother Teresa. By this time the congregation had grown so rapidly that there was no longer any room for them in the house in Creek Lane. Father Henry, a Roman Catholic priest, helped them find a house at 54a Lower Circular Road. They were able to buy the house because of the generosity of the Archbishop of Calcutta, who, on the security of faith alone, lent them the money. At last, they were able to settle into a home of their own, a home which was to become their Mother House. For Mother Teresa, fully aware that many priests and nuns had been refused authorization to found their own order, all of this was a miracle.

The aim of the new congregation was "to quench the thirst of Jesus Christ on the Cross." Above the crucifix in every chapel of the Missionaries of Charity are the words "I Thirst." Those aspiring to join the order are required to observe four vows. To follow Christ with undivided love in chastity and in total obedience. To love unconditionally without seeking returns or results. To love in chastity and in a spirit of total surrender. To love in poverty. Poverty is an expression of love; it means total dependence on the will of God. In obedience the Missionaries of Charity dedicate to their Lord their own will, as Christ did, who saved men through his obedience to the will of his Father. The fourth vow, to offer wholehearted, free service to the poorest of the poor, is special to the order.

The sisters observe their vows enthusiastically, living as the poor live, eating no more than they do, owning the barest necessities—a thin mattress, a pair of sandals, two cotton saris, underwear, and a pail to wash in. The one exception is the crucifix pinned to their left shoulder as a reminder of the sacrificial love of Jesus suffering on the cross. "Poverty," says Mother Teresa, "is our only safeguard. We do not want to begin by serving the poor only to end up by unconsciously serving the rich. . . . In order to understand and help those who have nothing we must live like them."

The day begins for the sisters at 4:30 in the morning with Mass followed by a half hour of meditation and morning prayer. Prayers continue in the afternoon, followed in the evening by a full hour of adoration. Echoing the words of St. Paul, Mother Teresa tells her sisters that they must see Jesus and love him in all people. The more repugnant the person, the greater must be their faith, love, and cheerful devotion in ministering to the Lord, however distressing his disguise. They are also enjoined to laugh. "Laughter is a way of communicating joy, and joy is a net of love by which we can catch souls." This is the spirit in which the nuns trip off smiling to run about the dark, squalid slums, to tend the sick and dying and bathe the maggot-infested sores of emaciated bodies. They have become known by some as the running nuns.

When Mother Teresa first moved into the new home, it seemed too big. But the congregation was expanding rapidly, and soon it was filled with new postulants and sister houses were being opened in many parts of India.

Already, in Calcutta, bridge-playing mem-sahibs and high-caste Indian ladies were leaving their elegant drawing rooms to join the sisters in their work among the poor and destitute and the outcast untouchables. By 1954, refugees were pouring into the town from East Pakistan. Hospitals and prisons were dangerously over-crowded; starving families made their homes on station platforms; the dead and dying lay about the streets; children and lepers picked their way among them, scavenging for food. But Mother Teresa and her sisters went out each morning, smiling their way through the filth, picking babies, dead and alive, out of dustbins, rescuing the abandoned and destitute to bring them to the deserted temple of Kali, the home for the dying which the health authorities had already made available for them. The old Hindu monks were not happy about this. One of them who had tried to get the sisters out told the monks: "I promised I would get these women out of the temple and I shall . . . but . . . I shall not get them out of this place before your mothers and sisters do the work these nuns are doing."

The sisters continued to bring the sick and dying either to be tenderly nursed back to health or to draw their last breath, held in loving arms, closing their eyes on a smiling human face. Hindu, Moslem, Buddhist, Catholic and Protestant alike are helped to die in peace with God, "like Angels."

Mother Teresa dispels all fear of death. "Dying is just going home to God," she says. She was asked once to pray for the late Barbara Ward, who was mortally ill. "Your name is up on the wall," she wrote, "and the whole house will pray for you, including me. St. Peter will be surprised at the avalanche of prayers for you and will, I'm sure, make you well again soon. Maybe, though, you are ready to go home to God. If so, he will be very happy to open the door for you and let you in for eternity. P.S. If you do go home before me, give Jesus and His Mother my love." Who would not look forward joyfully to such a welcome?

In 1963, the Congregation of the Missionary Brothers was formed, headed by Brother Andrew, a Jesuit, and the House of the Dying was handed over to them. Some of the work done was considered more suited to men than to women, but the new order has always remained closely associated with the sisters.

In 1955 the first of many children's homes, Shishu Bhavan, was opened, close to the Mother House in Circular Road, which became the refuge for unwanted babies, abandoned waifs, and starving children brought by mothers who had no food for them. None were refused, none died uncared for or unloved. Many grew up to be adopted or fostered. In the film *Something Beautiful for God,* Mother Teresa is seen holding a tiny human curved in the palm of her hand. "See," she cries exultantly, "there's life in her!" The assumptions of over-population are nonsensical to her and she refuses to countenance abortion.

The sisters had already installed a group of lepers on some unused railway property from which the authorities were ashamed to expel them. Their first leper colony, Shantinagar, was officially opened in 1957, and a fund was started to support it. The collection boxes were inscribed with these words: "Touch a leper with your compassion." Someone remarked: "I wouldn't touch a leper for a thousand pounds." Mother Teresa's prompt reply was: "Neither would I. But I would be willing to touch him for the love of God."

Politics are irrelevant for Mother Teresa. "There are those," she says, "who struggle for justice in the world and for human rights and try to change structures. . . . Our mission is to look at the problem individually. If a person feels that God wants him to pledge for the collective change of the social structures, this is a question between him and God." For her, revolution "comes from God and is made of love." Mother Teresa is not a woman who judges others. The harshest comment she ever makes about even the most villainous person is that she has met "Jesus in a *very* distressing disguise." And so the Missionaries of Charity have opened houses in the third world, among the victims of want and despair, and in the West, among the victims of consumerism who are suffering from surfeit and in even greater need of their loving care. They have also opened houses in communist countries such as East Germany and Yugoslavia, and in South America, and, indeed, in countries all over the world. The one exception is Belfast, Northern Ireland, where, after a short stay, the sisters were asked to leave. As it happened, Mother Teresa, as always on the lookout for where her sisters might be needed, had just applied for permission from Haile Selassie for her Missionaries of Charity to work in Ethiopia, which was suffering from a disastrous drought at the time. Before this was granted, she was asked these questions:

"What do you want from the Government?"

"Nothing. I have only come to offer my sisters to work among the poorest suffering people."

"What will your sisters do?"

"We give wholehearted free service to the poorest of the poor."

"What qualifications do you have?"

"We try to bring tender love and compassion to the unwanted and the unloved."

"I see you have quite a different approach. Do you preach to the people, trying to convert them?"

"Our work of love reveals to the suffering poor the love of God for them."

In the short interview that followed, the eighty-year-old Emperor's response was: "I have heard about the good work you do. I am very happy you have come. Yes, let your sisters come to Ethiopia."

So Mother Teresa was able to write to her workers in Belfast, telling them that through the intervention of divine providence the sisters who were excluded from Ireland were now to go to Ethiopia to "feed the hungry Christ . . . [to give] His love and compassion to the suffering people of Ethiopia."

It was now evident that outside help was needed to administer the internationally established convents of the Missionaries of Charity. This was especially the case if the sisters were to continue their life of prayer and meditation, as essential a part of their rule as "feeding the hungry for Christ" in the form of the sick and suffering. For this purpose, a secular branch of the Missionaries of Charity was set up to manage business affairs and organize the collection and distribution of the many gifts and donations arriving daily. One suggestion for the name of the group was the Friends of Mother Teresa. No, Mother Teresa did not want friends, she wanted workers. Finally, the name of Co-Workers was chosen, an expression which Mahatma Ghandi had applied to his helpers.

Accordingly, in 1969, The Association of Co-Workers was formed. It is now under the chairmanship of Mrs. Anne Blaikie, one of the very first helpers in the early days in Calcutta. Mother Teresa, however, does not consider the Co-Workers merely an association concerned with management and organization. She urges them to avoid spending too much time on fund-raising. If it is God's will, he will supply the money they need. They are not like social workers, laboring for a cause. They are working for a person.

Because they belong to God, their work is not an end but a means whereby they can put their love into action, seeing Christ in every person they touch because he has said: "I was hungry, I was thirsty, I was naked, I was sick, I was lonely and you took me." They are a "family united in their purpose to come closer to God and one another through prayer and loving service to their fellow men."

Mother Teresa's whole being is suffused with the beauty of holiness, which she shares in common with all saints. She also possesses what might be called the logic of holiness and the humor of holiness. When the two are combined, they have an irresistible power of persuasion.

For example, when her first novitiate was about to open in England, Mother Teresa invited Cardinal Heenan to open it, giving it his blessing. She wrote to him, saying that she knew he was a very busy man with many important engagements. Even so, she hoped he would come, as Jesus would be there. He came. He had to.

Then again, her brother Lazar recalls a trip he made to the Rome airport to say goodbye to Mother Teresa and her sisters, who were returning to Calcutta. He found them surrounded by a pile of bundles and brown paper parcels, bursting with everything they had collected to take back to the poorest of the poor. Excited officials were standing over them, frantically waving their arms about and flatly refusing to allow the baggage to be taken on the plane. The nuns were paying no attention. Their heads were bowed, their eyes closed, their hands folded in prayer. Presently up came another set of officials, who with resigned shrugs agreed to let the baggage through. Lazar asked his sister what they were praying about. "We were asking God to send other officials," she replied.

He also tells of the time when one of the sisters was in a state of great agitation on account of the theft of a large sum of money. Mother Teresa made no fuss. "Why worry? The money doesn't matter. That is not important. Nobody has stolen you. That would have been something to worry about!"

Mother Teresa always speaks with utmost simplicity. On one occasion she confronted the famous French geneticist, Jack

Monod, on Canadian television. While Monod expounded his faith in genes, Mother Teresa, as is her custom, sat quietly meditating. When he had come to the end of his testimony she was asked what she had to say. Replying to the wisdom of science with the wisdom of holiness she replied: "I believe in love and compassion." The professor left the studio muttering that if he saw more of that woman he'd be in bad trouble. He is now dead, and certainly Mother Teresa will have said a prayer for him.

Many books have been written and many anecdotes told about this amazing nun. She travels far and wide installing new houses and receiving homage from heads of state and those in high places, always returning home with joy and relief to be once again with the poor and suffering, whom she loves. She has appeared on television everywhere, has won nearly every known award, and has established convents in many countries. While other orders have relaxed their rules and found it difficult to attract new members, her convents, with their strict rules of poverty and discipline, are overflowing with novices. Mother Teresa's vast organization of sisters, with branches all over the world, is administered without offices or equipment of any kind and with no overhead. Mother Teresa contradicts in word and deed every cherished fantasy and lie of the twentieth-century consensus, fostered by the media in an overwhelmingly materialistic age. Most remarkable of all, while she is hailed by one and all as a saint, neither media publicity nor worldwide praise have falsified or devalued the sublime truth of her words.

Despite her indifference to fame and her deep humility and total surrender to God, she by no means lacks sound business sense. In 1964, when the Pope presented her with the white Lincoln Continental convertible in which he had been touring India, she knew exactly what to do with it. It was obviously unsuitable for her sisters to drive around the slums in; sold second-hand it would not fetch much, so she held a raffle and collected half a million rupees.

Mother Teresa loves to pray. She lives by prayer. Her favorite, and the one which best expresses the aims of her order, is the prayer attributed to St. Francis of Assisi. It is repeated each day by the Missionaries of Charity:

> Lord, make me an instrument of your peace,
> Where there is hatred, let me sow love.
> Where there is injury, pardon;
> Where there is doubt, faith;
> Where there is despair, hope;
> Where there is darkness, light;
> Where there is sadness, joy.
> O divine Master, grant that I may not
> So much seek to be consoled as to console;
> To be understood as to understand;
> To be loved as to love;
> For it is in giving that we receive;
> It is pardoning that we are pardoned;
> And it is in dying that we are born to eternal life.

She has also written many prayers herself:

> Dearest Lord, may I see you today and every day in the person of your sick, and, whilst nursing them, minister unto you. Though you hide yourself behind the unattractive disguise of the irritable, the exacting, the unreasonable, may I still recognize you, and say: "Jesus, my patient, how sweet it is to serve you."
>
> Lord, help us to see in your crucifixion and resurrection an example of how to endure and seemingly to die in the agony and conflict of daily life, so that we may live more fully and creatively. You accepted patiently and humbly the rebuffs of human life, as well as the tortures of your crucifixion and passion. Help us to accept the pains and conflicts that come to us each day as opportunities to grow as people and become more like you. Enable us to go through them patiently and bravely, trusting that you will support us. Make us realize that it is only by frequent deaths of ourselves and our self-centered desires

that we can come to live more fully; for it is only by dying with you that we can rise with you.

These words speak of the intent of her soul, and we listen to them.

Mother Teresa has become a legendary figure. Her role in the world today is beautifully described in the foreword to *A Gift for God*: "God never leaves us in total darkness, at all times and in all circumstances, by one means or another, the alternative to the dreadful assumptions and devices of godless men get demonstrated. Thus, just when it looks as though power is truly the only dynamic in a lost world, a Mother Teresa crops up, with no worldly resources, no special gifts of eloquence or charisma, to assert the dynamic of love. And all the world, instead of ridiculing her and rejecting her, falls in love with her."

In December 1979, the Nobel Prize Committee awarded the Nobel Prize for Peace to Mother Teresa. When her name was first put up the response was: "What has this woman done for peace?" The question is best answered by Mother Teresa herself in her Nobel Lecture, a shortened version of which is quoted below, when, after some delay, she finally won the award.

Having requested beforehand that the usual banquet should not be held and that the money which would have been spent on it be used to feed the hungry, she addressed her distinguished audience, which included the King of Norway. Her brother Lazar was there too. He had come up from Italy to join in the tribute being paid to his famous sister, about whom he had been so mistaken years ago. She spoke simply with her usual unsophisticated eloquence which went straight to the heart of her listeners.

"As we have gathered here together to thank God for the Nobel Peace Prize, I think it will be beautiful that we pray the prayer of St. Francis of Assisi which always surprises me very much and I always wonder that 400 or 500 years ago when St. Francis of Assisi composed it they had the same difficulties that we have today. As we compose this prayer that fits very nicely us also, I think some of you know it—so we will pray together. . . .

"Let us thank God for the opportunity that we all have together today for this gift of peace that reminds us that we have been created to live that peace and that Jesus became man to bring the good news to the poor.

"The news was peace to all of good will, and this is something that we all want—the peace of heart. Today the greatest means, the greatest destroyer of peace is abortion, and we who are standing here, our parents wanted us. Millions are dying deliberately by the will of the mother, and this is the greatest destroyer of peace today. Because if a mother can kill her own child what is left? For me to kill you and you to kill me. We are fighting abortion by adoption, and we have a tremendous demand for families who have no children. We are doing another thing which is very beautiful. We are teaching our people natural family planning. They practice this natural way by abstaining and self-control, by chastity, without destroying the life that God created in us.

"I think that we in our family, we don't need bombs or guns to destroy or to bring peace—just get together, love one another, bring that peace, that joy, that strength of presence of each other in the home and we will be able to overcome the evil that is in the world.

"Love begins at home, it is not how much we do, but how much love we put in the action that we do. To God Almighty how much we do does not matter, but how much love we put in that action. How much we do to Him in the person that we are serving. And let us all meet each other with a smile, for the smile is the beginning of love. Let us keep that joy of loving Jesus in our hearts and share the joy with all that we come in touch with. [And, then with a touch of holy irony] Just as I have said today, if I don't get to heaven for anything else, I will be going to heaven for all the publicity because it has purified me and sacrificed me and made me really ready to go to heaven."

She closed her address with these words: "I think that this is something; that we must live life beautifully. We have Jesus with us and he loves us. If we could only remember that God loves us, and we have an opportunity to love others as he loves us, not in big things but in small things with great love, then Norway becomes a nest of love. And how beautiful it will be that from here a center for peace from war has been given. If you become a burning light of peace in the world, then really the Nobel Peace Prize is a gift of the Norwegian people. God bless you."

And so Mother Teresa flew home from Norway bearing that gift of peace to her people, her beloved poor. It was something beautiful for God.

Brother Lazar returned to his home in Palermo where he has by now retired from the army; but Mother Teresa fights on for her King with her guided missiles of love. And should she be asked: "What will happen to your order when you 'go home,' Mother?" she would say: "God will decide."

Sources

Desmond Diog, *Mother Teresa: Her Work and Her People* (San Francisco: Harper and Row, 1980).

Malcolm Muggeridge, *Something Beautiful for God* (New York: Double-day, 1977).

Robert Serrou, *Teresa of Calcutta: A Pictorial Biography* (New York: McGraw Hill Book Co., 1980).

Kathryn Spink, *Brotherhood of Man under the Fatherhood of God* (New Malden, England: Colour Library International Ltd., 1981).

Mother Teresa of Calcutta, *A Gift for God* (San Francisco: Harper and Row, 1974).

TWO

Amy Carmichael of India

by Elisabeth Elliot

WHEN I WAS FOURTEEN years old, a student in boarding school, I first heard of Amy Carmichael. The headmistress of the school often quoted her writings and told of her amazing work in India for the rescue of little children in moral danger. No other single individual has had a more powerful influence on my own life and writing than Amy Carmichael. No one else put the missionary call more clearly.

Of the thirty-six books she wrote, I think it was the little book *If* that I read first, and found in it the source of an exhortation we heard often in the evening vespers services: Hold your friends to the highest. *If* is a series of statements about love, given to her sentence by sentence, Amy Carmichael claimed, "almost as if spoken aloud to the inward ear." Each page holds a single sentence, with the rest of the page blank. Someone has suggested that the blank space is for each of us to write in large letters GUILTY. I was seared by the words.

"If I fear to hold another to the highest because it is so much easier to avoid doing so, then I know nothing of Calvary love." I was guilty.

"If I can enjoy a joke at the expense of another; if I can in any way slight another in conversation, or even in thought, then I know nothing of Calvary love." Such jokes, such slights were habitual with me.

"If I make much of anything appointed, magnify it secretly to myself or insidiously to others . . . then I know nothing of Calvary love." Every page pointed up my guilt, but every page aroused in me a deep longing to know that love, to be like the One who showed it to us on Calvary, and to follow him.

As a student in college I wrestled with the desperate desire to be married. I had promised the Lord I would go to some foreign land as a missionary, but I hoped I would not be required to go single. By this time I had memorized many of the poems in *Toward Jerusalem.* One of those that became my prayer then, articulating what my heart wanted to say but could not have found the words for was,

Hold us in quiet through the age-long minute
While Thou art silent and the wind is shrill:
Can the boat sink while Thou, dear Lord, art in it?
Can the heart faint that waiteth on Thy will?

There was a strong and practical everyday sort of faith that ran through all her writings, an immediate appropriation of the promises of God and an exquisite artistic sensitivity that drew me like a magnet. I read everything of hers that I could get my hands on, and soon my diaries were peppered with quotations labeled "AC."

She was born on December 16, 1867, in Millisle, Northern Ireland, of a Scottish Presbyterian flour miller named David Carmichael and his wife Catherine Jane Felson, a doctor's daughter. The eldest of seven children, she often led the rest of them in wild escapades, such as the time she suggested they all eat laburnum pods. She had been told that the pods were poisonous, and thought it would be fun to see how long it would take them to die. They were discovered, and a powerful emetic was administered in time to foil their plans for suicide. Once she led her little brothers up through a skylight onto the slate roof. They slid to the lead gutters and were walking gaily around the edge when they looked down to see their horrified parents staring up at them.

She was educated by governesses before she attended a Wesleyan Methodist boarding school in Harrogate, Yorkshire. It was there she saw that there was something more to do than merely "nestle" in the love of God, "something that may be called," she wrote later, "coming to Him, or opening the door to Him, or giving oneself to Him.... Afterwards, when I began to understand more of what all this meant, I found words which satisfied me. I do not know who wrote them:

Upon a life I did not live,
Upon a death I did not die,
Another's life, Another's death,
I stake my whole eternity."

When she was seventeen, seeing on the street in Belfast a poor woman in rags, carrying a heavy bundle, she had what amounted almost to a vision of the things that really matter in life. She and her two brothers, moved with pity for the poor soul, helped her along, though they were embarrassed to be seen with her. Amy described it as a horrid moment, for they were "not at all exalted Christians," but on they plodded through the gray drizzle. Suddenly words came to her, "Gold, silver, precious stones, wood, hay, stubble... the fire shall try every man's work of what sort it is. If any man's work abide...." From that moment, for the rest of her life, it was eternal things that mattered.

She began children's meetings at home, then moved on to work at the Belfast City Mission, where she taught a boys' class and founded a group for the encouragement of Bible study and prayer called the Morning Watch. On Sunday mornings she taught a class for "shawlies," working girls who wore shawls because they could not afford hats.

One brother described her as "a wonderfully sincere, downright, unafraid, and sympathetic sister." Another said, "She was determined to get down to the root of things." Her sister's strongest impression of Amy concerned her enthusiasms. Nothing was impossible.

Her father died when she was eighteen, and the following year brought with it another moment of illumination. At a convention in Glasgow, when her soul seemed to be in a fog, she heard the words of the closing prayer, "O Lord, we know Thou art able to keep us from falling." It was as if a light shone for her. When her hostess took her to a restaurant for lunch and the mutton chop was not properly cooked, she remembered years later how trivial the chop was by comparison with those shining words, *able to keep us from falling.*

Her work with the shawlies grew so rapidly that a hall was soon needed that would seat five hundred people. The story of how that hall was paid for by one lady and how the land to put it on was given by the head of the biggest mill in the city is only the beginning of a lifetime of seeing a Heavenly Father's faithful provision for material needs as well as spiritual. She decided against receiving any money from those who were not utterly one with her aims, accepting it only when it was truly given to God. Amy Carmichael prayed for money and it came. She soon saw Bible classes, girls' meetings, mothers' meetings, sewing classes, and Gospel meetings being held in the hall which was called "The Welcome."

In 1888 all the family's money was lost, and they moved to England where Amy began another work for factory girls in Manchester.

It was on a snowy evening in January 1892 that a call which she could not escape and dared not resist came clearly: *Go ye.* A long and spiritually harrowing period followed as she sought to weigh her responsibilities to those who had never heard of Christ against responsibilities to her mother and, most agonizingly, to Mr. Robert Wilson, one of the founders of the Keswick Convention in England, to whom she had become like a beloved daughter. His wife and only daughter had died and Amy moved into the house. Although the situation was unusual, and not entirely to the liking of Wilson's two bachelor sons who also lived there, she believed it was God's place for her for a time. She loved and revered him, calling him "the D.O.M." (Dear Old Man) and "Fatherie" in letters to her mother. The thought of leaving him was a keen, sharp pain, something she had to lay on the altar, as it were, and trust God to take care of.

She thought of going to Ceylon, but then the knowledge that a million were dying every month without God in China prompted her to offer herself for that land. In July of 1892 she became the first missionary to be supported by the Keswick Convention, and went in September to the China Inland Mission headquarters in London. Geraldine Guinness, who later became the daughter-in-law of the mission's founder, Hudson Taylor, was one of those who encouraged and prayed for her there. She had purchased and packed her outfit when she received word that the doctor refused to pass her for service in China.

It must have been a blow, but did not in the least deter her in her purpose. She knew she had been called, and had no doubt that she would go—somewhere.

She sailed for Japan in 1893 to work under the Reverend Barclay F. Buxton of the Church Missionary Society and plunged into the work with joy, studying the language and adopting Japanese dress almost at once. It was there that she received a letter from her mother, asking whether she loved anybody very much. She gave an evasive answer. This is the only hint to be found anywhere that she might have had a chance to marry and perhaps was forced to choose between a man she loved and the call of God. Of course I am reading a great deal into the few words her biographer uses to cover this question, but because in my own experience it was such a burning one, I often longed to know more. I wished with all my heart that she had not been so everlastingly self-effacing and cautious in keeping herself out of her books.

Within a year, ill health took her to Shanghai, then to Ceylon, and a few months later she returned to England because the D.O.M. had had a stroke. His hopes were raised once more that she would remain with him.

During this time her first book was published, *From Sunrise Land,* a collection of letters she had written in Japan, illustrated with her own sketches. Again she received a medical rejection, and again she faced the unknown, still sure that the Lord who had called her so clearly would open a way somewhere, somehow. At last she was accepted by the Church of England Zenana Missionary Society at Keswick in July 1895 and arrived in Bangalore, India, in December with dengue fever and a temperature of 105. Some missionaries prophesied that she would not last six months. She lasted fifty-five years without a furlough.

Nearly a year later she met a missionary named Walker, who suggested that his district, Tinnevelly, was a much better place than Bangalore to learn Tamil, the language which the mission had assigned her to learn. Walker offered to be her teacher, and so it was in December 1896 that she reached the place which would be home for the rest of her life.

She was an excellent student. It was not that the language came easily to her. She prayed and trusted God for help, but she did what God could not do for her—she studied. She took comfort from the words of Numbers 22:28, "The Lord opened the mouth of the ass."

Amy lived with the Walkers in two different towns, where the number of Christians was pitifully small. She gathered together a band of Indian women to itinerate with her, among which was Ponnammal, who was to become an intimate, lifelong friend. They traveled at the rate of two or three miles an hour in a bullock bandy, a two-wheeled springless cart with a mat roof, "bang over stones and slabs of rock, down on one side, up on the other. Once we went smoothly down a bank and into a shallow swollen pool, and the water swished in at the lower end and floated our books out quietly" (*Things as They Are,* p. 5). They camped near the village at night, visiting in homes or wherever they could find women or children to talk to. Sometimes Walker and some of the men joined them for open-air meetings in the evening.

It was no lark. They found themselves in battle—the Lord's battle, to be sure, but one in which they were his warriors, up against a stupendous Force comprising principalities, powers, rulers of darkness, potentialities unknown and unimagined. She tried to describe it in a book called *Things as They Are,* but "How can we describe it?" she wrote. "What we have seen and tried to describe is only an indication of Something undescribed, and is as nothing in comparison with it." Nevertheless, even the understatement that she did put down on paper was rejected by publishers. It was much too discouraging. People wanted pleasanter stories, happier endings, so the manuscript was put in a drawer for several years until some English friends visited her, saw with their own eyes the truth of things, and begged her to allow them to try again to find a publisher willing to risk it. The book appeared in 1903. Its accuracy was questioned, so when a fourth edition was called for, letters were included from missionaries in India confirming in the strongest terms what she had written.

Amy had a clear eye and a keen ear. She wrote what she saw and heard, not what missionary magazines might have conditioned her to see and hear. One of them, for example, stated that Indian women think English women "fairer and more divine than anything imagined." But Amy heard them say when they saw her, "What an appalling spectacle! A great white man!" "Why no jewels? What relations? Where are they all? Why have you left them and come here? What does the government give you for coming here?"

"An old lady with fluffy white hair leaned forward and gazed at me with a beautiful, earnest gaze. She did not speak; she just listened and gazed, 'drinking it all in.' And then she raised a skeleton claw, grabbed her hair and pointed to mine. 'Are you a widow too,' she asked, 'that you have no oil on yours?' After a few such experiences that beautiful gaze loses its charm."

The notion of hungry "souls" eagerly thronging to hear the Gospel story is an appealing one and perhaps represents a true picture in some places but certainly not in South India, or, I found, in South America. I was very thankful for that book. *Things as They Are* told it to me straight, and thus prepared me for my own missionary work as few other books besides the Bible had done. It told of the great fortresses which are Hindu temples, and of the wickedness practiced there. It told of the utter indifference of most of the people when told of the love of Jesus. It told, too, of the few who wanted to hear.

"Tell me, what is the good of your Way? Will it fill the cavity within me?" one old woman asked, striking herself a resounding smack on the stomach. "Will it stock my paddy-pots or nourish my bulls or cause my palms to bear good juice? If it will not do all these good things, what is the use of it?"

It told of a boy who confessed Christ, an only son, heir to considerable property. He was tied up and flogged but he never wavered. At last he had to choose between his home and Christ. He chose Christ. The whole clan descended on the missionaries' bungalow, sat on the floor in a circle and pleaded. "A single pulse seemed to beat in the room, so tense was the tension, until he spoke out bravely. 'I will not go back,' he said." Though they promised him everything—houses, lands, a rich wife with many jewels—if only he would not break caste, though they told him how his mother neither ate nor slept but sat with hair undone, wailing the death-wail for her son, he would not go back. Later, Shining of Life (for that was his name) was baptized, and within a few weeks was dead of cholera. As he lay dying they taunted him. "This is your reward for breaking your caste!" "Do not trouble me," he answered, pointing upward. "This is the way by which I am going to Jesus."

During those first years, Amy Carmichael learned of the hideous traffic in little girls for temple prostitution. Calling them "the most defenceless of God's innocent little creatures" she gave herself to save them. She prayed for a way—she had not the least idea how it could be done, but she knew her Master, knew his limitless power, and believed him to show her.

She wrote letters (veiled, always, because the things she saw and heard were unprintable then) asking for prayer. She asked God to give her the words to say which would arouse Christians.

> And thus God answered me: "Thou shalt have words,
> But at this cost, that thou must first be burnt,
> Burnt by red embers from a secret fire,
> Scorched by fierce heats and withering winds that sweep
> Through all thy being, carrying thee afar
> From old delights. . . ."

In 1900 Amy went with the Walkers to camp in a quiet, out-of-the-way village called Dohnavur, and a year later the first temple child was brought to Amy, a girl of seven named Preena, whose hands had been branded with hot irons when she once attempted to escape. Gradually the child learned that she was to be "married to the god." She knew enough to detest the prospect and fled to a Christian woman who took her to Amy Carmichael. "When she saw me," Preena wrote fifty years later, "the first thing she did was to put me on her lap and kiss me. I thought, 'my mother used to put me on her lap and kiss me—who is this person who kisses me like my mother?' From that day she became my mother, body and soul."

And from that time on Amy Carmichael was called *Amma* (accent on the last syllable), the Tamil word for mother.

She began to uncover the facts of temple life. It was a system that had obtained from the ninth or tenth century. The girls trained for this service were sometimes given by their families, sometimes sold, usually between the ages of five and eight, but often when they were babies. They were certainly not "unwanted" children. They were very much wanted. In order to insure that they did not try to run away, they were shut up in back rooms, carefully watched, and, if they tried to escape, tortured as Preena was. They were trained in music and dancing, and, of course, introduced to the mysteries of the oldest profession in the world.

Amma's search for the children covered three years, but at last, one by one, they began to be brought to her. Soon it became necessary for her to have a settled place. Dohnavur, which she had thought of only as a campsite, proved to be the perfect answer. Indian women joined her, willing to do the humble, humdrum, relentless work of caring for children, work that they saw as truly spiritual work because it was done first of all for the love of Christ.

By 1906 there were fifteen babies, three nurses, and five convert girls training as nurses. There were no doctors or nurses to begin with, of course, not even any wet-nurses to help with the babies, since it was not the custom for village women to nurse a child other than their own. A number of babies died, some because they were frail when they arrived, some due to epidemics, some for lack of human milk. Amma grieved as any mother grieves, for they were her very own children. When one of the loveliest of them, a baby girl named Indraneela, died, Amma wrote,

> Dear little hands, outstretched in eager welcome,
> Dear little head, that close against me lay—
> Father, to Thee I give my Indraneela,
> Thou wilt take care of her until That Day.

In 1907 came the first gift of money to build a nursery. It was not long before Amma learned that boys, too, were being used for immoral purposes in the dramatic societies. Prayer began to go up for them, and by 1918 the work expanded to include them.

There were no salaried workers, either Indian or foreign, in the Dohnavur Fellowship. All gave themselves for love of the Lord, and no appeal was ever made for funds. When one sentence in a book she had written might have been construed as an appeal, Amma withdrew the book from circulation. No one was ever authorized to make pleas for money on their behalf. Needs were mentioned only to God, and God supplied them. The work grew until by 1950 or thereabouts the "Family" numbered over nine hundred people, including children and Indian and European workers. There was a hospital, many nurseries and bungalows for the children and their *accals* (sisters, as the Indian workers were called), a House of Prayer, classrooms, workrooms, storehouses, hostels, playing fields, fruit and vegetable gardens, farm and pasture lands. It was all "given." The financial policy has not changed to this day. The Unseen Leader is still in charge, and from him comes all that is needed from day to day, from hammocks in which the tiniest newborns swing, to modern equipment for the hospital. There are doctors, nurses, teachers, builders, engineers, farmers, craftsmen, cooks. There are none who are *only* preachers. A Hindu had once said to someone in the Dohnavur Fellowship, "We have heard the preaching, but *can you show us the life of your Lord Jesus?*" Each worker, whatever his practical task, seeks to show that life as he offers his service to his Lord.

The books *Nor Scrip, Tables in the Wilderness, Meal in a Barrel,* and *Windows* are records of God's constant provision for material needs, story after amazing story of his timing, his resources, his chosen instruments. The God who could provide food for a prophet through the instrumentality of ravens and a poor widow was trusted to meet the daily needs of children and those who cared for them, a few rupees here, a few thousand pounds there.

"An immense amount of rice is required for a family of nearly eight hundred," she wrote in 1943, "not counting guests and the poorest of the ill in the Place of Healing. Rice is brought from the fields unhusked. There has to be room for parboiling, drying, husking, and storing. Quantities of other things have to be stored; palmyra-palm sugar, coconuts, tamarind-pods, vegetables and fruit from our gardens, besides the spices which make curry what it is. And there are tins of oil, sacks of salt, shelves of soap. Then there are the miscellanea usually called sundries, such as lanterns, lamp-oil, rope, mats, extra cooking vessels, brass vessels, stocks of pots and pans, buckets and so on." (*Though the Mountains Shake*, p. 233)

"And He said to them, 'When I sent you out with no purse or bag or sandals, did you lack anything?' They said, 'Nothing.'" (Lk 22:35)

Amma was a woman of great reserve. Loving, unselfish, and outgoing to others, she was acutely aware of the dangers of drawing attention to herself in any way, or of drawing people to herself rather than to Christ. She could easily have become a cult figure, having great gifts of personality, leadership, and the ability to encourage the gifts of others. But she held strictly to Christ as Leader and Lord, and "coveted no place on earth but the dust at the foot of the Cross." In January 1919, her name appeared on the Royal Birthday Honours List. She wrote to Lord Pentland, "Would it be unpardonably rude to ask to be allowed not to have it? . . . I have done nothing to make it fitting, and cannot understand it at all. It troubles me to have an experience so different from His Who was despised and rejected—not kindly honoured." She was persuaded at last that she could not refuse it, but she did not go to Madras for the presentation ceremony.

There are a few pictures of her in the biography, but too few. I would love to have seen many more, but she refused to allow them to be taken, and although there are many pictures of the children and Indian workers in the books she wrote, none are included of herself or of other European workers.

Her biographer, Bishop Frank Houghton, tells us only that she was of medium height with brown eyes and brown hair. When I asked a member of the Fellowship to describe her she smiled. All she could think to say was, "She had wonderful eyes."

The light that seemed to shine in and through and around this woman was love. When asked what they remembered best about her, many people answered *love.* There is hardly a page of her books that does not speak of it in some way. Her poems are full of it.

> Love through me, Love of God . . .
> O love that faileth not, break forth,
> And flood this world of Thine. (*Toward Jerusalem,* p. 11)
>
> Pour through me now: I yield myself to Thee,
> Love, blessed Love, do as Thou wilt with me. (p. 69)
>
> O the Passion of Thy Loving,
> O the Flame of Thy desire!
> Melt my heart with Thy great loving,
> Set me all aglow, afire. (p. 83)

When she thought her time on earth was nearly up she began to write letters to each one of the Family, which she put into a box to be opened after her death. These letters are steeped in love. One of them speaks of a misunderstanding that had arisen between two members of the Fellowship, and how deeply it had hurt her to hear of it. "Refuse it. Hate it," she wrote. "It may seem a trifle, but it is of hell. . . . If this were the last time I could speak to you I should say just these words, 'Beloved, let us love!' My children, our comrades in the War of the Lord, I say these words to you again, 'Beloved, let us love!' . . . We perish if we do not love."

The kind of love she lived and taught was no mere matter of feelings. It was steel. Though for many years she made it a practice to give each child a good-night kiss, she also believed in canings when canings were called for, but then she would wipe away the tears with her handkerchief. Sometimes she would pray with the child first, that the punishment might help her, and, after she had administered it, she found on at least one occasion that a glass of water effectively silenced the howls.

In her book about the spiritual training of an Indian nurse named Kohila she writes, "It was when she was given charge of a nursery with younger girls to train and to influence that the first difficulty appeared. . . . The alloy that was discovered in her gold was a weakness which leaned towards shielding a wrongdoer, or even sympathising with her, rather than taking the harder way of love without dissimulation, the noblest kind of help that soul can offer soul, and by far the most costly.

"Once, and this was indeed a grevious time, a special friend of Kohila's caused a younger one to stumble by teaching her to deceive. Kohila's judgment was influenced by her fondness for her friend. She admitted the wrongdoing but condoned it. . . . She forgot her Lord's solemn words about the millstone and the sea. Her sympathy was rather with the offender than with Him who was offended in the offence done to His little one.

"But syrupy affection never yet led to spiritual integrity. And though it looks so like the charity which is greater than faith and hope that it is 'admired of many,' it is not admirable. It is sin. And it is blinding sin." (*Kohila*, p. 75)

Again, in the little book *If*: "If I am afraid to speak the truth, lest I lose affection, or lest the one concerned should say, 'You do not understand,' or because I fear to lose my reputation for kindness; if I put my own good name before the other's highest good, then I know nothing of Calvary love" (p. 24).

One day in 1916 when the World War shadowed them with fear for the future, a group of seven Indian girls met with Amma to join themselves together as "The Sisters of the Common Life." They were young women who wanted to live a life of unreserved devotion, "a life without fences." They took their name from the Brotherhood of the Common Life, a religious community founded about 1380 in Holland by Gerhard Groot. They determined that there would be no line drawn between the spiritual and the secular, for Jesus drew no such line. Amma believed that the usual teaching about Mary and Martha was all wrong. It was not service that the Lord rebuked, but fuss. "The spirit can sit at the Master's feet while the hands are at work for others. Come unto Me and rest—take My yoke upon you."

If a job was to be done that nobody else wanted to do, someone would say, "Ask her. She is a Sister of the Common Life." They were ready to go to any lengths and to lay down their lives for others. They read books together in English, for the spiritual classics that had put iron into Amma's soul were not translated into Tamil. They were single women who believed it was God's will for them to remain single in order to serve him without distraction. Theirs was meant to be a life of joy, with nothing "dreary and doubtful" about it. It was a soldier's life. "The nearer the soldier is to the Captain the more he will be attacked by the enemy." (*Amy Carmichael of Dohnavur*, Frank Houghton, p. 219)

There were no vows in the technical sense. If any of them felt that God was giving them marriage, they could leave with no stigma attached to their leaving, but as long as they were in the group they acknowledged the Cross as the attraction. These were their rules:

> *My Vow:* Whatsoever Thou sayest unto me, by Thy grace I will do it.
> *My Constraint:* Thy love, O Christ my Lord.
> *My Confidence:* Thou art able to keep that which I have committed unto Thee.
> *My Joy:* To do Thy will, O God.
> *My Discipline:* That which I would not choose, but which Thy love appoints.
> *My Prayer:* Conform my will to Thine.
> *My Motto:* Love to live: Live to love.
> *My Portion:* The Lord is the portion of mine inheritance.

Teach us, good Lord, to serve Thee more faithfully; to give and not to count the cost; to fight and not to heed the wounds; to toil and not to seek for rest; to labor and not to ask for any reward, save that of knowing that we do Thy will, O Lord our God.

Amy Carmichael has been accused of opposing marriage as though it were God's "second best." It is a false accusation. She understood the power of the influence of a Christian home, and many of the children from Dohnavur as well as many of the workers have married. Some of these have continued as a part of the D.F. But she believed exactly what Paul believed, that those who do marry will have "trouble in the flesh," and cannot possibly be as free as the unmarried for certain tasks in the Lord's service. Many single women were needed to mother the hundreds of children. As boys were included, men were needed also, but the number of men who regarded celibacy as a divine call was small.

Amma was a woman peculiarly sensitive to beauty, as not only her writings but everything she touched will show. She was determined, as plans for each building were drawn up, that they should be beautiful. When they were planning the hospital, Dr. Murray Webb-Peploe asked if it might be too expensive. She hesitated to answer, but next day was June 4, for which the verse in the *Daily Light*, that marvelous little book of collected scriptures, was, "The house that is to be builded for the Lord must be exceeding magnifical." She took the word magnifical to mean "perfect for its purpose of glorifying the God of love, so that men and women will be drawn to Him. He is also the God of beauty, and it follows that ugliness jars. He has no pleasure in it—nor in dirt."

The long poems, *Pools* and *The Valley of Vision*, contain exquisite descriptions of the loveliness of the world around her, but delve deep into the mystery of its sorrow and suffering,

I saw a scarf of rainbow water-lace,
Blue-green, green-blue, lilac and violet.
Light, water, air, it trailed, a phantom thing,
An iridescence, vanishing as I gazed;
Like wings of dragonflies, a hint and gone—
Discovery was very near me then.
But no unseemly, no irreverent haste
Perplexes him who stands alone with God
In upland places. Presently I saw . . .

Father, who speakest to us by the way,
Now from a burning bush, now by a stream. . . .

Hers was a mystical mind. A true mystic is an utterly practical person, for he sees the Real as no pedant can ever see it, he finds the spiritual in the material (what T.S. Eliot calls "fear in a handful of dust," or Thomas Howard, "splendor in the ordinary"). George MacDonald said, "A mystical mind is one which, having perceived that the highest expression of which truth admits, lies in the symbolism of nature and the human customs that result from human necessities, prosecutes thought about truth so embodied by dealing with the symbols themselves after logical forms" (*Unspoken Sermons*).

She was logical. She was incisive, vigorous, utterly clear. She could write of a "scarf of rainbow water-lace," or she could use words that stab like a dagger or scorch like fire: "And we talked of the difference between the fleshly love and the spiritual; the two loves stood out in sharp distinction. In such an hour the fire of the love of God is searching. It knows just where to find the clay in us. That clay must be turned to crystal." (*Ploughed Under*, p. 187)

To a modern American it seems marvelous that a woman with what would seem to us little formal education and with no "degrees" should be able to use the English language so flawlessly, to shape a phrase so finely, and to write (very rapidly—sometimes twelve to fifteen hours a day) with such apparent ease and fluidity. There is not a word in any book or poem which Amy Carmichael had not bought by suffering. There is not an empty word, a superfluous word, a glib word. Every word, every line, has work to do.

In my recent rereading of the biography I found illumination of many passages which echo in my memory from her own writings. I found the circumstances which gave rise to those writings, the context in which she learned the lessons so lucidly set forth. Words given to her in the heat of battle have spoken strongly to me in the heat of my own experiences. They have been, in fact, the very voice of God to me, alive and powerful and sharp today as they were thirty or twenty-five or ten years ago.

There are markings, of course, in my copies of Amy Carmichael's books, as there are markings in every book on my shelves in which I have found real meat. The Amy Carmichael books in their uniform blue covers with lotus motif take up only half a shelf now, which makes me sad. Some of them have been "borrowed" and never found their way home. Others, to my great consternation, I left in a jungle house in Ecuador. Those I have are well-worn. Most bear the marks of mould and mildew and crickets, but they are my trusted friends. When I was in the throes of decision as to whether, newly widowed, I should take my small daughter and go to live with a remote tribe of Indians, I circled these words:

> His thoughts said, How can I know that it is the time to move?
> His Father said, And it shall be when thou shalt hear a sound of going in the tops of mulberry trees, that then thou shalt go out to battle. Thou shalt certainly hear that sound. [That sentence is underlined.] There will be a quiet sense of sureness and a sense of peace. (*His Thoughts Said,* 16)

I remember feeling doubtful about that "sound of going" in mulberry trees. There were no such trees in our jungle. Of course I knew that the words came from scripture (2 Sm 5:24 AV), but Amma had a disconcerting habit of quoting from many diverse sources, including the Bible, without citing the reference, and often without using quotation marks. It is flattering to the reader that she supposed us to be as well-read as she, and as spiritually advanced. I wasn't and I'm not, but I can testify to the Truth of what she wrote. The "sound of going" was different for her at different times, I'm sure, and the sign given to me in 1958 which led to my going to those Indians was not in any mulberry trees. But I found the promise fulfilled, "Thou shalt certainly hear that sound." God made it perfectly plain when the time came. I understood then her confidence, the sense of sureness and peace.

But subsequent decisions have put me in the same sort of quandary, and I have gone back again to the same little book.

But the son still wondered what he should do if he did not hear a Voice directing him, till he came to understand that, as he waited, his Father would work and would so shape the events of common life that they would become indications of His will. He has shown also that they would be in accord with some word of Scripture which would be laid upon his heart. (19)

That made sense to me. No audible voices have ever told me what to do, but the providential shaping of events and corroborating scriptures given to me at the time have proved again and again the trustworthiness of the Shepherd.

There have been one or two occasions when I have been falsely accused by people on whom I had once had an influence for good. It is a hard lesson to learn, and I am a slow disciple. There is a circle around this one:

> Was He, whom he called Master and Lord, always understood? Was He never misjudged? They laid to His charge things that He knew not, to the great discomfiture of His spirit. Is it not enough for the disciple that he be as his Master and the servant as his Lord? (57)

Amma was visiting one day in 1931 in a nearby village where there had been hostility to Christians. She fell into a pit which had been dug "where no pit should be." The injuries did not heal, and she suffered acute neuritis in her right arm, arthritis in her back, chronic infections, and the cumulative effects of stress for the rest of her life, hardly leaving her room until she died in January 1951 at the age of eighty-three. During those twenty years as an invalid, in nearly constant pain, she wrote fifteen books "out of the furnace," as it were, and the words of 2 Corinthians 1 show a part of the service God gave her to do:

"Praise be to the God and Father of our Lord Jesus Christ, the all-merciful Father, the God whose consolation never fails us! He comforts us in all our troubles, so that we in turn may be able to comfort others in any trouble of theirs and to share with them the consolation we ourselves receive from God. As Christ's cup of suffering overflows, and we suffer with him, so also through Christ our consolation overflows. If distress be our lot, it is the price we pay for your consolation, for your salvation." (2 Cor 1:3-6)

I am one of the many thousands, surely, for whose consolation and salvation Amy Carmichael paid a heavy price. That she paid it with gladness and a whole heart no one who has read even a page of hers could possibly doubt.

As I write these pages, my husband hands me a newspaper telling of the life of Henry Morrison Flagler, the American millionaire responsible for developing Palm Beach, Florida, as a playground for the very rich. In the early 1890s, the account states, he was looking for his life's "crowning challenge." It was, I remembered, a snowy night in 1892 when Amy Carmichael heard the call she could not escape and dared not resist: *Go ye.*

In 1894 Flagler built the Royal Poinciana, the world's largest resort hotel, accommodating two thousand. In that year Amy Carmichael was in Japan, where she wrote,

O for a passionate passion for souls,
O for a pity that yearns!
O for the love that loves unto death,
O for the fire that burns!

In 1896 Flagler opened his Palm Beach Inn, later to become The Breakers. That was the year in which Amma reached Tinnevelly, the part of South India where she would live out the rest of her life of service.

In 1901 Flagler's luxurious Whitehall, a marble palace built for his third wife, had been completed at the cost of four million dollars. In 1901 Preena, the first temple child, came to Amma, which meant the beginning of what would become the Dohnavur Fellowship.

"The Vanderbilts, Wanamakers, Astors, Goulds, Belmonts, and European royalty come to the magic island," the newspaper goes on, "awash in Caribbean splendor and Henry Morrison Flagler's grandeur."

"Gold, silver, precious stones, wood, hay, stubble . . . the fire shall try every man's work of what sort it is." These were the words that had come to Amy as a girl, when she stumbled along that Belfast street with the ragged old woman, words that defined for her forever the nature of man's choices. "If any man's work abide... he shall receive a reward." (1 Cor 3:14)

Like the mountaineer whose epitaph she loved to quote, she "died climbing." Now she is one of the great cloud of witnesses whose course has been finished, and who cheer us on to run the race that is set before us, looking as they did to Jesus, "who for the joy that was set before him, endured the Cross."

Sources

For information about the life of Amy Carmichael, I have relied on Frank Houghton's *Amy Carmichael of Dohnavur* (Fort Washington, Pennsylvania: Christian Literature Crusade, 1979) and on the following books by Amy Carmichael.

His Thoughts Said (Fort Washington, Pennsylvania: Christian Literature Crusade, 1949).

If (Grand Rapids, Michigan: Zondervan, 1968).

Kohila (London: SPCK, 1939).

Ploughed Under (Fort Washington, Pennsylvania: Christian Literature Crusade).

Things as They Are (Old Tappan, New Jersey: Revel, 1904).

Though the Mountains Shake (New York: Loizeaux Bros., 1946).

Toward Jerusalem (Fort Washington, Pennsylvania: Christian Literature Crusade).

THREE

Catherine Marshall

by Kathryn Koob

NOVEMBER 4, 1979—that day news reports raced across continents to reach a stunned American populace with the headline: "Americans Held Hostage in Iran. American Embassy Falls to Student Militants."

A diplomat in the American Foreign Service, my office was only two miles distant from the embassy. The report, phoned to me by an Iranian, was confirmed when I called the switchboard at the embassy in response to reports of student riots. *Embassy Occupied*—these words spoken by an Iranian voice at the end of the line confirmed the incredible truth. An international crisis of tremendous import was underway.

Along with some of the other members of my staff at the Iran-America Society, I spent the following thirty hours operating an ad hoc wire service to Washington, doing my best to keep the State Department abreast of developments reported on Iran radio and television. If we played our cards right, we could keep the lines of communication open for a few more hours before slipping off to safety. It seemed that the militants had forgotten about our office—at least for the present.

But by mid-afternoon November 5, all hope of safety was lost to us. The students came streaming into the building, and we were rounded up and taken by car through screaming mobs and into the American embassy compound.

Thus began 444 days of captivity. These days were not all filled with fear and hardship. Certainly, there was great fear, particularly in those first several hours, as well as hardship, but there was also consolation and blessing, the solace of knowing that God was God and that he cared. In the months that followed, he gave me numerous opportunities to recognize his faithfulness and to be thankful for his gifts, both great and small. Not the least of these was a book that came into my possession six months after I was taken captive—*The Helper* by Catherine Marshall. And what a helper it proved to be! Let me tell you about its author.

Catherine Marshall LeSourd has comforted, strenghtened, and encouraged millions of people who have read her books. This woman, who as a child was so shy that she hid whenever guests came to the manse to visit, acquired, as an adult, the rare gift of opening herself to the world, especially through her writing. In one of her most recent books she says, "Over the years a recurring theme in letters from the readers of my books has been, 'Dear Catherine: Forgive me for calling you by your first name, but through your books I feel I know you, that you are my friend'" (*Meeting God at Every Turn*, p. 15). Her joy has been that "the Spirit of God does reach down through the printed page . . . to speak to individuals in their own difficulties."

Born in Johnson City, Tennessee, she was christened Sarah Catherine, the first child of John Wood and Leonora Hazeltine Whitaker. Catherine's parents were far from wealthy, but they were rich in terms of their love for each other and for their three children, and they lived a full life as they moved from parish to parish in Tennessee, Mississippi, and West Virginia.

Catherine describes her father as a scholar, a disciplined but loving individual who would dirty his fingers in coal dust to make his parishoners feel more comfortable shaking hands with him. His study was the center of their home wherever they lived, and it was always open to the children.

Her mother had a strong and steady influence on Catherine's life. In fact, she was the model for the heroine of Catherine's novel, *Christy*. It would be difficult to imagine anyone growing up under Leonora Wood's roof without adopting her attitudes toward marriage and family and her firm faith in God's goodness and love.

In *Meeting God at Every Turn*, Catherine entitled the chapter about her mother "Mother Never Thought We Were Poor." She compares her family's bounty to Mama's checking account in *I Remember Mama* by Kathryn Forbes. It was a nonexistent fund that kept the family going through many a crisis just because it was "there." Catherine describes her mother's account like this: "Suddenly in a blazing revelation it occurred to me that my own mother also had a bank account that kept us—her children—from being afraid. Her bank account too was real—as real as the mountain air we breathed and the nourishing bread she baked, as solid as the gold in Fort Knox. Mother's family bank account was her faith in the Lord, her absolute trust that the promise of give and it shall be given unto you was as eternal as the mountains around us" (*Meeting God at Every Turn*, p. 42).

When Catherine reached the age of seven, the Wood family grew with the arrival of a baby brother, Bob. Fourteen months later, a sister, Emmy, completed the family picture. Theirs was a "normal" family, deeply attached to one another, but not above the tensions, rebellions, anxieties, and problems that face all families. Inevitably the children played pranks and the parents lost their tempers and made an occasional unwise decision. But these momentary lapses were overshadowed by the strong, deep, mutual love that was expressed for one another and was a reflection of the love of Christ for each of his lambs.

Catherine's deep and abiding faith in the goodness of God—his ability to turn tragedy into promise—and his faithfulness began here, in this home. As a child she wondered at the source of her mother's strength and discovered that it was grounded in prayer. Determined that she, too, would know God's presence and love, Catherine asked her father if she could "join the church." She found that more was required than simply belonging to an organization; she must commit her whole life. When she gave it, she gave spontaneously and with deep conviction. Her future was in God's hands.

Encouraged to do her best at whatever she tried, Catherine decided to go to college. But it wasn't until she was accepted by the school of her choice, Agnes Scott College in Decatur, Georgia, that she realized there was not enough money to pay her tuition. Discouraged by this sudden insight, she threw herself across her bed, weeping tears of bitter regret. Her mother found her there and together they committed the problem to the Lord. Both parents decided that she should plan to go anyway. Almost miraculously, funds became available and Catherine went off to study.

During the years in Atlanta, she gave expression to a long-felt ambition to write. She steeped herself in literature and composition courses and began keeping a journal in earnest. "In it I would try to put down as accurately and memorably as I could my deepest feelings and reactions to life. A great earnestness about this had carried me through four years and several volumes." (*To Live Again*, p. 73)

While at Agnes Scott she met the pastor of Westminster Church—a popular young bachelor preacher. His name was Peter Marshall. The ensuing romance wasn't without its rough spots, at least from Catherine's point of view. On two different occasions she left Atlanta for summer vacation, determined to put the intriguing Peter Marshall out of her mind. But her efforts failed. Finally, during her senior year, he proposed to her and she accepted. They were married in November of 1936 and immediately moved to Peter's new parish in Washington, D.C.

It must have been a startling change for the young college graduate, barely out of her teens, to move from the campus of a fine women's school to the manse of one of the nation's most prestigious churches. But she did it graciously. She and Peter had committed their marriage to the Lord long before the ceremony ever took place. Determined to seek his will in their lives, they were sure that he would guide them in this venture.

Life in the manse was not unfamiliar to Catherine. She had lived in one all her life. But the duties incumbent on a minister's wife in the small southern congregations where she had grown up must have been far different than those in a large, metropolitan congregation. Yet, with the help of good friends, Peter's love for her, and her own background of love and good breeding, she bridged that chasm and the years of their Washington, D.C., ministry at New York Avenue Presbyterian Church were filled to overflowing.

Three years after their marriage, a son, Peter John, was born to them. By now Peter Marshall had become one of the nation's most influential ministers. He was the confidant of senators and congressmen and had been invited to become the chaplain of the United States Senate. He traveled across the country preaching and teaching. His presence at the New York Avenue church had resulted in expanded programs there. Life was full and busy.

Then, without warning, illness struck. The doctors could not diagnose Catherine's lung problem. Possibly tuberculosis. If so, it was not infectious, but it required total bed rest. This was a blow to Catherine, by now an active wife and mother. Yet she had no choice, and instead of the three or four months of immobility predicted by the doctor, she had to fight against the disease for almost two years.

Yet the time was not lost. She calls this period a time of "continuation in depth of the voyage of self-discovery and God-discovery begun in college" (*Meeting God at Every Turn*, p. 86). The most dramatic of these discoveries was the special power of the prayer of relinquishment. Catherine spent considerable time reading and studying what the Bible had to say about healing, and she prayed regularly to be healed. But her prayers seemed to go unanswered, and she became discouraged. Would she never again resume her activities as mother and wife? How could she face such a prospect?

In the midst of her discouragement she picked up the story of a missionary who had been ill for eight years. In a last, futile gesture, the missionary had given up everything to the Lord, including her wish to be well. This prayer of relinquishment inspired Catherine Marshall, and she prayed her own prayer: "I'm beaten, finished. God, You decide what You want for me." (*Adventures in Prayer*, p. 61)

The experience that followed is one that she relates in detail in

A Man Called Peter. Later that night she wakened. "Past all credible belief, suddenly, unaccountably, Christ was there, in Person, standing by the right side of my bed. I could see nothing but that deep, velvety blackness, but the bedroom was filled with an intensity of power, as if the Dynamo of the Universe was there. Every nerve in my body tingled with it, as with a shock of electricity. I knew that Jesus was smiling at me tenderly, lovingly, whimsically—a trifle amused at my too-intense seriousness about myself." (p. 168)

She was told to go and tell her mother about her experience, and she followed her Lord's command. The next step was to wait and see what the X-rays would reveal. Usually she awaited this test with anxiety. But not now. Perhaps she sensed that the healing process had begun. Her return to health was not instantaneous, but the X-rays indicated that real progress was being made against the disease. Slowly but surely Catherine Marshall was mending.

Prior to this extraordinary nighttime experience, she had been no stranger to the Lord and to his works and ways. Yet, this moment was so special that the memory of it must often have given her confidence and courage to strike out in new directions—to undertake the impossible and to rest secure in his wisdom during the storms of her lifetime.

The presence of God does not always seem as real as it did to Catherine Marshall that night, but the memory of that reality can give inspiration and courage long after the event.

This illness behind them, great things seemed in store for the Marshalls. But even as Catherine's own healing was underway, Peter was stricken with a heart attack. The taxing demands of a too-busy life were taking their toll. It was March of 1946 and the lessons learned in the prayer of relinquishment were needed once again. Catherine's was not the only prayer offered for her husband's life. People throughout the country prayed for Dr. Peter Marshall to recover, and he did.

Peter's doctors advised him to slow down if he wanted to live longer. But this was a difficult thing to ask of a man like Peter. As soon as he could, he was back at his schedule, working, traveling, and preaching as though he had never been ill.

Almost three years were to pass. Busy times, full of love, work, and play. The Marshall's spent pleasant summers at *Waverley*, their cottage on Cape Cod, where they could rest and relax and where Peter could work in his garden. Peter John was growing: a curious, vital, intelligent child. He and his father delighted in their time together, sharing in private nonsense games and sports.

Then, suddenly, this happy existence was shattered. Peter Marshall was stricken with another heart attack in January 1949. The sparkling eyes, the warm voice, the man dedicated to the will of God ceased to exist on this earth. Catherine was a widow, her son fatherless.

The fruit of Catherine's love for God and her search for his will in her life came to her aid. During the first days of her loss, she was sustained by an overwhelming sense of God's presence. Having lived her life so close to God, it is not surprising that the first thing she did when her husband was taken to the hospital was to pray. During this prayer, she experienced the "mother love" that God as Creator expresses for all his creatures. She was gathered into his arms and given the impression that all would be well. She describes it this way: "Suddenly the unexpected happened. Over the turbulent emotions there crept a strange all-pervading peace. And through and around me flowed love as I had never before experienced it. It was as if body and spirit were floating on a cloud, resting—as if Someone who loved me very much were wrapping me round and round with His love." (*To Live Again*, p. 27)

But all was not well. A few hours later, Peter Marshall went home to his Father. Even so, Catherine was sustained by the knowledge that her loving Father had not left her alone but was there with her—even in moments of deepest grief and anxiety.

Later, as she gazed on the still face, the shell of what was once the man she loved, she knew suddenly that the room was not empty. Again, her own words describe the sense: "I was not alone. For a while there was a transcendent glory. Though I did not understand it then and cannot explain it now, I knew Peter was near me. And beside him, another Presence, the Lord he had served through long years." (*To Live Again*, p. 14)

These experiences were to carry her through the days immediately following Peter's death. They gave her the inner strength and comfort necessary to make arrangements for the funeral service, to attend church services the first Sunday after that, and to meet the many people who demonstrated their love to the Marshall family at the time of this tragedy.

God was at her side. She knew he would be. But never had she expected such magnificent demonstrations of his love and strength. It must have been the knowledge of his care that helped her to quietly assess the assistance given her by the church board in sorting out her business affairs. With hard-headed practicality they pointed out the limited income available to her, the cost of maintaining a car, and the cost of dwelling space.

After the practicalities and good wishes had come to an end and the door closed behind these men, Catherine started thinking again. Perhaps her mind returned to that time years ago when a college education seemed impossibly out of reach. She would remember her mother's straightforward solution to that problem. God's will would be done.

It can't have been easy for the young widow to have sorted out her life and started over. And this certainly was complicated by the fact that Dr. Marshall had been so well-known and a bit of him claimed by so many people. Yet, from many sources a single idea began to evolve.

Peter Marshall had refused to have his sermons printed in book form during his lifetime. He had often been asked for reprints, and these requests did not stop with his death. Was there sufficient interest to warrant the publication of a book? The answer was yes, and Catherine set out, with the aid of many friends, to begin the complicated task of sorting, selecting, and editing the sermons for publication.

Mr. Jones, Meet the Master was the result, and it sold out rapidly. It is still in print, and still offering words of inspiration, encouragement, and hope to thousands of readers. Catherine wrote the introduction. Here was an opportunity to talk about the spirit of the man who had been her husband. Her years of journal-keeping and her long interest in writing stood her in good stead for the task. This brief introduction represented the beginning of an entirely new ministry for her.

Through the swirl of autograph parties, best-seller lists, and thousands of letters from those who responded to the book, Catherine still had to deal with the very real problems of finding a place to live, of caring for her son, and coping with life as a single person. The extraordinary popularity of *Mr. Jones, Meet the Master* led to a request for a second volume.

After careful thought, Catherine proposed, instead, a biography of her famous husband. This venture took a tremendous amount of time and emotional energy, yet it filled her days with remembered love. The result was *A Man Called Peter.*

As Catherine began writing the story she had lived, she evaluated her desire to write. She had always felt compelled to put her thoughts on paper and writing had become as essential as breathing. During her life she had struggled with the question of why she wanted to be a writer. She wanted to write for the good of others, to make a contribution of lasting value.

Now she had the chance to tell Peter's story. A book about a wonderful man. But more than that, it would be the story of one of God's servants. A book that would be written to God's glory. Her aim was to use the "life of this one man then, this fallible man, Peter Marshall, . . . to answer the average person's questions about God and how He deals with each of us." (*To Live Again*, p. 139)

Catherine Marshall has never deviated from this decision in any of the books she has written. For this reason, more than any other, they speak to the ordinary individual. The problems she talks about are real. The people in her books have personalities and feelings, and they are just like one's own family. Her commitment to God and his will is simple, direct, and personal. There is room for human error and she opens herself wide to observation—exposing her faults, foibles, and successes.

A Man Called Peter was a resounding success. Close to the top of the *New York Times* best-seller list for a year and a half, it reached the hearts and minds not only of those who knew him, but of countless thousands of others. God was at work in a marvelous way. One of the greatest surprises was that the book appealed to so many teenagers.

I was one of them. I have always loved books, reading anything that came to hand. My mother bought a copy and the entire family read it, cried over it, and were inspired by it. I remember thinking that it was a beautiful story written about a servant of God by another of his servants. In the early years of the 1950s ecumenism was not a word that was known widely in church circles, at least not in Jubilee, Iowa, where I grew up, but here was a book that transcended denominational lines and spoke to the matter of servanthood. And besides, it was a good story. We were proud that a Christian book could be a best-seller.

This was my first encounter with Catherine Marshall. She didn't enter my life again for many years. Occasionally I would see magazine articles written by her, always lovely to read, but so were a lot of other things. I can almost see her smile at this point, and I can hear her say softly, "But in God's own time. . . ."

What was Catherine's life like after she published her second book? She was a celebrity with two best-sellers to her credit, though she insisted that *Mr. Jones, Meet the Master* was really Peter's. There was talk of a film and incessant demands were made on her for autograph parties, tours, and public appearances. She tried to answer personally the letters that came her way. So many of them were filled with wonderful insights, sharing the innermost secrets of the writers.

Though she had become a celebrity, she was still a young widow, learning to cope with grief. Dealing with the problems of being a single parent were an everyday event. Her books *To Live Again* and *Beyond Ourselves* are filled with vignettes from her life during those lonely years and with stories of how she sought to deal with those problems. Most striking is her constant willingness to "go to the one place I could count on for final authoritative truth—the Bible." She disciplined herself daily, whether writing, researching, or establishing a special quiet time for study, prayer, and meditation.

Catherine had an incredible capacity for growth and was not

afraid to admit her shortcomings. She knew firsthand the temptation and weakness that challenge all of us and related these freely in her books.

When asked about her candor and willingness to share many of the details of her private life, she put her answer squarely in the context of God's will. "It is important," she says, "that we should be utterly frank with ourselves in establishing a relationship with Jesus Christ. It is the only way to establish a true relationship with him. This frees us to confess our shortcomings, and it is this freedom which helps us realize that we are very important spirits living in this body here on earth. Then we can make connections. It's only then that we find the spirit of the other person and share at that level. That's when we find this kind of candor. This is truly the communion of saints."

Loneliness is something we all must deal with and Catherine Marshall had to deal with it—as a celebrity. Being in the public eye is often much lonelier than you might think. Someone is almost always looking over your shoulder with the result that you are haunted by a horrible feeling that if you slip into a peevish tone of voice, or even worse, have a temper tantrum, the whole incident will be blown out of proportion.

And then there are the times when you sit alone because people are sure you have so many invitations that theirs would be an imposition. All of this is compounded by the self-imposed loneliness that occurs when you cannot bring yourself to shake one more hand or smile sweetly for one more minute.

Catherine had experienced a loving and fruitful marriage. She was human, and she longed for the companionship of a husband. In seeking God's will, she put herself in his hands. She says, "I stopped thinking about remarriage. Not that the desire was wiped out, just that it had become much less important to me. My perspective had changed. This was the Lord's doing, of course, and came about because I was able to give the matter over to Him to handle." (*Meeting God at Every Turn*, p. 172)

In 1959 Catherine Marshall married Leonard LeSourd, then the Executive Editor of *Guideposts* magazine, and thus began another chapter in her life. The frustrations and joys of life with the LeSourd family led her to plumb even more deeply the strength and wisdom of the Lord.

While all this was happening in her life, my own life was developing, sometimes along parallel lines. I, too, was dealing with the problem of loneliness and seeking patience and the wisdom of God for my life's direction. My learning and growth had not been as disciplined as Catherine's, but I had learned certain lessons in my travels.

God had been good. My life was full and rich. He had blessed my career beyond my wildest childhood ambitions. I was no longer the speech and drama teacher I had dreamed of becoming as a third-grader, but a diplomat in the Foreign Service of my country.

My job had taken me to many places. I was traveling and meeting people—all kinds, including missionaries who had given their lives to the work of the Lord in remote, underdeveloped areas. I had talked with people who served God under repressive governments. My own country's freedoms, particularly of speech and worship, had taken on new significance for me.

The interludes when I was in the States on assignment and could be in contact with my own church were increasingly precious as I met with Bible study groups, taught Sunday School, and gathered strength for the next long dry spell away from my own religious community.

In 1979, knowing that my next assignment was to a country that was 95 percent Muslim, I studied a bit about Islam and poured over the Old Testament history books to see how many biblical sites I might actually be able to visit. Little did I know that on this trip to Iran I would never see the place where Esther, that courageous Jewish woman, had lived. Instead, amid the clamor of militant Iranian crowds, I would encounter another courageous woman, Catherine Marshall!

My first day of captivity was November 5, 1979. Only one other woman was held for the full 444 days. Her name was Elizabeth Ann Swift (Ann), and she became my roommate in March of 1980. Shortly after that, sometime after Easter, we were taken to a room in the embassy which had been established as a "library." The sections were labeled fiction, biography, science fiction, sports, and religion.

We stood there for a moment, our blindfolds in our hands, looking in awe at the books. Up to that time we had had less than a choice selection brought around to our rooms in a grocery cart. From that cart I had selected and read such fascinating works as *Scuba Diving in Caves, The 1976 Football Yearbook,* and *A History of Bell Telephone.* Here was wealth! We looked the titles over, carefully selecting some old favorites and some new authors, too.

I moved to the religion shelf. What would be there? Just a few weeks earlier we had been given some books sent by a friend of mine: *Clap Your Hands!* by Larry Tomczak, *God Did Not Ordain Silence,* and a concordance of New Testament scripture passages relating to the Holy Spirit. All three books had been filled with the fruits of the Spirit and had been so important to us as we studied them during Holy Week. Would there be something on the shelf that would carry on our study?

"Ann, look," I said. "Thomas à Kempis' *Imitation of Christ.* Shall I take it?" She nodded and I slipped it onto the stack of books in my arms.

"This looks like a new book," I said pulling another slim volume off the shelf. "Catherine Marshall . . . might be good." I opened the cover and there, printed at the top of the page and leaping out at me were the words, "Love from your niece, Emma Louise."

I could hardly contain my joy—or my anger! This was *my* book from my ten-year-old niece and *they* hadn't given it to me!

When we got back to the room, I filled Ann in on what happened. I still didn't realize what the subject of this little volume called *The Helper* was.

My joy at finally receiving this gift from Emma Lou overcame my anger at the students, and I placed the book with my Bible to await next morning's study time. That night my prayers included a "thank you" for the book.

The next morning I opened *The Helper* and read the foreword. I discovered that it was about the Third Person of the Trinity—the Comforter on whose presence I had been relying so heavily since the first day of my captivity. The Giver of heavenly gifts, the Spirit who guides and leads our lives was the subject of this book.

I had experienced his manifestation in so many ways, and here was a systematic look at him, telling who he is and how he helps us. I was quite sure Catherine Marshall would not get carried away in an ecstasy of emotion. Anyone who had come from her background wouldn't. And in her foreword she had explained the deliberate method of study she had used to prepare this manuscript. Besides, she and Peter Marshall had initiated this study together.

My dilemma was whether to read slowly and savor, or to give in to the urge to take in as much of it as I could, as quickly as possible. I compromised. Never more than two short chapters at a time, but I could (and did) go back more than once a day. By now I had read the New Testament several times and the Old Testament in its entirety at least once, and some parts many times. I welcomed the guide this study would give me. I really wanted to find out how this woman, so much in the public eye, had dealt with a subject that was so sensitive to some people, particularly in the so-called conservative mainline denominations.

I knew from my own experience the wonderful presence of God in moments of severe stress, and I was anxious to see what I would find. I could understand the concept of God the Creator, Father and Giver of Life. And Jesus had been part of my life since I was very young. Since the day after my capture, the Holy Spirit's presence had been a constant source of comfort—yet there was something so mysterious and frightening to me about the Spirit, especially about his gifts. I knew that the gifts of healing and tongues had torn congregations and families apart.

Still, from catechetical instruction, I understood that my own faith was the work of the Holy Spirit. How often had I said those words of Dr. Martin Luther's, explaining the Third Article of the Creed, Sanctification:

> I believe that I cannot by my own reason or strength believe in Jesus Christ my Lord or come to Him, but the Holy Ghost has called me through the Gospel, enlightened me with His gifts and sanctified and preserved me in the true faith. . . .

But this did not spell out those gifts which Paul talks about so clearly in Galatians 5:22: "But the fruit of the Spirit is love, joy, peace, patience [did I need that one!]." And again in 1 Corinthians 12:8-10, Paul says "... to another gifts of healing by that one Spirit, to another miraculous powers, to another prophecy. . . ."

What would I find in *The Helper*? I started reading eagerly. In the summer of 1944, Catherine Marshall was led to do an exhaustive study of the Holy Spirit. Aware of the limited materials available on this subject, she made what I have come to regard as one of her trademark decisions. She tells about it in the foreword of the book:

"I decided to go to the one place I could count on for final authoritative truth—the Bible. Scripture had never yet deceived me or led me astray. From long experience I knew that the well-worn words from an old church ordinance had it exactly right—the Bible still is 'the only infallible rule of faith and practice.'

"At the same time I also knew that the search in Scripture could be no random dipping in; it had to be thorough and all inclusive. A Bible, a Cruden's concordance, a loose-leaf notebook, pen and colored pencils were my only tools." (pp. 11-12)

One chapter particularly made an impression. It was called "He Is My Remembrancer." The biblical basis for this concept is John 14:26: "But the Counselor, the Holy Spirit, whom the Father will send in my name, will teach you all things and *will remind* you of everything I have said to you." (Italics mine.)

I had already experienced a multitude of these remembrances as I filled my days by searching my mind for the scripture verses and hymns I had learned as a child. Here was Catherine Marshall encouraging me to lean more heavily on this gift, and I did. Bits and pieces of the catechism learned years before floated into place and notes from college Bible classes seemed to rise up to challenge my thinking. I have continued to rely on this help even since my return as I plow through piles of accumulated letters, clippings, and notes.

One of the most important passages for me during this time was Luke 21:12, 14-15: "And you will be brought before kings and governors and all on account of my name. . . . But make up your mind not to worry beforehand how you will defend yourselves. For I will give you words and wisdom that none of your adversaries will be able to resist or contradict."

It was easy to borrow trouble by wondering what questions the student militants would ask next. Could this passage have bearing on my own situation? The students weren't kings, but they were in power. I wasn't being held because I was a Christian, but I knew that this promise was for me here and now.

Reading *The Helper* reaffirmed my own thoughts and actions. Here was written witness to the strength, power, and variety of the Holy Spirit's ministry in many lives, and particularly from one who had experienced many trials and still looked to God for comfort and direction.

From then on it was a treasure hunt each time we went to the library. Would we find another book by Catherine Marshall? We did. *Something More, To Live Again, Beyond Ourselves*—all sent by "friends" of hers. They paid her the greatest compliment they could, sending us their well-worn, underlined, and annotated books. We also found *Christy* and kept looking for more.

Reading about Catherine Marshall's methodical habits of study and record-keeping, of maintaining prayer diaries and lists, encouraged me to keep a spiritual diary during the latter part of my captivity. In it I recorded my feelings and struggles, and I have come to consider this spiritual "note-taking" an important part of my spiritual life even now. I am not as faithful as I was in Iran, but I know the value of writing down my thoughts, my questions, and God's answers.

In the book *Something More* I found the prayer that has helped many Christians in dangerous and troublesome spots. Here was a prayer that was so short, so simple, that I could carry it in my head. It was really an affirmation of faith.

The Light of God surrounds me.
The Love of God enfolds me.
The Power of God protects me.
The Presence of God watches over me.
Wherever I am, God is.

I repeated this affirmation/prayer of faith as a litany each day during my exercise period. I would think of the blessings that had been bestowed on me during this time—of how God had protected his saints through the ages and surrounded them even in death with his presence. This prayer was a wonderful gift.

During my captivity, I was faced with a major challenge—to obey the Lord's command to love my enemies. This was perhaps the most difficult lesson I had to cope with in my captivity. Catherine Marshall offered insight and wisdom here, too. She reminded me that God's forgiveness to man is related to man's forgiveness to his fellow man. As my experience in Iran recedes, this lesson stands out, and it is one that grows in magnitude with each passing day. As Catherine Marshall points out, the need is not only for one person to forgive another, it is for nations and peoples to look to each other with compassion and forgiveness rather than with envy, hatred, and a longing for revenge.

Catherine's ability to open her life to so many has certainly been a model for me since my return. How I have longed to turn my back on requests for a speech or "just one more question," until I remember how she has turned many private and personal events to public witness and gave of her life so that God might instruct and teach others.

Her ability to see God in action in the ordinary events of everyday life, and to relate this in a simple, direct fashion understandable to anyone who seeks guidance is a great gift. She has been a good steward of her talents. When I am distraught because I have too much to do, or I think I would like to escape to a community retreat for meditation and study, I am reminded by this woman that as Christ's followers we are in this world. When Christ came he did not establish a retreat center—though he sought a place apart regularly—but he moved and worked among the people of his time. Like the One she loves, Catherine Marshall works among the people of her time and place.

She says she could receive no greater compliment than being thought of as a friend because of her writings. But I think there is something more important than that. I am sure that the greatest compliment one could pay Catherine Marshall is to say, "Through you I saw God a little bit clearer." For that is her life's mission, and it was to his glory that her work has begun, and it is in his name that it will be completed.

Thank you, Catherine, for helping me to see God more clearly.

† † †

I was in Washinton, D.C., when the first reports of Catherine Marshall's death reached me. What a sense of loss, and of regret. I had hoped to meet her for the first time in the coming months. Now that hope had dissolved in an instant. "But wait a minute," I could almost hear Catherine saying. "Aren't you forgetting that we're bound to meet—in glory? And what a meeting that will be, when neither of us need worry about any shortcoming, any earthly limitation!"

Yes, I reminded myself, my meeting with Catherine Marshall had only been postponed, not canceled. I laughed at myself for thinking anything else, and as I laughed I knew that it would be a meeting worth waiting for.

Sources

Adventures in Prayer (Lincoln, Virginia: Chosen Books, 1975).

The Helper (Lincoln, Virginia: Chosen Books, 1978).

Meeting God at Every Turn (Lincoln, Virginia: Chosen Books, 1980).

To Live Again (Lincoln, Virginia: Chosen Books, 1957).

FOUR

Adrienne de Lafayette

by Elizabeth Sherrill

IN 1794, IN PARIS, the French Revolution entered on its second phase. The makeshift prisons remained crowded, but their population changed: instead of former nobles, they now housed petty thieves, looters, and black-market profiteers, as the revolutionary government instituted basic reforms.

In one of the mansions-turned-prison, however, lived an exception. Everything about this prisoner—the way she walked, ate, spoke—marked her as a noblewoman. And the greatest difference between her and her fellow inmates was not even visible: a small silver crucifix pinned out of sight beneath her dress.

Here is the story I imagine her telling . . .

† † †

The crowd outside the dining room was already beginning to shove, though the door would not be opened for an hour. Usually I stayed out of it, waiting in my garret room on the fifth floor until the drum for the single meal of the day sounded. It didn't take a great deal of food, after all, to keep me alive.

Today, though, I struggled to keep my place near the door. Today

I must get to the bread tray before it is empty.

Verminous bodies pressed against me until I could scarcely breathe. If only I were taller, big enough to shove back! It was only since I'd been a prisoner that I had been aware of my size. I'd known, of course, that my husband stood far, far above me, but that was because he was extraordinarily tall, at six-feet-three-inches always the tallest man in any room, stooping a bit as though trying to get in touch with the rest of the world.

Gilbert . . . my love . . . are you still alive?

With the press of people jostling, suffocating, I closed my eyes and saw my husband looking down at me. The long, narrow nose, the high, sloping forehead, the powder from his wig drifting in a gentle snowfall onto the epaulets of his uniform. On tiptoe I would stretch up to brush them off. And he would smile that shy awkward smile: "Where did I ever find such a tiny wife?"

In those days it was a joke. When had I ever needed to reach for anything? As long as I could remember there had been footmen to place my food in front of me, pages to run my errands. Only in these last two terrible years had I learned that those with the longest legs got to the table first, those with the longest arms filled their soup bowls.

"Hi! Look who's here!"

With a sinking heart I knew that I had been spotted. Other voices took up the cry, gleefully passing on the news: "The great lady is dining with the serfs today!"

"What an honor!"

"She'll soil her satin gown"—a woman's voice—"rubbing shoulders with us riffraff!"

How long had it been, I wondered, since I had worn satin? The only clothes I owned were this rumpled linen dress and this torn woolen shawl, no match for the midwinter cold.

At last, the rat-tat-tat of the drum! The double doors swung inward; the crowd surged forward. Running, stumbling, I struggled toward the wooden bread-trencher.

"Look! The noble lady can scrap for her supper like any fishwife!" A wooden shoe came down painfully on my instep. It didn't matter.

My hand had closed around a chunk of coarse black bread.

From the rear door the pot of barley gruel was carried in and the crowd turned in that direction. I would not even try for a bowlful today: I would eat some of the bread. After all, it wasn't a very big piece that I needed for . . . tonight.

Tenderly I broke off a portion and tucked it into the sash of my dress. Then I found a place on one of the benches ringing the walls and began to gnaw on my prize.

This must have been a charming room once, I thought, gazing up at the painted ceiling. High above the wine-spattered floor the god Apollo still pursued the nymph Daphne across a forest glade. That hook in the very center had doubtless held a crystal chandelier, and there would have been vases on that green marble mantel. All gone now, of course, and the house turned into a prison, as so many great homes in Paris had been since the Revolution.

Somehow the unused fireplace made the room colder still. I thought of our own home, Gilbert's and mine, only four streets away, where at this time of year, December, there were always fires crackling on every hearth. Not December, I corrected myself, looking around guiltily. There was no month of December. This was the month of Frimaire, in the year three of the new world of Liberty, Equality, and Fraternity.

I swallowed another mouthful of the bitter black bread. For months the bakers had been mixing plaster with flour to increase the weight of their loaves, but this bread was maggoty as well.

The hollow-cheeked old woman beside me on the bench seemed to read my thoughts. "Criminals, that's what these bakers are, Citizeness! Not that I could chew it anyway—not if it was cake baked by Marie Antoinette herself!" She opened her mouth to reveal toothless gums and a winey breath.

I swallowed again, willing my stomach not to revolt. *You may be alive, Gilbert! You must be alive! And therefore I too want to live.* My companion hobbled off to join the group around the wine jar. I forced down the last of the bread and followed her. That was the other thing I needed for this night of nights, a little wine—though in this case the problem would not be getting it, but carrying it unnoticed up to my room. Bread and soup disappeared as soon as they arrived, but there was a seemingly inexhaustible supply of thin vinegary red wine.

I took a wooden bowl from the table and wiped the greasy rim as unobtrusively as I could. My concern for cleanliness had often brought hoots from my fellow prisoners.

"May I have some wine, Citizen?" I asked the sullen-faced trusty who occupied a three-legged stool beside the big wine jar.

He appeared not to see me.

"May I have wine, please?"

The man aimed a stream of tobacco juice at the green marble fireplace.

"Some wine, please, Citizen," I repeated hopelessly.

"*Please* will get you nowhere with the likes of him!" It was the old woman from the bench. "Out of the way, you lazy ox! If you won't do your job, I'll do it for you!"

She refilled her own bowl, then mine. And now . . . how to get it up to my room unseen! The daily meal was over; until the doors opened at this time tomorrow there would be nothing more to eat. But people lingered in the room, drawing at least an illusion of warmth from the nearness of other bodies.

A trusty was collecting wooden bowls from tables and benches; I thrust mine out of sight beneath my shawl. Another duty-prisoner began herding people toward the door. "Closing! Closing! Time to clean up!"

"Aye! There's time to clean up!" my toothless friend called back. "There's all the time in the world! Why don't you do it, then, to earn the rations you steal from the rest of us?"

"Out you go, granny," said the man, not unkindly. Besides being the oldest prisoner in the Maison Delmas she was a general favorite, a washerwoman who had stripped clothes from the headless victims of the guillotine to sell on the black market.

I edged with the others out the door, trying to keep my bowl with its precious contents from being bumped. Out in the vestibule people were settling down for the long, dull afternoon, reluctant to return to the icy rooms on the upper floors. I inched toward the stairs. Card players had settled on the bottom steps. But I must get past them to reach my room before Pere Carrichon arrived! For he would come, tonight, as soon as it grew dark enough to walk in the streets. If everyone else in Paris had forgotten what night this was, Pere Carrichon would remember.

At the foot of the broad, curved staircase I gathered my skirt into my free hand. "Pardon me, Citizens. May I disturb your game long enough to pass?"

"Her ladyship desires to pass, Emil!"

"On your knees, serfs!"

Would they never tire of the same stale jokes? Or of rushing to the foot of the stairs each time a woman started up? There were only a handful of us female prisoners in the Maison Delmas—mostly small shopkeepers convicted of hoarding—and the others handled the leering men with jeers of their own. Even the old washerwoman was more than a match for them, lifting her skirt around her bony knees and lamenting that there was not a man there who could inspire her to lift it any farther.

I alone was unable to control the tears that all my life had betrayed my feelings. Cheeks burning, I stepped over the sprawling figure of one of the card players and started the endless, circling climb. Usually I held my skirt tight against my side, but with the bowl held beneath my shawl, the other hand clutching the railing, I could only scramble up the stairs as fast as my legs would carry me, to the shrieks of merriment below.

The second landing. I circled the stairwell and groped up the third flight, hot tears blinding me. American women wouldn't cry, I thought suddenly, unexpectedly. They never cried, Gilbert said. The fourth landing. One more flight. This final stairway was narrow and steep, without a handrail. *Oh Gilbert! If I had been that kind of woman, would you have loved me more?*

The fifth floor at last. Mere cubicles of rooms up here. I hurried to the fourth one on the right and closed the door gratefully behind me. The glass was broken in the tiny dormer window and street noises from the Rue Notre Dame des Champs rose clearly: carts bumping over the pavement, the shouts of drivers. I set the wooden bowl tenderly on the chair that was the room's one piece of furniture, then knelt and groped in a corner for two stumps of candles I had hoarded there.

Already, at three o'clock this winter afternoon, it was growing dark. Here was the little pile of papers and quills with which I wrote every day, all day, to anyone who might know where my husband was. Not enough light for another letter today.

I found the candle ends and the tinderbox and stood up. Then, removing my shawl, I lifted the bowl of wine and spread the shawl over the seat of the chair. I put the bowl down again, precisely in the center, then took the piece of bread from my sash and placed it in front of the bowl. A candle on either side, the tinderbox on the floor close at hand.

One thing more. I unpinned from its hiding place beneath my bodice the silver crucifix Mamma had given on the day of my marriage. Gently I propped it against the chairback, feeling rather than seeing in the growing gloom, the figure of the Lord Jesus stretched upon the cross. It was far too small, of course, but a chair covered with a shawl was hardly a proper communion table, either. It was all I had, and Pere Carrichon, traveling the streets every day, liable to be stopped and searched at any corner, could carry nothing except what any carpenter might have in his tool bag.

A freezing rain drummed on the roof. I picked up the tattered blanket from the straw-filled sleeping pallet and wrapped it around my shoulders in place of the shawl.

And now that everything was ready I was seized with terror that Pere Carrichon would not come. What if he had been arrested . . . deported to the Indies! Surely in all this time someone would have reported him as a priest who had refused to take the oath of first-loyalty to the state. And even if he was free, he could be sick—starving. It wasn't only in the prisons that people were hungry: they said half of Paris was begging for bread this terrible winter.

Or . . . what if the guard downstairs at the door was not deceived by his carpenter disguise? Or suppose he had simply forgotten? No! Of that at least I was certain. He had not forgotten! If he was alive and if he was not in prison, he would try to come to me tonight. The rest of Paris might have forgotten. To the rest of France it might be only the thirteenth of Frimaire, year three of the Republic. To the two of us it was Christmas Eve in the year of our Lord 1794.

The chill rain gusted through the broken window. I crawled onto the straw and tucked my legs beneath me. What was the warmest thing I could think of? A blazing fire—Yes! Both dining-room fires crackling and glowing, on Christmas Eve in the Rue Bourbon. Just four streets away . . .

There would have been Americans at our table, of course. Americans were always homesick at Christmas and so we invited all who were in the city. Monsieur and Madame John Adams. Monsieur Thomas Jefferson. Monsieur Gouveneur Morris. I smiled, remembering how shocked our servants had been, one year, when Monsieur Benjamin Franklin appeared at the table without a wig, and no decorations on his dinner jacket.

And after dinner, *four* fires lighted in the long ballroom. And in the midst of the dancing, my excuses to our guests as I left for midnight Mass. The gentlemen bending low over my hand, Gilbert's half indulgent, half apologetic explanation:

"My wife finds comfort in the ancient customs."

Smiles behind the ladies' fans. Was it possible that an educated person took church seriously enough to leave in the middle of a party? My coach waiting in the courtyard, footmen leaping up behind, the swift ride through the dark streets.

A wagon rattled past in the Rue Notre Dame des Champs five floors below. I leaned against the attic wall, imagining I was on my way to church. This threadbare blanket was a bearskin rug; on my lap was the sack of coins for the poor who crowded the church porch on Christmas Eve.

And at home, when the Mass was over, an immense fire roaring in our bedroom, and Gilbert in the satin dressing gown that brought out the green of his eyes.

The old longing, the present fear, swept over me. No! Don't start to cry! Gilbert would not want you to cry. . . .

† † †

The woman shivering in that icy attic room so many years ago was Adrienne de Lafayette; the husband she ached for, the hero of the American Revolution. Thirteen years had passed since Gilbert de Lafayette returned in triumph from the United States, his role in the winning of our independence inscribed forever in our hearts and our history books.

What is not so well-known on our side of the Atlantic is what happened in the remaining fifty years of his eventful life. And still less, the part played in all of this by his wife.

In fact, until I encountered her name on the grave slab next to his in a tiny, out-of-the-way cemetery in Paris, I had not even known that he *had* a wife. Neither, apparently, did most people. "Was Lafayette married?" was the usual response when I tried to learn more about her.

It was enough to get my fairness-to-women flags flying. By then I'd unearthed some facts about Adrienne de Lafayette in dusty library stacks in Paris and Auvergne. I had met a woman every bit as courageous as her husband, a realist while he saw things as he wished them to be. I'd met a home lover who asked nothing but the companionship of her husband and the chance to raise their three children in peace. She was given instead: fame, adventure, and a role in history.

What I learned made me want to know more. Not just because her life was filled with stirring events, but because I was convinced that Adrienne had learned things about living in a time of catastrophic change that we in the final years of *this* century need to know.

For in spite of the immense differences between her world and ours, there are strange parallels, too. The world in which Adrienne grew up was as sophisticated as our own, and a great deal more graceful—probably the most elegant and cultured society the world has ever known. (It was this for the few, of course, not for the many; but Adrienne was one of those few.)

As today, ferment was everywhere—in science, in politics, in heady new ideas about equality and liberation. Many of the fabulously rich, people like Adrienne and Gilbert, were in the forefront of the movement to see the world's goods more fairly divided. Never before had there been such optimism, such faith in human potential. Science was at last revealing its secrets; poverty, disease, injustice would soon be things of the past.

Only a few of those working so hard to bring all this about had private doubts. Adrienne was one of them. She shared her husband's passionate commitment to democracy. She did not share his certainty that it would mean an end to human misery.

Adrienne suspected the existence in mankind of something darker, deeper than laws could reach, something only God could touch. For she was that rarity in 18th-century France, an educated person who believed the teachings of the church. Nobody who was anybody—not even bishops and archbishops—believed all those old dogmas. The peasants did, of course, but that was because up till now they'd been without hope in this world. When unjust laws were repealed and man's natural goodness allowed to express itself, then all these primitive beliefs about God becoming man—and dying on a cross for something called *sin*—would vanish like mist in the sunshine.

But Adrienne, so modern in most things, was stubbornly old-fashioned in this. With her mother and her sister Louise she persisted in attending daily mass and in daily Bible reading and prayer.

There was another way in which she was hopelessly out of step with her day: her view of marriage. Quite ridiculous, of course. She had been betrothed to Gilbert, as was only natural, before they ever laid eyes on one another: unions of the high nobility were not individual decisions so much as corporate mergers.

Love, of course, existed—was preeminent, in France!—but what did that have to do with the business arrangement called marriage? Adrienne was fourteen, Gilbert sixteen, when their marriage was consummated. Soon Adrienne discovered—somewhat to her alarm, earnest young Christian that she was—that she was also a rapturously passionate person. The awkward thing, in 18th-century France, was that the man she loved so desperately was her own husband.

And he loved her. But Lafayette was a hero—and a Frenchman. And French women were the most enticing in the world, and, except for the few like Adrienne, the least attached to their husbands. Gilbert's love for Adrienne was genuine, but it was not exclusive, while hers for him was, along with her love of God, the fixed passion of her life.

Christian commitment in an age that worshipped science, faithfulness in marriage when it was neither expected nor fashionable—Christians at the end of the twentieth century can recognize Adrienne's predicament. And into the midst of these private tensions burst the public upheaval called the French Revolution.

What a lot, I kept thinking, Adrienne would have to tell us about living through violent times. How I wished that I could sit down with her, as I've had a chance to do with outstanding Christians of our own day, to ask the intimate, painful questions.

And then I realized that I could. Whatever else was going on—in peace and in war, by sunlight and candlelight—the people of the 18th-century wrote letters. Physically separated much of their married life, Gilbert and Adrienne wrote each other constantly. They wrote to their parents, their children, their families, their business partners, their servants. And all of these people wrote back.

An astonishing number of these letters survived shipwreck and revolution—to end in those poorly lit library archives. It was there that I began my "interviews" with Adrienne, at first simply sketching a chronology of her life. She was seventeen and already the mother of fifteen-month-old Henriette, when her husband—only nineteen himself—sailed to fight in the American cause. Her second child, Anastasie, was born six months later, before she even knew that her husband's ship had reached the shores of the New World safely. The following winter, while Gilbert shivered in the snows of Valley Forge, little Henriette died in her mother's arms of a childhood disease.

On Gilbert's return from the United States, two more children were born to the young couple: George Washington Lafayette, named for Gilbert's favorite general, and Virginia, for the state where the British surrender occured. It was Adrienne's dearest wish—and Gilbert's often-stated one—to bring up their three children on his ancestral estate in the peaceful province of Auvergne, in southern France.

Again and again Adrienne made the 400-mile journey to get the château ready. And each time, some new public crisis kept Gilbert in Paris, and Adrienne and the children would return to be near him. The Lafayettes' townhouse on the Rue Bourbon became home away from home for Americans in France, while at the aristocratic French court Gilbert and Adrienne became the most ardent advocates of the fledgling experiment in democracy across the sea.

And slowly, haltingly, France's own experiment in democracy got underway. Gilbert was elected to the national assembly, the first representative body in France in 150 years. With the other assemblymen he plunged into the staggering task of converting an absolute monarchy into a constitutional one.

As the months of debate and speechmaking went on, however, the poor of Paris took to the streets in a kind of hysteria of hope too long deferred. Looting, burning, lynching—it was clear that only military force could put down the riots.

But who could command such a force? He would have to be a nobleman, or the officers would not follow. And a friend of liberty, or the common soldiers would rebel. Lafayette was the one man in France sufficiently esteemed by both sides. Mounted on a milk-white horse at the head of his newly formed National Guard, he restored order to the capital, safeguarded the meetings of the assembly, protected the king and queen from the mob.

Coaxing her children to sleep to the sound of gunfire in the streets, Adrienne's heart sang with pride. The whole world at last saw her husband as she did: the gallant knight on a white horse, the perfect hero.

It was her one lapse into idealism. About everything except the man she loved, Adrienne was a realist. She knew all too well that the perfect hero was performing his deeds in an imperfect world.

Lafayette did not know it. When the Constitution was at last complete—approved by the Assembly, signed by the king—he believed that the job was done. At that moment he was the most powerful man in France. But he had as his ideal his commander-in-chief in the American struggle. As George Washington, victory won, had refused the title of king and retired to Mt. Vernon as a simple private citizen, so Gilbert hastened to give up all military and civil authority.

Once more, Adrienne packed her household into coaches and carriages for the long journey to Auvergne, "this time, ma petite Adrienne, for good."

"For good" lasted two and a half months.

Autocratic governments all across Europe were threatening to invade the new democracy; Frenchmen were summoned to defend the homeland. On his white horse Lafayette galloped north to take command of the army near the presentday Belgian border.

What he did not realize was that in the few weeks since his "retirement," the political picture had continued to change. Forgotten were the lofty and equitable laws he and the others had hammered out with such care; the revolution which he had helped to set in motion was sweeping on. This was not America, with its self-sufficient frontiersmen and independent farmers. This was France, a nation of landless peasants and wretched city-dwellers. Lafayette's sublime, all-reforming Constitution was just so many words on paper.

To his army camp came the news that the king and queen had been arrested and placed in prison. As individuals, Lafayette did not admire Louis XVI and Marie Antoinette. As an institution, he disliked the whole idea of monarchy. He personally had wanted a republic under an elected chief executive, as in America where his beloved Washington was now president. But the Constitution named the king as head of the state. And Lafayette believed that the Constitution mattered.

When he asked his troops to pledge loyalty to the king, he was charged with treason. A few hours ahead of the agents sent to bring him to Paris for trial and execution, he escaped across the border.

Into the arms of an Austrian patrol. Hated now in France as a king-lover, he was loathed in the rest of Europe as a revolutionary.

He was incarcerated in Namur, moved to Nivelle, from there transferred, some said to Wesel, some Magdeburg, then—rumor had it—to Olmutz in far-off Moravia. But nobody knew, nobody could say for sure, whether he was alive or dead.

And meanwhile in France the Terror took shape. Any member of the "former nobility" was automatically suspect of antirevolutionary sentiments. Adrienne was at first kept under house arrest in the château in Auvergne, later in a local jail where at least a sympathetic turnkey permitted her children occasional visits. Eventually, however, she was transported to Paris and placed in one of the prisons that were mere waiting-rooms for the guillotine. The king was beheaded in January 1793, the queen the following October. Twenty thousand men and women mounted those same wooden steps, among them Adrienne's mother, who had devoted her life to deeds of charity, her deaf and senile old grandmother, and her beloved sister Louise.

Only the appeals of the American ambassador kept Adrienne from the same sentence. "Her name is revered in America," James Monroe reminded government authorities.

And then France itself recoiled from blood and horror. In August 1794 the radicals were overthrown, replaced by a more moderate group of revolutionaries. The remaining nobility were released from prison, while into jail went the radicals themselves, along with black marketeers and other lawbreakers, in the sweeping reforms carried out by the new government. The population of the prisons made an almost total turnabout—except for the woman who bore the name Lafayette. Extremists on both sides hated that name—but so did the new moderate leadership. Compromise, adjustment, bending of principles was their approach, and Lafayette had repeatedly refused to give an inch on principle.

But, after all, since the start of the Terror thousands of French women had dropped their married names. In September a little committee from the new regime visited Adrienne in prison to inform her that she could be released immediately under her maiden name . . . her mother's name . . . any name in the world but Lafayette. "And as your husband is in all probability dead, Citizeness. . . ."

"I believe my husband to be alive, sirs. And if he is not, then I will bear his name all the more devotedly."

Brave words, in sunny September. But now it was midwinter, the coldest in memory, with freezing rain gusting through the broken window. Had she regretted them? I wondered as I gazed at the portrait of a diminutive woman with prematurely grey hair and large, brooding eyes.

I imagined myself putting that question to her, heard her indignant: "No! Never! Not for a single minute!"

"Not even at night? I can see how you could get through the days, writing letters, keeping busy. But those dark, endless nights!"

"I had memories, you see, of joyful nights."

"And yet the memories themselves must have been painful? So much was lost. So much had changed."

"Yes. Yes, thinking of the past could bring on those hateful tears. And thinking of the future was worse! But there was another way, you see . . . the best one. I discovered it that Christmas Eve."

"Yes, you were telling me about that night . . ."

She would close her eyes, remembering. Remembering that little room on the top floor of a house-turned-prison. . . .

† † †

The straw was scratchy beneath my legs. It had grown so dark I could see nothing but the white candle-stubs on the chair seat. How many hundreds of candle-ends, longer than these precious two, would our servants toss away every morning in the great house where I grew up!

If I could not think about my husband without starting to cry, I would think about Christmas Eve in that house. I saw the chandeliers in our entrance hall showering light from a thousand crystal prisms, and myself, age seven, dressed for my first midnight Mass at the church of St. Roch across the street.

Louise, age eight, tied a fur-trimmed bonnet over her dark curls, while Mama's wide, wide skirt preceded us out the door. Our major-domo led the way across the broad forecourt, aglow with lanterns, his tall staff tap-tap-tapping on the marble pavement. In the street beyond, it looked as though all the poor of Paris had gathered. There were always beggars outside our house, for Mama's generosity was known, but never so many as this—snatching off their caps, thrusting their hands almost in our faces. We were on foot because Mama would never be carried in her traveling chair to church. "Our Lord walked the dusty streets when He was on earth. Are we to set ourselves above Him?"

"The Countess!" the people cried. "Alms, Madame la Comtesse! Alms for the birth of the sweet Savior!"

The major-domo distributed the coins from Mama's purse, then started up the steps into the church, tapping, tapping with his ivory staff.

I sat up straight. Surely I had really heard that! Tap, tap, tap . . . there it came again—the floor below!

I sprang to my feet and felt for the door. A murmur of conversation rose from five floors below as I groped down the black corridor. Again, three short taps! "Citizen carpenter!" I hissed down the dark stairs. "Up here, that leak in the roof! Up here!"

"Ah, one moment, Citizeness! It is so dark. . . ."

That voice I had known since childhood! Now I heard his footsteps on the steep, narrow stairs. Reaching out, I found his hand. I led him swiftly down the lightless corridor to my room, and soundlessly closed the door behind us.

He raised my fingers to his lips. "Madame la Marquise!"

"Your blessing, Reverend Father!"

The forbidden titles seemed to ring in the night air, although we had spoken in whispers. And then titles were forgotten as we embraced. "Praise God!" the old man kept saying. "Praise God for his goodness!"

For my part, I was too shocked to speak. Beneath his workman's smock my arms encircled not the portly, comfortable figure I remembered, but a skeleton clothed in skin. Could this be the good Pere Carrichon, the round-cheeked priest who was forever popping the buttons down the front of his cassock?

"Your children are well, Madame! I bring messages. . . ." Of family and friends he had much welcome news. Only of my husband, only of Gilbert did he know nothing.

Suddenly I could bear the darkness no longer. I had to light at least one of the candles, after so many months of seeing only the faces of strangers. I groped for the chair, found the larger of the two little stubs, and felt on the floor for the tinderbox. Whether from cold or excitement my hands shook so that I could hardly strike a spark. At last the candle caught. I lifted it toward him . . . and caught my breath.

If it had not been for his voice I would have thought there was some awful mistake. The good-natured ruddy face I remembered was ash gray, the skin of the cheeks hung in folds. His hair which I recalled as gray and close-cropped, was shoulder length and quite white. Pere Carrichon could not be more than sixty; the man in front of me looked eighty.

"Dear friend," I began—and then saw that he also was staring in disbelief. Had I too, then, changed so very much?

The old man's horrified gaze traveled from me to the spartan little room: the single chair, the straw-filled pallet. "Is this—where you live, my lady?"

"I requested this room, Father. In the large ones below they put eight or nine people. Here I can write, I can pray."

"Your pardon, Madame la Marquise. I did not mean to question the all-seeing providence of God. It was just that, for a moment, comparing this room with—"

Both of us froze. Loud voices rang out somewhere below. A shout and then a crash . . . a fight, no doubt. They broke out often during the long supperless evenings. There was still no sound here on this floor, but it was a reminder of how swiftly our moments together might end.

Hastily we turned to the makeshift communion table. Pere Carrichon unwrapped several loops of a long, ragged scarf from around his neck and with an apologetic smile draped it evenly down the front of his carpenter's smock, making of it a priestly stole. With the lighted candle he lit the other and placed them on either side of the wooden "chalice."

Now he rummaged in his leather sack and drew out a hammer and nails. "If someone comes, you must pick up the candles as if you were lighting my work, and fold the shawl over the rest." Then he raised his hand in blessing:

"Dominus vobiscum," he whispered.

"Et cum spiritu tuo," I replied.

Turning back to the chair he launched into the ancient liturgy. "Te Deum laudamus. . . ."

As the rhythmic Latin phrases poured into the little room, I closed my eyes and sank to my knees. I did not see the wooden bowl and the black bread on the woolen shawl. I saw the high altar at St. Roch, its golden vessels glimmering . . .

So rapt in the well-remembered scene was I that I did not realize that Father Carrichon had stopped speaking. I opened my eyes to see him looking at me in puzzlement. "We confess our sins to Almighty God," he repeated.

Yes, of course, he was awaiting my response. What were the Latin words that summed up all guilt, all remorse? It had been so long. . . . There! I had them. I opened my mouth to speak the stately Latin formula, but what came out was a rush of ordinary words.

"Father, I failed him! I failed my husband! I did not know how to keep his love! And now it's too late—he may be dead, he—"

"My child! My child!" the old priest broke into my outburst. "Your Father in heaven knows the griefs of your heart. If you are in any way at fault, make your confession and he will forgive you."

I clasped my hands together, trying to steady my thoughts as well. "Lord," I began in Latin, "I am heartily sorry for having offended you. . . ." Swiftly the ancient words worked their healing calm. And now the holiest moment of the Mass had come. Pere Carrichon raised the bread high above his head, asking the Lord of life to enter this attic room. I swallowed the bitter black loaf, and it was the Bread of Life. I touched my lips to the wooden bowl, and it was the Cup of Salvation.

Afterwards, when the final prayers of praise and thanksgiving were said, when Pere Carrichon had drawn off his stole, we embraced again for the sheer joy of our great celebration. One of the candles wavered, flamed briefly, and went out; perhaps another five minutes of light remained in the other.

Pere Carrichon fixed his care-rimmed eyes on mine. "Dear Madame la Marquise, these alarms and regrets for your husband are not the product of faith. Can you not commit him, past, present and future, to God's never-failing care?"

"I do, Father. Every day, every hour. And God tells me that I must go to him! If ever I'm released from this hateful place, it will be to search the world until I find him! Wherever he is, in prison, in a hospital—in the grave—at his side is the only place on earth I can be happy!"

"My dear lady, I tell you again that these transports of passion are not the fruit of submission to God's will. What of your three children, praying daily on their knees that you will be restored to them?"

"They are never for a moment out of my mind. But they do not need me, Pere Carrichon, as my husband needs me."

"Not need you! Why, Mademoiselle Virginie cannot be more than twelve!"

"Dear Father Carrichon, must I quote your own words back to you? The ones you spoke to *my* mother when she had smallpox, and the doctors despaired, and she wept at the thought of leaving her children?"

He shook his head. "I don't recall them. And I don't see how you can. You were only a child."

"But Mama quoted them often to us, afterward. And I have repeated them to myself every day I've spent in prison."

"What were these wonderful words, then?"

"You said to her, 'Do you think you are so indispensable to God that he cannot provide all your children will ever need, both for their bodies and their souls, whether you are there or whether you are not?'"

"Well . . . and very truly said it was! But, Madame, does the same wisdom not apply to your husband? Why can you trust God for your children's welfare and not for his?"

"Because—" How could I explain to Pere Carrichon what I did not understand myself? My children would find God, each in his own way, of that I felt sure. As for Gilbert . . . "Because he trusts only in reason. He believes human beings can be made perfect. He thinks we can create paradise ourselves, without—"

Blackness sprang between us as the second candle guttered out. "I have stayed too long!" Pere Carrichon exclaimed. "I must go!"

Our time was over, and neither of us had spoken of the tragedy looming blacker than the night around us. I groped for my friend's hand in the dark. "Pere Carrichon, they wrote me you were there when Mama and Grandmother and Louise . . . they said you followed the cart."

His hand tightened on mine; he did not answer.

"You were there?" I persisted.

"I was there."

"And were they—did you . . ."

"I saw it all," he said, "and someday I will tell you all, dear, dear lady. But not tonight. Not on the eve of our dear Lord's birth when your mind is distressed with many things. You must not think of the past tonight!" He dropped my hand to search in the dark for his hammer and tool bag. "When you are well, Madame! When you are free and far from this dismal Paris—then will be time to speak of such things."

"But . . . will such a time ever come?" I felt my courage deserting me as he moved toward the door. "The future seems as terrible as the past . . . in the nighttime."

"Do not think of the future, lady! The future is God's. Do not occupy your mind with it!"

"But, dear friend and father, if I may not think of the past, and must not dwell on the future—what is left?"

"Why . . . everything is left, lady! God is left! Do you not know that God exists only and eternally in the now? God exists today—not yesterday, not tomorrow—and as long as you live in the present, you live in him."

Footsteps in the corridor made us both catch our breath. "I will try," I whispered.

Once again his lips brushed my fingers. Then the door opened, closed, and I was alone. I listened at the door with pounding heart, heard his "Good evening, Citizen," as he passed someone in the dark hall, then his footsteps descending the stairs. Nothing else. No sound, no outcry of challenge.

I crossed to the outside wall and stood at the shattered window, straining for the sound of the street gate opening. How silent the city had become! No clatter of hooves in the rue Notre Dame des Champs; no sound of footsteps. The creak of rusty hinges, the slam of the gate! Then no further sound from the strangely quiet street. Dear God, protect your servant! A carriage lumbered past, oddly muffled.

I felt for the chair, set the empty wooden bowl on the floor and drew the shawl once again around my shoulders. Then I knelt on the pallet for my evening prayers. Don't think of the future! Don't remember the past. God exists today.

But . . . how often and how clearly I had seen God this day! If once more no news had come of my husband, at least there was no bad news either. And that meant—that had to mean—that he was alive. And Pere Carrichon had come, God himself had come, to this small room tonight.

I wrapped the shawl tighter, wrapped myself in the wondrous Christmas gift Pere Carrichon had left behind. Christmas was not a long-ago event. Christmas was now. Once more you have come in the dark and cold of night, Lord Jesus! Once more straw has been your bed. . . . You know how it scratches and gets in the nose. The very earth is hushed tonight because you have come.

A feather-soft presence blew in at the window and caressed my cheek, and I understood the strangely silent night. The dismal rain had turned with nightfall to snow. God's pure white covering lay over the bloodstained streets, his Christmas benediction over our heartsick world.

† † †

Adrienne was released from the Maison Delmas in 1795. Although ill, she refused the asylum of her home in Auvergne, staying on in Paris until she could arrange to send fifteen-year-old George Washington to the care of his namesake in America. By then she knew reliably that her husband was imprisoned in the fortress of Olmutz, in Moravia. With her two young daughters she made the difficult trip across Germany and Austria, winning from

Emperor Francis II the only thing on earth she desired: to share her husband's cell.

She found Lafayette wasted and ill from three years' solitary confinement. With Anastasie and Virginia she nursed him back to health, in spite of appalling conditions. Not for another two years were the four of them finally set free.

Lafayette and the two girls speedily recovered from the effects of their harsh captivity. Adrienne—ill when she entered Olmutz—did not. For the remaining eight years of her life she suffered blood poisoning, impaired breathing, swollen and painful arms and legs. None of it altered the joy she felt each day she could spend at her husband's side.

They were still all too few. Lafayette remained persona non grata in France. The family settled in Holland while Adrienne, ill and lame, traveled repeatedly to Paris on behalf of family, friends, former servants, and the family's innumerable creditors. In Paris she located Pere Carrichon, who had survived his dangerous role as a priest-in-hiding, and in 1802 officiated at George Washington Lafayette's marriage.

After months of secret inquiry she also succeeded in locating the mass grave where 1300 headless bodies, including those of her mother, sister, and grandmother, had been unceremoniously dumped. With other relatives of the victims she arranged for a wall to be built around the tragic site and daily prayers to be recited in an adjacent chapel.

Adrienne died, surrounded by her family, on Christmas Eve 1807. She was buried in a plot next to that hallowed wall. Her husband lived to play a part in the peace that followed Napoleon's defeat at Waterloo, to tour the United States half a century after independence, to resume command of the National Guard after the Revolution of 1830. Twenty-seven years after Adrienne's death, honored by two nations, loved by innumerable beauties, Gilbert was laid to rest beside the woman who had loved him best.

FIVE

Johanna Lind Hult

by Ingrid Trobisch

HER ONLY CLAIM TO FAME was a photograph of herself on the front page of the *New York Herald Tribune* on Monday, May 19, 1941. It was also the darkest day of her life. Two of her children, a son-in-law, and three grandchildren were reported to have gone to their graves off the coast of Africa. They had been travelling on an Egyptian ship which was sunk by a German raider. It is of such tragedies that news is made.

I remember the events of the day well, for she was my grandmother and I lived through them with her. One of the passengers reported lost was my own dear father.

A sophomore in high school, I was dismissed from classes so that I could be with her. Calm and controlled, she listened to the radio reports hour after hour on that black Monday. At the age of seventy-seven she was by nature an energetic little woman with hands that didn't know how to be idle. She had acquired the discipline of "just being quiet" with difficulty.

The words of farewell she spoke to my father just a month before came back to me. Her head barely even with his shoulders, she had looked up at him and said: "Ralph, remember when you left for Africa that first time, more than twenty years ago? I told you then it was the happiest day of my life. Today I want to say the same thing again."

Now the radio was telling her that she had lost not only a son but also a daughter, and all of her daughter's family.

That day was the longest I had ever lived through. The late news brought us the thinnest ray of hope, suggesting that some passengers may have survived and been taken aboard a prison ship.

The next morning I awoke to the ringing of the phone. As I picked up the receiver, I heard the operator say: "Long distance calling."

An unfamiliar voice came on: "This is Dr. Swanson from mission headquarters in Minneapolis." Why was he calling me? I wondered. Then he said: "We've just received good news from the United Press. Your father is alive and safe! So are your aunt and uncle, and all the other missionaries and passengers. Will you tell your mother and your grandmother?"

Black Monday had given way to a Tuesday of good tidings! The sun was shining. Birds were singing in the maple trees. The world went round and round. It was like Easter joy.

My grandmother's face was serene as she heard the message. It was a serenity that told of suffering overcome.

My earliest memory was of finding refuge in my grandmother's house. It was to me a place of security, love, and warmth.

My parents had returned from their mission post at Moshi, Tanzania, on the slopes of Mt. Kilimanjaro in East Africa. I was born there just in time to make a long boat trip through the Red Sea, the Mediterranean, and then to Sweden. Here we spent a wonderful three months, which brought healing of body, mind, and soul to my battle-worn parents. Along with my two older brothers, I kept them well-occupied. When we reached the States, we settled in Wahoo, Nebraska, where my father did deputation work for the mission.

I am told that I cried often as a young child. My parents rarely picked me up to comfort me since the rules of child-rearing advised against it. I have often wondered if that "weeping child," which my husband said he sometimes detected in me, would have been healed earlier if my mother had ignored the "experts." By the time her last child arrived, she had forgotten those rules and had learned to listen to her own inner mother-voice. At any rate, it must have been a difficult time, and my grandmother, living next door, realized it. She took me in from time to time, and I had "only child" status in her home.

My playthings were stored in a box tucked underneath the legs of her electric stove. The stove was a table model, under which I found the quietness and shelter I needed. After a period of "hiding out" under her watchful eye, I was ready to return to the company of my brothers and my new baby sister. Perhaps that is what grandmothers do best—taking each child separately and giving them the individual attention that a busy mother cannot always provide.

The bond that began to be forged in these first years of my life was completed when I lived with her for two years as a young teenager. I loved her with a love founded on deep respect. Now, four decades later, I realize that her life has formed the pattern for my own. She has become for me, consciously or unconsciously, the model on which I base my life.

My grandmother, Johanna Lind Hult, affectionately known as Tilda, was born in Sweden as the Civil War was drawing to a close in the United States. Her father, Svante Lind, born in a humble tenant home near Skara, Sweden, had a lively sense of humor, which his daughter was to inherit. Her mother, Anna Kajse Larsdotter was born in the city of Skara in somewhat more comfortable circumstances than her future husband. But her father lost the family property when in good faith he signed a note for a friend which dragged them into poverty.

This misfortune prevented Anna from completing school. However, she had a great talent for music and was invited to sing at elite parties of noble families. Since she was not of the noble class herself, she was requested to sing off stage and stand behind a curtain. Eventually, she took a job as a household maid at Harlunda where Svante worked as a hired man. Before long he had fallen in love with the pretty redhead. Anna's mistress presented her with a wedding dress and prepared her for her upcoming marriage. After their wedding in 1856, Svante had to join the

Swedish army and the young couple moved into a small house. The rent amounted to two days of his soldier's pay per week. He kept his own little garden plot which he worked with his milk cow.

Thirteen years later he fled from the army service, since it was impossible in those days to get permission for a release. He sold the family cow and scraped together enough for his passage to America, promising God that he would eventually send for his family and that he would pay back every cent of the money he had borrowed for the trip.

As he travelled across England by train, his knapsack with his food and all his clothes for the voyage fell off the top of the train. Months later he arrived in Hampton, Illinois, where he worked in the coal mines earning enough to pay his debts and the passage to America for his family. Finally, he wrote to his wife in Sweden, advising her to sell the household goods, and even the precious loom which had helped her earn an income by weaving fine linens and selling them. Unfortunately, Svante was not a good business man. He ordered the tickets from a swindler who never delivered them to Anna and the five children.

The impoverished family had to move out of their little house to a yet smaller one and work by the day. The older children were forced to beg. Rye porridge, dark bread, and turnips were often all they had to eat. It was some time before Svante realized that he had been cheated. When Anna's letter came, explaining that no tickets had arrived, he had to start all over again earning their passage. At last he succeeded. Three years after his arrival, on June 17, 1872, he welcomed his family to their new home, a cabin in Hampton Hills, East Moline. Then, in 1879, the family moved to Phelps County, Nebraska, where Svante built a two-room sod house.

Johanna Mathilda Lind, born March 23, 1864, was eight years old on the trip to America. She grew to be a happy and generous child, who loved to help her mother take care of her baby sister. As a young girl she left the family home in Nebraska for a time to attend school in Illinois. She told her mother that the only thing better than going to school in Illinois was rocking her little sister to sleep. But in less than three years the little schoolhouse she attended went up in smoke. The end of the schoolhouse spelled the end of her formal education. From then on she had to work for her living. In Moline she found jobs helping professors and friends from the church where she took confirmation instruction. Though her formal education was limited, she was a bright girl, and she learned much from her contacts with educated people. But before long she was called back to Nebraska.

Her mother had fallen from a ladder and broken her arm at the wrist. Tilda was needed at home. By now she had become a pretty young woman. Bachelors were plentiful and she had quite a few admirers. Before long, she became engaged to a gifted young student who preached at their church one Christmas. He arranged for her to stay with a pastor's family so that she could learn the duties of a pastor's wife. So it was back to Illinois for a time. Shortly after she returned in 1884 her fiance died of tuberculosis. Her youthful hopes were crushed. It seemed that the way of life that was opening before her had suddenly collapsed, just as her hopes for an education had been demolished with the destruction of the schoolhouse. Once again, she took her misfortune in a "stately" mood, as the Swedes would say. God must have other plans for her life.

The Lutheran Church in Kearney was now built and Tilda attended all the meetings and services. A young man by the name of Henry Hult was also a faithful attender. One day Henry asked Tilda's brother-in-law, who frequented the hardware store where he worked, whether she would be interested in forming an acquaintance with him. When her brother-in-law posed the question to Tilda, she simply replied, "Let him ask me. I will give him the answer myself."

Henry and Tilda's wedding took place at her parent's home on the 28th of August, 1887. A comfortable bower was built for the festivities because the sod house was too crowded. Six witnesses stood up for them. "When all had been fed, a powerful thunder and lightning broke loose," writes one of the relatives. "And the water stood like a lake upon the yard. The guests gathered in several small groups. We had to vacate the leafy bower since the roof didn't keep out the rain. But the guests were happy. At the time it was quite an aristocratic wedding." Tilda's younger sister Ida adds these details: "Father and the boys made a frame out of tree branches, a sort of canopy. Benches and chairs were brought from church, and tables were set in the sod home. Mother cooked a whole lamb in the wash boiler, which we ate with potatoes, vegetables, and lemon pie. Augusta and I sang, 'Farewell dear sister.' We had new pink sateen dresses with a small design in the material. Very pretty, of course. Tilda had sewed them."

The newlyweds made their home in Kearney. It was here that their first son, my father, was born on July 9, 1888. They named him Ralph. The heat was terrible, but since so many people were dying of swamp fever (malaria) Henry had asked Tilda to keep the windows closed. He didn't want his wife and child to be infected. She suffered more from the heat than from anything else, she said.

Both parents had dedicated Ralph to the Lord even before he was born. They prayed that he would be a pastor, and, later, God heard their prayers.

Even as a young wife, Tilda was active with her husband in their church. They both taught Sunday School, taking turns so that one could teach while the other watched the little ones in their growing family.

One of my aunts describes Henry and Tilda: "Both Mother and Father were deeply spiritual. Church attendance was an accepted rule, and only sickness kept a member of the family at home. Family devotions were a regular part of our lives at home. Every day began and ended with moments at the family altar. Both our parents served God with deep devotion. Father served on church boards and just before his death was elected to the Luther College Board.

"Good literature and learning were also part of our home life. Mother practically went through school with us, reading history, geography, and other of our textbooks. Father would often read aloud for Mother's benefit, as she was busy knitting, mending, or sewing.

"Father was a man of discipline. He was a man of order and care. But he was also loving and tender. Whenever one of us had a birthday, we had a special treat in store—the birthday child would climb into Father's comfortable lap during morning devotions.

There was no better place. At Christmas he was a child along with us."

In August, 1907, Henry and Tilda moved to Wahoo so that their children could be educated at Luther College. By now they had five sons and three daughters. However, Henry did not live to see his hopes fulfilled. He had gone back to Kearney again to see that his pledge to give the first wagonload of wheat to missions was carried out. This accomplished, he was riding in the wagon which had been used to haul the wheat to the elevator. The horses became frightened and ran wild. Henry fell to the ground and landed on his back. Peritonitis set in after he reached home in Wahoo. He died at home, October 28, 1907.

Their marriage had lasted for twenty years. At the age of forty-three Tilda was a widow with eight children, from the ages of two to nineteen, to raise alone. Again her dreams went up in smoke. Within weeks after Henry's death, her third son died of peritonitis after a ruptured appendix. Shortly after, her brother John, a bachelor who planned to come and live with her and the children, died the next spring. Three deaths within five months—and yet she refused to give up.

She remained in Wahoo, as Henry would have wanted, so that her seven children could be educated there. My aunt describes these years: "Soon after Father's death, Mother bought a house on the western edge of Wahoo. It had four acres, a barn, and a good house. Just north of this was a ten-acre apple orchard. Mother purchased this too. She was determined that none of us would have to quit school. It was Father's wish that we all be educated in our church school, Luther College.

"Mother worked hard. We always had plenty of good meals, we were well-dressed. She made many of our dresses out of good used clothes that Aunt Lou sent us. Mother would rip them and wash the cloth, careful to preserve any of the lovely trimmings which could be used again. She used apples in every possible way, canning and drying them for winter. She had two cows, whose calves she would sell to the local butcher. She also raised a litter of pigs to sell each year, feeding them completely on apples (not a kernel of corn). She also sold milk and cider that we made on our own cider press.

"We were never hungry or in need, even though the crop yield was minimal some years. We had a wonderful place to live. Throughout her thirty-eight years as a widow, Mother kept a happy and good home for us children."

One of her nephews said of her: "She spoke so advisedly, always with a deep and natural Christian accent." She was a living example of Proverbs 31:25-26:

> Strength and dignity are her clothing, and she laughs at the time to come. She opens her mouth with wisdom, and the teaching of kindness is on her tongue.

During the time that I lived with her, she taught me that all Saturday work—cleaning, baking, preparations for Sunday—must be finished by noon. This was her unswerving rule. Then, as she told me, "I go to my bedroom and close the door. My Lord and I have time to fellowship and I study His word." On Sunday morning she would stand in front of the young people's class at church, and they would listen to this wise woman. She spoke out of her long experience, and her words carried authority. One of her former students wrote this about her: "Mrs. Hult—I don't even know her first name—in the 'old days' women weren't called by their given names. I can just picture her walking so stately and dignified, a beautiful woman with a soft speaking voice. She was one of those pioneer women who gave us so much. What a rich heritage we have and how I thank the Lord for it!"

My grandmother took pride in her appearance. I heard her called the best-dressed lady in church. For a poor widow, she was very elegant, because she had a sense of creativity, especially when it came to decorating her hats and remaking her dresses. She was a lady in the best sense of the word, great in the art of self-acceptance. She had learned the secret of Simone de Beauvoir's words: "It is the task of every woman to forget herself, but how can she do that if she doesn't know who she is? Some women never learn to know who they are; and that's why they have so little to give others." My grandmother knew who she was, and this made her one who could speak wisely and with authority.

After the death of her husband, son, and brother she would sometimes express her sorrow by playing Swedish hymns on the organ. Many of them were based on melancholy folk song melodies. Once when she began to play, her youngest child, not yet four, lay on the rug and sobbed, "Mother, that makes me so sad." She never played them again.

Tilda was a good mother of sons. As a child, I sensed that her four sons, one of them a pastor and the others successful businessmen, were very proud of her.

Her sense of humor endeared her to others and restored perspective in difficult situations. I remember one story she liked to tell about herself. She occasionally suffered from dizzy spells. One day she had an attack of dizziness while shopping. To prevent herself from falling down, she held on tight to the bar outside the store. Only after she recovered and walked on did she realize that she had been standing outside the saloon and holding herself up on the bar meant for drunks.

She was an orderly woman, but not a perfectionist. When I threw the dish towel over the hanger after drying the dishes, she would show me how to fold it carefully, so that the kitchen had a "straightened-up" look. But she knew that "nothing is 100% on this earth," and she could be satisfied when something was less than perfect.

Even in her seventies she was a woman of action. When something had to be done, she did it. I recall travelling with her and my father through the Ozarks. We would see sheds in great disrepair. "Let me out," she told my father. "I'd just like to push that one over."

Instead of deploring a situation, she thought of how it could be bettered. If she saw a fruit tree in our orchard with saplings, she broke them off herself instead of telling someone it should be done.

I remember how she praised my own mother: "Ingrid, no one can prepare a good meal with so little to do it with like your mother." Daughters need to hear these words for they don't always have the perspective of someone outside the home.

My grandmother was seventy-eight when she bade farewell to my father as he set out for Africa, this time never to return. Shortly afterwards my mother became desperately ill. She had tularemia, an infectious disease transmitted by insect bites. In 1942, with few drugs to combat it, the doctors gave her little chance of survival.

My grandmother wrote to us children (I was sixteen, the eldest daughter with seven younger brothers and sisters at home): "When I heard about your mother and how terribly ill she was, I went into my bedroom by myself and pleaded with my Lord for help. I asked Him to spare her if possible. I felt relieved and got the assurance that she would get well."

These words gave me more comfort than if the doctor had pronounced my mother's life out of danger. I had great respect for my grandmother's Lord although I didn't have a personal relationship with him myself at that time.

My younger sister told me of the first letter she received from Grandmother. It came when she was spending a year with one of our cousins in order to take confirmation training and to help in the family of small children. Grandmother wrote: "It's your first time away from home and I know you're lonesome and miss your family, but you're with good people." At the end of the letter was the footnote, "P.S. I'm sending you mittens." It was this tangible sign of her love which comforted her granddaughter the most.

At the time he was leaving the States to go to Africa in the midst of World War II my father wrote to his younger brother: "Have received a wonderful letter from Mother. . . . That letter means so much to me right now." My father was to die from a heart attack after contracting malaria. He died in Dar es Salaam, Africa. I had to break the news to Grandmother on her seventy-ninth birthday. It was a hard blow for both of us, and I leaned on her strength.

Two years later as I walked home from church with her, she turned to me and said, "Ingrid, this is my last week on earth. Soon I shall be with Henry and with your father, Ralph." There was no sentiment—just a matter-of-fact statement.

We had grown especially close after my experience of faith at the end of my freshman year in college. An avid reader all her life, she shared with me the biographies of the great missionary pioneers. When her eyes were tired, I read to her and knew that deep joy of kinship and mutual understanding that comes from being related on a spiritual as well as physical level.

One of the last days of her life, she called me to her bedside. My two sisters and I had come to sing for her and she had requested the song, "Under His Wings, I Am Safely Abiding." Then she asked me, "Ingrid, you want to go to the Sudan, don't you? You feel that this is your calling, to carry on there where your father did pioneer work—but where he could not stay?" I assured her that this was my wish. "Then may I bless you to this end," she said and laid her hands upon me.

I thought of the promise of Psalm 103:17: "But the steadfast love of the Lord is from everlasting to everlasting upon those who fear him, and his righteousness to children's children, to those who keep his covenant and remember to do his commandments."

I was with her as she died in her home, her children around her bedside. It was the first time that I had seen a loved one departing from this life. There was the gasp for air and then a look of great peace came over her. My nine-year-old sister was with us. Later, she said to me, "Ingrid, I don't know whether to cry or to be happy. I am sad to lose my grandma but I know she's happy now."

Because I saw my grandmother die, I realized that death, for a believer, is not to be feared. Therefore, I did not panic when I saw my own husband, so alive one minute, leave this world for good the next. I could imagine the reunion they must have had—my father, my grandmother, and Walter. Knowing that they are together before God's throne, I sometimes feel as though I have a peephole into heaven, something which keeps me going when things seem difficult here.

Grandmother's words comforted me in my own time of trial at Walter's death. One of my aunts wrote to me then and quoted her, saying, "God never places a burden or sorrow on shoulders unfit to carry them." Certainly her shoulders had been strong enough for sorrows and now mine must be too.

In her last years, Grandmother made me a quilt out of the dresses she had sewn for me throughout the years. It was a labor of love and demonstrated her skill with the needle. She gave it to me knowing that she wouldn't be able to quilt it. Her three daughters sat together the days after her death and finished it for me. It has been on my bed in Africa, Germany, Austria, and now in my home in Springfield, Missouri. Maybe this too is a task of grandmothers—to make things of lasting beauty for their children and grandchildren. Still today her tangible love keeps me warm.

After my grandmother's death, one of my aunts said, "How we will miss her prayers for us all, for she's no longer here on earth!" I am convinced that although we are separated in body, we are not separated in spirit and that her blessing is with us even more than before. How often I have felt her invisible hand of blessing as I have undertaken a project which seemed humanly impossible. An Episcopalian friend wrote to me recently that the prayers of the Saints are even more powerful than when they were on earth: "Your dear and much loved husband, Walter, prays for you daily and his prayers and the prayers of the Saints allotted each day to pray for your work sustain you and enable you to do what you must here on earth. Because so few people understand the role that the Saints and loved ones who have gone before us are able to play in the lives of those still on earth, much joy is missed and much appreciation, too, of their regard and interest and help."

Gertrude le Fort has said that men are like monuments. Rarely does a famous man have a famous son, because he is likely to burn himself out in his work. But mothers are like rivers, flowing from one generation to the next. "Like a Gulf Stream," they said about Sarah Edwards, the wife of Jonathan Edwards, and her influence on future generations. The same could be said about my grandmother, with all her pioneer qualities, her steadfastness, serenity, stamina, and strength.

I find myself in the middle of this stream. I can reach out one arm and touch my grandmother, carrying with me her example of courage in the face of sorrow and with the other arm touch my grandchildren and pass on to them the heritage of their great-great grandmother.

SIX

Elizabeth Rooney

by Luci Shaw

THE BELL RANG and the poetry workshop closed with a flurry of final questions. As I gathered my lecture notes together and walked out of the classroom with a group of students, a woman who had been waiting quietly by the door came up to me somewhat apologetically to ask if I would look at one of her poems. I was not surprised. People are always doing this. The poem she handed me was simple and short—nine lines. I read it through twice and felt at once the tingling certainty that this was writing beyond the commonplace. I noted the name typed at the bottom—Elizabeth B. Rooney. For me it was a moment of recognition, not of the name—I had never heard it before—but of a kindred spirit, one whose work had a poetic quality that lifted me out of that noisy, academic hallway at the heart of a writers' conference into the limitless blue of an evening sky patterned with darting chimney swifts:

The chimney swifts cut patterns in the sky.
They snip, snip, snip
Great soaring circles of the hanging blue
And carry them away to line their nests
So fledgling chimney swifts,
Born in the dark, soot-blinded,
Will be reminded of the sky

And know which way to go
When they begin to fly.

I heard myself voicing a remark rare for me: "Mrs. Rooney, this is extraordinarily good stuff! Can I see more of your poems?" Appearing genuinely surprised, though pleased, she handed me two other typed sheets. I read them both through with rising excitement. The first was called "Cream."

From the white depths
The poem's richness rises,
Clotting in thickened skins
Across my soul.

I rise and skim
The spirit-filled surprises
And fill with cream
The paper's empty bowl.

Next was "Eschaton":

I saw the world end yesterday!
A flight of angels tore
Its cover off and heaven lay
Where earth had been before.

I walked about the countryside
And saw a cricket pass.
Then, bending closer, I espied
An ecstasy of grass.

I looked at the writer more closely. Elizabeth Rooney was an unpretentious woman with short, nearly white hair and a face of singular sweetness, tranquility, and strength. In the brief conversation that followed she told me some things about herself which intrigued and moved me.

The most striking fact to emerge was that in August 1978 during her induction into a lay order of Episcopal women known as the

Society of the Companions of the Holy Cross, and during the retreat that had followed, she had experienced a sudden, astonishing joy, an awareness of God's presence and his sweetness that affected her profoundly. "I fell in love with God," she told me simply. "It was as if my veins were bubbling with champagne."

As this spiritual and emotional exaltation grew in the following weeks, she came to realize that she had been supernaturally overwhelmed by the Holy Spirit in a way she had neither expected nor asked for. One of the results was that she began to write poetry, something she had not done since college days.

I asked her about this new gift. "How often do you write these verses? And how many?" "Oh, all the time," she replied with a laugh, "sometimes as many as four or five a day." The amazing thing to me was not only the number of poems she was writing, but their literary quality, their sharply focused intensity, if these samples were representative. They reminded me of Emily Dickinson.

Of course, I thought, this is the sort of thing that *should* happen—first the Holy Spirit's visitation, then the spiritual release spilling into the intellect—the holy overflow resulting in a surge of creative thoughts and images and words. Why was this coalescing of spirit, intelligence, and imagination so rare? I had often been urgently assured by writers who were Christians that "the Holy Spirit gave me this poem," only to be shown writing of such banality or sentimentality, work so stale or derivative, that I blushed for the Holy Spirit. But here was writing that resonated. It was fresh, vivid, richly packed with meaning, imaginative—real poetry. The seed ideas had been *shaped* into works of art. A poet is, by definition, a "maker," one who works the "given" images and concepts into arrangements of words, not just a human CRT on line with the Main Computer.

How had this gentle, unassuming woman been able so spontaneously to combine real faith with creativity? I sensed a mystery at work; the word "mystic" even came to mind. Yet though there was an otherworldly dimension to Elizabeth Rooney, it was fused with a practical earthiness that was appealing—comfortable and comforting.

But other workshops were beginning that afternoon. Our time

was gone. We exchanged addresses and after I asked her to send me more of her writing we said goodbye and blessed each other in Christ's name.

In the following months our contacts were infrequent, occurring in the cracks of our two very crowded lives—a letter or two, a phone call. I realized I knew little about the details of either her present life or her background, but her chimney swifts kept darting through my thinking.

The following winter Elizabeth phoned me one snowy night to say that she was in Wheaton for a trade show (A trade show? This contemplative dreamer?) but that this one evening was free. Could she come over and visit us? "Yes, if you'll bring me some more poems!" A delighted chuckle—she just happened to have some with her! When she arrived, the trade show mystery was solved; she explained that her family farm in Blue Mounds, Wisconsin, overlies a natural underground cave, the Cave of the Mounds, containing scores of limestone formations—a tourist attraction, with a gift shop and restaurant. Elizabeth was at the Dupage County Fairgrounds near us for a Winter Sports Show, to publicize the Brigham Farm cross-country ski trails, newly developed for winter tourists.

That evening, with an oak wood fire blazing in our family room fireplace, we spread out her poems on the couch and began to explore together the shared country of the spirit and the imagination. We discovered how much we have in common, our acquaintance with and deep admiration for people like Madeleine L'Engle and Winifred Couchman, our wholehearted response to the created world that greenly surrounds us both, our passionate love for good literature, our perfectionism—the compulsion to get things *right*, our vulnerability to the demands of other people's needs, our hunger for personal approval and acceptance, our fascination with the metaphysical poets, our equivocal responses to the constant pulls from several directions—God, family, vocation, occupation (to put it another way—from prayer, people, writing, and daily work).

It was an evening rich with shared realities. I confessed to her my delight at finding, at our first meeting, a Christian whose writing seemed to flower so naturally out of closeness to God and nature—human and otherwise—that there seemed to be no dichotomy between faith and art. We discussed how poetry rises most authentically from the events and impressions of ordinary life, the specifics—what C.S. Lewis called "the tether and pang of the particular"—and in a letter following our time together, Elizabeth quoted to me a current entry from her journal: "The more I strive for pure holiness, the more I am plunked back into the ordinary—the miracle of rain and of green, the essential toadness of a toad. Yes, the end *is* the beginning but with this difference—at the end you comprehend the sacramental quality of the beginning and rediscover that though ordinariness is all there is, ordinariness is no longer ordinary, it is, rather, sacred and infinitely significant. The carrot I peel is no longer merely a carrot."

In a later letter she commented on the arrival of poems: "Mine seem to come like butterflies, and I try to net them and get them on paper without knocking too many bright bits of color off their wings. My problem is to know how to improve them without destroying them. I do hope they can open to me more friendships like yours and chances to tell people about the Lord to whose love we all respond."

As Elizabeth Rooney continued to send me new poems and as we discussed ways to strengthen them further, I encouraged her to share them with a wider circle. She had already been urged to do this by friends and critics such as Margaret Sheets and Virginia Huntington. But her hesitation is typical of new poets. "I must confess I feel timid about sharing my poems with anyone; it's a step toward intimacy, somehow." Coupled with her natural diffidence was the problem of finding quiet time to write and rewrite, let alone time to type and retype, then submit the work to editors. There was also the sense that a precious, private vision would, in the process of publication, become commercialized. But gradually she gained confidence that God's gifts of insight are not meant to be guarded and hidden, but broadcast like seeds so that they might root in other fertile minds.

When the opportunity came for me to write this chapter, I knew I wanted to write about a woman who was both Christian and poet.

Rather than telling of the impact on my life of an internationally known personality, I felt a growing conviction that I would rather talk about someone like Elizabeth Rooney, an "ordinary" woman, hardly known beyond her own circle of friends and colleagues, though uniquely gifted by God. Her experience would, I was sure, suggest to other women with earthbound, unremarkable lives that he could lift the most mundane existence into his own beauty and glory. What he requires are eyes open to his brightness and ears alert for his voice.

My discovery of Elizabeth was furthered through the reading of some of her journals, generously lent at my request. Never intended for publication, but written purely as a series of personal reflections, they are diaries of soul-growth rather than historical records, pinning down on paper her day-to-day responses and insights and the seemingly trivial events that might otherwise evaporate and be forgotten. A large proportion of her entries are poems in different stages of composition, often distilling into verse the content of the prose entry for that day. In her small, neat writing she gave me a series of provocative hints and clues to her circumstances, the people she loved, the web of her activities spread between the Cave, her church, her prayer group, her home and family. Even more intriguing was the record of her developing inner life with God.

To fill in some of the gaps in my understanding, I drove the three hours northwest from West Chicago to Blue Mounds through a green and golden day in early May 1982. I recognized the Mounds from several miles away, curving up like two gentle breasts from the rolling Wisconsin terrain that surrounds them. Elizabeth had told me to follow the signs to Cave of the Mounds and to come directly to the Cave to find her. I left my car in the tree-circled parking lot and walked down the sloping track. I liked the cultivated wildness of the landscape, bright with local wildflowers and alive with the sounds of birds and wind-chimes. The gift shop, ivy-covered, against a low cliff face, was charming, inside and out. (Elizabeth had told me that, as the buyer, she chooses half the kind of gifts she likes herself and half the kind most tourists seem to demand, such as T-shirts emblazoned with the legend "Cave of the Mounds.")

And there I found her, at the back of the shop near the entrance to the subterranean Cave. A warm hug, a "Welcome!" and I felt at home. It was lunchtime, and after joining Mike, her charming, witty, down-to-earth husband, we crossed a sparkling stream to the Brigham Farm Kitchen where we had bowls of the best chili I'd ever eaten, with homemade brown bread. Later I was to go on a tour of the Cave with Mike, but first Elizabeth and I drove up the hill to their home where I was installed in the guest room.

Brigham Farm, high on the side of one of the Blue Mounds, looks south across a green lawn and through a fringe of trees to the barns and outbuildings of the Cave and its surrounding parkland, and over distant levels of fields and forests. It is an old, comfortable, two-story frame house, complete with dogs (Jiggs, Gretel, and Flopsy) and a well-used front verandah with steps good for sitting on in the early morning and drinking coffee. Throughout the house the windows are large and uncurtained ("It's O.K. The people all look out; only deer and trees look in.") A portrait of Ebenezer Brigham, one of the family patriarchs, monitors the large living room with its rich, worn, oriental rugs, shelves overflowing with books, and a wood stove that radiates a warmth as real as Elizabeth's and Mike's.

We sat on the porch steps in the afternoon sun and got down to the important business of discussing life. Our conversation ranged far and dug as deep as time would allow. We found more things in common: we both are the children of older parents and both have had life-changing encounters with the Holy Spirit. Other facts were highlighted in our conversation. Elizabeth grew up in that very house, with parents who were upright, gentle, widely read, and churchgoing. Their daughter's journal notes: "I was too young to realize how exceptional my childhood was. I remember in high school wishing I had ordinary parents who lived in a little brown house in town and went bowling and to the movies instead of parents who lived in a big white house in the country and read poetry and Dickens and the *Atlantic Monthly* aloud to each other and listened to the sermons on the Sunday Evening Club."

They were always quite poor, until the discovery of the Cave on the property began to bring in money from tourists. Elizabeth, who had learned to read at home, started her formal education in the second grade in the two-room country school in Blue Mounds. She was too bright to be happy among her peers, who viewed her as conceited. As she put it, "I was pretty miserable except that I loved to learn."

After she graduated, her class's salutatorian, from high school in Madison, she went East to Smith College. One of her professors there was Mary Ellen Chase, a writer and English teacher who dedicated her book *The Bible and the Common Reader* to Elizabeth and the three other Smith girls who were in her honors seminar when she was writing the book. Miss Chase tried to persuade Elizabeth to make writing her career, but Elizabeth felt she had nothing worthwhile to say, a feeling that changed only as she came to know God many years later.

Her time at Smith was a time of religious growth, however. She discovered the Episcopal Church, was confirmed, and headed the New England Student Christian Movement before graduating Phi Beta Kappa. Later she earned her M.A. in Christian Education from Columbia and Union Theological Seminary. Though she studied under Niebuhr, Tillich, and Van Dusen, she recalls, "I always felt that we were learning about God as if we were learning about algebra. We had brilliant propositional teaching about God, but there was no sense of God as a personal intimate."

Edwin J. Rooney—Mike—entered her life as a student at General Theological Seminary while she was at Union. As soon as they both graduated, they were married and lived, for the next thirty years, in the East, where their four children, Mark, Jonny, Betsy, and Patty were born and where Mike served as an Episcopal priest in several parishes, on the staff of the Diocese of New York, and on the Executive Council of the Episcopal Church.

In 1972 the family moved back to Wisconsin to manage Brigham Farm and the Cave of the Mounds. Elizabeth Rooney, always an active church worker, began her years as an employment counselor, helping disadvantaged youth and welfare clients. She was also a devoted and creative mother. A yellowed, pencilled school report from Patty, then seven years old, reads: "If I did not have my mother I would not be living. My mother has black hair. She mostly wears skirts. She has brown eyes. If I did not have my mother to cook my meals I would starve. My mother helps our house to be happy. She teaches me the things I want to know and should know. She likes to help the hurt people. My mother is a kind person. She loves me and I love her." It was Patty who remarked to her mother as a small child, "Everything you say goes into me and I think about it."

The second day of my visit, Patty's elder sister Betsy—small, sunny, quick, and warmly affectionate—filled me in some more. "Mom always showed us how to climb for things rather than just bringing them within our reach." The children were appreciated by their parents as homegrown friends and eager discussion partners. When I asked Betsy if her mother had any faults she hesitated. Finally, "Mother needs to learn to be angry!" she laughed.

Of course, these biographical facts only skim the surface. Elizabeth had matured beautifully in many areas in her life. Spiritually, however, she felt that she had been "marching in place." Oh, there had been gleams of spiritual insight, moments when God seemed real and close, longings for the freedom of spiritual wings. Her poem, "Wild Geese," echoes this heart cry:

Barking and calling courage to each other,
The singing skein sweeps south across the sky.
We hear their legendary cry
Saying goodbye to summer swamps and sweetness.
They know some ancient mystery of weather,
Of daring and of caring for each other,
Which we have lost.
Shrouded in sheets and city streets,
Our stifled hearts half waken at their sound.
Something within us trembles, flaps its wings,
Falls back against the ground.
We dress for breakfast, start the daily round
And wonder, why
Must we know only fenced yards,
And shelled corn, until we die?

But in God's time came God's initiative—at Adelynrood, in Byfield, Massachusetts. Elizabeth arrived there after a year's probation and study, to become a member of a very special group of lay women—the Society of the Companions of the Holy Cross, whose lives are committed to intercession, thanksgiving, and simplicity of life.

And now, because she has said it all so much more truly and cleanly, firsthand, than I could describe it for her, here are some "bits of bright color" from the butterfly wings of Elizabeth Rooney's journals—excerpts I have chosen thematically rather than in any strict, chronological order.

† † †

"How does someone feel when the God of Love moves into her life?" I had wondered. These were some of Elizabeth's first responses:

From her journal entry for August 11, 1978:

"Invite a tornado in and what do you get? You get swept away, that's what—'A mighty, rushing wind.' I hadn't really thought of inviting you in, Lord. I sort of thought I'd just keep handing you bits and peices of my life, like feeding a tramp at the back door without letting him in to mess up the kitchen. You know and I know that I need to let you in. So here goes everything. . . ."

Her first poem, "Adelynrood":

The winter of my heart
Melts here.
Rivulets run
Beneath the ice of fear.

Pierced by your warmth
Life moves.
Spring has begun.
I feel the sun, the sun!

"I am overjoyed—literally bursting with joy. I could caper like a young lamb, except that, not being a young lamb, I would look ridiculous."

RECRUITED

I didn't mean to get into this army of yours, Lord.
I didn't bargain on joy, and on all of this love.
How do I follow these barely perceptible signals
That frequently seem to be coming to me from above?

I've been a good Christian soldier for plenty of years, Lord,
Careful and steady and dull, always marching in place.
I've made very sure that I never would get any closer,
Never so close as to hear you or look in your face.

I thought we were only supposed to be playing a game, Lord,
There on the shore, asking "What would you have me to do?"
Now nothing about me will ever again be the same, Lord,
And it will be ages and ages before you are through!

"My whole purpose and training has been toward excelling, and certainly part of the joy of all this has been a newfound courage that frees me to excel more than I ever did before. But if I start taking credit for this I betray the situation. I feel presumptuous saying that this is the work of the Holy Spirit, but dishonest if I pretend that good old EBR suddenly, all on her own, got her act together and began writing letters and poetry and saying her prayers and getting dishes done promptly and losing weight and being more hospitable and less critical and needing less sleep. And all of this has, in fact been happening with no effort of will on my part. I've just felt so energized by love and joy that I can't obey quickly enough."

"One thing that makes me feel a little daffy and which I hesitate to admit is that I'm inclined to take God entirely literally. When we make everything symbolic we create distance between ourselves and him and I do think God wants closeness. Somehow, this is an appalling idea! When I think of the awesome majesty of God and then that he wants to know me personally, to share my life, to enter my being, to be part of my simple, domestic, earthbound existence, not just symbolically but literally, I feel so inappropriate for such a friendship."

"He doesn't love me *because of me*—my great loveableness; he loves me *because of him*—his great capacity for love."

"The world today is full of charismatic Christians who have the courage to witness to the Lord. I am tempted to be private and special, holier than them, to accuse them of phoniness, bad taste, lack of discretion—any excuse to avoid identifying myself as one who has been with Jesus. The cock that crew for Peter crows for me."

†

Always a keen observer and lover of nature, Elizabeth felt her response to creation and the commonplace augmented by her new closeness to the Creator:

"I'm so glad God loves color. What a generous distributor of it he is—but also, always the ultimate artist, never picture-postcard color. Vulgarity and Puritanism are alike in denying God—the one, his artistry and restraint, and the other, his joy and exuberance."

"The sun has come over the horizon and the eastern side of every leaf and branch and tree trunk is glistening with gold. I feel like that. I'm always the same twig, but to the extent that I allow myself to be suffused with God as the trees are with sunlight I am transformed, golden and glistening. I don't have to do anything except stay in the same place and be still and let him come."

All of the bushes are burning now!
All of the trees are aflame!
The woods are alive with the glory of God
And the leaves are telling his name!

"I am trying for simplicity of life and every day gets richer and more peopled, more alive with beauty and tenderness. Mike is so dear and loving, Jonny and Mark and Patty and Betsy so fond and promising; the Companions pour affection into my life; and Grace Church is blossoming with love and prayer. And this benign weather—this gentle, golden Fall! A sunset tonight like a great, rose-colored wing curved over the edge of the world."

JOSEPH

Joseph was a good man.
It's hard to be

A good man here below.
Joseph was true,
True as a tree is true.
He did what the angel
Told him to do.
When Mary needed his shelter,
He was there,
Strong as a tree,
Four square.
Joseph knew how to obey.
We'd call him Joe
If he were living today—
"Hey Joe, can you mend
My hay rack?"
"Why Joe, you've done
a beautiful job on my chair!"
Yes, Joseph was a good man.
When God needed him,
He was there.

"The Baltimore orioles are back—three at least, whistling their triple whistles and flashing in and out among the new leaves, leaves so new that they run through all possible variations of lemon and lime. And the leaves of one oak tree are distinctly and delicately pink. Imagine making something as useful as a tree, as efficient at converting sunlight into food and fuel, as huge and tough as a white oak that can live 300 years, and then decorating it with tiny, pink leaves and pale green tassels of blossoms. Until men can make solar convertors as beautiful and functional as oak trees, we had better remember to feel humble."

†

Did her growth toward holiness and her new clearness of vision negate Elizabeth's individuality and personhood? Emphatically no! Listen to the humanity that vibrates from these entries:

"Today I am—'fifty-four and ready for more!' Mike says I remind him of the *New Yorker* cartoon of the very rich, very fat man kneeling by his bed in his silk dressing gown and saying, 'I want more!' "

"Today I couldn't do anything right and all my pretensions have been pretty well knocked from under me. God knows the pretensions are ridiculous and so he mercifully relieved me of them. But I feel pretty blah, like a pricked balloon. I guess deflated is the opposite of elated."

"Mother used to say regularly, 'What have you done today to justify your existence?' When I told the prayer group this last week, they shuddered visibly. The question epitomizes the pre-redemption dilemma—how do I earn my own salvation? All through school I worked so hard to achieve, to prove my worth, to please my mother. But the goal was self-centered—*my* success, *my* worth."

"I know now that I can never justify my existence, or deserve God's friendship. Instead I think about him and am overwhelmed. I want to be as good, as pure, as humble, as useful, as obedient as he can make me—not to justify my existence but to say Thank You."

"The important thing is not whether my will is crossed (lovely verb!) but whether I yield to anger, self-pity, revenge when I am crossed, or whether I can attain gentleness and humility and unselfishness."

"Our old, faithful dog just died within the last twenty minutes. We each work out our grief in our own way. I'm trying to get as much of mine as I can out through words. Jonny has taken a chain saw and retreated into the woods north of the house where he is working his out on the logs."

FARM DOG

The chain saw bites through the skin and flesh of the log.
The sawdust spills bright on the fallen snow,
Bright as the blood of the farmer's favorite dog
When she came staggering back from the road below.

She was already dying, there at the door,
Still wagging her tail, still trusting his love to save her.
He had not known what kind of a morning chore
Awaited him. Still, he was there, and gave her

All of the love he could—called the vet,
Carried her out to the truck.

They sutured the gaping wound but her heart gave out.
And now he is out in the woods
In his old green coat, tackling the logs for relief—Sawing
and sawing and sawing away at his grief.

"It's so important to live fully. Since grief is my assignment for today, Lord, help me to grieve wholeheartedly, allowing the reality of the grief to possess me until it becomes appropriate to move beyond it."

†

For Christian women with family responsibilities as well as the call to be accountable for a creative gift and its development, there will always be an ongoing conflict. Which stands highest on the priority scale—the urgent or the important? What do you give your time to—God, family, gift, or a needy world? Here are Elizabeth's thoughts, as one finite individual responding to multiple demands:

"We are part of the web of the world and God wants to redeem the whole web. (The cat just threw up and a squirrel has arrived on the bird feeder. Some web! I have also fed Jiggs and the cats, plugged in the truck, and started the dishwasher.) That's in parentheses but it's relevant. These are the realities of the web I'm meshed in and it's not for me to say or feel that it's more important for me to write poetry than to mop up after the cat. There's no doubt about what I'd *rather* do but the important thing is what God would rather I did. Some choices are obvious, but right now, should I get Mike's breakfast or keep on writing? It's 7:50 and I've been writing for three hours. I'll write until 8:00 and then cope with domesticity."

"The trouble with falling in love with you, Lord, is that I miss you so terribly unless I am with you all the time. Looking back I can see I am like Peter in his attempt to walk on water. The minute I begin to hoard anything—my strength, my time, my energy, the pleasures of feeling filled with the Spirit—I lose my peace, begin again to worry and complain. Right down into the water of failure I go."

"Moments of aloneness are so precious. What shall I do first—pray or write? To write without praying seems so precipitate and unblessed and yet, if I always begin with praying when I have so little time for writing, I will never get the writing done at all."

OH, BOTHER!

Why don't you give up, God?
You know me by now—
The churning restlessness,
The worrying, and how
Tense and distracted I am.

You keep asking me
To stop fussing and play,
To relax and rejoice
And admire your new day.
I'm *busy*, Lord.
I have things to do.
Like Martha, I am never through.

Yes, I know Mary chose
The better part,
Simply stopped still
And opened up her heart.
It's something I would really
Like to do
But not right now. Right now
I'm much too busy
For you.

"Today I ache all the way from toe to head. Menopause? Accumulated fatigue? Guilt? Evil spirits? I think I'll assume normal accumulated fatigue and just offer the remnants of my energy to the Lord and proceed in low gear for the day. There are a lot of useful things I can get done while in low gear."

"Today I cleaned the orange juice machine. The ironing is undone. We have an ozone alert. Skylab is falling. My feet hurt. Mike keeps asking me to complete the corporation minute book. Betsy looks so tired it hurts. But do these things really matter when I know that the children are moral and good, and believing

Christians, when I know that my Redeemer liveth? I need to learn over and over that the things that are happening to me in this life are the raw materials of which our Lord wants me to build a grace-filled life."

"When I left Adelynrood I was thinking that the poetry was a kind of reward for promising to follow Christ and that I must be very obedient and stick close to him so that the poetry would come. That was getting my priorities exactly backwards. If writing is a means of growing closer to God, lovely, but the goal is not writing but learning to conform my will to his. Maybe he intends me to be a frustrated poet but an obedient wife, housekeeper, ticket seller, and servant for him."

†

But it was becoming clearer to Elizabeth and to those who read her writing that she was not meant to be "a frustrated poet." The poems and insights continued to come, and with them an increased understanding of the role and the craft of the writer:

"I know what I want to say. I want to write about God, about the intense tenderness manifest in the world wherever goodness, truth, and beauty allow it to shine through, about the essence of things—Plato's ideals showing forth not just in the relative dullness of tables but in bicycles and keys and gardens and loving people. (My apologies to tables. They aren't dull either.) I want to keep saying it while it's fresh. The question is, how am I to find the time? I find myself a constant refugee from my family. I love them, need them, want them, but saying my prayers and writing poetry, the two activities of greatest importance to me at the moment, are not communal activities."

"Emily Dickinson wasn't a recluse; she was trying to concentrate."

"Writing is like praying. It doesn't come to much unless you do it every day."

"We saw an old-fashioned copper still in Horse Cave, Kentucky. The mash goes in a tightly covered kettle, a fire burns underneath, steam rises and runs downhill through a covered eavestrough and recondenses as it circulates inside a copper pipe coiled round within a barrel of cold water. The condensed steam comes out a spigot at 180 proof.

"In order to say anything significant, a writer has to operate on much the same principle. All of life's emotions, excitement, stimuli must be contained, brought to a boil, prevented from leaking out in casual conversation but instead distilled and cooled through the writing. If the experiences are rich and the writer both passionate and disciplined and, especially, also skilled with words, he can distill life as he knows it and make of it a heady potion for his readers, a rich liqueur. Writing takes solitude—and not just aloneness filled with housework and busy work and radio. Solitude has to be aloneness in which you allow all the stirred up dust of your thoughts to settle into patterns. Then, you try to describe the patterns."

†

A poet's merit is largely dependent on sensitivity. But sensitivity is openness not only to images and ideas, not only to the music of the spheres and the melody of a single phrase, but to expressions of need in other people's lives:

"'Bear ye one another's burdens and so fulfill the law of Christ.' *We are* one another's burdens and when we relate to someone, we bear *him*, not just his burdens. This concept gives significance to the most casual contact, between the customer in front of the counter and the clerk behind it, the driver waiting for a traffic light and the man in the car behind him. We have a responsibility toward all who touch our lives, even casually."

"I am beginning to learn more about the Cross. I always thought that to walk the way of the Cross meant to seek suffering, and this seemed perverse. I am beginning to realize that it means to learn to love and the more people I love and the more intensely and tenderly I love them, the more opportunities for suffering are presented, as life happens to them and as I learn to share their burdens and care about their cares. Intercession goes well with this because praying for people does make you love them more and more."

"These days it's as if everyone I meet has the potential for becoming a close and dear friend. Is it perhaps by this magic that Christians come truly to love their enemies, so instead of your enemies being people whom you hate, they are reduced to being only people who hate you—far less lethal to the soul, regardless of the effect on the body."

"If God can cure someone's cancer, why doesn't he just do it? Why include some human intercessor? I think because the cure, if cure comes, is more beautiful and intricate this way. He prefers to work through us not by force but by asking and waiting and inspiring and hoping. It's the concept of The Great Dance."

†

Ever since Elizabeth's life had been lovingly invaded by God, closeness to him had become not only the central joy but the necessity of her days. And it was in prayer that this closeness was best nourished:

MUTE

Must we use words for everything?
Can there not be
A silent, flaming leap of heart
Toward thee?

"Praying is like swimming. I have trouble getting into depth in either because I am unable or unwilling to let go and trust the element I'm moving in—whether it's water or God. I need to learn abandonment."

"I used to worry when I woke up off schedule, but now I assume that our Lord has something in mind for me, and so I rise and wait."

"Yesterday I patched Jonny's blue jeans instead of saying my prayers because it seemed closer to what God would want."

†

C.S. Lewis talked of moving further up and further in; a phrase that has often come to my mind to describe the divine-human integration is "the in-Godding of man"; however it is described, it involves the increasing intimacy of a love relationship. In her journal and poems Elizabeth Rooney talks of the process of her own growing toward God:

"Virginia Huntington uses the words 'Brim me!' in one of her poems. I think we can be filled with the Holy Spirit quite as literally as a glass is filled with water or a cup with coffee. But you can't pour anything into a cup unless it is held still. We miss the streams of grace, or they miss us, because we can't hold still enough for long enough so God has a chance to fill us with himself."

"God intends us for himself and with our eager cooperation or with our rebellious reluctance he works to achieve this. He respects the reluctance; he will hint and then wait, ask and then wait, urge and then wait. And wait and wait!"

"As I develop an ever-growing, ever-closer relationship with God, immediate mercies are swallowed up in The Mercy, immediate goods are overwhelmed by The Goodness."

"This evening my heart and veins and arteries and my whole system have been filled with a joyousness I can hardly contain. I want to pray or read but feel as though I shall explode. I need to tell someone how wonderful God is!"

I haven't cleaned the cellar,
I forgot to sweep the stair,
There's a button off my jacket,
Jonny's blue jeans have a tear,
There's an old, arthritic lady
Whom I should uphold in prayer,
And I'm sitting in the moonlight,
The moonlight, the moonlight,
Adoring you by moonlight,
As if I had no care!

"Four A.M. I got up and found it had stopped snowing, leaving about a foot of new-fallen snow in great white billows under a full moon. Mike woke up and asked what I was going to do and I said, 'Go to the bathroom,' which was a deception, since after I went to the bathroom I was going to pray and write and wander about as usual. I have to stop lying to people about how much God means to me, just because I'm embarrassed by it or think they won't understand. What if Sts. Peter and Paul had acted like that? Stroke victims have to practice and practice speaking in order to learn to speak again. I need to practice speaking about God, his love, his immanence, his active presence, his willingness to participate in our lives if we'll only let him."

"The story of the talents used to make me feel sick to my stomach because I always identified with the fellow who buried his talent. Now, after this blessed time of total commitment to Christ, I have reread the parable and find I identify with the man who had the ten talents and on whom God kept pouring out more and more good things."

"Reading Catherine Marshall's *Beyond Ourselves* is a great help. It confirms that I have come to admit with considerable timidity, that I did receive the gift of the Holy Spirit during the service when I was admitted as a Companion and that all these perceptions and emotions and sensations and guidings which have marked my life since are not just fantasies and symptoms of mental illness on my part (I have never felt more whole or healthy) but are the usual tokens of the Holy Spirit at work in a life. It's reassuring to know that other people have gone through this and grown and changed and glorified God."

"The sights and sounds of Christmas are beginning. I am like the shepherds—'The glory of the Lord shone round about them and they were sore afraid.' Being sore afraid is the only appropriate human reaction to the glory of God, but we must go toward it in spite of the fear."

"I believe that God wants to enter each of our lives as fully as he entered Mary's. Not that we're all going to get pregnant, but that the concept of incarnation is to be carried into all of creation, not just in some spiritualized way. God doesn't want a Platonic friendship. He wants to become literally incarnate in each of us. The Eucharist is the epitome of his physical identification with us. How can you become more perfectly a part of someone than by letting yourself be eaten by him?"

ENCOUNTER

I stand beneath a night of stars
And see
As far as I can look

Into infinity.
I kneel at the communion rail
And meet
That very infinite
Come down to me—
His flesh to be part of my flesh,
His blood to flow with mine,
His love come from beyond
Creation's farthest sky
As bread and wine.

† † †

It has not been hard for me to see the infinite Son of God in my finite friend Elizabeth Rooney. The more time I spend with her, the more I recognize the vibrancy of Christ living in this "ordinary saint."

Sometimes it is good to have a human model. Elizabeth is just a few years my senior (I have just reached the "fifty-four and ready for more" stage myself), but in my thinking and behavior I find myself imitating her as she herself imitates Christ. Any human contact modifies, shifts, changes us, not always for good. One of the fruits of this continuing friendship is that I sense myself to be different, better, because of Elizabeth. For me, the possibilities of the Christian life are enlarged because of her. By the gentle persuasion of her own clearly focused life she has nudged me into loving Jesus more deeply, openly, constantly, happily, wholeheartedly.

Wholehearted—that's the word. I have been searching for a precise description of this unique friend. *Enthusiastic* is a word that fits her well; its root speaks of the ardor of an in-Godded human. But even more closely, the words wholesome, healthy, healed, hale, whole—all words with a single source can unreservedly be applied to her. They bring to mind the body full of light because of its single eye, as St. Matthew expressed it. As I see her pulling into one the twin strands of the contemplative and active life (not without struggle), she seems to be finding the secret of holding the inner and outer Elizabeth in a whole, and holy, balance. In her the beauty of spirit and the clarity of disciplined intellect seem to translate freely into decisive actions, firm relationships, lucidly spoken words, imaginative prose and verse. In turn, the voice of God speaks to her through the created universe, the church, other people, literature, and the Bible, informing and shaping her inner growth, worship, and belief.

This dynamic ebb and flow moves me profoundly because of its simplicity and naturalness. Elizabeth Rooney, for all her sensitivity and awareness, seems devoid of unhealthy self-consciousness and hubris. For her, the Christian life has not been a human achievement so much as a fervent response to a divine initiative—the outpouring of Gift and Grace to which she holds up her earthen vessel for filling; or, to change the metaphor, the shining Sun towards which she tilts her mirror. Titus describes the process like this: "When the kindness and love of God our Savior appeared, he saved us, not because of righteous things we had done, but because of his mercy. He saved us through the washing of rebirth and renewal by the Holy Spirit, whom he poured out on us generously through Jesus Christ our Savior, so that, having been justified by his grace, we might become heirs having the hope of eternal life" (Ti 3:4-7).

In her journal Elizabeth supplies a vivid analogy for this divine-human joining: "Today in the Cave parking lot there was a puddle—a muddy, shallow puddle on the blacktop, not more than an inch deep at best and perhaps four feet across. When looked at from a certain angle, it reflected all the tree tops and clouds and sky, all the way to infinity. I think I'm like the puddle—muddy, shallow, insignificant—but, by God's grace, capable of the miracle of reflecting him and, in him, all the wonder of the universe. 'We have this treasure in earthen vessels that the glory may be of God and not of man. . . .'"

Hope, in a muddy flower,
Infinity, caught in a shallow pool,
Eternity, in every passing hour,
And you, Creator God, in every fool.

SEVEN

Evelyn Harris Brand

by Gladys Hunt

NO ONE WHO KNEW EVELYN HARRIS during the first thirty years of her life would have guessed that she would one day be a pioneer in missions, an indomitable figure in the hills of South India. Yet no one who knew her during the last thirty years of her life could imagine her as anything else, so single-minded was her concern for the people of the hills. From "retirement" at age seventy until she died at age ninety-five, this wisp of a woman trekked the hills on her pony spreading the Good News, caring for people few others seemed to love. Evelyn Harris Brand is God's kind of surprise in human history.

I first heard of Evelyn from her son, Dr. Paul Brand, a well-known authority on the rehabilitation of lepers. Later, I read the story of Dr. Brand's amazing achievements in India in a book entitled *Ten Fingers for God*, by Dorothy Clarke Wilson. It told of his success with the surgical reconstruction of limbs impaired by leprosy. No author could tell his story without telling something of his mother, and so I read more about Evelyn Brand. I felt unaccountably drawn to this unusual woman, and shortly after reading the book drove with my husband to the leprosarium in Carville, Louisiana, where Paul Brand was working. Subsequently, I entered into correspondence with Evelyn Brand. She was eighty-five years old when she began writing to me, telling me how she and Jesse

Brand had committed themselves to carry the Gospel to the malaria-ridden hills of the Kolli range. Her letters fairly crackled with the fire of her passion for the hill people and for God. But I am getting ahead of my story, which begins in England in 1879.

Evie, as the family called her, was born ninth among eleven children, only two of whom were boys. Both parents were deeply spiritual, and their commitment to God and to his church was of greatest important in their family life. In the loving environment of this home, the children learned to pray, to care about the needy and the lost, and to know the Bible. Evelyn spent time at her mother's knee, learning the scripture and hearing the story of Jesus' love. She came to trust Christ while still very young, feeling a strange stirring in her own heart as she repeated the Beatitudes to her mother. "Blessed are they who hunger and thirst after righteousness, for they shall be filled." She never forgot the importance of that moment, writing to me years later, "Mother brought me to Christ by that word in Matthew, showing me how desire is the proof of the new life to which Jesus was calling those who were thirsty." She was baptized at age eleven in the Strict Baptist Church of England, where her father was superintendent of a thriving Sunday school for unchurched boys and girls.

Mr. Harris, a prosperous London merchant, provided well for his family. All their needs would be met. Servants did the cooking and scrubbing; maids waited on their personal needs. Mr. Harris educated the girls according to the custom of the Victorian age. Their schooling included the three basic R's, a foreign language, and additional training in the arts. He himself possessed a keen artistic sense and collected various works of art, among which were several paintings, a passion Evelyn later shared.

In this loving, supportive environment Evelyn came to womanhood, greatly influenced by the members of her family, caught in a web of dependencies. She had all she needed and more. She was serious-minded, talented in art, and very beautiful. Not only did she excel at painting, but she often sat as a model for others.

Evelyn painted landscapes, broad vistas, sweeping colors, the changing mood of the sky. She liked what Turner did with sunsets and sunrises and sought to model her own work after his. She put together a small book of her water colors, and her oils were in some demand. Her life was full as she tended to various good works and social obligations befitting her standing in society. She loved pretty clothes and, bedecked in gowns of lace and silks, wearing stylish flounces and feathered hats, she cut an attractive figure. She was not unhappy, only restless as time passed. Life did not seem to be heading anywhere, and she found no adequate outlet for the stream of creativity and energy within her. She was now almost thirty years old.

Evelyn later wrote about her childhood: "My girlhood was a happy one, with no hindrances or shortages of anything that was appreciated by girls of that generation. But it was so often overshadowed by self. Years later I found in my childish hand, written when I was about ten, this verse:

> Oh, why are children called such
> When higher heights they run
> In thought and mind
> Than many more experienced one?

Jesse Mann Brand both directly and indirectly changed the shape of Evelyn's life. Evelyn had heard about Jesse when he had gone out to India with the Strict Baptist Mission three years earlier. Now she read a booklet he had written in which he described a survey trip he and a Mr. Morling had made to the Kollis Malai, a range of mountains in South India. So graphic was his description of these inaccessible, malaria-ridden mountains and their people that Evelyn felt that she, too, had climbed over the rocks and through the thick undergrowth. She lived vicariously in such adventures and her interest in missions grew. She began to wonder if she could ever be a missionary.

About this time Evelyn accompanied her sister Florrie on a six-week voyage to Australia. Florrie had married an Australian and was returning to him after a short visit to England. This was the first exciting step in uprooting Evelyn for foreign service. Suddenly life was far from ordinary; she was seeing the world, rushing from one side of the ship to the other with her paints and canvas, trying to capture the beauty she saw on every hand as the ship sailed through the Mediterranean Sea, along the coast of Africa, and around the tip of India. On the return journey a fellow passenger, a missionary, told her about Africa and its need. Sensing a responsive spirit in her, he began recruiting her for missionary service. He sought Evelyn out with such fervor that she began to wonder whether it was a missionary call or interest in the man himself that stirred her response—until he casually mentioned his wife. Hurt and embarrassed by her mistaken emotions, Evelyn decided this was not her call. Still, the idea of going abroad to serve Christ became increasingly appealing. The Evelyn who arrived home in England was a freer, more determined Evelyn than the one who had left.

On her return, she went directly to Keswick, to attend the annual Christian conference held there. Her sisters also attended. When the invitation was given for those who felt called to mission service, Evelyn rose to her feet to indicate her willingness. Even so, she made sure she was standing behind a post so that her sisters could not see her and report her decision to their father before she could summon the courage to tell him. She would probably go to India, she thought, for most of her church's mission work was there. But how could she tell her father?

Then, unexpectedly (the way God often works), Jesse Brand, home on furlough, came to speak at the St. Johns Wood Chapel, to which the Harris family belonged. He described his life in Sendamangalam, a small village on the plains of South India, where open sores, disease, poverty, and starvation were the common lot of thousands. He told of epidemics of plague and cholera, of the pressure to minister that kept him from going to thousands on the mountains of death, as the Kollis Malai were called. Evie drank in the details of India's need.

Later Jesse Brand came to the Harris home for tea. Evelyn had many questions to ask, but something about his male vitality and eagerness intimidated her. He seemed to be staring at her with his black eyes, as though he were addressing everything he said solely to her. She shrank back to the edge of the gathering, leaving her sisters to serve the sandwiches and cakes. Everything about Jesse

Brand—his mustache, his eyes, his tone of voice, his dark good looks—seemed a bit overwhelming. Jesse told of how the people of the hills had begged him to come and settle among them.

From that day on Evelyn knew she must tell her father. It was the hardest thing she had ever done. He seemed to grow older before her eyes. Must she go? Weren't there enough heathen in London to convert? *Haven't I provided you with all you need?* He had wanted to keep her safe from the cruel world and make her *comfortable.* But she was choosing a life of discomfort, turning her back on all he offered. She stood before him, beautifully radiant, so eager to serve God. But he had not walked with God all these years to no avail. He, too, cared about the lost. But to send Evelyn? He delayed his decision by asking a doctor to examine her to determine whether she was fit to work in the tropics. To his disappointment, the doctor pronounced her hearty and able to do what her sheltered life had never allowed.

She was accepted by the Church Mission Board, and her passage was booked on a ship to Bombay. As she dressed for a farewell party in her honor, she wondered if she would ever again wear the satins and laces she had thought so important in her life. In the end, it was Evelyn who wept most bitterly at parting from her family. She had not realized how hard it would be. She could not know that she would never see her father again on earth.

In India at last, Evelyn absorbed the sights, sounds, and smells of a totally different world than the one she had known. Hardest of all was learning Tamil. The Strict Baptist Mission had high standards for language study, and this proved a trial for Evelyn, who found languages a snare. And it was so hot in Madras! The students were awakened before dawn when the temperature would already be in the low nineties. If she rested her hands on the table, a puddle formed from her perspiration. The long-sleeved, full-skirted dresses the missionaries wore were oppressive, and at night, crawling under mosquito netting seemed akin to smothering.

But gradually, she adjusted to both the study and the heat, and later began making visits in the city with the Bible women. Then young Jesse Brand appeared in Madras. His appointment had been to Sendamangalam, which was several hundred miles to the

Southwest. Now he was to take over the work in Madras. Evelyn wondered how she could ever have been intimidated by him; he was so fun-loving and attractive. One day he said to her, "I knew you'd be coming. I could see it on your face when I spoke about the hill people."

Evelyn's fascination with the hill people drew them together. He helped her with language study, and they began to share plans and dreams, discovering a common love for nature and for beauty and a deep dedication to God. When Evie went to Coonoor in the Nilgiri Hills, Jesse began courting her by mail. His plans for medical study were changing, he said. He was requesting that the Mission Board allow him to begin work in the hills as soon as the Booths returned from furlough. His letters contained endearments and, at last, a proposal for marriage. Evelyn and Jesse were deeply in love.

Mrs. Elnaugh, the widow who was to accompany Evelyn to the hills, became ill and had to return to England. Now, in the incredible way God works in human lives, she would go with Jesse. "I would gladly have gone alone," she said, "but with Jesse! Where could one get closer to heaven!" Only these two felt such a strong call to the hill people.

Suddenly Evie became desperately ill with typhoid. For days she was delirious with fever and pain. Just as she was on the point of undertaking what seemed her life's work, she was struck down by illness. Would her hopes end in ruin? The answer came—a definite no. With the help of friends she was nursed back to health and recovered her strength.

Meanwhile, Jesse had been up in the hills building their simple house, which he had framed on the plains in Sendamangalam. Coolies had carried the house in sections up the tortuous paths to the hilltop where Jesse and Evelyn would begin life together in "the mountains of death." It was the same house from which she wrote to me fifty years later.

Evelyn never tired of telling the story of their wedding day, recounting the events with amusement and nostalgia. It was August 1913. The chapel in Sendamangalam was packed with the grateful patients of Jesse Brand, who had done medical work among them. Evelyn was amazed and humbled by their love for Jesse, which was now showered on her as garland after garland was placed around her neck. She was so weighed down that she had to take one lot off to make way for the second. Here at Sendamangalam she saw the hills for the first time, misty blue against the sky. She and Jesse planned to spend their honeymoon in their new home on the hills.

Wedding dress and all, they rode the first rough five miles in a jutkka cart to the foot of the Kollis Hills. Jesse had arranged for bearers to meet them and carry the two of them in dholies to their home. He had said it would be a real wedding procession. It was late afternoon when they approached the base of the hill. The dholies were there, but the coolies were missing. They had gone off on a pig hunt, said the anxious sahib who helped make the arrangements. While Evelyn sat on the jungle path guarding the baggage, Jesse and the sahib rushed off to find other bearers. Thunder sounded in the distant sky, and monsoon clouds gathered.

Jesse returned with four bearers for Evelyn and enough men to carry the baggage. Sitting on the dholie—a rough hammock of canvas fastened to bamboo poles—with her wedding dress tucked over her knees, Evelyn clung to the bamboo poles. Eager to get up the steep paths before dark, the coolies began to jog along. The rolling motion and the heat gave her a wilted, sick feeling. The paths became steeper and thorns tore at her dress. Then the clouds opened and the rain came, transforming the dholie into a veritable bath tub. She sat there rocking along in sodden grace.

"Are you all right?" Jesse asked worriedly. This was not the wedding night he had so carefully planned.

"Fine," said Evelyn. "I was needing a bath."

They laughed together, both aware that they would need their sense of humor often in adjusting to this life. They finally arrived, both of them mud-streaked and soaked to the skin.

Well, thought Evelyn, this is not going to be easy, and I might just as well know it now. Later, Jesse presented her with their prayer book, entitled *Evie's and My Prayer Book.* It is her most precious memory of that eventful day. One column was for prayer requests, the other for praise when the prayers were answered. It was the first of many such books they would keep as a witness to God's faithfulness to them.

Engraved inside Evelyn's wedding band are the words *Trust and Triumph.* Jesse Brand had taken courage from these words on a wall motto when Evelyn's life was threatened by typhoid fever in Coonoor. In their new home, Evelyn made her own wall motto with those words, forming them out of eucalyptus leaves, and fastening them to a board. For the next sixty years those words directed her life. At eighty-nine she made them the title of a small autobiography she wrote.

Jesse Mann Brand was a gifted man, if not a genius. He was a clever builder, making their home not only weathertight, but enjoyably liveable in its simple fashion. He taught young men in the villages to build, and the results of his skill dot the mountains of South India. He built huts, schools, dispensaries, and chapels to meet the needs of the various stations he and Evelyn established. Before leaving England he had taken a missionary medical course at Livingston College, and had an intuitive sense for diagnosing and treating illnesses. His strategy for reaching the hill people included opening schools, teaching trades, instructing people in basic hygiene, cleaning their wells, and introducing new agricultural techniques and products. As time went on he taught the people to make tiles to replace the thatch on the roofs, which provided breeding places for rats and vermin and which frequently went up in smoke from the torches people carried at night. He planted orange trees and sugar cane and taught the people how to market them. He raised poultry and sheep. Both he and Evelyn had a resourcefulness and determination that equipped them for this work.

Evelyn wrote about him, "Jesse seemed made for the hills." He not only had the vision, but the energy to carry out his plans. He was a teacher, preacher, naturalist, and scholar. Evie constantly marvelled at this man she had married. In his spare time he read books like Carlyle's *French Revolution*, Bunyan's *Grace Abounding*, and books on relativity and mathematics. Evelyn once commented on the folly of the struggle to gain knowledge when death would only cut it all short.

Jesse responded, "Why, you infidel, this is only the beginning. I think of Heaven as going on to learn and know that after which we can seek but feebly here!"

Nothing about the hills made for an easy mission field. To say that the terrain was rugged is a monstrous understatement. The people were animistic, caught in the worship of devils. They had a "pig cult"—not worshipping the pig, but pouring out the blood as a libation to Karapen, the head of devils. The witch doctor or priest (the *poosari*) was greatly feared, and his word had great authority, especially in the matter of illness. Without education and contact with the outside world, the people lived in fear, bound by caste. Few government officials ever spent the night on the hills, even though bungalows were provided for the forestry department. They feared contracting malaria, the deadly plague of the mountains. To make matters worse, bears, leopards, and other wild beasts made travel dangerous.

Evelyn tells a bear story that happened early in their stay in the Kollis. A bear attacked a woman as she and her husband walked through the jungle. The man ran to her rescue, and the bear turned on him, felling him with one blow. The man would have been killed had not his tiny, timid, pregnant wife kept pushing at the bear until it ran off. The man was brought to the Brands the next day. Jesse stitched for hours, closing the torn scalp and leg and setting the arm. The man stayed on for further treatments, and they were able to tell him the gospel again and again. They had not yet built a place for in-patients to stay, and took advantage of the poosari's offer to house their patients in his grain shed. It seemed generous of him until they realized that the poosari had frightened the man, threatening him not to listen to the white man's religion.

But the man recovered and spread Jesse's fame as a doctor throughout the villages. People began coming from all over the Kollis. In one year the Brands treated 1,500 patients.

Evelyn and Jesse went on extensive camping trips to reach

people across the Kollis range. Everywhere they went, crowds gathered for medical help and heard the Good News. While Jesse treated the sick, Evie would teach the women about clean water and mosquito nets or other needs she saw in their lives. When Jesse preached, eager crowds gathered to hear. Their hopes would rise as they answered inquirers. But, in the end, no one was willing to break caste and become a Christian.

Evelyn wrote to Mrs. Booth in Madras, asking her to send a lady's sidesaddle, for she was expecting a baby. Mrs. Booth was aghast that she would travel those "wild hills" on a horse when she was pregnant. She did go down to Ooctacamond, about a hundred miles away, when the time for delivery came. On July 17, 1914, Evelyn Harris Brand, age thirty-five, gave birth to Paul Wilson Brand, who was promptly dedicated to God's service. It was a gruelling business to have a baby so far from home. Getting back up the hills with a baby meant first a carriage ride, then the train, then bullock cart, and finally the dholie up the rough, steep terrain. But she was home at last, and her beautiful baby boy gave her many more opportunities to minister to the women. Two years later, a daughter, Connie, was born into the family. Both children accompanied them on the camping trips across the Kollis Range.

As the years went on, Jesse and Evie became increasingly incensed at the evil ways of the hill people. It was common practice to marry small children to adults in order to get more farm workers. A mature girl might be married to a small boy so that the father could have an extra worker. Then she would be forced to bear children for his use by any man available. This man would be a "kept man" and also work the land. Immorality and venereal disease were widespread, and it was the women who suffered most. Evie's solution was to get the children into schools, to teach them the joy of study. It was only then that they would be able to resist early marriages, she reasoned.

Still no converts came. The poosaris kept the people away. They knew what belief in the Yesu-Swami would do to their own power over the people. "Believe in the Yesu-Swami if you choose," they said, "but you must worship the other swamis, too."

It was 1919, the year of the worldwide influenza epidemic.

People were baffled by this unknown illness, and there were no sulfa drugs to help fight the epidemic. The hill people simply fled from each other, rather than trying to deal with it. Left to die alone, the sick struggled and succumbed with no one to feed them or give them so much as a drink of water. Jesse and Evie took around rice gruel to keep the people from dehydration. Even so the death rate was high. The poosari was frightened and would not even take part in the funerals.

Then one day news came that the poosari and his family were sick. Evelyn ran to their compound and found the wife in the middle of the court, clinging to a string cot, struggling for breath. The poosari lay on the mud verandah of his swami-hut, panting with pneumonia. On the verandah of their own home, crying by herself, lay their unfed nine-month-old baby girl. Evie offered them hot rice gruel, but the poosari had lost all hope. "You must take our baby," he gasped. "Don't give it to the village people. If God lets me live, I will come to the bungalow to worship Jesus."

The poosari and his wife died shortly thereafter, the poosari calling on the name of Jesus. Jesse and Evelyn named the little girl Ruth, for long ago Ruth left her kindred to join the people of God. This was the breakthrough for which they had prayed, and it came from an unexpected quarter.

They continued camping, treating the sick, building schools, facing disappointments, and embracing new hope. While they were camping in the hills, Ruth's brother came and brought another boy with him. Both of them wanted to live with the Brands. Later a boy with a chronic face ulcer got permission from his grandfather to join them. They were now feeding and clothing four children besides their own. Eventually they sent the boys to be educated in a Brethren School for Boys. Years later those boys were among those the mission sent to work with their people in the hills.

Another triumph came when a hill man, Solomon, joined them, despite the threats of his poosari. He boldly announced he was leaving his old ways and following the Yesu-Swami. He brought his reluctant wife, who later also became a believer. His father, David, joined him in the faith. The door was swinging open.

Jesse and Evelyn taught their own children in lieu of formal schooling. What an exciting pair they were! Jesse fed the children's curiosity about nature, telling them stories, taking apart a white ant's tower, examining insects or whatever came into their path. Evelyn carried her canvas and boards in a knapsack, and while she was painting would teach the children to notice the world around them. "Look at the sky! How can I capture those colors?" She let Paul do his arithmetic up in his favorite tree, dropping his finished paper to his mother, who sat below. They would soon return to England on furlough. In accordance with mission rules they would have to leave the children behind when they returned to India. Both parents were determined to make the most of every minute spent with their children.

From the outset, the children shared their parents' concerns for the hill people. They did their best to teach baby Ruth. "Mother, we are teaching her that she must leave her old swamis and pray to Jesus." Returning home after visiting in several villages, Paul wanted to stop at yet another village. Evelyn protested that she was too tired. Paul said, "But, Mummy, we must or they will go on worshipping their false gods."

They prayed together about the problems in the work, about their joys and sorrows. Evelyn said, "We did not teach our children how to pray. We simply included them in our prayers from their earliest years." Later, separated from the children, their letters kept those close ties alive. Jesse wrote to Paul: "Yesterday when I was riding over the wind-swept hilltops around Kulivalavu, I could not help thinking of an old hymn that begins 'Heaven above is deeper blue, flowers with purer beauty glow.' When I am alone on these long rides, I just love the sweet-smelling world, the dear brown earth, the lichen on the rocks, the heaps of dead brown leaves drifted like snow in the hollows. God means us to delight in his world. Just observe. Remember. Compare. And be always looking to God with thankfulness and worship for having placed you in such a delightful corner of the universe as Planet Earth."

The work kept growing. Teachers and preachers came from the plains to staff the schools. Five stations were open with schools and chapels. Jesse used hill men to build, teaching them to be sawyers and carpenters. Those who became Christians were often forced out of their own villages and came to live near the Brand's compound, making it a strong Christian settlement.

By 1923 they had spent ten years on the hills. It was time to leave for a year. A year too late for Evelyn to see her father. A letter had come saying that he had collapsed while leading his beloved Sunday school and had never regained consciousness. When Evelyn told the children, "We're going home," they looked at her in wonder. "But this is home, Mummy." It was all they knew. Nevertheless they were going for their first journey out—home to England.

Evelyn's culture shock at England was as great as her children's. Rooms full of furniture, fancy clothes, wearing gloves to church, and shoes! It seemed a confining world. Damask, fine china, and silver, for two uninhibited small creatures from the jungle, took some getting used to. The long, polished balustrade was an irresistible slide. The family invaded the placid life of Evelyn's two unmarried sisters, who cared for their elderly mother, and who would care for Paul and Connie when they returned to India.

Jesse was away in the churches, reporting on the work in the hills. It was a good year, and it passed all too quickly. The children were enrolled in schools, and it was time to leave them behind. Paul and Connie were to recite five Tamil Bible verses every Sunday morning at breakfast. Evie painted other texts by their beds. . . . *I will be a father unto you. . . . As one whom a mother comforteth, so I will comfort you.* Leaving them behind was the greatest test of loyalty she ever had to face.

A month later Jesse and Evelyn were back at their little settlement. An eager crowd greeted them with music and garlands. They were home. *Stottherum, stottherum*—Praise, praise. These words were more and more on Evie's lips.

Jesse had collected money in England for a girls' home, and he set about to build it. Little Ruth came back to be with them. Word soon spread over the hills that there was a place for unwanted children. Because of the practice of marrying children at an early age, an unwanted child-wife might later be evicted. One after another of these children came to the Brands. Babies left to die on rubbish heaps were brought to Evie. Some did not live, but she loved and cared for them as they came to her home until the girls' home was finished in 1925. This home grew to twenty girls, ranging from infants to adolescents. They were given an elementary education by a Tamil teacher from the plains. Many of them became Christians. When they were older, marriages were arranged for them with young Christian men. "The first sound of every day in the Settlement, as dawn is breaking, is a song of praise from the girls in the Home," Jesse wrote in a report to the churches back home.

A small boys' hostel was also begun. A Mission Industrial School taught both boys and girls practical skills. Jesse planted two acres with mulberry bushes and bought silk worms. He discovered what government aid was available for the hill people in order to receive help for his projects. Dr. Samuel, a Syrian Christian from the ancient church in Travancore, came to work with them. The fact that the government paid his salary is a comment on their esteem for the work the Brands were doing.

Sometimes Evelyn traveled with Jesse to the plains when he was asked to speak. He wrote to the children on the occasion of one train journey, "Mother nearly frantic because she could not paint both sides at once."

The work was becoming more demanding. Jesse was preaching in over ninety hamlets surrounding their six stations. Over 25,000 people were given medical attention in a year's time. He spent hours reading law books to obtain rights for the hill people. He took a band of simply clad men from the hills to a government office to protest their exploitation by landlords living on the plains and got rulings that prohibited ownership of hill land by absentee landlords. He formed a cooperative society at a bank so that farmers would not need to pay ruinous 35% interest rates to moneylenders on the plains.

One day, in 1928, Jesse stood with Evie on a high crest near one of their stations. They looked beyond the Kollis to the horizon where, ranged in stark grandeur and mystery, stood four other mountain ranges—the Pachais, the Kalyrans, and beyond them, the Peria Malai and the Chitteris. "We must go to them," said Jesse, "to all five of them. Before we die we must go to all five ranges and take the saving message of Jesus Christ." It was a vision they shared, a commitment they made together.

By 1928 the Christian community in the settlement on the Kollis had grown to fifty. There were nine schools on the Kollis. The mission farm was feeding the whole community. The carpenter shop and the silk industry were thriving. The Brands were due for furlough in 1929, but, as had happened before, another missionary family seemed to need it more, so they agreed to postpone it for a year. "It will pass quickly," Jesse said cheerfully to Evelyn, who was thinking of the children. "Who knows? This one year may bring the greatest blessing of all."

The mission was facing difficulties and Jesse was asked to visit the churches of South India. He was gone for two months. He returned more tired than Evelyn had ever seen him, yet even more full of hope. When he complained of a fever, his temperature at 106, the doctor thought it was malaria. Never having seen blackwater fever, both the doctor and Evie were slow to realize what was happening. In the tortuous days and nights that followed, Evie listened to her beloved Jesse calling for water he could not possibly retain, saw his flesh turn dry and yellow, his eyes glaze, and his blood drain away. Now it was too late to take him out of the hills to a hospital. It was unbelievable. Four days later, on June 15, Jesse Brand died of blackwater fever at age forty-four. Evelyn was too dazed to respond.

In a letter written to me when she was eighty-five, she was still asking herself why she had not taken Jesse away for a rest. Why hadn't she known it was so serious? She said, "As I write this I have just asked my Indian co-worker Paul Chakkaravathy these questions and he answered me, 'Did you not teach me that our Lord said that one sparrow does not fall to the ground without the Father seeing it, and cannot you see that it was all according to God's will?' God is the first and the last. He never makes a mistake."

Evelyn did what needed doing. She said the right words and encouraged the community, saw to it that the funeral service focused on Christian hope, but she felt dead inside. The Mission Board expected her to leave at once, but she stayed on, stubbornly refusing to leave.

Evelyn had one resolve: to see that the work in the hills continued. She must save the work for which Jesse gave his life. The Mission Board had never given it more than half-hearted support. She would wait until someone else was appointed. She was bewildered at this terrible sweeping break in their plans to reach the hills. Writing to me about Jesse's death she enclosed this poem, and the pain in her letter seemed as fresh as it might have been thirty-five years earlier:

We were only one
So when the sun shone,
Shone on us,
It shone on one.

And when the rain came
It was just the same
It rained on one
It fell on one.

When He withheld from us
'Twas ever thus,
We were but one
To feel the miss
Of any bliss
Under the sun.

Then came the storm
The cold and bitter weather.
It hurt us not,
For we were one together.

When He took him away
Nothing was left
But a heart bereft
With no one to share
No one to care.

No, He who took him is here,
No one by my side,
But He is my guide.

One day in her misery she set out on a lonely trek riding Jesse's horse. She had never ridden this high-spirited animal, preferring her own plodding mare. She seemed to have lost all fear, thinking it would be better to die than to face life alone. On her way to a distant village she remembered that Jesse had told her just before his death that he had found a new way, a path that avoided the steep outcropping of rocks that made the way a narrow ledge. She had always been frightened on this path, even when Jesse was with her. Now, she thought, I will never find it. Suddenly Jesse's horse turned at a right angle and entered into the jungle bushes and trees. She gave it rein. Hardly breathing, she sat quietly while the horse crossed a stream and went through the woods, arriving at the village. Tears blurred her vision as these words came to her, "I will bring the blind by a way they know not; I will lead them in paths they have not known. These things I will do unto them and not forsake them." (Is 42:16) It was a promise from God for the future.

Before long, Evelyn decided that it was time to return to England on furlough. She seemed suspended between two worlds when she arrived in England to find Paul a boy of fifteen and Connie thirteen. Her arms were starved for these precious children she had so reluctantly left behind a few years earlier. Connie with the same golden hair, and Paul, a reserved, self-conscious young man. Connie flew into her arms, sobbing. Paul was more remote, almost in shock.

Years later he told me his reaction to that meeting. He was almost giddy with excitement on the way to the boat. He pictured his mother as she had been when he last saw her—tall, beautiful, vibrantly alive. Instead he saw this unbelievably shrunken, *little*, old lady coming down the gangplank. He had to keep telling himself, "This is my mother!" He felt torn with grief over his father's death—and now this reality of what his father's death had done to his beautiful mother. He couldn't believe it was true.

In the year that she remained in England, Evie encouraged her children, particularly Paul, to become missionaries. Both have done so. Through all their separations they remained close, united in their concern to spread the Good News. Evelyn wrote in a letter to me, "No earthly relationship can be like the one where mother and child meet at the footstool of the same Lord."

Evie knew she must return to India. Her commitment was to God and, although she might be less than half a person, she knew that even a broken vessel can carry living water. The Mission Board refused to return her to the Kollis Malai. It was not sound policy, they said. But her arguments were persuasive. She had helped create the work on the Kollis, and she wanted to return. They had built most of the work with their own hands—she and Jesse—and with their own money which she received in a trust from her father. Finally it was agreed that she could go to the Kollis. She sailed in the autumn of 1930. Feeling fearfully alone and weak, she expressed herself in a poem.

And must I now go on alone with You,
And is there no one near to hold my hand?
And no one who can really understand?
"I'll do it all for you."
But there'll be silence round me all the time,
Silence which even You with all your infinite resource
Cannot break through.

"Silence to hear My voice, that's all,
And I have planned it all for you.
You have been speaking all the time,
You would not listen, now no other choice
But to sit still and hear My voice."

Speak, Lord, thy servant waits to hear
Thy gentle whisper, strong and clear.

The hill people came from all over the Kollis, bearing gifts and garlands of flowers. Their Mother had come home. She ploughed into the work—loving, teaching, exhorting, feeding on the beauty of the hills. But this five-year term on the Kollis for which she had fought was filled with tension and frustration. First one couple and then another were in charge of the work, and none of them had Jesse's gifts. She had been co-creator and co-manager of the work for over sixteen years, and now she was under the authority of others who did not understand the people as she did—and who made policies she did not approve. She didn't hesitate to speak out. And it couldn't have been easy for other dedicated missionaries to see their predecessor honored and sought after while they were bypassed. The people called her *Mother* or *Honored Lady*.

She knew she must give these hills to others. But what of the other mountain ranges they claimed for God? Perhaps she should go to the Pachais where she and Jesse had already camped. Or to the Kalyrans?

Her mind was busy with all kinds of ideas. She even drew plans for a house, with a dispensary attached. But her mission refused to consider it. The leaders even questioned the value of work on the Kollis. She wrote to Connie: "Do you know, Con, I feel like a mother with a baby, and when you see a crowd of people seize it, feel its pulse, shake it a bit . . . and discuss whether it should live or die!" She was hot in her protest.

Again in 1936 she went home to England for a furlough. She cared little for clothes or fashion—she who had once been so conscious of lace and frills. Even though her sisters badgered her about her wardrobe, she would pick an unbecoming dress, hopelessly outmoded. Her disregard for the amenities of life were more and more part of their non-conformist sister. But when she spoke, she held her audience spellbound. She was radiant with love for the Lord.

She returned to India in 1937, assigned to work on the plains in Sendamangalam—she who loved the hills. At least she was in sight of them here, and whenever she could, she went up to the mountains to camp. She returned to the Peria Malai, believing it offered the best possibilities for developing a work. She searched the hills for a good place to begin, but the mission frowned on her interest and sent her to Madras. It was like leaving the promised land to go back into the wilderness for three years.

Almost ten years had passed since she was in England, and the war was over. When she arrived home again in England, Paul noticed, to his surprise, that she did not really seem to age after fifty-five. She was frail-looking, her features pared to the bone. She wore her grey hair short, straight, and tied with a ribbon. Her eyes were young and piercing. She met David Wilmshurst and Connie's baby Jessica, and Paul's wife Margaret and their two-year-old Christopher. For the first time she was called Granny, somewhat to her dismay. From that day on people everywhere began referring to her as Granny Brand, a name she never really agreed to.

She was now near retirement age. The board suggested she stay in England. She was getting *too old for the work,* they said. She seethed at that remark—she who had gone up the mountains, lain in her mosquito net hut through drenching rains, traveled on horseback from village to village. She begged the mission to send her back to India for one year. Reluctantly they yielded to her request. But Granny Brand had a plan. She would give the mission the required year in Sendamangalam and then she would retire—in India. She would take the Gospel to the next of the five ranges as she and Jesse had planned to do. The Kollis had come first. She would go the Kalyrans, then the Pachais. The income from her father would support her work.

And that is exactly what Evelyn Brand did. Up until now her story may be no more or less remarkable than that of many missionaries of her caliber. At seventy she began to finish what she and Jesse had begun. She had arranged for a mud hut with a thatched roof to be built for her. Up the mountains she went, with a small caravan of coolies carrying her goods. Later two retired Indian workers came to live with her and, for a time, her daughter Ruth and Ruth's husband, John Michael.

As in the Kollis, the people came flocking to her for medical help, and she ferreted out those who did not come. She battled epidemics of typhoid, dengue, and even cholera. She delivered babies and fought malnutrition. A procession of adopted children came into her life, children who needed education to serve God.

On the way down hill in a dholi one day Evelyn was careless, neglecting to hold firmly to the side poles. When one of the bearers fell, Evelyn pitched forward and hit her head on a rock. The pain was almost intolerable, but she had to travel miles further by dholi, then by bus, then a train ride of a hundred miles and then another crowded bus. She was in a daze when she arrived at the hospital. The doctors treated her and took X-rays of her injured spine, but did not discover the seriousness of the fall. She never completely recovered from that fall, and her feet were partially paralyzed from then on.

Walking became difficult. Back in the village sometime later she tripped over the doorway and broke her leg. After that she needed to wear special shoes with braces, and walked with two unmatched bamboo sticks—a terrible nuisance, she said. But at least she could still ride a horse. Over the next years, fifteen workers came to help in the mountains, and only two stayed.

The work began growing in the Kalyrans. A few hill people became Christians. Evie worked four different stations. Following Jesse's model she cleared land and consulted with the government horticulturists to find supplements for the diet of the villagers. Schools were established, and the government agreed to pay the teacher's salaries if she would find the teachers. She paid for much of the school land from her own meager income. She had a nose for sin on the one hand, and a trusting spirit—to the point of gullibility—on the other. She was cheated and bilked out of money and property by people who saw she was careless in keeping accounts.

Paul despaired of the way his mother gave things away. Once he visited her and brought two dozen blankets. On his next visit she scarcely had one for herself. Connie chided her and said it was wrong to give so much away. Granny's comment: "Well, I'm glad the Lord hasn't shown *me* it's wrong."

Three young women under the New Tribes Mission started a station on the Chitteris range and worked in cooperation with the Hill Gospel Fellowship. Three of the five ranges now had a witness. Only two more to go, thought Evie. She was taking on more workers for the hills.

When Evelyn was eighty-five, Paul made one of his treks to find her. He climbed for hours, rigorous climbing that left him exhausted. He talked at length about the work, telling her how much had been accomplished, how well the work was going in the Kalyrans. It was time to leave now, he said. Granny agreed. It *was* time to leave, so she packed up and headed for the Pachais, her third mountain range. Here in a crude hut, with the same opposition, the same need, the hundreds of miles over stony trails, camping out in all kinds of weather, she began again.

When Granny wrote letters, she used a wretched old typewriter that evidently didn't secure the lines. And often in her haste she typed over the previous line, making it an "adventure-in-understanding" to read her letters. When someone offered to type her letter to me, she refused and wrote, "It's all true. I've been careless not putting full stops, etc., sending disgraceful letters everywhere—people not able to read, etc., but . . ." She assumed I knew the people about whom she wrote and her letters were full of half-stories and allusions. She preached to me, wanting to make certain the college students with whom I worked truly were converted to Christ, that I wasn't just polishing the dirt off, as she said.

"It's terribly marvelous to be used by God," she wrote. For those who were worried about her walking over such rough terrain she wrote, "I can wobble along with my canes, but this is my text, 'Thou hast beset me behind and before, and laid thine hand upon me.' That's a great Psalm to learn by heart. . . . The all-enclosing power of God."

Later she wrote, "I am more conscious of failure than success and see the need for confessions more than congratulations."

No one worked in the hills if they were afraid of sacrifice. Granny herself was a tough reed. She seemed immune to illness, riding across the hills on her pony and entering squalid huts to treat fearful diseases. When she tired, she tethered her pony in a beautiful spot, took off the saddle and used it for a pillow. On one occasion she was advised not to come to a meeting of the Hill Fellowship because monsoon rains made the paths too slippery for her horse. The steady downpour continued and the group couldn't believe she would come. Yet, knowing her, they were hesitant to begin without her. Just then a postal runner arrived with the news that Evie had reached the last and largest river, which was swollen with waters up to a man's armpits, and the bearers of her dholi had refused to go further.

Just as they were leaving to investigate how she was faring, along came four men bearing a dholi at a rapid trot, a tiny figure on board, dripping muddy water. *How*? they asked. It was simple, she said. Taking off her shoes and braces, she had crawled to the edge of the rushing stream, grabbed hold of the rope that went across the river and let herself into the river. Seeing this, the bearers rushed to her aid and carried her across because her legs got tangled up in her ballooning skirt. She'd just have a small wash and a change of clothes and they could get on with the meeting.

In addition to the five ranges she and Jesse claimed for God, she discovered the Gothais and the Paithur Hills. By 1967 Granny was working on all seven ranges. That year she made fourteen trips up and down on horse or in a dholi.

For years Evelyn had hoped to find a doctor who felt called to the hills. Whenever she spoke at the Vellore Medical College, she gave the challenge. Now a young man, Dr. David Lister, a descendant of the great Sir Joseph Lister, heard that call. In Granny he recognized a quality of selfless dedication akin to his own. "She was happier and more alive than anyone I had ever met," he said. "When she looks at you, it's as if she could see right through you."

When she was ninety-five, her frail body seemed to be kept active only by the intensity of her inner zeal. She could scarcely rise to a standing position without help, especially since her favorite sitting place was on the floor.

In the fall of 1974, hearing of an adulterous relationship between two hill people on the Kollis, she went up to her wooden bungalow in the settlement to help solve the issue. There, on her way to chapel, she fell and gashed her head on the corner of the house, but still she insisted on speaking. From the Kollis, she went to the Kalyrans. Granny sent message after message to backsliding Christians, exhorting and forgiving.

She was excited that Paul would be visiting in October in Vellore, and then impatient to get back to the hills in November. Then she fell again. "The Sands of Time are sinking fast," said

Granny, and repeated most of the sixteen stanzas of that hymn. Her speech became jumbled, but she remained strong otherwise. Her pulse, which had been an irregular forty, now became a regular eighty, as if she were climbing that last Summit. On December 18, 1974, she gave one deep sigh and went to heaven.

The next morning a thanksgiving service was held in the Vellore Hospital Chapel. Then a procession began up the Kolli Malai, where in the chapel Jesse built sixty years before, the sorrowful community paid tribute to her. Late that afternoon she was laid to rest beside Jesse Mann Brand. She had written:

You'll say it's a dream that must come true
For the promise is sure to me and to you
That the seed that is sown and watered with tears
Must produce a harvest in after years.

For Evelyn Harris Brand, it proved to be *Trust and Triumph.*

Sources

In telling Evelyn Brand's story, I have relied heavily on the careful research of Dorothy Clarke Wilson and her exciting full-length book, *Granny Brand* (Christian Herald Books: Chappaqua, N.Y., 1976). Regrettably, this is no longer in print.

Evelyn Brand's autobiography, *Trust and Triumph,* published by the International Gospel League, 854 East Washington Boulevard, Pasadena, California 91102, gives colorful insights into her life and the lives of the hill people.

I am also indepted to Dr. Howard T. Lewis of the International Gospel League for his help in getting materials to me—and beyond that, for his vision for Granny Brand's work and for taking on the funding of these needy projects in India.

And last, but surely not least, I want to thank Dr. Paul and Dr. Margaret Brand for sharing so much information and for letting me know Granny through them.

EIGHT

Wilma Burton

by Karen Burton Mains

MY MOTHER DIED UNEXPECTEDLY at her winter residence in Florida. The phone call came from far away bearing the terrible news. My brother-in-law's voice. The awful words.

"Lord . . . Lord . . ." I prayed, then remembered. *Today is my birthday.*

This year I will turn forty on the first anniversary of my mother's death.

First anniversaries after any death are hard. I remember the first Christmas, the first baby born, the first wedding day after my father died. What is missing, what is absent, what is so wounding? Where are the bouyant, familiar sounds? The grand words? The deep pride in family? The laughter? The hilarity? The serious, intense discussions?

Naturally, I am wary about marking this midlife date, cautious about this coming junction of birth and death.

We have always measured our births by decades—Gram, my mother, myself, my son. Mother was a firstborn child, as was I, as is he. My grandmother was twenty when her first, a daughter, was born. Mother was thirty at my birth. I turned twenty in the hospital. In fact, mother was forty at the birth of my brother.

So by this arithmetic, we counted our days. Randall, my son, will be twenty. Craig, my brother, will be thirty. Mother would have been seventy. Gram will be ninety. I will turn forty on the first anniversary of my mother's death.

As a child, poking through bureau drawers, I found a letter, sealed and hidden beneath the paper lining. It was addressed: "To Dick." My father. Lacking propriety like most young, I opened it. Mother's handwriting is tight and small; without bold loops and slashes. The letter was to have been read posthumously, in case of death at childbirth.

The letter is gone now. I have not found it in the sorting we have done after death. The remains—such a euphemism; the remains are not the body from which breath and warmth have fled. The remains are the contents of drawers and files and cupboards and closets.

We made three lists. One for myself. One for Valerie, my sister, and one for Craig. Valerie will take the Roseville vase. I will take the blue and white china cannister set. The maple bedroom furniture goes to Craig. This jewelry to mother's close friends. These boxes for the garage sale. This pile of junk is to be thrown into the dumpster.

We are also the remains, we three. We remain.

One finds old pictures and thinks, "Mother must have been my age. Craig was just a baby." In my heart, I beg secret forgiveness for being the eldest child with the longest memory and not knowing how young, how lovely Mother was at forty.

We remain... and soon I will turn forty, and in the middle of this fresh and early grief I must understand the meaning of my mother's life and the essence of it for me.

Doctors told my mother, Wilma Inez Wicklund Burton, not to have children. Rheumatic fever had bedridden her for a year in her early twenties, threatening her life. She survived but with damage to the valves of her heart.

One fiancee had been tall and slender, dark with wavy hair, a literature major and a student of Shakespeare. I can hear mother repeating to me his long-ago words, "Well, it's every man's right to have children." The wedding was cancelled.

One of life's many ironies is that mother, who the doctors said should never have children, gave birth to three, while he, a man I never met whose picture is in the boxes in the attic, never had any.

Wilfred Burton, "Dick" to his aunts and uncles who raised him and nicknamed him after the death of his own mother, on the other hand, was not reluctant at all about Wilma Wicklund.

"I want you all to meet the woman I'm going to marry," he announced at a gathering of the Burton clan.

Mother was stupefied. She protested the rain of congratulations. I can see her in my mind's eye, flustered, her peach complexion blushing. They had never talked about marriage. She had only known this man a short time. She was not at all sure, recovering from a broken engagement, that this was the man *she* wanted to marry.

My father-to-be was a music professor, slightly balding and short of stature. (I can remember him saying once with surprise in his eyes, "All my life, on the inside, I've *felt* like a big man, like a tall man.") The possibility that this woman he loved might never be able to have children seemed not to have fazed him at all.

I know *I* would have preferred the forthright music teacher to the literary aesthete. It is wonderful to be wanted, to be really wanted.

So mother wrote a letter to the man who loved her enough to risk birth. It was to be read in case her heart failed, in case she died in labor. "To Dick," her tight handwriting scribbled. And I, a child, found it unopened and split the seal because I was so much a part of my mother I never dreamed she would hold any secrets from me, her firstborn. And I discovered, what weight this knowledge, that she had risked death at my birth.

Her heart did fail on my birthday—thirty-nine years later, two-and-a-half years after my father's death. My parents, though eternal now, are probably still surprised by this chronicle of earthly events. I think they expected another order in dying.

People often ask me, "How did you start writing?" My answer has always been, "I have this mother who never said to me, 'How are you doing?' but always asked, 'What are you writing?' "

Most certainly, it was mother who, more than any other,

influenced my earliest attempts at writing. She gave me the love of the rhythm of words. She identified my innate ability. She encouraged me to enter writing contests. She planted in my heart the knowledge that reading is wonderful.

Wilma Burton was a published and prize-winning poet. During her life she belonged to many professional writer's organizations like The Poets Club of Chicago, The Chicago Poets and Patrons, and especially The National League of American Pen Women, whose magazine, *The Pen Woman*, she edited for many years, beginning in 1974.

Numerous honors came in tribute to her skills as a teacher at writers' conferences in more than half a dozen states, as an award-winning contestant herself and a judge in poetry contests, and as a writer of four books: *I Need a Miracle Today, Lord*; *Sidewalk Psalms and Some from Country Lanes*; *Without a Man in the House*; and *Living Without Fear*.

In July of 1981, at the Fifth World Congress of Poets in San Francisco, the World Academy of Arts and Culture of Taipei, Republic of China, awarded my mother an honorary doctorate of literature for her contributions to world poetry.

Perhaps most intriguing of all, these accomplishments all happened after Mother was forty, the majority taking place in her fifth and sixth decade. In addition, her books were written and published during a period of tortuous duress, the four years of my father's institutionalization after he suffered brain damage due to encephalitis, and in the two years of grief immediately following his death.

She wrote a poem a day; poems were her prayer language. She rose early—4:00 or 4:30 A.M., as do I. The phone call that came at 6:00 A.M. was invariably from mother. In those fresh hours she gave expression to the lyricism that lay on her soul.

I am the inheritor of twenty black, zippered notebooks filled with my mother's language, sonnets and free verse and a new form she created, the burtonelle. There is a nearly finished manuscript titled *Living with Joy*, an unpublished book of love poems, letters and filing cabinets and several years of daily journals—all my mother's writings.

Obviously this has influenced me, but I am also aware that had my parents been mute, even illiterate, I would have written or at least have been a teller of folk tales. I am convinced that the urge to express is impressed in the composite of my DNA.

Mother's influence in my life is more subtle, more profound than merely encouraging me to take pen to paper. It was her vision of life, her voice—to use writer's terminology, the intimate viewpoint of the author as he communicates through word form—that has incomprehensibly formed my own worldview and, consequently, molded my writing by means of which I will probably never really be aware.

In many ways, mother's background was disadvantaged. She was born in Des Moines, Iowa, December 1, 1912, to Nellie Brown Wicklund and Robert Wicklund. Her father was a lightning rod salesman who turned to drink after watching a youth in his employ fall to death while fixing rods to the pitched roof of a building.

Mother said that the memories from these years were too painful to share, and she never did speak specifically of them to me but only alluded to the fear and shame caused by her father's alcoholism. During her late teens, he converted to Christianity and was miraculously enabled to overcome his alcoholism, but within a year, he had died of pneumonia, leaving behind a family of five with no visible means of support.

At this time, mother gave up plans for college and went to work to help support her family. Eventually, her own body rebelled at the stress of death and poverty and anxiety. She became a victim of the rheumatic fever that damaged her heart. She recovered and returned to work. After some years, the literary fiancee entered, then exited, then my father appeared.

At this point, as well as I can construct, there evolved a determination on my parents' part that they were not going to live their life together hampered by an invalid mentality.

That is the profound influence that has shaped me more than mother's dogged question, "Karen, what are you writing?" It was this remarkable conspiracy on the part of my parents to daily choose life over death, despite the disadvantages of their backgrounds, the many emotional quirks of their own personalities, or the potential negations in their circumstances.

Mother was a romantic, a poetical lyricist who saw moondust and apple blossoms in all of life, who endowed her closest associates, her friends and children with superhuman qualities, then was disillusioned when the moondust was discovered to be artificial kleig lights, when the poison spray on the apple trees killed the birds, and when the gods and goddesses of her world displayed plain human tendencies.

She felt everything deeply, was intuitive, sensitive, and idealistic. She accumulated learning by osmosis and without a master plan, and she was dependent upon my father's cool logic and psychological analysis to interpret to her the factual, realistic meaning of the world, and of the people in it.

Dad was rudder to mother's sailing ship. He was also most frequently her ballast. Interestingly, she came into her own after the ballast had been pirated and her rudder snapped by high seas. Three months after their joint retirement, my father became ill with encephalitis, infection to the brain itself.

The years mother spent as an executive secretary while I was a child, later an adolescent, and then newly married are not as integral to an understanding of her personal influence on me as were her later years.

I often regret my parents' inability to recognize mother's very real creative abilities earlier, that she used her gifts typing letters and board reports, composing newsletters. Heavily involved in parachurch organizations, each of my parents held to a ministry mentality. They both actively served their Lord full-time, in ways that eventually bore fruit in the lives of their own children. All three of us are ministering families. My brother is a pastor. My sister is married to a minister as am I.

When I feel disappointment about this lack of vision regarding mother's gifts, I soon remind myself that neither of my parents had the parents I had.

It was in those agonizing years following the shipwreck which cast my father's body and personality, broken and disordered, upon the shores that the meaning of my mother's life became focused to me. Under this extreme stress, illness and dementia and death, mother's flaws and strengths became exaggerated, clear for me to examine and see.

For a time, mother needed all her energies. She was flailing in high waters. During this rationing of personality, I often felt the loss of both parents. But even in those early days of illness, those slow hours of inquisition in the hospital when doctors searched for a diagnosis and my father's condition rapidly worsened until he was nothing but a comatose form whose chest the nurses punched to regulate the irregular pull of lungs—even then, mother wrote poetry in the waiting rooms. These poems, about long hospital corridors and wildernesses of the soul, became the basis for her book, *I Need a Miracle Today, Lord.*

SONNET OF THE MIDGET CROSSES

To die upon a charred and burning cross—
I am unworthy, Lord, the martyr's name!
To count all this world's gain but pauper loss,
could my weak soul bear out the Hus-like shame:
Each day holds midget crosses, one by one.
Let me not flinch, as fingers point the match,
and I, the object of my torment's fun,
behold the blue-white flame leap from the scratch.
As the wood chars deep within my soul,
burn out the worthless chaff of my desire:
the choking dross of every human goal
be now consumed upon Your altar fire.
And through the midget crosses of each day,
let me now walk the living martyr's way.

I am convinced that the miracle of my mother, Wilma Burton, was that after shipwreck, after floundering on the sands of a castaway's shore, she eventually built her own little boat, unfurled her mast, and plied her way, alone, back onto the open sea.

Obviously, the going was not smooth sailing. Storms swamped her little dinghy. Further hurricanes cast her overboard; she lost her balance and frequently swallowed bitter salt water, but, amazingly, mother always climbed back into the bobbing vessel, dried herself out, set sail, and caught a windstream.

In the face of adversity, mother's tenacity was remarkable. What would have drowned a lesser person became ocean for mother to swim. The life pattern of refusing to be invalid in any way, in body or in emotion or in spirit, became her survival vest. Having lost her human rudder, my father, I watched her increasing dependency on the Ocean Master, the One who controls all the waves.

Not only did she hold on, her tenacity became productive.

LET THERE BE NO GRAY CURTAINS TODAY, LORD

shutting out Your face
and the world of light
on light on light that You
have made.
  This world has far too many curtains:
  iron, bamboo and ghetto
  to name a few, but purple curtains
  of the heart and gray ones of the mind
  are far more prevalent.
Defying boundaries
they suddenly appear
and hang on rods of words
or lack of words
to do their silent work
of shutting in and shutting out.
  Yours the hands adept
  at rending curtains
  in temples of stone or flesh:
Let there be no curtains, Lord, today.

Making decisions on her own was one of the areas in which she floundered. She had never made a major purchase without consultation with my father. Just mention "mother buying a car" in my family and brows lift, eyes roll in an appeal toward heaven. Oh, the convolutions of complications she invented! Car-buying became the symbol on which hung all the haplessness of her awkward non-widowhood. The act became akin to an emotional cyclone. She over-researched the products, reading endless consumer reports, discussing increasing options with friends, conferring with her children *ad infinitum*—and taking *none* of our advice. One wanted to shout, "Buy it! Buy anything! Take our car!"

A purchase was finally made, but not until the whole family had been involved in weeks of emotional indecision, which we discovered to be typical for a while of most of her decision-making.

How often mother would phone, those early morning calls, swamped by some improbable storm of personal dilemma. "I need something good to happen today," she would wail. Stress had made her forget that we humans are empowered to create our own good happenings.

After time, mother learned to negotiate the decision-making seas. The next car, a few years later, was purchased with a minimum of advice seeking, and she even bought something slightly impractical, something my father would not have chosen.

Three or four years after my father's initial illness, she was a far different woman than the one she had been. Entering vigorously into the world of publishing, she established a wide circle of friends, fellow poets, and writers. She traveled the country conducting poetry workshops and speaking in writers' conferences. Her responsibilities as the editor of *The Pen Woman* took her to Washington, D.C., for national board meetings. She learned to manage the properties my father had left awaiting his attention until retirement, the family residence, the ninety-four-acre farm, a small rental property, the trailer in Florida.

During all this, she continued to make daily trips to the nursing home except for winters, which she spent in the south because the severe northern climate aggravated her anginal heart condition. While my father was still ambulatory, mother attempted to get him outside of the institutional environment as much as possible. She brought him home, took him out to restaurants, to concerts, to supermarkets—anything to prevent vegetation. Navigating a brain-damaged, incontinent adult was an undertaking demanding incredible power of will and deep loyalty.

My father's condition slowly degenerated, however, despite all efforts, and mother's professional life blossomed against the private torture which increased proportionately to the degree of my father's dementia.

Actually, an intriguing phenomenon was occurring in my mother. The sociological process of self-actualization which normally takes place in the twenties and thirties was going on in mother in her late fifties and sixties. All becomings are awkward; when they are three decades late, they may at times look preposterous.

Jokingly, my oldest child would call her "my teenage grandmother." The two of them considered this verbal badge to be one of commendation, and though I laughed, I was sometimes chagrined by how near the truth it was.

At times, mother's emerging propensities looked decidedly auntie-mamish. She loved gatherings of people, was garrulous and animated, never considered at any time that she might be an outsider, thought nothing of pushing her own books and accomplishments, was an unabashed name-dropper, often monopolized conversations.

Once Craig had mother come for Sunday dinner along with another woman her age from his church. When asked for a report on how the afternoon had proceeded he replied, "Oh, just fine! Mother talked. The other woman talked. Neither of them listened for a moment to what the other was saying and they *both* had a wonderful time!"

Mother spent hours on the phone with her friends, and my sister and I detected a generational style of dress that began to develop. Valerie dubbed it "dowdy-queen-of-England." Jewelry was worn for jewelry's sake, never to particularly accessorize an outfit, and large hats began to emerge as a costume must.

We noticed that she slightly stretched the truth to enlarge the reputation of her children. All events were marked with poetry, *her poetry*, sometimes decoupaged, sometimes unpolished.

Without my father to interpret humans for her, to enlarge their fatal flaws with laughter, mother was often snowed by some obnoxious types—like the woman who said she was Elvis Presley's aunt. She may have been, for all I know. I took her with a grain of salt; mother swallowed her hook, line, and sinker. She was particularly susceptible to the self-proclaimed "artist" types. She believed everyone's press releases, like the gentleman who specialized in sculpturing madonnas. His home was filled with his own art. Mother thought he was marvelous.

Mother was so caught up, on the one hand, with the crisis that was my father, and on the other hand, with her thrilling emerging professionalism, that until her death, I never again felt that I had her full attention. If I had read something, it reminded her of something *she* had read. If I had a personal achievement, she was more enthusiastic about her own. Finally I stopped telling, opting to wait until this too had passed.

Once, during those years, I had her full attention. One of the children, doing an experiment in the backyard, ignited the gasoline in the lawn-mower can. Attempting to beat out the flames which were charring the backside of our house, the child was burned himself.

Because we had been having a series of near brushes with death, I fell apart over this minor disaster, crying over the phone, painting the horror of my blackened world.

Mother was sympathetic, made warm noises, rushed over with dinner. Somehow this fleeting restoration of roles stabilized my sanity. For a while, I was child; mother was parent.

The more that mother self-authenticated, the more I individuated. We were both come-lately in certain sociological processes. The problem with having loving, supportive parents is that a child feels no need to cut umbilical ties. One must separate in order to find identity, the way my mother discovered who she was after my father's illness.

My identity demanded separateness at this time of my mother's own self-discovery. In some ways, it was painful to us both, and without her interpreter, my father, to explain the psychological journey we were both undertaking, I think mother was wounded by me without knowing exactly why. (Without dad, mother had no one to tell her that the gentleman with all the madonnas was, (1) not a very good artist, and (2) looney as a bird to boot!)

Enough of this insistence on truth. All saints are strange. All holy things are wacky.

So what that mother took up bicycle riding and broke her ankle—I gave her the bicycle! No matter that my sister gave her a lovely pleated houserobe and she wore it (belted) to a formal dinner. ("She didn't!" protested my sister. "She did," I replied. "I have a picture right here. She received a prize or something.")

No matter that she not only dropped her names, she dropped *our* names, the well-known people *we* had met or associated with, names we children would never mention ourselves, all of us being extremely diffident.

So what if she and her friends went traipsing off to all corners and mother thought they were all raving beauties and people of accomplishment. So what if her romantic frame of mind prevented her from understanding that she was getting old. No, she was ageless; her associates were ageless.

So what if we children were sometimes embarrassed and had to "come to terms."

So what if all of our friends loved our auntie-mame mother. My sister once offered a helpful explanation: "It's not at all threatening if it's not your mother acting that way."

We continually heard from them: "Your mother's such a character." "Your mother is simply fascinating." "Your mother is so warm and loving."

I am well aware, student of human nature that I am, that all of our weaknesses are only the shadow side of our strengths.

This garrulous woman was also a woman of great verbal intelligence who could converse on a wide range of topics with a wide variety of people. Her learning never peaked; it never reached a high-water mark, then began to recede. Without higher education herself, she taught poetry symposiums on many a college campus.

She loved people and even though she tended to romanticize them, her positive approval brought out many of their best points. She collected friends by the tens and hundreds. I was continually amazed by the quantities (if not always the qualities) of my mother's friends.

She was quick-witted. At one writers' conference, she saved a man's life by administering CPR after he suffered a heart attack. I was in her kitchen the day roses from his wife were delivered. The card read something like, "For the gift of the life of my husband." Mother burst into tears.

She loved life and participated in it fully, never conserving herself, never really recognizing her own limitations (she suffered her limitations, but she never recognized them). "Let's go . . . let's do something interesting," were some of her favorite phrases. She never came to terms with the truth that you fall as low emotionally as you rise high. She was often depleted from her expenditures of energy. It confused her. "I don't know why I'm feeling so exhausted," she would comment. The reasons were obvious to everyone but herself.

Mother was always up hours before the rest of the world. She wrote in her diary, composed poetry, prayed. Often by the time the rest of us were functioning, she had worked on the magazine, written a chapter for a book, picked strawberries or made rice pudding, noticed birdsong, watched the sun rise. It was wonderful, really, her loving the gift of life so.

My firstborn, the one five decades younger than his grandmother, named her Dobie when he was barely lisping his first words; and Dobie she became to all the grandchildren. My children loved her. They were like my friends—if it's not your own mother doing those outrageous things, it's not embarrassing.

The teens gave a party and mother chaperoned because I was out of town. "Really, Mother!" reported my daughter. "I think we should have had a chaperone for Dobie. She had as much fun as the kids. And she got kind of carried away during the scrabble marathon. You should have seen the words she was using."

They all have Dobie stories. Every outing with her ended in misadventure.

Mother *always* emerged from under her flood waters because she loved life. She greeted this great gift of life each new day. She taught me to identify the lovely, anguished gift of being. With a leaking heart and a brain-damaged husband, the real Wilma Burton nevertheless emerged, with all her vagaries and wonder. She chased after life, she chased it hard.

Mother was a woman of deep faith who verbalized it with the greatest of ease on all occasions, with strangers and with familiars. She saw the holiness in the firm world around her, struggled to find it in its bramble side as well.

I AM NOT SATISFIED
WITH CRUMBS

from Your banquet table.
I would know Your full-course meal
complete with aperitif
of sweet communion wine
and over all the frescoed banner
of Your love
   stretching
from dawn to sunset
with the sunlit, starlit, moonlit
wonder of Your presence.

Mother was square-dancing the night she died. She was planning to remarry. Some of her last words were, "Isn't this fun?"

She slid suddenly from her chair and was gone—but I know that on my birthday, a death she had anticipated thirty-nine years before, she went dancing into heaven.

With a heritage such as this, who am I to fear forty?

Mother was a woman of deep faith, a faith that was tested in the last years of her life. Many people of deep faith become serene and sedate as they age. Mother just became more of herself, and with that she honored her Creator.

Actually, serene and sedate saints are rather dull.

Despite the aberrations, I would rather age like my mother. None of this sweet little old lady bit for me. I would rather be a tough old bird—but holy.

Mother never stopped becoming. Please God, neither shall I.

NINE

Mary McKenna O'Connell

by Madeleine L'Engle

IT IS MY GREAT PRIVILEGE to have known a saint. She was not, perhaps, an obvious candidate for sainthood (like Dorothy Day, or one of her own favorites, Mother Seton), because she lived a life of almost complete anonymity. But nobody who had the privilege of knowing her will ever forget her. And she is probably the most powerful single spiritual influence in my life.

After her death I was given her simple rosary, and it is one of my greatest treasures, the beads worn with prayer. But when Mary McKenna O'Connell looked at the cross it was not to weep over the wounds but to laugh with the joy of the resurrection. The joy of the living Christ shone from her, putting all the events of life into perspective and proportion.

She came into my life, and as a great blessing, very early. My parents had been childless for nearly twenty years before my mother was able to complete a pregnancy and bring forth a live and healthy baby.

Mother told me that once she and Father had had their long-awaited baby, I became a bone of contention between them. They disagreed completely on how I ought to be brought up.

Father wanted a strict English childhood for me, and this is more or less what I got—nanny, governesses, supper on a tray in the nursery, dancing lessons, music lessons, skating lessons, art lessons . . .

Mother had the idea that she wanted me trained by a circus performer, that it would give me grace and coordination and self-assurance, but Father was horrified. I wish Mother had had her way. However, I did have Mrs. O.

Mrs. O., Nanny: odd, obsolete, un-American idea. But Mrs. O. is worth a book in herself. She was English, a Liverpudlian. I was always comfortably certain that she loved me, but it was a typically Anglo-Saxon love which did not indulge in demonstrativeness. She did not, as I remember, kiss me at bedtime when I was a small child. One of our pleasant jokes, after my marriage, was Hugh's attempts to give her a kiss; despite much laughter, she managed to avoid the kisses. Nor was she ever a handholder.

Her family for generations had belonged to the highest order of English servants—and there is nothing more rigid or more snobbish than the English servant class system. It started to break down during World War I and vanished during World War II. There are a few nannies left, but not many. Mine was ninety-one the summer my mother died, still completely *compos mentis*, and passionately concerned with all the doings of my family. She clucked with me many times about Mother's decline, and somehow she always managed to phone me on a day when things had been particularly difficult, and by the end of the conversation we were both laughing.

She was born Mary McKenna and came to the New World when she was fifteen, to spend a summer on Prince Edward Island taking care of four small children. At summer's end she went to visit one of her aunts, who was housekeeper for a wealthy family on Park Avenue; the enormous house is still in existence, now a club. There were four in the family, and forty on the staff, which included gardeners, coachmen, and outdoor laborers. The staff ate dinner at noon, around a long table below stairs, having a "joint" each day, bowls of potatoes, vegetables, salad. They were well-fed, if hard-worked. The family dined at night. One of the daughters of the family, Miss Amy, fourteen, was blind as a result of scarlet fever. She was spoiled and demanding. Young Mary McKenna's aunt suggested that Mary take Miss Amy for a walk. When Miss Amy began to be difficult, not wanting to walk, whining and demanding to go home, Mary said, "My aunt said that you are supposed to walk for an hour, doctor's orders."

Miss Amy said, "I won't."

Mary said, "You will."

Miss Amy said, "I'll lie down in the street."

Mary said, "Go ahead, for all the good it will do you." It was the first time anybody had crossed Miss Amy since her blindness.

They walked for a full hour, and when they got home Miss Amy said to her mother, "I want Mary."

So Mary McKenna, barely older than blind Miss Amy, became a lady's maid. The next day the family left for a trip abroad, and Mary sat at the captain's table with Miss Amy, to help her. The family arrived in Paris earlier than expected, and the floor of the hotel which was usually reserved for their use had not yet been emptied, so the servants were sent, just for one night, up to the top of the hotel, under the eaves.

Mary McKenna announced to one of the others, "I've never slept in a place like this before, and I'm not going to begin now." So she went looking for some way to summon help and express her displeasure. At one end of the attic she saw a series of brass bells, took a broomstick and began whacking away at them, making a considerable din. It was not until firemen came rushing upstairs with hoses and hatchets that she knew which bells she had rung.

However, she had made her point. She did not sleep in the attic.

With Miss Amy she traveled all over Europe, went to formal dinner parties, to the opera, to the theatre; because of Miss Amy's blindness she saw far more of the above-stairs world than would most lady's maids.

Then she met and married John O'Connell, whose brother is still remembered in Ireland as one of the great fighters of the Irish revolution. They had three daughters, and then the O'Connell family fell on hard times, and in order to help feed and clothe the children she went back to work, and the only work she could get was as a charwoman—the lowest rung of the English servant caste system. It was a humiliation to her that few could understand.

She worked on Wall Street cleaning offices at night. My godfather often worked late and got to talking with this rather unusual cleaning woman, and once when his wife was having a large party and needed extra help, he asked Mrs. O'Connell if she could come to their house and help out. My parents were at that party, and later Mother phoned to find out who the splendid extra helper had been, and if she would come help at a party Mother and Father were giving.

When she arrived at our apartment, Mother smiled and said, "I don't even know your name."

"My name is Mrs. O'Connell, but I expect you will want to call me Mary."

"I'd be delighted to call you Mrs. O'Connell," Mother said, and that was the beginning of a friendship between the two women, and my nanny's entrance into my life. I was only a baby, and when I began to talk I called her "O," and a little later "Mrs. O," and Mrs. O she has remained, and there are many people who don't know her by any other name. Wherever she was, she brought laughter, and a sense of fun, although her life, after she left Miss Amy, was full of pain and tragedy.

Until arthritis prevented her from traveling, she spent several weeks with us, three or four times a year, and I treasure a small snapshot of Mother and Mrs. O sitting on the sofa, side by side, nattering away. They shared many of the same memories—of operas all over Europe, of singers; Mrs. O refers casually to Madam Melba, Jean de Reszke, Chalijapin. If Mother knew the people above-stairs, so did Mrs. O, and from the point of view of below-stairs, so she was able to tell Mother all kinds of little tidbits she'd never have heard otherwise. She also enjoyed telling stories on herself, such as the time she was sent out to buy pâté de foie gras; when she reached the grocer she couldn't remember the French words, "but it sounds like Paddy Fogarty." The closest she has ever come to being vulgar is when she said, "Ah, well, I must go and shed a tear for Ireland," and headed for the bathroom.

She thought my father a prince, and treated him accordingly. She loved to tell of one summer when Mother and I were out of the city and Father was preparing to sail to Europe on an assignment. He couldn't find some things he needed, and knew that Mrs. O would know where they were. She didn't have a phone, so he sent her a telegram: "Come at once."

She came, and there he was, she said, sitting alone at the dining table, eating scrambled eggs by candlelight.

She also liked to tell of the times she met him on the street, when he would stand leaning on his cane and passing the time of day, "as though he didn't have anything better to do."

She was deeply religious, in a quiet way, and sometimes when she had a special concern on her mind, she would take me to church with her. She also thought—quite rightly—that I was overprotected, and took me on my first subway rides. She didn't like the fact that Mother would allow no sugar in my breakfast oatmeal; Mother always tasted the oatmeal to make sure no softhearted member of the household had sugared it; Mrs. O got around that by putting the sugar in the bottom of the porringer, and the oatmeal on top of it, and stirring it in after the porridge had been tasted, and Mother never knew, until we told her a few years ago, why I would always eat my oatmeal for Mrs. O. For I never told of the subway rides, or the visits to church, or the sugar in the cereal, or the little packets of butterscotch in the park; all I knew then and all I know now is that Mrs. O never taught me anything but good.

I used to say to her, "Will you help me take care of my children when I grow up?" And she would remind me of this on her visits to us.

When *A Night to Remember*, about the sinking of the *Titanic*, was on television, she sat and watched and rocked and clucked; she knew most of the passengers from Miss Amy's family; the captain had been to the house many a time for dinner, and the young Mary would go to the ship bearing the invitation; some of the crew she knew this way, and some from family and acquaintances in Liverpool; the movie seemed to have been filmed especially for her, and all of us watching it with her were far more moved by it than if we had not been seeing it through her eyes.

She was probably the most normal part of my childhood, and I will always be grateful for her. I think I realized that I was a subject of disagreement between my parents, and yet I managed to think that both of them were always right, and I'm sure Mrs. O had something to do with this.

The day after my mother died, I phoned one of Mrs. O's daughters, and she immediately said that she would call her mother and have her call me, which was a wise decision. When Mrs. O got on the phone she was in charge, telling me what to do, just as she had done all my life.

Last spring Mrs. O was ninety-five, and for the past several years has been in a home for elderly nuns, the Convent of Mary the Queen.

Two of her three daughters are nuns, Sister Miriam Ambrose and Sister Anastasia Marie, and it was because of them that she was given her pleasant room and bath. During these years of her old age I have been called three times to her deathbed, and each time she has surprised doctors and nurses by recovering. It isn't that she is clinging to life, like a brown and brittle leaf clinging to the tree; she is very ready to go home. When she has been on the road to recovery she has each time remarked with good-humored resignation, "Well, God doesn't want me and the devil won't have me."

The Sisters call me regularly to report on her condition, and we all try to go see her as often as possible, and to bring the little girls, my granddaughters, for a state visit once a year. This spring she became very weak, and her mind began to wander, but the Sisters urged me not to come. "If there's a day when she's alert and will recognize you, we'll call."

In August I suddenly had a tremendous urge to go to her, and my friend Gillian said that she'd love to take a day off from work and drive to the convent with me. So when Sister Ambrose called to say that her mother seemed a little stronger and might recognize me, we decided to go.

It was a brilliant summer day. There had been a lot of rain, so the leaves were a lush rich green, not dry and dusty as they sometimes are in August.

When we reached the convent, I fell silent. A voice called

upstairs on a loudspeaker to announce our visit. We walked through a long room with two rows of rocking chairs where ancient Sisters sit to watch television. When Hugh comes to the convent with me, it is an added glory for Mrs. O, for not only do the Sisters watch his show, but most of the nurses, and many of them come hurrying for autographs or simply to shake hands with "Dr. Tyler."

Gillian and I go up on the elevator to the fourth floor. Mrs. O's room is just around the corner. From there she has been able to watch all the comings and goings on the floor. It is hot in the summer, and we have wanted to give her an air-conditioner, but she won't have one because she'd have to keep her door closed and thus be isolated from the life bustling around her.

Wherever she is, she always brings with her the gift of laughter. The nurses on the night shift say, when they are tired or discouraged, "I think I'll go to Mrs. O'Connell's room. She's always good for a laugh." The orderlies and cleaning women love her; whenever there has been a crisis in her condition there have been tears, open and unashamed. Perhaps she is being kept here on earth for so long because her gift of laughter is desperately needed. Ill and difficult patients may well be treated with more tenderness because of Mrs. O.

Never very large, each year she has become smaller and smaller. But there is today a startling change since my last visit. She has eaten nothing solid for three months; a little tea, a little thin soup, the Holy Mysteries; on these she has been kept alive. But there is nothing now between skin and bones. The body on the hospital bed looks like pictures of victims of Belsen, Auschwitz, Ravensbruck.

When I first bend over her she does not know me. I wait while she makes the slow journey from the past to the present. I put my hand on hers and say, "It's Madeleine, Mrs. O. It's Madeleine." Suddenly she is fully with me, and she puts her arms around me as she would never have done in the old days, and says, "Oh, Madeleine, my Madeleine, oh, my Madeleine," and I no longer see the ancient wasted body. I have my arms about her so that I am holding her sitting up, with the fragile body leaning against me like a child's, and yet she is still holding me; we are both child, both mother.

She moves in and out of time. We talk in low voices and she asks me how the children are. Does Bion still have his nice girlfriend? How are the little girls? She hasn't seen Gillian for at least fifteen years and yet she is completely aware of her presence and knows who she is, and asks about her family.

Once she gets lost in chronology and asks me, "Are you downstairs in your carriage?" But the next moment she is back in the present and says, "How's the boss?" (Her pet name for Hugh.) "How could I have forgotten to ask about the boss?"

I stay for an hour, much longer than I had expected, but we are in *kairos,* Mrs. O and I, in God's time, free, for the rest of the hour, from *chronos.* "And the extraordinary thing," I wrote in my journal, "was the electric current of love, powerful and beautiful, flowing back and forth between Mrs. O and me. Gillie had expected to step outside and write letters, but she too felt the lovely light of love which was uniting Mrs. O and me, so she stayed, remarking later what a privilege it had been for her to be present. I cannot set down in words the strength and joy of that river of love; it was something which can happen only in *kairos;* it was a time of Transfiguration—and in the octave of Transfiguration, too—I just thought about that."

So we are given our glimpses of what it is really like, how things are really meant to be. There in that wasted body I saw at the same time the transfigured body, something visible to the spirit and not to the eyes.

These glimpses of reality are the foundation stones of faith.

Mrs. O was, for me, *is* for me, a true saint. As far as worldly success is concerned, she is nobody. But she knows who she is. She had no hesitation in ringing the fire bells of an elegant Paris hotel if she didn't think her quarters fitting. She was not overawed by hobnobbing with the Greats in the world of opera or theatre or society. She simply took it for granted. If she liked people, she liked them on her own terms, regardless of their public reputation. It never occurred to her that her opinion was not valid. She had a totally unselfconscious and humble sense of *amour propre.*

But perhaps the most telling quality of sainthood is laughter. She brought laughter with her, no matter how serious or tragic the surroundings. Since in God's good time "all shall be well and all shall be well and all manner of things shall be well" (as Lady Julian of Norwich, another of my favorite saints, and a remarkably liberated woman, wrote in the fifteenth century), there is nothing that cannot in some measure be redeemed by holy laughter.

She would have been comfortably at home with St. Teresa of Avila. And she would have been equally at home with the other Thérèse, the Little Flower. Because her true home was heaven (and heaven was wherever God chose to put her, no matter how hellish to the casual observer it might seem), there was no place on earth where she was not comfortably at home. And there was no place where she did not bring her gift of loving, compassionate laughter. And, with Mrs. O, laughter was always with and for, never *at*. It was always healing, never destructive.

I have known many women more important in the world's eyes than Mary McKenna O'Connell. Like Jesus, she was not interested in causes, or starting movements which would bring her prominence, but she was passionately interested in people. Anyone who came into her orbit received the gift of a greater sense of self than they had had before; they felt more named, more real. And that is the gift of the saint, for that reality is always tied in with an awareness that we are God's, children of light, meant to walk in the light. I will always be grateful that in my own lifetime I have known a true saint, and have been made more real by that knowing.

And I am certain that she is giving the angels some good laughs, and that there is more joy in heaven because of her presence.

TEN

Ethel Renwick

by Rebecca Manley Pippert

IF ONLY MY PARENTS could find happiness, I thought, then I would be happy too. I was a teenager, watching their marriage dissolve. What I had believed to be the most secure aspect of our life together was in fact the least. But the pain I experienced drove me to ultimate questions. When everything seemed at peace again (although they later divorced), I was still left feeling a strange, gnawing emptiness. I was surprised to realize that what I had longed for the most, a secure family structure, was simply not big enough to build my life upon. So the search began for a foundation strong and trustworthy enough on which to base my life. Although the roots of my search were emotional, the process itself was intellectual.

I studied every system of thought I came across—philosophies, world religions—everything, that is, *except* Christianity. I assumed I knew about Christianity. After all, hadn't I been raised in America? I had even been a Girl Scout!

Although I was raised with a great deal of love, ours was not a particularly religious home. I went to Sunday school and to church sporadically as a young teen. But Evangelical theology and lifestyle were foreign to me.

Everything I studied left me unsatisfied, even despairing. I had wanted logical, defensible answers. I recall asking a believer how he knew his faith was true. "It's a feeling in my heart," he said.

"But what about my head? I have a head as well as a heart!" I exclaimed.

Then I stumbled across a book I was surprised to find in my family's library, *Mere Christianity* by C.S. Lewis. In Lewis I found myself face-to-face with an intellect so disciplined, so lucid, so relentlessly logical, that all of my intellectual pride at not being a "mindless simple believer" was quickly squelched.

I read Lewis, line by line, with intensity and hunger. The issue finally became clear: Could Jesus really be God? Not a prophet, a great teacher, but *God himself?* My conclusion was twofold: First, if Jesus was God, then the final proof of his God-nature must be his physical resurrection. Second, a Christian was one who not only believed in this Jesus, but actually *knew* him. And if those two propositions were true, then as far as I could tell, I had never met a Christian. At least I had never met anyone who talked about knowing Jesus personally. I poured out my frustrations to my pastor, Malcolm Nygren, whom I had not seen in a long time. His final words were, "Come to Sunday school. There's a couple you must meet."

I walked into class that morning feeling awkward. I wanted solid answers, not pat Sunday school rhetoric. Without knowing it, I took a seat next to the teacher—a tall, dignified woman named Ethel Renwick. She was elegant, bright-eyed, and chock full of energy. Her graciousness put me at ease immediately.

Three questions burned in me. But before I had a chance to ask them, she answered them—in sequence. And she answered them well. I was spellbound. As I ventured to ask her other questions, she seemed to take genuine delight in them. I was intrigued to realize that this woman, with so vast a knowledge of the world, was yet a convinced Christian.

She began to talk about knowing Jesus—not as an ethic, or a code of laws, but as a *living* Lord. As I watched her, I perceived a radiance and a presence that spoke to my depths. I felt drawn to her in a way I had never experienced with anyone else. Suddenly it dawned on me that this inexplicable attraction I felt was not to her—it was to Christ in her. Christ *must* have risen, I thought, because he is so alive in her! It was my first glimpse of Jesus, and I loved him instantly. My mind and my heart connected. It was true and I knew it. Relief and joy flooded me as I said to God, "This is it. This really is it. I'm home . . . at last."

I had just been converted.

That afternoon I drove over to her house and drank in her words as she read scripture to me. We met together uncounted times in the weeks that followed, reading the Bible and praying. I grew to know her family well. Her husband, Frank, and their three children, George, Margo, and Robert, have all played significant roles in my life. From that Sunday morning fifteen years ago until now, a day has not passed when Ethel has not prayed for me. What impressed me then still impresses me. She is a woman who has fallen hopelessly in love with God. She celebrates his world and the gifts he has given us to enjoy. And she respects the way he intends life to be lived. I have never once heard her give a glib answer. She is a model of godly wholeness.

One of five children, Ethel was raised in Chicago. Her father, Milan Hulbert, was a noted architect and inventor, decorated by eight countries. Her mother, Olive, was an American raised in Europe, an artist fluent in five languages. She was the President of Alliance Francaise and one of only two women outside of France ever to receive the French Legion of Honor. The other woman, Madame Curie, was a personal friend.

Prior to World War II, Madame Curie came to America to promote the French Red Cross. During her stay, she stood in endless reception lines, always shaking hands with her gloves on. Underneath those gloves were hands badly eaten by radium. But when it came time to say goodbye to Ethel's mother, she took off her gloves to embrace her—a poignant gesture from an otherwise restrained and quiet woman.

Ethel can remember the infectious excitement among the servants and the children whenever special guests came. They would peek over the banister for a glimpse of Sarah Bernhart or Madame Curie.

By training, Ethel was herself more European than American.

She spoke only French until she entered school. Each child in the Hulbert family had a governess to take care of practical needs so that the parents could devote extra time to developing their children's minds and forming their values. Ethel remembers her home as a place of great security and love, where discipline was firm, but love stronger.

Dinner time was a cherished event. Everyone dressed for dinner, wearing a coat and tie or a dress. During the meal, her father would introduce a topic and a lively discussion would ensue. Each child was expected to be well-read and conversant, and all opinions were regarded with respect.

The atmosphere in the Hulbert home was one of tremendous curiosity, characterized by a fervor for knowledge and truth and a deep appreciation of other cultures and ways of life. Each member of the family played an instrument, and together they formed a family orchestra, with Olive Hulbert on the harp and Milan Hulbert on the cello.

Life was good and meant to be appreciated. "Never be afraid of truth," her father would say. He made it a practice never to punish the children for telling the truth.

The children's manners were impeccable, and their mother taught them that good manners were a reminder that others were important. She instructed them to make life as easy as possible for others. "Manners are always motivated by thoughtfulness to others—a reminder that we are not the center of the universe," she would say.

Ethel's parents were Episcopalians who trained their children in the ways of the church. But it was not their custom to discuss faith and God. They baptized their children, sent them to Sunday school, and taught them to say their prayers. Faith was assumed, not probed.

Two events in Ethel's life proved to have a profound impact on her. The first happened when she was only thirteen years old. A team of physicians in Chicago had examined her father and concluded that he had only six months to live. Ethel remembers the verdict: "There is nothing medicine can do." The children were packed off to boarding schools while the parents, following doctors' orders, went to California. Rather than give up all hope of recovery, Milan Hulbert studied nutrition and devised a diet based on whole grains and other natural foods. "The doctors said it wouldn't help," Ethel recalled. "But it did and he lived to a ripe old age."

While Ethel was at boarding school, her father sent her wheat germ and bran. "Sprinkle this stuff on your cereal," he wrote. His advice hardly seems remarkable today, but it was astonishing for the 1930s. The impact of her father's cure and his determination to eat natural foods was to have far-reaching implications for Ethel's life and ministry.

Another major event in her life took place in 1932. Her father's view of education, much akin to his pioneer spirit, was that life was meant to be understood and experienced. He wanted his children to see the whole of life—not to perceive it simply through American eyes. To achieve this goal, he encouraged them to travel, to visit different countries, meet the people, study the language, religion, and food. "While my parents' friends spent enormous amounts of money on elaborate balls for their daughters," explained Ethel, "my parents supported us in our endeavors to appreciate and understand the world."

Mrs. Hulbert and her four tall daughters journeyed not once but three times around the world. In those days, travel was fairly primitive and slow, which meant that the four women had ample time to study the various countries and cultures in which they found themselves. Ethel had always been especially interested in philosophy and religion in college. Now she was able to study each religion close up. She was fascinated by what she saw, and she realized, subsequently, that she was searching for God even then.

The five travelers embarked on their journeys prior to the spread of communism and the spread of industrialization to many of the remote regions of the world. They took freighters through tropical isles and rode narrow-gauge railroads and all manner of motor vehicles across distant landscapes. They sat atop elephants as they swayed through the jungles of the deserted city of Rajputan, blazing with vivid colors and reverberating with the cries of the wild peacocks, parrots, and monkeys. Later, the five women booked passage on an onion freighter, which sailed through the South Pacific, stopping at Borneo and the exotic islands of Mindanao, Jolo, Zamboagna, and Ilo Ilo.

Her father's approach to eating made Ethel curious about the food people ate. The most elaborate meal she encountered was hosted by the burgomaster of Brussels and consisted of eight courses, including everything from pâtè to bombe.

But they ate the simplest and probably the most nutritious meal seated on the ground with a tribal chief of Iloilo, in the Philippines. There were delicious chunks of roast pork, tapioca kneaded in a large wooden trough, bread, fruit, coconut meat from the shell, and fresh vegetables steamed over hot rocks. The natives ate only what their forebears ate, and seemed strong, healthy, and happy. And they had sparkling teeth.

But on her return trips, Ethel also saw people who had converted to the Western diet. To her surprise, many of them were not only unhealthy, flabby, and surly, but their teeth were rotten as well. These people had no dentists to counteract the damage done by eating sweets and other such foods. Ethel concluded that the culprit was an unnatural diet. She has not changed her mind.

Eventually, Ethel returned to live in America. The first crisis she faced came when she was still a young adult. Like so many others in the Great Depression, her father's business failed, due in part to a dishonest employee. The Hulbert family went from having everything to nothing. Ethel was forced to go to work immediately, managing a hotel in Chicago. Her reaction to the crisis was twofold: "On the one hand our parents never let us think that money or material things were important. We were taught to value ideas, culture, music, and art. So it was not so much a devastation as a challenge. However, up until that time, my life had been fairly sheltered. I trusted people and believed they were good. But this experience forced me to see that people were not inherently good. I learned that I needed to become more astute in my judgment of character. I couldn't trust everyone I met."

Later, she met a handsome young man by the name of Frank Renwick, her brother's roommate at military academy. They married after a friendship blossomed into courtship while he studied law. Later, they settled in Colorado Springs, where Frank joined a legal firm.

Ethel was satisfied and content. Her marriage was a happy one, her three children a delight to her. She didn't question God's existence, but neither did she seek him. She sent the children to Sunday school, even though she and Frank never attended church.

One day her eldest child, George, came home from Sunday school and asked, "Mother, was Jesus really raised from the dead?" George's simple question took her by surprise. She considered herself a Christian, one whose family had placed great importance on truth. But she felt unable to answer this earnest question from her nine-year-old child.

She asked herself, "Did Jesus rise from the dead or not?" If so, she would admit the truth and proclaim it to others. If not, she would take her children out of Sunday school. She was determined to find the answer. (Fascinating to me, this same question was the one that, years later, was to drive me to her Sunday school class.)

The next Sunday, she attended church and heard a minister ask: "Did you come here to find Christ? Unless Christ lives in you, you won't find him in a building." She kept mulling over what he said. "Christ in you." But how can Christ be in a person, she pondered?

She discussed her questions with her husband. She and Frank had always been close. If one was interested in a topic then the other wanted to study it as well. They agreed that it was important to find answers. So they searched. They attended church regularly and Ethel began reading books on Christianity. What she read thrilled her.

"I knew the universe was interrelated, interdependent, and integrated. Christianity made sense of the universe by explaining that God was at the center. All of nature, all of creation obeyed God, except humans who, having their own will and intellect, went their own way and chose not to fit into his plan. For the first time I saw that sin consisted not simply of an isolated act of wrongdoing but of a state of brokenness and separation from God that resulted in our going our own way. I saw that Christ came for the purpose of making us *one* with God. Christ could live in me through his Holy Spirit abiding in me. If I followed Jesus, I could be empowered by God himself to be a part of his whole purpose for the world.

"I was thrilled to discover a system that made sense. I had seen people of other religions clamoring for God's attention. They were so terrified of God that they hung food outside their huts to keep the Devil away. I'd seen fear and superstition. Now I saw that God *wanted* to live in us. He'd sent Jesus to show us the way."

Privately, she surrendered and accepted Christ. At once, she felt peace and joy at her decision. It wasn't until two weeks later that she realized she had been converted.

In the meantime, Frank had become warden of a new chapel. At a coffee hour after the chapel service, Ethel spotted three newcomers. She was intrigued to see that they were carrying Bibles. She introduced herself and discovered that they were British—Reverend David Steele and two friends. The three seemed pleasant enough, and she quickly telephoned her Latvian cook, asking her to set three more places for dinner.

During the meal, the Renwicks learned that their guests worked for the Navigators and were in town only for the summer. As Ethel peppered the three with questions, David Steele opened his Bible, showed her a passage, and said, "Does this answer it for you?" Instead of giving her his opinion, he gave her God's Word, and God's Word spoke to her. David Steele's visit confirmed to Ethel that she had indeed become a Christian. Moreover, through them, she had been introduced to the power of the scriptures.

Ethel spoke freely to her husband about her new faith. He was eager to read what she had. With his keen legal mind and open heart, he, too, was soon convinced and converted. Their three children were, at this time, all under twelve years of age. "We didn't preach at them," Ethel says. "We simply shared our delight and joy in the Lord. Jesus was real in our home. Each child came to know God and love him. When people ask how we did it, I answer honestly that it was the grace of God. Of course we prayed daily for them and tried to live a life worthy of the Gospel. But it was God's goodness that brought each one."

Ethel and Frank were a team. If Ethel spoke to a group by herself, she could always count on Frank's prayers. And Frank could always rely on her prayers. They were immensely involved in one another's lives. They left articles and pamphlets for each other to read. When they were apart they read the same scriptures or devotional material. And when they were together, they delighted in sharing the details of their day. I recall once helping Ethel prepare an unexpected dinner. We were in a hurry, and I was a bit frantic when Frank began telling her about his day. Putting down her knife, she gave him her undivided attention. Later she confided to me, "Having dinner on time is only a *thing*, Becky. But Frank is my husband. Never put things ahead of your husband."

An intriguing aspect of their relationship had to do with the fact that they both had strong wills. Neither hesitated to state a conviction forcefully. Indeed, there is not one member of the Renwick family who could be called passive. A marriage between two strong-willed people can easily lead to frequent conflict. But this was not true of Ethel and Frank Renwick. Neither of them was volatile by nature. But more than that, they seemed to share a great oneness of mind and spirit. I remember noticing the slightest frown steal across Ethel's brow one night at dinner. Frank immediately verbalized the problem that Ethel was grappling with. Clearly, he understood what was going on in Ethel's mind.

Despite this mutual understanding, they had their share of problems to work through and lessons to learn. When I asked Ethel for advice about being a good wife while helping to juggle two busy schedules, she replied, "Be careful of too much busyness for the Lord. You can end up serving the Devil instead of God." She told me that one of her first mistakes as a young believer was to become involved in so many Christian activities that Frank began to take second place. "Living by proper priorities isn't a battle that is won once and then forgotten. It involves the daily discipline of reminding oneself who the most important people to serve and love are. You must *choose* your husband each day," she explained.

David Steele and the Navigators taught the Renwicks how to study the Bible and impressed upon them the value of memorizing scripture. After meeting David, they signed up immediately for a couple's conference led by a young minister, Dr. Richard Halverson (now chaplain to the U.S. Senate). Dick Halverson had a great impact on both of them. He suggested that they become acquainted with International Christian Leadership (the "Prayer Breakfast" movement). When Ethel attended one of the first Presidential Prayer Breakfasts for women she found herself sitting next to a twinkly eyed, spunky Dutch woman by the name of Corrie ten Boom. Corrie and she became lifelong friends, and their friendship provided Ethel with ongoing spiritual nurture.

As a new Christian, Ethel could have been tempted to isolate herself from her "worldly" friends. Wisdom, as well as the desire to see others come to Christ, kept her from making that mistake. Ethel's love for God was so radiant and apparent that her country club friends soon noticed the change in her. She did not try to sneak the Gospel into every conversation or to force it on people. An approach like that was alien to her gracious nature. And she knew that theologically it was wrong. She believed that God was seeking others as he had sought her. She knew she was cooperating with her Creator, so she expected him to work. She had been raised to view the universe as a whole. Now that she was a Christian, she saw that God was to be glorified in all of life—in her love of people, literature, music, ideas—not just in church and Bible studies. And because she was interested in so many things, it gave God the opportunity to be glorified in many things.

A glance around Ethel's apartment says much about the scope of her life. In one corner is a hand-carved elephant table from India. On a bookshelf stands an antique piece of cloisonne china, a jade bowl from Nepal, and a Chinese silver box. In the background is an Italian oil-painted, three-panel screen from the 1800s. On one wall hangs an autographed picture of Victor Hugo, a gift from him to her parents. On another wall is a lovely portrait of "Madame Le Brun," painted by Ethel's mother at the Louvre. Atop a Peking rug, the coffee table bears books about Chinese art, Quebec, and several early maps. On the sofa lies her latest manuscript on nutrition from a biblical basis—now a foremost passion. One need only look around to see that she is fascinated by all of life: music, literature, the arts, other cultures, nutrition, health, and most importantly, faith.

By her example Ethel convinced me that for the sake of Jesus Christ we must be interesting people. If our only interest is the Bible—as marvelous and important as that is—we will find ourselves limited in our ability to relate to others and even to God himself. As Ethel related God to all of life, without imposing but simply exposing what she believed, people noticed. Her love for God was contagious.

Before long, her friends began asking questions about her faith. They even asked if she would help them understand the Bible. Feeling inadequate to the task, she told them, "I can't teach you the Bible, but I'll show you how to study it and the Bible will teach you!" From the moment of her first encounter with David Steele, she knew that the Bible could speak for itself; it was "sharper than any two-edged sword."

So began her first Bible study. She has ministered through Bible studies ever since. "Many things take place in a Bible study," she says. "First, remember that people often come from liberal but nominal religious backgrounds. They are well-educated, and yet often essentially unaware of the Gospel of Jesus Christ. So in a Bible study they see who Jesus is, what he is really like, often for the first time. And Jesus is irresistible! Furthermore, the Gospel message is spelled out. Sin is explained. They begin to see the thrill of being a Christian as well as the commitment required. As the leader, I learned firsthand that God empowers us with the Holy Spirit for his tasks."

One by one, nearly every participant in that first Bible study became a Christian. What started as a Bible study for the purpose of evangelism ended up as a Bible study to nurture and disciple new believers.

Her Bible study ministry led to a speaking ministry. Through the Prayer Breakfast movement she spoke to groups across the country. Then she and Frank moved from Colorado to Arizona, where she organized and became chairperson for the Governor's Wife's prayer luncheon, which included 800 women. Simultaneously, she started several new Bible studies, at one time leading as many as five a week.

How did she do it? She simply prayed that God would guide her to the people he was seeking. She had no strategy, other than what God provided.

Both Frank and Ethel led several classes for couples. And both had a vital ministry in Arizona, leading groups alone as well as together.

Because of her keen interest in food, Ethel wrote a book at that time entitled *A World of Good Cooking* (Simon and Schuster), which was awarded the bronze medal at the International Cookbook Fair in Frankfurt, Germany.

Then Frank was asked to be the director of the Executive Development Center at the University of Illinois. So they moved to Champaign, Illinois for two years. The reverberation of their ministry there is still being felt. In Champaign they attended a large, mainline Presbyterian church. Reverend Malcolm Nygren, the pastor who baptized me and performed my wedding and who has a unique gift for incorporating and using the gifts of others, welcomed the Renwicks warmly.

Both of them taught adult Sunday school classes, in which many, including myself, were converted. They led Bible studies and taught us how to study scripture on our own. I can remember Ethel saying as I was preparing for my first year of college: "Now it's your turn to lead a Bible study, Becky." I gulped, but her suggestion that I pray about it inspired me to be on the lookout for the people God would give me.

The Renwicks believed that most Evangelicals tend to flock to the same church, often leaving more liberal congregations devoid of vibrant, committed Evangelicals. They themselves found mainline churches full of open and spiritually hungry people. Ethel told of one example: "I recall meeting a woman for lunch who was a pillar of the church. We talked about programs and organizational details. But on the way home, she began pouring out her personal problems. After we had discussed them, I simply said, 'Let's pray about this. The Lord cares so much about you. He'll show us the way for you.' She looked at me in stunned silence, then said, 'No one has ever prayed for me before.' The woman began to weep. She had gone to church all her life, yet she had never realized that Jesus was alive and personal, that Christ could live in us and love us and guide us."

"If only Christians could see the power they have in the Holy Spirit," Ethel says. "We are small and weak. But God himself lives in us! And he will multiply what we do. We may be only one small pebble in a pond, but that one plunk of obedience causes motion in the rest of the water. God multiplies what we do!"

Hazel Offner, a woman who has also shaped my life and has had a profound impact through her Bible study leadership in the Champaign-Urbana area, says of Ethel: "I have never met anyone who so stretched my vision. Together, we drew up a chart of my neighborhood and prayed for each family by name. We wrote down the names of people in the neighborhood and prayed for each family by name. We wrote down the names of people in the Presbyterian church whom Ethel had just met and prayed for them. Ethel had never met my neighbors, and I had never met her Presbyterian friends, but, together, we believed God to accomplish great things in them and in us as we prayed. The result for me was a neighborhood Bible study which turned into an all-community study of forty-five small groups. My life—and my understanding of God—was never the same again.

"Ethel's faith was contagious. There wasn't any dream too big for her to dream and to believe that God would cause to become reality. She knew that there was marvelous untapped potential in everyone around her, and she was so expectant—both before God in prayer and demonstrably to the persons themselves as her soul touched theirs—that it was impossible not to catch her faith and her vision and to become expectant, too. She seldom expressed negative feelings; rather, there was constant, pervasive expectancy that God was just waiting and was eager to change and use people. I can recall several times when a name would come to her as we were talking and she would interrupt the conversation for a moment and spontaneously lift that person to God. By the time she left Champaign, after two years there, one life after another had been deeply affected and changed by God."

When Ethel and Frank returned to Arizona, where she now lives, she worked at the International Food Bazaar, managing fourteen kitchens representing nine different nationalities. Her knowledge of international cuisines stood her in good stead—and so did her knowledge of people. "Waitresses and busboys would ask me if we could talk. They told me they were addicted to drugs and wanted to stop. They asked for my help." Ethel would listen intently to convey a genuine concern as well as God's love for each person. She also invited a guest speaker, a physician, to lecture to the entire staff on why drugs led only to a dead end. And she regularly scheduled Christian speakers who had been on drugs themselves to come and speak to the staff on various subjects, including faith in Christ.

As she recounted this story, I marvelled at the thought of teenagers admitting such a problem to their boss. After all, she could have fired them. But they sensed that they could trust her. Such trust says a great deal about Ethel, but she insists that it says much more about God. "It's Jesus in me that enabled me to see pain I might otherwise have missed. He gives us a love that truly comes from above. If you'd told me in college that I would love a drug addict much less know one—I would have been amazed." "But when God lives in you, what draws you into people's lives isn't duty or social work, it's his love that keeps penetrating the barrier," she says.

Part of her sensitivity to pain comes from the presence of God in her life and part comes from firsthand experience. Throughout the years, her life has been marked by pain as well as privilege.

Several of her close friends have suffered from alcoholism. She has cleaned up after them, held them, and provided hour-to-hour emotional support as well as physical nurture. She has had the painful experience of telling some that they were addicted to alcohol and needed professional help, only to be avoided by them from that time on.

Her own family suffered tragic automobile accidents, serious physical problems, and other crushing blows, resulting in the premature deaths of three of her five brothers and sisters. Perhaps her deepest grief has been over the death of her husband Frank.

In a way that only God could order, I was home one night, contrary to my previous expectations, when George Renwick called me with the sad news that his father was gravely ill. Abruptly, George said, "Becky, call mother, right now, please." I hung up, dialed, and Ethel answered, having been informed only seconds before that her husband had died.

Later, she said, "There are so many stages one goes through with the death of a spouse. At first, I felt that half of me had died. My major human support was buried. Nothing else seemed to matter. I felt I had no place, no mooring, apart from the constancy of God's love and the comfort of my children. Six months later the phone would ring, and I would begin immediately to recount in my mind all that I wanted to tell Frank. As I leapt to the receiver, I would remember that he was gone. It's hard to describe just how deeply the loss of someone you love can affect you. But as I received God's love, as well as the tremendous care of my children and friends, I began to be healed. The numbness started to leave."

One of the friends to offer comfort was Corrie ten Boom. It was a remarkable experience for me to sit in a living room with Ethel, her sister Adele, her three children, and Corrie. It was obvious that Corrie loved Ethel and knew only too well the pain that comes from the death of a loved one. But her eyes shone as she said in her heavy Dutch accent, "My dear sister, vee don't vant him back. Frank ist vith our Jesus now! *Think* of it."

After the initial pain, Ethel experienced yet another level of grief. "I had to deal with my new social status. People treated me differently as a widow. I was no longer invited to all the social gatherings that I had been. Businesses did not take me as seriously. A male voice on the telephone carries more clout, I discovered, than a female voice. So I had to learn to deal with that.

"The third, unexpected stage of recovery happened when God gave me a new ministry. My book on nutrition *Let's Eat Real Food* was published in 1977 and is now in its eighth edition (Grand Rapids: Zondervan). I began leading seminars for individual Christians as well as for schools and secular groups, teaching others how to eat sensibly and responsibly. After that, all kinds of opportunities opened up."

All kinds of opportunities, indeed! One week before I flew to Arizona to interview her, I was speaking at a conference in

Pennsylvania. As I was autographing books, a woman came up to me and said, "I couldn't believe you mentioned Ethel Renwick in the foreword to your book. She changed your life spiritually and my life physically. My family suffered from headaches, hypoglycemia, and poor eating habits. Reading her book changed our eating patterns. We feel like new people. We keep her book on our coffee table and have given copies to our friends."

In short, there is life after tragedy and loss. "Sorrow," relates Ethel, "is God's greatest opportunity to deal with us. Because in those times we are so defenseless. We know that we simply cannot continue on our own. We can't heal ourselves or fill the gap. But God can meet us on our knees. He can have deeper access to us in our pain. And he does heal the brokenhearted and bind up their wounds."

What exactly is her present ministry? "In many ways, I believe God has taken all the strands of my life and made them come together, to do what he called me to now," she says.

Perhaps a story will best illustrate. I told the Lord as I fell asleep in Ethel's apartment on the night of my interview with her that I wanted to convey the depth and significance of what she does. I was awakened early the next morning by a telephone call for Ethel. It was from a woman who had recently brought a friend to see Ethel. The friend had attempted suicide twice. Ethel had spent four hours listening to her spill out her problems. Ethel asked her spiritual questions, but she also inquired about her eating and drinking habits. It became clear that in addition to being emotionally and spiritually troubled, she was also a physical wreck. She was living on colas and valium.

So Ethel suggested that this young woman change her eating patterns and begin filling her body with nutritious foods. She told her that God cared for her physically and emotionally as well as spiritually. If she wanted real health, in every dimension, she needed to be invaded by God through Jesus Christ. It was clear that the distraught woman was moved, almost astonished by the kind of God who loved every part of her. She had never heard the Gospel presented in such an integrated way. She thought Christianity was just for the soul. She had not realized that God made provision for every dimension of life—body and soul. He wanted her to be whole and she knew she was fragmented. She left, saying she was determined to change her physical habits and to seek God as well.

That morning's telephone call related the news that the troubled woman was on the road to physical recovery and spiritual renewal. For the first time, she felt hope and not despair. Ironically, the person telephoning with the good news had, herself, gone to Ethel only months before with many of the same problems: suicidal, addicted to valium. Through Ethel's help, she, too, rededicated her life to Jesus Christ.

Says Ethel: "We say we're concerned about wholeness as Christians, yet we so often avoid the physical dimension. The only thing that nourishes the brain and the nervous system is food. Yet it never occurs to us to check what a depressed person has been eating, as one indication of the source of the problem. Food affects how we see the world. It can make our minds clear or fuzzy. If we load our bodies with sugar and caffeine, we get a lift only to crash later. How can we be a vital witness to God? God wants his children to be strong and healthy and clear-minded—not addicts."

How did Ethel's ministry come to include a concern for people's physical well-being? "It was because I kept meeting people who didn't feel well. It was especially alarming how many of them were Christians who told me they were tired, with little energy and feeling depressed." They often felt the culprit was spiritual inadequacy. As Ethel questioned them about their diet she was disheartened by how poorly they ate. They cared deeply about the Kingdom, yet they ignored and even abused the vessel God works through to build his Kingdom—our bodies."

In our nation's diet, Ethel warns, "we eat more candy than eggs, more sugar than vegetables, fruits, and eggs combined; we drink more soft drinks than milk. And since 1971, we eat more processed foods than fresh foods. We send our children off to school carrying a lunch box filled with a sandwich made of fluffy enriched white bread, potato chips and a couple of cookies, not even stopping to think what ingredients or chemicals are in those basic ingredients. We often reward children with destructive food, and then we wonder why they seem so high-strung and irritable. We have bake sales at church to raise money for the poor by selling impoverished, nutrient-less food."

Strong words? Then hear what she has to say about Christians!

"The Lord recently sent me someone who loves him—a pastor's wife—who was in great need. Her story is the same I hear from so many—unexplained anxiety, depression, fatigue, increased mental problems. The doctors after many tests, found nothing wrong with her. Yet her diet was atrocious! (but very usual)."

Ethel believes that our ignorance of today's food has serious consequences and that Christians are especially accountable for these consequences. Her latest book, *Feeding the Faithful* (Keats Publishing), rises out of just this conviction. From the book she writes, "There has been a radical departure in many ways from the food which God designed for our bodies and the food we accept today with little question. . . . Perhaps one reason that scripture mentions eating and drinking to the glory of God is because, when we disobey this, we self-destruct to some degree; we are less than we could be for Him."

The strands have, indeed, come together—personal commitment to Christ, energetic witness in the world, the understanding of the relationship between physical and spiritual well-being. Through her life, Ethel has provided an example of tireless dedication and caring love to countless individuals. Hers is an example that merits close examination.

The underlying assumption of this book is that in addition to needing heroes and role-models we must be ones for others.

Ours is a strange age. Never have we hungered more for heroes or tried so hard to defame them. We lived through the nightmare of Watergate, but it has left us more cynical than before. Nevertheless, we still ache for heroes, even if we are no longer comfortable with them. Pete Dawkins, all-American football player, Rhodes scholar, the most luminous graduate of West Point, and now, at age forty-three, the youngest general in the U.S. Army, said in an interview with my husband, Wesley: "A lot of things that are central parts of our lives are transcendent or abstract. But it's hard for us to deal with courage or dedication or sacrifice in the abstract.

We need to have people who embody those qualities, who are reassuring and real. What we really want is to believe in people." Yet we live in an age of the "anti-hero." As Hawkins says, "We seem to turn on our's [heroes] with special fervor, driven by an almost compulsive need to scratch and rub anyone of heroic dimension until we find a wart or flaw. We microscopically examine people in public life until we find something about them that is flawed."

Yet the human heart cannot seem to resist the desire to elevate someone above the masses: whether this tendency is realized in the exuberant outpouring of joy and enthusiasm for the Pope; the poignant scene where hundreds kept vigil outside Yoko Ono's home the night John Lennon was slain, or the wearing of hideous T-shirts for Gary Gilmore or Claus van Bulow. As disparate as these examples are, we must listen to what our culture is telling us. We need heroes. People want to believe in someone.

We must distinguish between *celebrities* and *heroes.* Never be ashamed of having a hero or of being one. But be leery of the celebrity-mania that exists in America today. There will always be an abundance of celebrities, but there is a paucity of genuine heroes in the land.

Garry Trudeau, the creator of the comic strip "Doonesbury," spoke of this in his 1981 commencement address at Colby College: "This is a deeply cynical age where generosity is in short supply. You will find that this technological society will soon reveal its limitations. It is a world where taking a stand has come to mean finding the nearest trap door for escape. . . . You will find that your worth is measured not by what you are, but by how you are perceived. There is something disturbing in our society when men wish not to be esteemed, but to be envied. . . . When that happens, God help us."

A popular television show was being broadcast in the nation's capital, just the kind of thing that Washington loves best: top news men and women questioning a news-making political celebrity. Senator Barry Goldwater was an exceptionally good guest that night. His answers were characteristically tough, feisty, and candid. As the program came to a close, one interviewer said, "We always ask this, sir, in the last thirty seconds, realizing it's not nearly as significant as the other things we've discussed, but who has been the greatest influence in your life? Who has been one of your heroes?" There was silence. One by one each reporter looked up. The silence became awkward. The camera zoomed in for a close-up and the reason for the silence became immediately apparent. Senator Goldwater was fighting back his emotions. His voice breaking, he apologized to the startled reporters.

Finally he said, "It's a man you've probably never heard of. I'm sure he himself had no idea the impact he made on me as a young man. But he modeled for me all the things I've ever aspired to be. He pointed me in the right direction. He believed in me and he cared for me. He was a great man."

That night a politically powerful man wept publically on television. Not because he won an election, or lost an election, or was indicted (as is too often the case!). He wept because he had a hero. That night I realized that Senator Goldwater and I have a great deal in common. The thought of my hero also makes me weep.

Part Two

Portraits of Ten Outstanding Christian Men

ELEVEN

C.S. Lewis

by Harry Blamires

I RECALL CLEARLY C.S. Lewis' first words to me when I knocked on his door at Magdalen College and entered his room some time early in 1936. He looked me up and down and said, "Ah, good; an Anglo-Saxon. I've had nothing but Celts lately." Presumably he was referring to the succession of new pupils he was introducing himself to. Looking back now, and trying to recall what they looked like, I can see that my fair hair and pale complexion perhaps distinguished me. Certainly one of my year, Gerald Brodribb, who was later to become known as a writer on cricket, had a shock of red hair that flamed like a sunset. Lewis of course was just trying to make me feel comfortable by a personal remark that put the relationship on a companionable footing and was calculated to ease the natural awe of student for tutor. In my case he was never one hundred percent successful in this respect. Though years later I got on terms of real friendship with him, I never overcame the reluctance to be too familiar with one so distinguished. "My friends all call me Jack," he said, but if it was meant to be a hint or an invitation I didn't take it up. And Lewis' delicacy was such that he wouldn't force a change like that. In tune with the habits of the time he remained "Lewis" to me and I was "Blamires" to him.

Lots of people have described what it was like to be Lewis' pupil. One point ought to be mentioned—his meticulous conscientiousness. Illness apart, he was always there precisely on the tutorial hour and as ready to keep you till the time was up, sometimes till the next student knocked on the door. At a time when many tutors were notoriously lax and one heard stories of dons who practiced golf strokes on the carpet throughout tutorials or caught up with their correspondence while students read aloud their essays to the unresponsive furniture, this was a great boon to a student. It is especially worth mentioning because Lewis' own view of a university such as Oxford was that its fellows were meant to live the "clerkly life." They were there to study. This was their vocation, and it had once been a celibate vocation. Dons were not there primarily to teach. They were not "educators," for education by teaching was something that happened to you at school. Dons were primarily men and women at work on their own studies. Students were there to pick up whatever crumbs of enlightenment might be found by tagging on behind them. It is characteristic of Lewis that he held this ideal notion of a university don's function, yet in practice discharged his teaching obligations with punctilious care and thoroughness.

For he must often have been bored by the tedium of listening to third-rate essays read to him by uninspired students who wrote their weekly assignments by adapting chapters from *The Cambridge History of English Literature.* I myself was a fairly late developer. My earliest essays must have been drearily obvious to listen to. But I have no recollection at all of a bored-looking auditor, let alone of anything like a snub, a rebuke, or any remark that ever made me feel small. I remember only the occasional compliment, the word of praise that stimulated me enormously. I had been having tutorials with him for a couple of terms when he said, "You're beginning to ply a very pretty pen," and the remark has stayed in my mind ever since. I found throughout all my dealings with Lewis that if he wanted to draw attention to a fault, he would combine his criticism with praise for some quality or virtue. Once, when I had expressed myself very badly in a tutorial, replying very lamely and haltingly to his attempts to make me argue, he said: "You're like Oliver Goldsmith, as Dr. Johnson described him—

Here lies Nolly Goldsmith
For shortness called "Noll"
Who wrote like an angel
And talked like poor Poll.

Years later, when he took to pieces my first attempt to write a book in the field of literary criticism, his letter of analysis began: "You have struck gold and made a real critical advance." Then, after a paragraph in praise of what there was to praise, he settled down to a severe dissection of the book's faults. Lewis' careful consideration of the effect of his words on the person he was dealing with was a model of charity and sympathy in action. No man I have ever met was more anxious not to hurt others. When people talk about an overbearing Lewis or a bullying Lewis, they describe a man I never met.

Lewis was acutely conscious of the power of Christian personal influence in this respect—the use of words. (He was fond of saying, "The tongue is man's most unruly member, except one.") He once remarked to me, "Have you ever noticed how, when we angrily try to hurt people directly, especially when we want to make them feel small, our rebuke generally misfires; but when we are speaking quite innocently and charitably we may unintentionally touch their consciences and sting them? It's the unintended rebuke that stings. It's the same with praise," he added. His implication was that a watchful Providence restricts our capacity to do damage out of ill-will, for the very good reason that a rebuke bred of anger or envy is a tainted rebuke even if it happens in substance to represent a justifiable correction. But the same Providence may use our innocent, malice-free remarks to prick someone's conscience whom we are not trying to hurt.

I often reflected on these words. I found them especially apt because one of Lewis' most crucial practical influences on me was exercised in exactly this oblique way. Sometime in 1946 I completed a study of the English novel from its earliest beginnings up to the death of Sir Walter Scott in 1832, and I wrote to Lewis to ask if he would look through it. Overwhelmed though he must have been by demands at this time, he at once agreed. I had of course approached him apologetically. It was characteristic of Lewis that he did not make me feel that I was imposing a burden. "Most people just send their manuscripts without asking first," he wrote, "and I don't even know them." I was made to feel considerate for having been gracious enough to ask something with a polite preliminary letter! In my study I had tried to show how novelists, by their implicit moral attitudes, reflected changing emphases and in particular how a current of what Lewis himself called "the old Christian thought" surfaced in Scott's *Waverley Novels.* Lewis treated this manuscript with great thoroughness as he would have dealt with a doctoral thesis. He pencilled in marginalia. He put crosses where he thought a matter of fact or style was faulty. He put ticks where he thought a point merited approval. Two ticks and even three ticks marked a point that especially excited his approval.

I was studying this typescript one day when it suddenly struck me that the ticks tended to occur at places where I had been making judgments of a moral, theological, or philosophical character rather than sticking to my role as a literary critic. Noting this, I said to myself, "So perhaps that's the kind of writer I am really!" And so it was the influence of those ticks that gave me confidence to start writing as a lay theologian. What an apt illustration of Lewis' own theory that you may exercise the most compelling influence as a by-product of what you are consciously about.

To go back to Lewis as a tutor, I have no memories of anything but the maximum kindness and good-humor. Good-humor especially. There was a lot of laughing in Lewis' company. At that date he was a very cheerful man indeed. His tutorial method was to give you a reading assignment for a week. You had to produce an essay on it the next week to be read aloud to him and then dissected. He didn't give you a title for your essay. You must choose your own line. One of my most amusing tutorial experiences occurred after Lewis had told me to spend the week on the seventeenth-century poet and essayist, Abraham Cowley. Among Cowley's works was a massive neoclassical biblical epic, *The Davideis,* which is generally agreed to be a heavily uninspired effort in the genre of Milton's *Paradise Lost.* The time came for me to read my essay on Cowley to Lewis. There I sat in an armchair, my book on my knees, while Lewis faced me, sitting in the middle of his immense settee, pipe and tobacco on one side, a packet of Wills Goldflake cigarettes on the other side, and the two served his purposes alternately. As usual he held a paper and pencil in hand, the paper resting on the back of a book, so that he could jot down notes in preparation for dissecting my work afterwards. Halfway through my essay I launched on a thorough analysis of Cowley's epic, *The Davideis.* As I pursued my eloquent way through section after section of this vast work I gradually became conscious of a faint restlessness on Lewis' part. Soon he began to shake a little and then to rock from side to side. I had to look up and I found his face suffused with the largest and most uncontrollable grin I had seen there. I stopped reading. Vainly trying to smother his laughter, Lewis said, "You don't mean to say that you've actually *read* the thing!" "Every word," I said. His smile disappeared. The large face assumed a look of great solemnity and a note of deep compassion sounded in his voice. "I'm sorry," he said. "I'm terribly sorry," as if nothing could recompense me for his failure to warn me in advance against so outrageous a waste of my time. Then he visibly brightened. He had found a crumb of consolation. "But think," he said, pointing his finger at me, "you must be the only man in England, perhaps the only man alive, to have read every word of Cowley's *Davideis.*"

Plainly Lewis did not believe in indiscriminate reading. On the other hand he did believe in repeated rereadings of what he most admired. As a student I once distinguished myself with an essay on Malory's *Le Morte D'Arthur* which caused him to slap his knee as I finished reading and declare, "That's an alpha!" Some twelve years later when I came into his orbit as a young writer and we were talking about books, he said, "I remember a very good essay you wrote on Malory." I don't know now what I said in reply, but it must have conveyed to Lewis that Malory was not much in my thoughts at present, for he stiffened, stared me in the face, and assumed an expression of utter astonishment. "You don't mean to say you've *stopped* reading Malory!" Ruefully I had to confess that I was one of those philistines who, in spite of his patient tutelage, could allow a year to begin and end without opening *Le Morte D'Arthur.*

Was Lewis especially sympathetic to students who were evidently Christians? Not unfairly so in my experience. It is true that by a fluke I had read Lewis' *The Pilgrim's Regress* before I went up to Oxford in 1935. *The Pilgrim's Regress,* his first prose book, published by Dent in 1933, sold very badly. It was little known, even in Oxford. I could not at first find a fellow-student who had read it, or heard of it until I mentioned it. (After Sheed and Ward took it over from Dent I heard Lewis say that he had never received a penny for it—and this cannot have been said earlier than 1936.) But naturally, learning that Lewis was to be my tutor, I reread the book carefully, pencil in hand. I cannot now recall how or when I made clear to Lewis that I had read and enjoyed the book; but obviously a student does not conceal so useful a fact from his tutor for long. I mention this because it has occurred to me since that I may have been marked as the student who had read *The Pilgrim's Regress* long before I became the student who had read *The Davideis.* However that may be, there were occasions when, after the tutorial was over, I engaged Lewis in conversation on other matters. One memorable conversation took place soon after the news came through that G.K. Chesterton had died, so it must have been at the end of the summer term of 1936. I said how I had devoured as much Chesterton as I could lay my hands on as a schoolboy. Lewis warmed to the praise of Chesterton and I felt a new sympathy between us. I recall this now when I read how many of Lewis' affinities and friendships started from common interest in favorite books and writers.

One thing that occurs to me now, but which never struck me while Lewis was alive, is that I was rarely with him in the presence of others—except of course other students, for he gathered us together as undergraduates for what he called his "Beer and Beowulf" evenings, when we all sat on the floor in his room to declaim and translate Anglo-Saxon poetry. But my regular tutorials with him were individual tutorials, and when I renewed contact with him as a young writer, it was to have long conversations with him alone. On one of those occasions Hugo Dyson was present with us for dinner at Magdalen, but after the meal he departed. So I do not have those personal pictures of Lewis in company which enliven so many people's recollections of him. I did not get any clear impressions of Lewis' life outside the tutorial room and the lecture room. I recall only one occasion during my student days when Lewis spoke to me of his domestic situation. I asked him if he had been to see a certain play that had been performed in Oxford the previous day. He hadn't been able to, he said. "You see my mother—I call her my mother though in fact she is not—insisted on my taking her to see that film of Anna Neagle as Queen Victoria." It was insufferably tedious, he said, as films generally were, and he laughed scornfully about the way the camera focused for the emotional climax on glycerine tears rolling down the actress' face. At that time I felt it somewhat strange that this "mother" could so command the great scholar to the cinema, but later on it added to my insight into Lewis' faithfulness in humoring the whims of this very demanding woman. One might be tempted to feel anger at the way he gave himself to the tasks of washing up, mowing lawns, cleaning shoes, and other such chores, simply to help and please her. One is tempted to say, "What a waste of the man's valuable time" were it not that he accomplished so much as a writer anyhow that it would be difficult to conceive of his achieving more.

We students were all of course very much aware of Warnie—"the Colonel" my familiars called him, for no one could have looked more like a former military man. We thought him a great joke. He inhabited an inner study approached through Lewis' sitting room. There he could often be heard typing. But there was no one whose tutorial was not from time to time interrupted by a stealthy opening of the study door. The "Colonel" emerged, walked across the sitting room to the outer door with that kind of contrived "unobtrusiveness" that makes itself heavily obvious while the student's reading or the dialogue between student and tutor continued uninterruptedly. Having gone out, of course, the "Colonel" had to come back. The student waited in suspense until the performance was repeated in reverse. We could not in our ignorance and our innocence imagine why a bachelor don should saddle himself with a character whose regular processions across his tutorial room reminded us for all the world of Groucho Marx.

Until I was asked to contribute to this volume I have been reluctant to put pen to paper on the subject of Lewis. This is because Lewis was such a generous and unselfish man that most of my later connections with him arose out of, and centered upon, books which I had written. This puts me in a quandary (the sort of quandary that would have tickled Lewis hugely). It is a poor way to pay tribute to a great writer if I turn it into an occasion for talking about my own works. Yet it was my own work that brought about a renewal of meetings between us. It happened like this. In 1948-49 I wrote what was to be my first published book, *Repair the Ruins* (reflections on education from the Christian point of view), and I offered it to the publisher, Collins. They turned it down and their letter of rejection made it clear to me that it had been read by some professor of education, or someone of that kind. "I must try a publisher who is not in the educational field but who might send it to a reader interested in theology," I said to myself, and promptly sent it off to Geoffrey Bles who at that time had a strong list, including such writers as Maritain and Berdyaev as well as Lewis. Bles accepted the book and asked me to go and see him. When it transpired that I was an ex-pupil of Lewis', Bles suggested that we should try to interest him in the book. (His aim at this time was to try to get Lewis to introduce every new writer who came along—but that's another story.) Lewis very kindly agreed to look through the typescript. When he had done so, he asked me to go along for "dinner, bed and breakfast" at Magdalen so that he could take up some points with me before the book was sent to the printer.

When I wrote my next book, *English in Education*, Bles, to my surprise, got Lewis again to read it, and he did the same with my third typescript, *A Christian Philosophy of Education*, which in fact was never published. The only thing more astonishing to me now than Lewis' readiness to spend precious time and energy on my early typescripts was the way he turned my indebtedness to him into something for which I myself could be commended. "I think you are a very patient man," he wrote to me. "You might very well feel that you had been ready to put up with my comments for two years as an undergraduate, but not for a life-long critique." However, the critique, I'm glad to say, did continue. For in 1954 and 1955 I published my three allegorical novels which trace the visits of the narrator to a kind of purgatory, hell, and heaven. Out of sheer kindness Lewis wrote an encouraging letter to me as each book was published.

I have never kept a diary and I was lax in preserving letters—even Lewis'. I do not know on how many occasions I took advantage of his hospitality. "You know there is always dinner, bed and breakfast to be had here?" he ended a letter to me in 1954. In fact I went rarely, supposing that he must be over-plagued with visitors, and with ex-pupils especially. When I did go, it was to be taken along to the Senior Common Room for a sherry, and then to dinner in the college hall (if it was term-time) or in the Senior Common Room (if it was the vacation). After dinner the port and the madeira circulated in the Common Room and Lewis would whisper, "I advise against the madeira unless you've got a very strong head." We then repaired to his room to talk. During the course of the evening he would boil a kettle of water on the floor and make tea. Next morning he would knock on my door at 7:30 to take me for a walk in the grounds before breakfast. After breakfast we shook hands and parted, Lewis to get down to work promptly at nine o'clock.

Odd snippets of conversation linger in my mind from these occasions. I remember once, before Tolkien had published *The*

Lord of the Rings and when he was little known as a writer, how we talked about *The Hobbit* and the way children took to it. "If you read it aloud, as I have done," I said, "there's only one false thing in the book, and it's that psychological stuff about the Took family at the beginning. It doesn't belong." Lewis was delighted to hear me say this. "How right you are," he said. "We all tried to get him to take it out. But he wouldn't." The remark conjures up an intriguing picture of Tolkien resisting the combined pressure of the Inklings.

I recall a visit I paid to Lewis shortly after the publication of my first theological novel, *The Devil's Hunting-Grounds,* in 1954. Perhaps I may repeat here something which I have recorded in my introduction to the reissue of the book. At the beginning of the story the narrator encounters his Guardian Angel who conducts him on a tour through localities in the hereafter where various heretics and half-believers go on indulging their misconceptions. The Guardian Angel is there to correct the earthbound notions of the narrator and other muddled characters. To suggest authoritativeness in modern terms I had made the angel, Lamiel, talk rather like a bureaucrat or a pedant. Why had I done this? Lewis asked me. "I thought it funny," I said. "It is, very funny indeed," Lewis grinned, but then went on to make a very serious point. Was I perhaps in danger of not treating angelhood seriously? This made me think. Especially since Lewis went on to say that when he first started to write *The Screwtape Letters,* he had intended to balance the correspondence between devils attacking the human soul with correspondence between angels protecting him. But when it came to the point and he tried to enter the angelic mind, he decided that the attempt was too presumptuous. Apparently I had rushed in among the angels where Lewis had feared to tread.

When talk turned to Lewis' theological works, he revealed how much hostile criticism had wounded him. "You don't know how I'm hated," he once said to me with feeling, adding as an afterthought, "loved too of course." No doubt envy and resentment were aroused in Oxford Senior Common Rooms by his popular success at the kind of polemical fisticuffs which donnish minds affected to despise. It has been said that Oxford dons objected to

Lewis, not for becoming a Christian, but for advertising the fact. Unspoken rules of English decorum require one to be secretive about religious conviction. Lewis' way of putting intellectual and moral pressure on people in print for the purpose of converting them was an offence against academic etiquette. One must remember that Lewis had no degree in theology and was therefore, in the eyes of some, trespassing into other people's rightful terrain, an amateur taking on the experts. Professional academic theologians could obviously not be expected to enjoy having their thunder stolen. Lewis appealed to a vast audience over the heads of the university establishment and in defiance of academic protocol. In the eyes of some critics he was using a donnish know-how to mesmerize the innocent masses with dialectical conjuring tricks.

As Christians we know that Lewis was right to do what he did. The message of the gospels is unmistakable in this respect. The disciples were told to spread the gospel throughout the world, and there was no mention of their need to graduate in theology first. By comparison with what Lewis had to tell his generation, the protocol of even the most exalted university was trivial and petty. As for the resistance he sometimes encountered within the church itself, one can only assume that it was vengefully engineered by Screwtape. I say this while recalling an account he gave me of an encounter with some trendy clergymen at a gathering he had been invited to address. They did not conceal their coolness towards him.

No doubt this kind of hostility helped to drive Lewis into writing the Narnia books. He certainly regarded these stories as continuing the work begun in his apologetic. He spoke to me once as though he were turning away from one generation to address another. He implied that perhaps there wasn't much more he could do against the aridly unimaginative unbelief of our contemporaries, but that there was always hope in the young. He reacted warmly to appreciative talk of the Narnia books, and especially to any suggestion of a possible influence on children that might prove fruitful in later life. He could talk about the

Narnia stories without self-consciousness. I remember one evening in his room how he dived down to the bottom of a bookshelf to dig out the French edition of *The Lion, the Witch, and the Wardrobe.* He was anxious to show me how the French artist had captured a totally different aspect of Aslan from that brought out in Pauline Baynes' drawings. He had nothing but praise for Pauline Baynes herself and for her illustrations. He thought them delightful. The lovableness of Aslan shone through her pictures. But the French artist had projected a more awesome, less cosy, indeed positively fearsome Aslan. The huggableness was gone. Here was a power you might well be advised to keep your distance from. Lewis' zest and pleasure in laying the book open before me to make the point stayed in my mind as such images sometimes do. It was a fit image of his own principle, that the Christian ought to be able to take the same delight—not greater, not less, not different—in his own good work as in someone else's. I suspect that the particular delight he took in praise of the Narnia books had something to do with the way their reception by readers and reviewers lifted him right out of the arena where the prophet and the preacher are sneered at and stoned.

I would not wish to make too much of the hostility to Lewis in academic theological circles. He had good friends in Oxford, high-powered theologians among them. I have two personal memories that illustrate this. On December 18, 1956, I took the train from Winchester to Oxford because I had been invited to have lunch with Eric Mascall at Christ Church. As I got off the train at Oxford, I came face to face with Lewis standing on the platform. He was ready to talk, but I could not linger because of my appointment to meet Mascall in Christ Church lodge. I explained this, and Lewis waved me off, saying, "Give my love to Eric." A memorable thing about these words is that I think they were the last I heard him say and the kind wave the last gesture I saw him make. When I returned home that evening I said to my wife, "I met Lewis on the station platform at Oxford, and I've never seen him look so utterly miserable. He looked tragic." Six days later he gave news of his marriage publicly in the *Times.* I was utterly bewildered. The image of Lewis' evident sadness and the news of the marriage did not fit together. Of course I assumed that he would no longer wish to be visited by ex-pupils. Only after a very long time did I come to understand that in the month of December 1956 Lewis had recently learned of Joy's fatal cancer and the decision to convert the civil marriage into a Christian marriage was being made.

Ten years later, in 1966, I was in Oxford one day for lunch with another distinguished theologian, Austin Farrer, then Warden of Keble College. Farrer and his wife, Katherine, gave me a graphic description of the remarkable occasion when Katherine felt that she simply must get in touch with Joy because something was wrong, and she called her by phone. At that very moment Joy had just collapsed on the floor, tripping over the telephone wire and bringing the telephone on to the floor beside her. As Katherine's call came through, she was able to reach the receiver and ask for help.

These two memories suggest to me that Eric Mascall and Austin Farrer, probably the two most distinguished Oxford theologians of their day, were among those Lewis had in mind when he made parenthetical deferential allusions to theologians more talented and more learned than himself. They figure several times among the speakers invited to address the Socratic Club. But of course Lewis was also surrounded by theologians of very different caliber—exponents of modernist heresies and subtly secularized uplift—and he was deeply aware that if he brought his readers into the fold only to leave them under the tutelage of such false teachers, he would not have served either God or them aright. So, for all his frontal attacks on atheism, he never ceased to adopt a strategy which allowed for a running battle on the side with the peddlers of soft-center liberalism.

Lewis certainly enjoyed the fray. Especially he relished puncturing pretentiousness, whether it was the pretentiousness of a theologian who thought the time was ripe for remodelling the Christian faith to suit the temper of the age, or the pretentiousness of a bumptious student. When a too-solemn undergraduate propounded some highfalutin theory on the nature and function of imaginative literature, he would nod gravely and say, "Yes. Now how would you apply that to *The Tale of Peter Rabbit*?" There was more than a touch of the Irishman here—and in his polemical combativeness, his irony, and his rich imaginative power. The English media have lately managed to give a somewhat pejorative flavor to the term "Ulster Protestant" which has been exploited by detractors of Lewis. Even Tolkien, alas, spoke rather disparagingly of Lewis' regression to his native "Ulster Protestantism" in preference to the Roman Catholicism for which he had hoped to win him as convert. But in fact the Anglo-Catholic strain in Lewis' churchmanship (though he would certainly not have used the label for himself) was so foreign to "Ulster Protestantism" that he could not be categorized in those terms, as Tolkien must surely have known. Lewis was regular in his use of the confessional. And I have a personal memory that is relevant here. Once he and I were talking about "churchmanship." I said that I was attending a rather "spiky" Anglo-Catholic church and that sometimes there were things that cut against the grain with me. I mentioned the Good Friday liturgy in which the congregation file up to the altar rail and each in turn kisses the foot of a crucifix held by the priest. "I don't really go for that kind of thing," I said. Lewis turned on this immediately. "Oh but you *should*," he said. "The body must do its homage."

Now I suspect that, had I been expressing reservations about some converse evangelical, low-church, protestant (call it what you will) practice, he might well have turned on what I said with equal promptness. His habit in this respect was to defend what was under attack, to correct whatever prejudice might be emerging, by pressing the converse. This was an aspect of his tutorial technique carried over into conversation. And anyway, so anxious was he not to have his churchmanship docketed and labelled—either Evangelical or Anglo-Catholic—that he tended to run this way and that way across the dialectical seesaw to forestall its dipping down decisively at either end. For far more important to Lewis as a writer was the content of "mere Christianity" or "deep Christianity" whose intensity and coherence, over against the flabbiness and fragmentariness of contemporary theological liberalism, made intraecclesiastical variations of emphasis of less account in the immediate strategy of evangelism.

It is this emphasis in Lewis which has recently and rightly captured the imagination of both Roman Catholics and Protestant Evangelicals in the United States, who are combining in defence of the new trans-denominational orthodoxy against the secularistic dilution of creed and dogma that afflicts all denominations. They derive immense strength from C.S. Lewis. One might add that culture is on their side. The friendship between Lewis and Tolkien exemplifies the fact. Where there is theology that is great literature, or great literature that is theology, whether it be St. Augustine or Newman, John Bunyan or Lewis, you will find that the theology is never reductionist. Imaginative literature has naught for the comfort of liberal theologians. Those qualities of insight, imagination, intellectual sinew, and wholeness of grasp which make great writers are qualities which, when brought to bear in the theological field, conduce to the kind of credal firmness that both Lewis and Tolkien were blessed with.

It is interesting to recollect now how students looked on Lewis and Tolkien before either of them had made a name as a writer. Lewis was certainly the most popular lecturer in the English school in 1936 to 1938. When he was due to lecture, one of the largest halls had to be made available. This was simply because he was a lucid, entertaining, and highly instructive lecturer. From no other tutor's lectures could a student go away with notes so clear, orderly, and meaty. The series he called "Prolegomena to the Study of Mediaeval and Renaissance Literature" (lectures which he later put into book form as *The Discarded Image*) left us all with batches of clearly tabulated notes, for Lewis used the blackboard impressively and repeated important quotations at dictation speed. Small wonder that these lectures drew such enthusiastic audiences.

Tolkien, by the way, was a very different lecturer. His expertise lay in a specialism into which only the most linguistically oriented English students wished to venture very far. The custom in those days was for one's tutor to recommend his pupils to attend certain of the series of lectures announced in the term's schedule. I recall one term when Lewis recommended that we should go to Tolkien's lectures on "The Finn and Hengest Episode in Beowulf." This sounded rather abstruse. Moreover, the lectures were to be given twice, not once, a week. We were not at all sure that we wanted two hours per week on this topic even from the Professor of Anglo-Saxon. However, Lewis' recommendations were not lightly to be disregarded, and a friend and I went along to Tolkien's first lecture. We were surprised to find ourselves directed to one of the smallest lecture rooms and to discover an audience of little more than a dozen students (if my memory serves me well). The discourse was mostly beyond us. Tolkien littered the blackboard with etymologies, with Norse, Anglo-Saxon, and Sanskrit. But he was most evidently a likeable, unpretentious man whose only misjudgement was to think us capable of advancing in philological studies. So my friend and I decided to attend a couple more of the sessions before detaching ourselves from the course, having shown a decent degree of preliminary interest. Alas, by the second week the audience was down to about half a dozen. In such a small band we were only too noticeable as individuals. No doubt we were recognizably Lewis' pupils. Was it kind, let alone wise, to deplete the audience further? So we stuck it out to the end of the term. How absurd it seems now! Who would not think it a privilege to sit at Tolkien's feet for a few hours and listen to his voice, however abstruse its message?

Lewis, by contrast, seemed to be warmly in touch with his whole audience, giving them exactly what they wanted. The liveliness, the eloquence, the lucidity, and the unfailing good-humor he exuded were those of a man bursting with confidence and professionalism. Yet, if one arrived in good time for his lecture, before the previous hour's lectures were finished, and it was necessary to hang around outside the Examination Schools where the lectures took place, Lewis could be seen pacing up and down the pavement of the High Street, glancing frequently at his wristwatch, and looking outwardly as tense, nervous, and grave as if he were about to lecture in public for the first time. A few moments later he would be the unfaltering maestro on the rostrum. There was something about this contrast between tension and relaxation, gravity and cheerfulness, self-containment and overflowing ebullience that is for me a powerful image of Lewis' character.

I am thinking of the personal burdens he shouldered, intensified as they were by Mrs. Moore's awkwardness and Warren's alcoholism, and how firmly they were prevented from saddening or souring any other aspects of his life. What an astonishing man he was at putting up with things! Childhood in Ireland, schooldays in England, war service in France were all marked at times by miseries which many a literary man would have turned into material for agonizing protest fiction. Yet how rarely is the note of grievance heard in Lewis' output! His own griefs and trials were mentioned only when mentioning them might help someone else to bear theirs.

I recall a curious little instance of this. After Lewis realized that the third book of my fictional trilogy, the vision of heaven, *Blessing Unbounded* (reissued as *Highway to Heaven*), had not attracted much notice from reviewers, he wrote a kind letter to me saying how much he himself had suffered when his early publications went unnoticed and unread. "Suffered" is not too strong a word, for he described graphically and feelingly what the aspiring writer goes through in this experience of grappling with early unsuccess—how the mind, reflecting on what is in store, tends by habit to move hopefully down familiar paths, and then has to be rudely checked and rebuffed, for those paths are now closed. This graphic description could have come only from someone who had felt his own disappointments keenly. But the record of it was unearthed only in order to sympathize helpfully with someone else.

For of course Lewis believed it a Christian duty to banish fruitless sadness. I recall how, in one of his more somber moods, he lamented to me the sad state of the church. "We're plagued with bad clergy," he said. "And it isn't just us. I'm told that the Roman

Catholics have the same worry." I think this was said on the same occasion when he spoke more personally about the difficulty of prayer during dry periods. It was a time when there was, as always, plenty to worry about in public life and in the life of the church, if one were so minded; and I can hear Lewis now very sadly repeating, "*Deus absconditus,* indeed!" ("God is indeed the hidden God!") But what was surely most characteristic of Lewis was the way this mood suddenly gave place to another, which positively swept it aside. "You know the story of Saint Teresa?" he asked, and went on to describe her vision of our Lord standing on the opposite bank of a river and beckoning her to cross over to him. She stepped into the water and got into ever greater difficulties as the river got deeper and the current more dangerous. She was barely saved from being swept away, and turned, on reaching the further bank, to remonstrate with our Lord. "That's how I treat all my friends," he said. And Saint Teresa replied, "No wonder you get such rotten friends!" This sentence Lewis declaimed with relish and immediately swung into rocking laughter. "No wonder you get such rotten friends!"

I believe it is in *The Everlasting Man* that G.K. Chesterton remarks how he was drawn to Christ by the fact that people who praised him praised him for so many different reasons. Since Lewis himself said that we are all called to be "little Christs," it may not be inappropriate to note how richly varied are the accounts that have been given of him by those who knew him personally. Every account seems to enrich the portrait. It is clearly the portrait of a saint. Through all the accounts there runs the theme of Lewis' immense generosity in helping others. I am thinking not just of the numerous instances of often hidden financial charity and the renowned quickness to assist those he lived with in the arduous chores of daily life, but of the sheer magnitude of his achievement in answering the letters of those who sought his advice, in reading the manuscripts of people like myself whom he hastened to encourage, in guiding, criticizing, and stimulating so many whose brains simply could not supply him—as could the brains of a Barfield or a Tolkien—with comparable counter-stimulus.

For myself I am of course deeply aware of my indebtedness to Lewis, and yet—such was his character and his way of helping people—that I never say to myself now, "I ought to have troubled him less." On the contrary I find myself saying, "I wish I'd visited him more." Especially I regret that I did not go to see him after his wife's death. I regret too that I did not preserve all his letters to me. Those that survived I gave to the collection at the Bodleian Library. I thought I had given them all. But recently a postcard has turned up among my papers which was certainly my last message from Lewis. It is clearly a reply to a letter of mine saying that I should be in Oxford on a certain day and suggesting that I might call on him. The card is dated March 26, 1962. The note is handwritten:

> The doctors hold out a hope of my being able to return to Cambridge on 24 April. If I do I shan't be here when you are. I'd v. much like a visit, however. Perhaps you'll be here some time in the vac? C.S.L.

I feel very sad now that I wasn't.

TWELVE

Paul Brand

by Philip Yancey

I FIRST MET Dr. Paul Brand on the grounds of the official U.S. Public Health Service leprosarium in Carville, Louisiana. To get there, I drove from New Orleans for two hours along the leveed banks of the Mississippi River, past crumbling old plantations, crawfish cafes, and gleaming new petrochemical factories. The Catholic sisters who had drained swamps and built the hospital buildings a hundred years before had deliberately located the leprosy center away from major population centers. Laid out in a sprawling, colonial style under huge oak trees, Carville resembled a movie set of a Philippine plantation.

I knew of Dr. Brand's stature in the world medical community: the offers to head up major medical centers, the distinguished lectureships in Great Britain and America, the surgical procedures named after him, the prestigious Albert Lasker award, his designation as Commander of the Order of the British Empire. But I waited for him in a cubbyhole of an office hardly suggestive of such renown. Stacks of medical journals, photographic slides, and unanswered correspondence covered every square inch of an ugly government-green metal desk. An antique window air conditioner throbbed at the decibel level of an unmuffled sports car. Charts of the labyrinthine government bureaucracy, not awards and citations, covered his office walls.

Finally, a slight man of less-than-average height entered the room. He had gray hair, bushy eyebrows, and a face that creased deeply when he smiled. In a British accent a striking contrast to the bayou accents heard in hospital corridors—he apologized for the flecks of blood on his lab coat, explaining that he had just been dissecting rabbit muscles.

That first visit with Dr. Brand lasted a week. We grabbed bits of conversations between management meetings, surgeries, clinical lectures, and animal research. I accompanied him on hospital rounds, leaving a wide berth in the hallways for the whirring electric wheelchairs and bicycles jerry-rigged with sidecars and extra wheels. I sat in the examination room as he studied the inflamed, ulcerated feet and hands of patients, trying to coax from them the cause of the injuries.

At night in his home, a rented wooden-frame bungalow on the grounds of the hospital, I would share an Indian-style meal with him and Mrs. Brand (also a doctor). Then Dr. Brand would prop up his bare feet (a trademark with him), and I would turn on the tape recorder for discussions that ranged from leprology and theology to world hunger and soil conservation.

In my role as editor of *Campus Life* magazine and writer for other magazines, I had interviewed many subjects over the years: rock music stars, successful business people, Pulitzer Prize winners, Olympic athletes. But something attracted me to Dr. Brand at a deeper level than I had felt with any other interview subject. I found in him a rich mixture of compassion, scientific precision, theological depth, and spiritual humility. In addition, his ideas on pain and pleasure were utterly different from any I had encountered in months of research.

My visit to Carville sparked a relationship that has grown and developed ever since. Later, when I left *Campus Life* to pursue freelance writing, I devoted the first five years to presenting the fruits of our dialogue: first in *Where Is God When It Hurts,* and then in two books we coauthored, *Fearfully and Wonderfully Made* and *In His Image.* I still maintain file folders labeled "Brand" stuffed with unused notes on topics we have never explored in print.

True friendship is measured, over time, by its effect on you. Has the association in some way changed your essential nature? As I compare the person I was in 1975, on our first meeting, and the person I am now, I realize that seismic changes have occurred within me, and Dr. Brand has been responsible for many of those tremors.

I was a college student during the 1960s. That tumultuous era awakened me to the ugly reality of poverty in the third world and here in American ghettos. Everything in America seemed to be cracking apart in those days: the Vietnam war chiseled away at our national ideals (and later Watergate proved the political cynics correct), revelations about pollution and the environment challenged the industrial ethic that had built our country, and the new counterculture exposed the hollow, image-conscious materialism that permeated business and the media. The issues are now so familiar as to become hackneyed. But to those of us who were forming a view of the world in that era, the sixties had a profound and permanent impact.

I recall my emotions in those years as being primarily anger, loneliness, and despair. I felt drawn toward books about the Holocaust, the Soviet Gulag, and other black holes of human history. I saw bright and talented friends give up on society and seek a different way through LSD and mescaline. Examining the church from such a jaded perspective, I noted mainly the hypocrisy of its members and their irrelevance to the world outside.

I now believe that God used Dr. Brand as one of his human agents to bring me out of that time with some stability. I was twenty-five when we first met; he was sixty. We made an odd pair, he with thinning gray hair and I with bushy hair in an Afro style. But somehow our friendship flourished. I look with deep appreciation on the privilege of learning from a great and humble man. I came to know him not through history, but as an actual living model, a man of God I could see in action—at Carville with his patients, in rural villages of India, as a husband and father, as a speaker at both medical and spiritual conferences. He, as much as anyone, has helped set my course in attitude, spirit, and ideals. In this tribute, I hope to identify partially how he has done so.

Dr. Brand achieved fame in the medical world mainly through his pioneering research on the disease leprosy. He had grown up in southern India, a child of missionary parents, and returned in 1946 after getting an education in England. During eighteen years in India he worked as a surgeon and teacher, directed the large Christian Medical College Hospital in Vellore, and founded a leprosy hospital known as Karigiri. Then, in 1965, he moved to the United States and began research work at the Carville hospital.

I did not expect to find gratitude as the chief characteristic of a man who had spent his life among victims of leprosy. Through the medical ignorance of others, those afflicted by leprosy are often isolated and reviled. In a place such as India, they are the outcasts of society, often doubly so as members of the untouchable caste.

Leprosy disproportionately afflicts the poor. Left untreated, its victims can develop the nerve damage and ulcers that eventually lead to facial disfigurement and loss of limbs. If anyone has a right to bitterness against the way the world is run, it should be someone who works with these unfortunates. And yet the single characteristic that most impressed me about Dr. Brand was his bedrock of gratitude.

For Paul Brand, gratitude began in childhood as simple appreciation of the natural world around him. He grew up in remote hill country, with none of civilization's normal barriers against nature. Snakes lived in the dark corners of the house and leopards stalked the forests outside, but apart from these dangers nature seemed wholly good. Until the age of nine he did his schoolwork sitting on a branch of a giant tamarind tree, dropping his completed assignments down to his mother on the ground below.

He spent childhood in a world of tropical fruit trees and of butterflies, insects, birds, and other animals. His artistic mother tried to capture its beauty visually, sometimes calling wildly to him to come and look at the sunset as she daubed watercolors on a canvas.

His father, a self-taught naturalist, saw nature as an awesome display of the genius of the Creator. He would lead his son to a towering four-foot termite mound and carefully expose the elaborate network of passages and their built-in cooling system, explaining the marvels of cooperative termite society. He would point to the sandy funnel of an ant lion trap, or the nest of a weaver bird, or a swarm of bees hanging from a tree.

The need for education interrupted Paul Brand's paradise, and he was sent to England at the age of nine. Five years later, as a fourteen-year-old student far from his native homeland, he received a cable that his father had died of blackwater fever. Two days after the cable, a letter from his father arrived, mailed by boat before his death. It described the hills around their home:

> Yesterday when I was riding over the windswept hilltops around Kulivalavu, I could not help thinking of an old hymn that begins, "Heaven above is deeper blue; flowers with purer beauty glow." When I am alone on these long rides, I love the sweet smelling wood, the dear brown earth, the lichen on the rocks, the heaps of dead brown leaves drifted like snow in the hollows. God means us to delight in his world. It isn't necessary to know botany or zoology or biology in order to enjoy the manifold life of nature. Just observe. And remember. And compare. And be always looking to God with thankfulness and worship for having placed you in such a delightful corner of the universe as the planet Earth.

Jesse Brand's son kept his advice, and keeps it to this day, whether hiking on the Olympic Peninsula or following birds around the swamps of Louisiana.

Another naturalist, the author Loren Eiseley, tells of an event he called the most significant learning experience of his long life. Caught on a beach in a sudden rainstorm, he sought shelter under a huge piece of driftwood. There, he found a tiny fox kitten, maybe ten weeks old. The kitten had no fear of humans. Within a few minutes it had engaged Eiseley in a playful game of tug-of-war, with Eiseley holding one end of a chicken bone in his mouth and the baby fox pulling on the other end.

The lesson he learned, said Eiseley, is that at the core of the universe, the face of God is a smile. Even the most ferocious animals—leopards and grizzlies and rhinoceroses—begin their lives playfully. Paul Brand, too, learned that lesson early. First in the hills of India, and later through a detailed study of the human body, he came to realize that at the heart of the natural world God could be found, and the God that he found was good.

Brand gained a sense of creatureliness, an awareness that he too had been willed into existence by a loving Creator and placed on a planet that, despite all its pain and fear, contained much beauty and goodness. He began to develop a consistent outlook of gratitude, undergirded by trust in the One who made the world.

My early conversations with Brand, coming as they did out of a time of personal searching, focused mainly on the dark spots and blemishes on the world. How could a truly good God allow such blemishes to exist? Dr. Brand took them on one by one. Disease? Did I know that 99 percent of all bacteria are healthful, not harmful? Plants could not produce oxygen and animals could not digest food without the assistance of bacteria. Most agents of disease, he explained, diverge from these necessary organisms only slight mutations.

What about birth defects? He went on to describe in detail the complex chemical changes that must work right to produce one healthy child. The great wonder is not that birth defects exist but that millions more do not occur. Could a mistake-proof world have been created so that DNA spirals would never err in transmission? No scientist could envision such a system without possibility of error in our world of physical laws.

Even at its worst, he continued, our natural world shows evidence of careful design. Imagine a world without tornadoes or hurricanes, calamities that carry the damning label "acts of God." When hurricanes and monsoons do not come, the delicate balance of weather conditions gets upset, and killer droughts inevitably follow. How would you improve upon the world? he asked.

Brand's professsional life has centered on perhaps the most problematic aspect of creation, the existence of pain. He emphatically insists on pain's great value, holding up as proof the terrible results of leprosy—damaged face, blindness, and loss of fingers, toes and limbs—which nearly all occur as side-effects of painlessness. Leprosy destroys nerve endings that carry pain signals. People who do not feel pain almost inevitably damage themselves; infection sets in, and no pain signals alert them to tend to the wounded area.

"Thank God for pain!" Brand declares with the utmost sincerity. "I cannot think of a greater gift I could give my leprosy patients." (Actually, he tried to give them the protective gift, in a three-year research program to manufacture an artificial pain system.) Even in this instance, so commonly held up as a challenge to a loving God, he sees reason for profound gratitude.

The Bible records a dramatic scene when the overwhelming questions raised by the problem of pain were asked of God himself, in the Book of Job. The long speech God gave in reply has endured as one of the great nature passages in literature, a wonderful celebration of wildness as seen in mountain goats, ostriches, wild horses, snowstorms. But to the problem of pain God gave no direct answer, only this challenge to Job: if I, as Creator, have produced such a marvelous world as this, which you can plainly observe, cannot you trust me with those areas you cannot comprehend?

In that spirit, Dr. Brand learned at an early age that God wanted from him gratitude and trust—gratitude for those things he could see and appreciate, and trust regarding those things he could not. To his surprise, that attitude in him deepened even as he worked among people least likely to feel gratitude: the poorest of the poor, leprosy victims in India. In many of them, he saw the transformations that the love of God can produce. The immense human problems he lived among did not dissolve, but his faith supplied a confidence and trust that enabled him to serve God with gratitude and even joy.

Although I have great respect for Dr. Brand and his service to God, I also confess relief that he is not from the mold of St. Francis or Mother Teresa. I have immense respect for those rare individuals in history who have lived on a different plane, forsaking all material possessions, withdrawing from the world, and devoting themselves singlemindedly to a prophetic ideal. I learn much from them. And yet as I study their lives I sometimes have the nagging sense that they do not live in my world.

In his lifestyle, Dr. Brand has chosen the middle way of balancing off the material and the mystical, the prophetic and the pragmatic. At the hospital he left behind in Vellore, Brand is remembered for his spiritual depth and sacrificial service, but also for his practical jokes, love for marmalade and mangoes, and fast driving. As I emerged from the sixties, a decade never accused of possessing a sense of balance, I needed an example of someone who lived a well-rounded life in the midst of modern society, not off in a monastery or *ashram.* Dr. Brand had struggled with both extremes of the tensions facing modern civilization, while not giving in to either. On the one hand, he lived a "counterculture" lifestyle long before such a word entered American vocabulary. The Brand family eats simply, relying mainly on homemade breads and vegetables grown in their garden. Dr. Brand acknowledges a few reasons for discarding clothes—unpatchable rips, for instance—but lack of stylishness is certainly not one of them. Furniture in his home and office is, to put it kindly, unpretentious.

On the other hand, he has learned to use the tools made available by modern technology. Under his leadership, a hospital in the dusty backwater town of Vellore grew into the most modern and sophisticated facility in all of southwest Asia. Later, Brand came to the Carville hospital in the United States because it offered the technological support needed to research treatment procedures that would benefit millions of leprosy patients worldwide. And when personal computers were introduced in the 1980s, he signed up with boyish enthusiasm for one of the first IBMs, to assist his research and writing.

My conversations with Dr. Brand have often strayed to the question of lifestyle, for his experiences in India and America have afforded him a unique perspective on that issue. He has lived in one of the poorest countries and one of the richest. Affluence in the West, he recognizes, offers a deadly temptation. The enormous gap in economic development can create a moat separating the West from the rest of the world. Wealth can dull us to cries of need and justice, and too much comfort can sap the life from Christian work.

The lifelong tension over lifestyle traces back to Brand's childhood in India. After her husband's death, Paul's mother, Evelyn (Granny) Brand, took on the life of a "saint" in the traditional form. She lived on a pittance, devoting her life to reach villagers in five mountain ranges. She cared nothing for her personal appearance, not even allowing a mirror in her house. She continued hazardous journeys on her pony even after suffering concussions and fractures from falls. Although tropical diseases ravaged her body, she gave all her energies to treating the diseases and injuries of the people around her.

Sometimes Granny Brand would embarrass Paul with an intemperate outburst; at an official function in Vellore, for example, she might ask in horror, "How could you possibly dine on such fine food when I have people back in the hills starving to death this very night!" She died at age ninety-five among the people she loved, leaving Paul an unforgettable legacy. (The book *Granny Brand* tells her full story.)

From childhood Paul learned that Christian love is best applied person-to-person. His parents traveled from village to village, teaching health, sanitation, farming, and the Christian gospel. They left behind no lasting institutions, only their permanent imprint on thousands of lives. Singlehandedly, Granny Brand rid huge areas of a guinea worm infection that had persisted for centuries. Trusting villagers followed her instructions on building stone walls around their wells; no government program could have been so effective.

Yet Paul Brand himself found his most lasting successes through rigid scientific disciplines. At Vellore he fought his wife Margaret for space in the icebox, preserving cadaver hands to study by lamplight and practice surgical techniques. For years he puzzled over the physiology of leprosy: which cells does it attack, and why?

His most important medical discovery came when he observed

that the leprosy bacillus did not destroy hands and feet but only attacked nerve tissue. Proving that theory required years of painstaking research. He had to keep track of patients and their injuries, searching whether all damage could indeed be traced to abuse of tissue, rather than the disease itself. The results of such research had a dramatic impact on the treatment of leprosy and other anesthetic diseases worldwide. Fifteen million victims of leprosy gained hope that, with proper care, they could preserve their toes and fingers and limbs. Damage was no longer inevitable.

Brand admits he would shed no tears if all advances from the industrial revolution onward suddenly disappeared—he prefers the simple village life in India, close to the outdoors. Yet unlike, say, Gandhi, he does not want to roll back modern civilization. He gratefully uses electron microscopes and thermograms and jet planes.

I sense in him a sort of "holy indifference" to many of the specifics that bother some sensitive Christians. He opposes waste in all forms. If an item is advertised as "disposable," he either refuses to buy it or else enjoys finding ways to make it last and last. He lives a remarkably disciplined and simple life. Yet, he says, "like the Apostle Paul, I have learned to be abased and to abound." To him technology, when used wisely and not destructively, offers a tool that helps advance the goals of the Kingdom.

A similar kind of balance characterizes other areas of Brand's life. His Christian faith developed through a combination of his parents' devout belief and his scientific training in medical school. The church he attended in England, a member of the "Strict and Particular Baptist" denomination, had not adequately equipped him for intellectual challenges to his faith. But his missionary parents had demonstrated love in action, and although he found no quick answers, his faith remained intact as he deferred the questions to a later date, when he could approach them with more wisdom.

Originally, Brand had planned to go to India as a missionary builder, until an unlikely series of circumstances caused by World War II landed him in medical school. He traces much of his spiritual formation to the period of time just before medical school when he signed on for a year with an austere organization called the Missionary Training Colony. The Colony sought to equip missionaries for any rigorous situation they might encounter. It assigned students to live in crude huts, each of which accommodated twelve trainees. Brand's hut had hand-hewn furniture and a tiny charcoal stove which hardly sufficed in the British winter.

The Colony used a simple method of Bible training: each group of twelve trainees would work through the Bible in two years, wrestling with the issues they found there. No classes in theology and homiletics were held—Colony directors believed the Bible alone supplied all that was needed for theology and living. At regular intervals, the trainees would go out into cities and towns to conduct services, open-air meetings, and camp programs. Prewar Britain offered unusual opportunities for confrontational evangelism: sometimes Brand would find his open-air service sandwiched in between a communist rally and a meeting of blackshirt fascists.

Each summer the Colony also sent the groups of twelve "on trek" for a period of ten straight weeks, a program designed to teach teamwork and endurance. Brand's team loaded a two-wheel cart with clothes, tents, and all their necessary belongings. The boys harnessed themselves to the cart with long tow-ropes and marched along the backroads of Britain, singing as they went. When they reached a town in the afternoon, they would check with local church authorities for permission to conduct meetings in the church or in the town square. They slept in tents or on the floors of churches. In ten weeks, Brand's team covered 600 miles along the border of England and Wales.

Looking back, Dr. Brand fondly recalls that ten-week course as one of the great experiences of his life. It gave him a living, working example of the Body of Christ in action, with each member dependent on the others. Also, it taught him about his own cynicism, and about faith.

The Colony had one absolute rule for the trek: it must be

conducted on faith. Each team began the trek with the equivalent of $100, sufficient to feed them for two or three days if no money or food came in. Otherwise, they depended entirely on what people gave to them, and they were never allowed to ask for gifts or take up a collection. The trek offered a chance for a sincere experiment in faith—for most of the boys at least.

Brand and two others viewed the faith rules of the Colony with considerable skepticism. The forced dependence seemed artificial to them—after all, they had relatives at home who could bail them out if necessary, so why starve for a principle? The three formed a secret club, each hiding away a few shillings. They made plans to sneak away from the group now and then to buy ice cream or a piece of cake.

After two or three such clandestine purchases, Brand and his friends realized they were wrong. The rest of the group was maturing into a deep sense of unity and faith, and the three knew their actions could poison that unity. They stopped their secret activities.

The next weeks offered Brand an unforgettable lesson in faith. After the stores and money supplies had run out, the twelve never knew whether they would have another meal. Yet supplies showed up, again and again, offered to them by villagers in astonishingly varied ways. They only missed one meal, a breakfast, but half an hour later a truck driver stopped beside them by the road and asked if they wanted some fresh melons. He had never done such a thing before.

Brand served as treasurer the last week of the trek, and after final expenses were paid, only three shillings and sixpence remained. As he went to the railroad station for final arrangements, one trunk suddenly turned up that had not been paid for. The price? Brand's jaw dropped open as the stationmaster quoted it: exactly three shillings and sixpence. The group of twelve headed back to the Colony, having never missed a meal, with no money but with a permanent lesson in faith.

The Colony taught Brand a lifelong pattern. He would use his own resources and intelligence as fully as possible but freely acknowledge dependence on God for the ultimate result. Later, in India, he had many opportunities to put faith into practice. The massive building plans at the Vellore hospital were all carried out with no sophisticated appeals for funds. Instead, the staff relied on simple prayer and belief. Brand also learned to seek wisdom from God during important research assignments, or in the midst of surgery. For him, faith became a daily habit that affected every part of his life. He no longer felt a dichotomy between the natural and spiritual realms.

During his time at the Missionary Training Colony, Paul Brand also gained a new perspective on the concept of "self-sacrifice." The Colony intentionally created difficult circumstances for its students in order to prepare them for conditions they might encounter in their mission assignments.

Primitive living conditions were not new to Brand. As a child, he had lived in a hand-built cabin with no water or electricity in a disease-infested region known as the "Mountains of Death." He had regularly fought off bouts of malaria. In bed at night he could hear rats crawling overhead. Yet when he arrived in England for schooling, he quickly saw that his own childhood had been far more adventurous and thrilling than the middle-class environment around him.

Gradually he learned an important part of his life philosophy: that pleasure and pain are not opposites, but rather mutually dependent parts of the richest experiences in life. Most often, the greatest pleasures come after great sacrifice, including considerable pain. The pattern holds true for musicians, who endure tedious hours of practice in order to produce great music, and for athletes, who willingly take on habitual pain in order to condition their bodies. Pleasure derived from producing great music and achieving athletic excellence can come in no other way except through pain.

Brand studied the life of the Apostle Paul, viewed the sufferings he endured in his attempts to preach the gospel as merely the cost required to fulfill his goals. Brand decided to stop looking at life as a polarity: avoid painful experiences, seek pleasurable ones.

Rather, he would first ask, "Is this what God wants me to do?" If so, whatever came along, whether unpleasant or pleasant, provided an opportunity for him to exercise faith. He tried to think of normally unpleasant experiences as something of an adventure.

Brand's family went through trials that would horrify a modern mission executive. His first child was born while he was on wartime duty at a London hospital, fire-watching from the roof in order to dispatch emergency crews to deal with bombing victims. His second came while he was packing for India. He left his wife and children behind in England for six months while he established himself at Vellore (volatile political conditions in India delayed his wife from coming).

Missionary service in India took its own toll. As his body adjusted to a new climate, he broke out in prickly heat in the 110-degree temperatures and suffered through a series of tropical diseases. He practiced surgery under a homemade operating lamp hammered out of a sheet of aluminum.

In India, Dr. Brand insisted that each of his children (eventually six in all) be raised with the same freedom and sense of adventure he had known in childhood. Only half in jest, he calculated that it would be far better to have only four of his children live to adulthood than to have all six survive by living sheltered, overly protected lives. He encouraged them to climb, explore, and enjoy fully the adventures that India offered. As the children reached a certain age, the Brands had the wrenching experience of separation, as they sent each child off to England for high school. Somehow, the family came through beautifully, and all six children survived.

The pattern I observed in Dr. Brand and his family reinforces a trend I have noted among various Christians I have interviewed for magazines. Not everyone fits the pattern, surely. But I have encountered it often enough that I can almost lump these interview subjects into two sets: Christian entertainers and Christian servants. The Christian entertainers—musicians, actors, speakers, comedians—fill our periodicals and television shows. We fawn over them, reward them with extravagant contracts and fan mail. They have everything they want, usually, including luxurious lifestyles. Yet many whom I've interviewed express to me deep longings and self-doubts.

In contrast, most of the Christian servants I have interviewed are not in the spotlight. People like the Brands toil unnoticed in remote parts of the country and the world. Relief workers, faithful pastors in communist lands, missionaries in the third world—these have all impressed me with a profound wisdom and deep-seated contentment strikingly absent from the entertainers. They work for low pay, long hours, no applause. They "waste" their talents and skills among the poor and uneducated. Yet in the very process of losing their lives, they find them. God reserves rewards for them which are unattainable in any other way.

Dr. Brand taught me that self-denial need not be viewed as an affliction, an opportunity for martyrdom. He adamantly refuses to look back on such experiences as sacrifice; they were, rather, challenges, tests of faith. They allowed an opportunity for God to redeem a hopeless situation.

At the hospital in Vellore he encountered seemingly insurmountable problems. Power failures and equipment breakdowns spoiled many of the research projects. He had to train unskilled Indian workers on the job. Attempts to treat leprosy patients ran into brick walls of opposition—initially, no one wanted them admitted to the main hospital.

Brand's theories on treatment and rehabilitation had to overcome centuries-old biases about the disease before they gained a foothold in the world medical community. Eventually, he had to find ways to provide new skills, housing, and employment for those leprosy victims who, even upon successful treatment and release, met hostility and rejection in their home villages. Yet, through it all, God's work was accomplished. Today, the leprosy facility at Karigiri, India, flourishes as a world-recognized training center, and its influence has spread to leprosy treatment centers across the earth.

A Christian ministry will require sacrifice—there are no exemptions. Human needs, whether social, spiritual, or physical, will guarantee that. But to a person committed to God, the very aspect of sacrifice can, paradoxically, become one of the most satisfying parts of service.

Dr. Brand expresses the guiding principle of his medical career this way: "The most precious possession any human being has is his spirit, his will to live, his sense of dignity, his personality. Once that has been lost, the opportunity for rehabilitation is lost. Though our profession may be a technical one, concerned with tendons, bones, and nerve endings, we must realize that it is the person behind them who is so important."

Although our conversations together cover a broad range of topics, inevitably they drift back to stories of individual human beings. The essentials of both his medical philosophy and theology had been worked out through constant contact with patients. Most often, these patients are the forgotten people, the poor and lonely who have been ostracized from family and village because of their illness. A medical staff can repair the marred facial features and fingers drawn into a claw-hand. They can provide that most basic human need: touch. But what can they do for the spirit of the patient, the corroded self-image?

It takes a few pennies a day to arrest leprosy's progress with sulfone drugs. But it takes thousands of dollars and the painstaking care of skilled professionals to restore to wholeness a patient in whom the disease has spread unchecked. In India, Dr. Brand began with hands, experimenting with tendon and muscle transfers until he found the very best combination to restore a full range of movement. The surgical procedures and rehabilitation stretched over months and sometimes years. He applied similar procedures to feet, correcting the deformities caused by years of walking without a sense of pain to guide the body in distributing weight and pressure.

New feet and hands gave a leprosy patient the capability to earn a living, but who would hire an employee bearing the scars of the dread disease? Brand's first patients returned to him in tears, asking that the effects of surgery be reversed so that they could get more sympathy as beggars. Then Dr. Brand and his wife saw the need to correct the cosmetic damage as well. They studied well-known techniques of surgery and modified them for the special problems of leprosy.

They learned to remake a human nose by entering it through the space between gum and upper lip (to utilize the moist lining inside) and fashioning a new nasal structure from transplanted bone. They learned to prevent blindness by restoring the possibility of blinking: the paralyzed eyelid was attached to a muscle normally used for chewing. Margaret Brand worked daily with those patients, teaching them to make a chewing motion with their jaw every thirty seconds, in order to operate their eyelids and thus prevent dehydration of the eye.

Finally, they learned to replace lost eyebrows on the faces of their patients by tunneling a piece of scalp, intact with its nerve and blood supply, under the skin of the forehead and sewing it in place above the eyes. The first patients proudly let their new eyebrows grow to absurd lengths.

All this elaborate medical care went to "nobodies," victims of leprosy who most commonly made their living from begging. Many who arrived at the hospital barely looked human. Their shoulders slumped, they cringed when other people approached. Light had faded from their eyes. But months of compassionate treatment from the staff at Vellore could restore that light. For years people had shrunk away from them in terror; at Vellore, nurses and doctors would hold their hands and talk to them. They became human again.

In his twenty years in India, Dr. Brand operated on perhaps 3,000 hands and did thousands of other surgical procedures. He cannot possibly recall the details of each patient he contacted. But some stand out, such as John Kermagan, an irredeemable social misfit who learned of Jesus Christ through Granny Brand. It was the love shown by members of a local church that brought John back to health. He doubted whether any nonpatients would accept him, but they did, and thus helped transform his life.

Another patient named John showed up, a near-blind old man with severe damage from the disease. When he begged for surgery to free his stiff hands, Dr. Brand hesitated—many younger patients with a full life ahead of them were waiting in line for treatment. But the old man got his surgery. Although blind, he somehow learned to play the organ with insensitive fingers. He spent his last years as official organist at a mission leprosy sanatorium.

There were failures, of course, such as one man who threw himself in a well when he learned two fingers must be amputated. But over time the Brands learned that the human spirit, no matter how battered, can be reawakened and set free. Even in the most ugly, suspicious, hate-filled patients, the image of God began to shine through.

This lesson on the image of God is perhaps the greatest gift Dr. Brand has given me. The great societies of the West have been gradually moving away from an underlying belief in the value of a single human soul. We tend to view history in terms of groups of people: classes, political parties, races, sociological groupings. We apply labels to each other, and explain behavior and ascribe worth on the basis of those labels. After prolonged exposure to Dr. Brand, I realized that I had been seeing large human problems in a mathematical model: percentages of Gross National Product, average annual income, mortality rate, doctors-per-thousand of population. I had been wrestling with "issues" facing "humanity." I had not, however, learned to love individuals—people created in the image of God.

I would not predict a leprosarium in India as the most likely place to learn about the infinite worth of human beings, but a visit there makes the lesson unavoidable. The love of God is not mathematical; we cannot precisely calculate the greatest possible good to be applied equally to the world's "poor and needy." We can only seek out a person, and then another, and then another, as objects for Christian love.

Gratitude. Balance. Sacrifice. The Image of God. In no way have I mastered these principles that Dr. Brand has demonstrated for me. I must remind myself of them every day. When I look outside my window in downtown Chicago I ask myself again, How can I be grateful in view of such human misery everywhere? How can I achieve a sense of balance in a world tilting toward chaos? Why should I worry about sacrifice or self-denial when my culture offers me an easier, more pleasurable way? And how can one individual matter? I ask these questions, and perhaps I always will.

But as I ask them, I also give thanks that I have had Dr. Brand to help lead me on the way to answers. He would not want me to impiy that these qualities have arisen from his own person. The same Holy Spirit that motivated his mother and father in India, and now animates him, is the One who wants to bring adventure and love of life to all who are willing to lose themselves in him. I hope that our collaboration in writing has made it possible for other persons to see those same principles and that same Spirit at work in Paul Brand.

THIRTEEN

William Wilberforce

by Charles Colson

SEVERAL HUNDRED MILES OFF THE COAST OF AFRICA, 1787. The scudding clouds obscured the moon as the heavy schooner pitched forward in the dark waters. The decks were empty save for the lone sailor on the late watch and a cluster of others at the wheel.

The rest of the crew tossed fitfully in their hammocks; in the main cabin a fat tallow candle burned low, flickering in the tropical air. The captain, a balding man with thick sideburns, squinted as he dipped his quill in a well of sepia ink and continued his log report, laboriously noting progress on their voyage to Jamaica. The flogging that day of the cabin boy was the only incident of note.

In the dark hold below, the heavy air was almost palpable with the stench of human waste and vomit. Five hundred and twelve black men and women lay on their sides in the filth, crammed so tightly together that the chest of each was pressed against the sweaty back of his neighbor, their legs drawn up, their feet on the heads of those in the next anguished row.

Moans, sobs, and feverish delirium combined with the creaks of the ship's aged timbers to transform the putrid hold into a scene from hell.

And for the slaves, it was. They were captured Africans, some the prisoners of tribal wars or petty criminals, others the unsuspecting dinner guests of visiting Englishmen. But all had been rounded up, chained and held in a stockade, then sold to the highest bidder who had come into port.

The elderly and unfit had been dispatched with a pistol shot or clubbed to death, their bodies dragged into the shallows, where they bobbed gently until caught in the flow of the tide.

Others were branded, then whipped and shoved into small boats to be ferried to the large oceangoing vessels laying at anchor offshore. Weeping, screaming for mercy, they were hoisted onto the tall ship and forced into the stinking hold, then shackled into irons.

But not all were immediately driven below. The crew, though diseased and ill-treated themselves, claimed the one sordid privilege of their trade—the pick of the slave women. Once off the coast, the ship became half bedlam, half brothel, as one captain put it.

Now on this cloudy night, several weeks into the voyage, sixty slaves were already dead. Some had succumbed to the fevers raging through the rotten hold. Others, driven insane by the horrors, were disposed of by the crew. Each morning as the lower decks were opened, the dead and the near-dead were removed, their bodies thrown overboard to the waiting sharks.

Whenever the captain watched this morning ritual, he cursed as each black body hit the choppy water, muttering as he calculated his lost profits. Certainly he had no legal worries, however, about throwing sick slaves to their deaths: in a celebrated case in England's high court only four years earlier, slaves had been described as "goods and chattels," the chief justice observing that it was "exactly as if horses had been thrown overboard." And in the colonies, the word of a black could not be taken over a white. That was the law.

At any rate, no slave remaining in the dark hold of that slave ship had any idea what was in store if he did survive the three-month journey: he would be auctioned naked in the marketplace, then—if he survived the treatment of his new master—life would be merely a dogged hold on survival in the cane fields. He would never know or see in his short lifespan the nation which would so richly profit from his misery: England.

London, 1787. In the city described as "one vast casino," the rich counted their profits from the slave trade while in a fog of claret. They lost and rewon their fortunes over gaming tables in prestigious private clubs; duels were the order of the day to preserve honor.

Corruption in government was so widespread that very few members of parliament thought twice about the usual practice of buying votes. And since the slave trade was not only considered successful business, but a national policy, political alliances revolved around commitment to the trade. It became euphemistically known as "the institution," the "pillar and support of British plantation industry in the West Indies."

The planters and gentlemen who grew rich through the profits of their trade investments became an increasingly powerful force in parliament, paying £3,000 to £5,000 to "buy" boroughs, which sent their representatives to the House of Commons; hence the term "rotten boroughs." Their influence grew until a large bloc of the House was controlled by the vested influence of the slave traders.

The same attitude reigned in the House of Lords. After all, the horrors of the trade were far away and unseen. But the returns on their investment were often 100 percent; the cotton and sugar and profits the slaves provided were very tangible. If the slave trade made England stronger—and the rich richer—it could not be a bad thing.

So they counted their returns and, when time weighed heavy on their hands, turned to whatever distraction took their fancy. The town's theaters were surrounded by clusters of brothels; hordes of prostitutes (estimated at one out of every four women in the city) specialized in any manner of perversion for those whose appetites had grown jaded.

High society similarly revolved around romantic intrigue and adulterous affairs. An upper class couple might not see one another in public for weeks during the social season; no self-respecting hostess would have such poor taste as to invite a husband and wife to the same social event.

The poor had no such opportunity to escape from one another. Crammed together in grimy cobblestoned neighborhoods, they sweated out a living as cogs in Britain's emerging industrial machines. Pale children worked as many as eighteen hours a day in the cotton mills or coal mines, bringing home a few shillings a month to their parents, who often spent it on cheap gin. One-eighth of the deaths in London were attributed to excessive drinking.

Highwaymen were folk heroes; Newgate and other infamous prisons overflowed with debtors, murderers, children, and rapists. A twelve-year-old thief might be hung the same day as a celebrated robber, with huge crowds relishing the expiration of the celebrity while scarcely noticing the life choking out of the other.

Frequent executions provided one form of public amusement, bull baiting another. Bulls were tortured with fire or acid to keep them lively; if the attacking dogs failed to be gored, their throats would be slashed to satisfy the crowd's thirst for blood. At county fairs, badgers, their tails nailed to the ground, were worried to death by dogs; sheep were slaughtered as savagely as possible for popular sport.

At one such event, the Duke of Bedford and a Lord Barrymore staged a bet in which the latter, for £500, brought forth a man who ate a live cat before a cheering crowd.

In short, London was the center of a country where unchecked human passions had run their course. Few were the voices raised in opposition.

#4 OLD PALACE YARD, LONDON, OCTOBER 25, 1787. It was still dark when the slight young man pulled the dressing gown around his small, thin frame and sat at the oak desk in the second floor library. As he adjusted the flame of his lamp, the warm light shone on his piercing blue eyes, oversized nose, and high wrinkling forehead—an agile face that reflected the turmoil of his thoughts as he eyed the jumble of pamphlets on the cluttered desk. They were all on the same subject—the horrors of the slave trade.

He ran his hand through his wavy hair and opened his well-worn Bible. He would begin this day, as was his custom, with a time of personal prayer and scripture reading. But his thoughts kept returning to the pamphlets' grisly accounts of human flesh being sold, like so much cattle, for the profit of his countrymen. He couldn't wipe the scenes from his mind. Something inside him—that insistent conviction he'd felt before—was telling him that all that had happened in his life had been for a purpose, preparing him to meet that barbaric evil head-on.

William Wilberforce was born in Hull in 1759, the only son of a prosperous merchant family. Though an average student at Cambridge, his quick wit made him a favorite among his fellows, including William Pitt, who shared his interest in politics. Often the two young men spent their evenings in the gallery of the House of Commons, watching the heated debates over the American war.

After graduation, Wilberforce ran as a conservative for a seat in parliament from his home county of Hull. He was only twenty-one—but the prominence of his family, his speaking ability, and a generous feast he sponsored for voters on election day carried the contest.

When he arrived in London, the city's elegant private clubs and societies welcomed him; Wilberforce soon fell in step, happily concentrating on the pursuit of pleasure and political advancement.

He spent his evenings with friends, consuming enormous dinners accompanied by multiple bottles of wine and then perhaps a play, dancing, or a night of gambling. His friendship with William Pitt and other young politicians flourished; then, in early 1784 Pitt, though only twenty-four, was elected prime minister. Inspired, Wilberforce took a big political gamble, surrendering his safe seat in Hull to stand for election in Yorkshire, the largest and most influential constituency in the country.

It was a grueling campaign, the outcome uncertain until the

closing day, when Wilberforce addressed a large rally. James Boswell, Samuel Johnson's celebrated biographer, stood in the cold rain and watched Wilberforce, barely over five feet tall, prepare to address the wet, bored crowd.

"I saw what seemed a mere shrimp mount upon the table," Boswell wrote later, "but as I listened, he grew and grew, until the shrimp became a whale."

Such was the power of the young parliamentarian's oratory; he was elected from Yorkshire. As an intimate of the prime minister, respected by both political parties, William Wilberforce seemed destined for power and prominence.

After the election, Wilberforce's mother invited him to join his sister and several cousins on a tour of the Continent. Wilberforce agreed, then ran into his old schoolmaster from Hull, Isaac Milner, and spontaneously asked him to join the traveling party.

That vacation was to change Wilberforce's life.

Isaac Milner was a stocky, big-boned man with a mind as robust as his body. He was eager to debate the quick young orator, though he could not match his skill. As their carriage ran over the rutted roads between Nice and the Swiss Alps, their lively discussion turned to religion. Wilberforce, who considered his flirtation with Methodists—as the religious enthusiasts of his day were known—a childish excess, treated the subject flippantly. Milner growled at his derisive wit, stared moodily out the carriage window, and declared, "I am no match for you . . . but if you really want to discuss these subjects seriously, I will gladly enter on them with you."

Provoked by the older man's remark, Wilberforce entered in, eventually agreeing to read the scriptures daily.

As the summer session of parliament got underway, Wilberforce returned to the whirl of the London social scene. But his diary reveals subtle changes in his tastes. One party, of the kind he routinely attended, was now described as "indecent"; his letters began to show concern for corruptions he had scarcely noticed before. The seeds of change had been planted.

That fall of 1785, as he and Milner returned to the Continent to continue their tour, Wilberforce was no longer frivolous. He pressed his companion about the scriptures. The rest of the party complained about their preoccupation as they studied a Greek New Testament on their coach between cities.

Wilberforce returned to London in early November 1785 faced with a decision he could no longer avoid. He knew the choice before him: on one hand his own ambition, his friends, his achievements; on the other a clear call from Jesus Christ.

Selections from his diary show the Holy Spirit's relentless pursuit:

> *Nov. 27:* I must awake to my dangerous state, and never be at rest till I have made my peace with God. My heart is so hard, my blindness so great, that I cannot get a due hatred of sin, though I see I am all corrupt, and blinded to the perception of spiritual things.
>
> *Nov. 28:* Lord, I am wretched, and miserable, and blind, and naked. What infinite love, that Christ should die to save such a sinner, and how necessary is it He should save us altogether, that we may appear before God with nothing of our own!
>
> *Nov. 29:* Pride is my greatest stumbling block . . .
>
> *Nov. 30:* Was very fervent in prayer this morning, and thought these warm impressions would never go off. Yet in vain endeavor in the evening to rouse myself. . . . What can so strongly show the stony heart? O God, give me a heart of flesh! . . .

On December 2, weary and in need of counsel, Wilberforce resolved to seek out a spiritual guide. He made a fascinating but unlikely choice: John Newton.

Son of a sailor, Newton had gone to sea at age eleven, where he eventually deserted, was flogged, and exchanged to a slave ship. Later Newton himself became a slave on an island off the coast of Africa. Rescued by his father, he sailed on a slave ship and in 1750 was given command of his own slaver. Then, on a passage to the West Indies, Newton was converted to Jesus Christ, later expressing his wonder at the gift of salvation to "a wretch like me" in his famous hymn, "Amazing Grace."

Newton was subsequently ordained in the Church of England; his outspoken singlemindedness in spiritual matters must have attracted a buffetted Wilberforce.

Though he cautioned Newton in a note to "remember that I must be in secret . . . the face of a member of parliament is pretty well known," he called on the old preacher. Newton reassured him and, prophetically, told Wilberforce to follow Christ but not to abandon public office: "The Lord has raised you up to the good of His church and for the good of the nation."

Wilberforce knew he had to share his new faith with his old friends. The responses were predictable: some thought his mind had snapped under the pressures of work; many were convinced his new-found belief would require him to retreat from public life. Still others were simply bewildered: how could a well-bred and educated young man, with so much promise, get caught up in the religious exuberance of Methodism, a sect appealing only to the common masses?

The reaction Wilberforce cared about most was Pitt's. He wrote to the prime minister, telling him that though he would remain his faithful friend, he could "no more be so much of a party man as before."

Pitt's understanding reply revealed the depth of their friendship; but after their first face-to-face discussion, Wilberforce wrote in his diary: "He tried to reason me out of my convictions but soon found himself unable to combat their correctness, if Christianity was true. The fact is, he was so absorbed in politics, that he had never given himself time for due reflection on religion."

Though Pitt and Wilberforce were to continue as friends and allies, their relationship would never again be the same. And, indeed, one of the great sorrows of Wilberforce's life was that the friend he cared for most never accepted the God he loved more.

On this foggy Sunday morning in 1787, as Wilberforce sat at his desk, he reflected that even if Pitt did not share his commitment to Christ, God had brought him brothers who did. He thought about Thomas Clarkson, the red-headed clergyman and brilliant essayist who had visited so often that year while Wilberforce had been ill—Clarkson, whose passion for justice and righteousness awed him.

These were Clarkson's pamphlets strewn across his desk, shocking papers detailing the brutality of the slave trade. Wilberforce had been poring over them for months. He stared out the window at the gray English drizzle, but all he could see were burdened slave ships leaving the sun-baked coasts of Africa.

Then, on the cobblestone street below, two cloaked figures stumbled into view, leaning heavily on one another. Their raucous voices jangled together in a few bars of a lewd song as they lurched toward home, near collapse after a long night of carousing. Such a common sight in London.

He turned back to the desk and the journal filled with tiny, cramped writing meant for no one's eyes but his own. He thought about his conversion—had God saved him only for the eternal rescue of his own soul, or also to bring his light to the world around him? He could not be content with the comfort of life at Palace Yard, the stimulating debates in parliament. . . . True Christianity must go deeper. It must not only save but serve; it must bring God's compassion to the oppressed, as well as oppose the oppressors.

His mind clicked, and he dipped his pen in the inkwell. "Almighty God has set before me two great objectives," he wrote, his heart suddenly pumping with passion, "the abolition of the slave trade and the reformation of manners."

With those words, the offensive was launched for one of the epic struggles of modern history. God's man, called to stand against the entrenched evils of his day: the self-indulgent hedonism of a society pockmarked by decadence and the trade which underwrote those excesses, the barbaric practice of trafficking human flesh for private gain.

From his discussions with Thomas Clarkson and others, Wilberforce knew the issue had to be faced head-on in parliament. "As soon as ever I had arrived thus far in my investigation of the slave trade," he wrote, "so enormous, so dreadful, so irremediable did its wickedness appear that my own mind was completely made up for the abolition. A trade founded in iniquity and carried on as this was, must be abolished, let the policy be what it might."

Thus, throughout the wet fall of 1787 he worked late into the nights, joined by others who saw in the young politician the man God had raised up to champion their cause in parliament.

There was Granville Sharpe, a hook-nosed attorney with a keen mind. He was already well-known for his successful court case making slavery illegal in England herself—ironic in a time when her economic strength depended on slavery abroad.

Zachary Macaulay, a silent, patient researcher, sifted through extraordinary stacks of evidence, organizing facts to build damning indictments against the slave trade. A dedicated worker who regularly took pen in hand at four o'clock every morning, he became a walking encyclopedia for the rest of the abolitionists; whenever Wilberforce needed information, he would look for his quiet, heavy-browed friend, saying, "Let us look it up in Macaulay!"

Thomas Clarkson, of course, was Wilberforce's right hand and scout, conducting various exhausting—and dangerous—trips to the African coast. He once needed some evidence from a particular sailor he knew by sight, though not by name. He searched through dozens of slave vessels in port after port, until finally, after searching 317 ships, he found his man.

Suddenly, in February of 1788, while working with these friends and others, Wilberforce fell gravely ill. Doctors warned he could not last more than two weeks; in Yorkshire the opposition party, cheered by such news, made plans to regain his seat in parliament.

By March he was somewhat better, though not well enough to return to parliament. He asked Pitt to introduce the issue of abolition in the House for him. Purely out of the warmth of their friendship, the prime minister agreed.

So in May of 1788, Pitt, lacking Wilberforce's passion but faithfully citing his facts, moved a resolution binding the House to discuss the slave trade in the next session.

His motion provoked a lukewarm debate, followed by a vote to duly consider the matter: those with interest in the trade were not worried about a mere motion to *discuss* abolition. Then Sir William Dolben, a friend of Wilberforce's, introduced a one-year experimental bill to regulate the number of slaves that could be transported per ship; after several MPs visited a slave ship lying in a London port, the debates grew heated, with cries for reform.

Now sensing the threat, the West Indian bloc rose in opposition. Tales of cruelty in the slave trade were mere fictions, they said; it was the happiest day of an African's life when he was shipped away from the barbarities of his homeland. The proposed measure, added Lord Penrhyn hysterically, would abolish the trade upon which "two thirds of the commerce of this country depended."

In response to such obstinate claims, Pitt himself grew passionate. Threatening to resign unless the bill was carried, he pushed Dolben's regulation through both Houses in June of 1788.

The success of Dolben's bill awakened the trade to the possibility of real danger. By the time a recovered Wilberforce returned to the scene, they were furious and ready to fight, shocked that Christian politicians had the audacity to press for religiously based reforms in the political realm. "Humanity is a private feeling, not a public principle to act upon," sniffed the Earl of Abingdon. Lord Melbourne angrily agreed: "Things have come to a pretty pass when religion is allowed to invade private life."

Wilberforce and the band of abolitionists knew that privatized faith, faith without action, meant nothing at all if they truly followed the God who mandated justice for the oppressed.

Wilberforce's first parliamentary speech for abolition on May 12, 1789, shows the passion of his convictions, as well as his characteristic humility:

> When I consider the magnitude of the subject which I am to bring before the House—a subject, in which the interests, not of this country, nor of Europe alone, but of the whole world, and of posterity, are involved . . . it is impossible for me not to feel both

terrified and concerned at my own inadequacy to such a task. But . . . I march forward with a firmer step in the full assurance that my cause will bear me out . . . the total abolition of the slave trade . . .

I mean not to accuse anyone, but to take the shame upon myself, in common, indeed, with the whole Parliament of Great Britain, for having suffered this horrid trade to be carried on under their authority. We are all guilty—we ought all to plead guilty, and not to exculpate ourselves by throwing the blame on others.

But the passionate advocacy of Wilberforce, Pitt, and others was not sufficient to deter the interests of commerce in the 1789 session. The West Indian traders and businessmen pressured the House of Commons, which voted not to decide.

The House's vote to postpone action spurred Wilberforce to gather exhaustive research. He and his coworkers spent nine and ten hours a day reading and abridging evidence; in early 1791 he again filled the House of Commons with his thundering yet sensitive eloquence.

Never, never will we desist till we have wiped away this scandal from the Christian name, released ourselves from the load of guilt under which we at present labour, and extinguish every trace of this bloody traffic, of which our posterity, looking back to the history of these enlightened times, will scarce believe that it has been suffered to exist so long a disgrace and dishonour to this country.

However, the slave traders were equally determined. One member argued:

Abolition would instantly annihilate a trade, which annually employed upwards of 5,500 sailors, upwards of 160 ships, and whose exports amount to 800,000 sterling; and would undoubtedly bring the West India trade to decay, whose exports and imports amount to upwards of 6,000,000 sterling, and which give employment in upwards of 160,000 tons of additional shipping, and sailors in proportion.

He paused, dramatically, and pointed up to the gallery, where a number of his slave-trading constituents watched approvingly, exclaiming brazenly, "These are my masters!"

Another member, citing the positive aspects of the trade, drew a chilling comparison: the slave trade "was not an amiable trade," he admitted, "but neither was the trade of a butcher . . . and yet a mutton chop was, nevertheless, a very good thing."

Incensed, Wilberforce and other abolitionists fought a bitter two-day battle; members shouted and harangued at one another, as spectators and press watched the fray. By the time the votes were cast, in the terse summation of one observer, "Commerce clinked its purse," and Wilberforce and his friends were again defeated.

After their loss in 1791, Wilberforce and his growing circle of Christian colleagues, grieved and angered by the unconscionable complacency of parliament, met to consider their strategy.

They were a varied group, marked by the common devotion to Christ and to one another. In addition to Wilberforce, the lawyer Sharpe, and researchers Clarkson and Macaulay, there was James Stephen, a handsome West Indian who had witnessed the evils of the slave trade firsthand. Stephen's passion for abolition could burst into fiery anger against those who propagated such evil; occasionally, in later years, he would even burst forth at Wilberforce when frustrated by the course of their battle.

Thomas Gisborne, a close friend of Wilberforce's at Cambridge, had lost touch with him after leaving college. Now a clergyman and gifted orator, Gisborne wrote to Wilberforce, asking to join with him in the movement.

Henry Thornton, a member of parliament, was a calm, wealthy banker who brought managerial ability to the diverse group. He also became one of Wilberforce's closest friends, ready to weather any political storms or disappointments that might lie ahead.

These men, along with Thomas Babington, Charles Grant, and

writer Hannah More were just a few of the personalities who gathered together to fight the slave trade. Committed to Christ as Lord above all, they began to form a bond based on more than the allegiance of a united political cause. They were, says one historian, "a unique phenomenon—this brotherhood of Christian politicians. There has never been anything like it since in British public life."

In 1792, as it became apparent that the fight for abolition would be long, Henry Thornton suggested to Wilberforce that they gather together at his home in Clapham, a village four miles south of Westminster, convenient to parliament yet set apart.

Thornton had thought out his plan and believed that living and worshiping together would draw the brotherhood closer to God and to one another. His home, "Battersea Rise," was a lively Queen Anne house on the grassy Clapham Common; as friends came to live or visit, Thornton added extra wings. Eventually Battersea Rise had thirty-four bedrooms, as well as a large, airy library designed by Prime Minister Pitt.

This oval, bookcase-lined room was the site of many an intense prayer meeting and late-night discussion. Here, in the heart of the house, Thomas Clarkson related the horrors he had witnessed on his fact-finding missions to the African coast; here Henry Thornton led in prayer as all knelt on the polished floor. Here they met in hours-long "cabinet councils," as they prepared for their parliamentary battles.

Wilberforce moved to Clapham to take up part-time residence in Thornton's home; then, after his marriage in 1797, he moved to Broomfield, a smaller house on the same property.

Clapham was also a place where the brothers sharpened and reproved one another. At several points the fiery James Stephen detailed several of Wilberforce's faults to him; to each such criticism Wilberforce replied, "Go on, my dear sir, and welcome.... Openness is the only foundation and preservative of friendship."

Such was Wilberforce's character—he welcomed not only the rebukes of his brothers, earnestly committing his failures to God, but he also brimmed over with the vitality which characterizes great saints.

In later years, this was often manifest in his attitudes toward his children and those of his colleagues. Sometimes he was "as restless and volatile as a child himself," Henry Thornton's eldest daughter, Marianne, recalled. "During the long and grave discussions that went on between him and my father and others he was most thankful to refresh himself by throwing a ball or a bunch of flowers at me, or... going off with me for a race on the lawn.... One of my first lessons was I must never disturb papa when he was talking or reading, but no such prohibition existed with Mr. Wilberforce."

Such was life at Clapham: a deeply committed and joyful community of Christian families, living in harmony as they pursued the great calls God had issued them: both the abolition of the slave trade and the reformation of a decadent society around them.

As the Clapham community analyzed their battle in 1792, they were painfully aware that many of their colleagues in parliament were puppets—unable or unwilling to stand against the powerful economic forces of their day.

So Wilberforce and his workers went to the people. In 1792 Wilberforce wrote, "It is on the general impression and feeling of the nation we must rely . . . so let the flame be fanned."

The abolitionists distributed thousands of pamphlets detailing the evils of slavery, spoke at public meetings, circulated petitions. The celebrated poet William Cowper had written "The Negro's Complaint," a poem that was set to music and sung in many a fashionable drawing room; Josiah Wedgwood designed a cameo—which became the equivalent of a modern-day campaign button—of a black man kneeling in bondage, whispering the plea that was to become famous: "Am I not a man and a brother?"

They organized a boycott of slave-grown sugar, a tactic even Wilberforce thought could not work, but which gained a surprising following of some 300,000 across England.

Later in 1792, incredibly, Wilberforce was able to bring 519 petitions for the total abolition of the slave trade, signed by thousands of British subjects, to the House of Commons. As their movement rode on a surging tide of public popularity, Wilberforce's usual impassioned eloquence on the subject profoundly disturbed the House.

> In the year 1788 in a ship in this trade, 650 persons were on board, out of whom 155 died. In another, 405 were on board, out of whom were lost 200. In another there were on board 402, out of whom 73 died. When captain Wilson was asked the causes of this mortality, he replied, that the slaves had a fixed melancholy and dejection; that they wished to die; that they refused all sustenance, till they were beaten in order to compel them to eat; and that when they had been so beaten, they looked in the faces of the whites, and said, piteously, "Soon we shall be no more."

Even the vested economic interests of the West Indian bloc could not gloss over these appalling facts or ignore the public support the abolitionists had gained. But again the slavers exercised their political muscle. The House moved that Wilberforce's motion should be qualified by the word "gradually" and it was thus carried. The slave traders had no real fear of a bill which could be indefinitely postponed by that simple yet powerful word.

Though Wilberforce was wounded at yet another defeat, he had a glimmer of new hope. For the first time the House had voted for an abolition motion; with the force of the people behind the cause, it would only be a matter of time.

Suddenly, the events of the day reversed that hope. Across the English Channel the fall of the Bastille in 1789 had heralded the people's revolution in France. By 1792 all idealism vanished; the September Massacres had loosed a tide of bloodshed in which the mob and the guillotine ruled France.

In England, fear of similar revolution abounded; any type of public agitation for reform was suspiciously labeled as "Jacobinic," after the extreme revolutionaries who fueled France's Reign of

Terror. This association, and ill-timed slave revolts in the West Indies, effectively turned back the tide of public activism for abolition.

The House of Commons, sensing this shift in the public mood, took the opportunity and rejected Wilberforce's motion for further consideration of the abolition of the trade. The House of Lords' attitude was summed up by the member who declared flatly, "All Abolitionists are Jacobins."

The abolitionists' success was quickly reversed; lampooned in popular cartoons and ridiculed by critics, Wilberforce could have no hope of success.

One can only imagine the grief and frustration he must have felt. Perhaps he went home late one night and sat at his old oak desk, staring into the flame of a single candle. "Should I give up?" he might have thought. He sighed, flipping through his Bible. A thin letter fell from between the pages.

Wilberforce stared at the shaky handwriting. Its writer was dead; in fact, this letter was probably the last he had ever written. Wilberforce had read and reread it dozens of times, but never had he needed its message so deeply: "My dear sir," it began,

> Unless the Divine power has raised you up to be as Athanasius contra mundum, I see not how you can go through your glorious enterprise, in opposing that execrable villainy, which is the scandal of religion, of England, and of human nature. Unless God has raised you up for this very thing, you will be worn out by the opposition of men and devils, but if God be for you who can be against you? Are all of them together stronger than God? Oh, be not weary of well-doing. Go on in the name of God, and in the power of his might, till even American slavery, the vilest that ever saw the sun, shall vanish away before it. That He that has guided you from your youth up may continue to strengthen in this and all things, is the prayer of,
>
> Your affectionate servant,
> John Wesley

"Be not weary in well-doing." Wilberforce's mind clicked; he took a deep breath, carefully refolded the letter, and blew out the candle. He needed to get to bed—he had a long fight ahead of him.

Wilberforce doggedly introduced motions each year for abolition; each year parliament threw them out. In late 1794 Wilberforce's advocacy for negotiating a peace in the war with France that had broken out the year before made him the subject of bitter public hostility. Even Pitt's friendship was temporarily shaken; the King disdained him, saying, "I always told Mr. Pitt they [the Clapham brothers] were hypocrites and not to be trusted." Others used this opportunity to heap derision on his chief cause, abolition, and circulated rumors that Wilberforce, unmarried at the time, was a wifebeater and that his wife was a former slave.

Another abrupt reversal came early in 1796, after the fall of Robespierre in France, with the swing of public sentiment toward peace. Fickle popular favor again turned toward Wilberforce, reinforced in a surprising majority vote in the House of Commons for his annual motion for abolition. With surprising swiftness, victory was suddenly within his reach.

Unfortunately the third reading of the bill took place on the night a long-awaited comic opera opened in London. A dozen supporters of abolition, supposing that the bill would surely be voted in this time, skipped parliament for the opera—and a grieving Wilberforce saw his bill defeated by just four votes.

So it went: 1797, 1798, 1799, 1800, 1801—the years passed with Wilberforce's motions, thwarted and sabotaged by political pressures, compromise, personal illness, and continuing war with France. By 1803, with the threat of imminent invasion by Napoleon's armies, the question of abolition was put aside for the more immediate concern of national security.

During those long years of struggle, however, Wilberforce and his friends never lost sight of their equally pressing objective—the reformation of English life.

John Wesley's indefatigable preaching over fifty years had produced a great revival a half-century earlier, with its effect still being felt in many areas, particularly among the poor. But many individuals within the Church of England were Christian in name only, religion simply part of their cultural dress.

Wilberforce would not accept a perversion of Christianity which treated Christ as Savior but not Lord. Of church people he wrote, "If Christianity were disproved, their behavior would alter little as a result." Thus Sunday morning worship that did not manifest itself in daily holy living was hollow faith.

Given the prevailing attitudes of his day, Wilberforce knew he needed some dramatic ways to capture public attention and decided to ask King George III to reissue a "Proclamation for the Encouragement of Piety and Virtue and for the Preventing of Vice, Profaneness and Immorality." Though such proclamations were usually nothing but perfunctory political gestures, Wilberforce had discovered in his research that a similar statement issued by William and Mary had been used by local societies to successfully rally grass roots support. Wilberforce believed the same thing could be repeated in his day.

Backed by Pitt and others, Wilberforce's proposal went to the King, who issued his proclamation on June 1, 1787, citing his concern at the deluge of "every kind of vice which, to the scandal of our holy religion, and to the evil example of our loving subjects, have broken upon this nation."

Copies of the proclamation were distributed to magistrates in every county; Wilberforce mounted his horse and followed after them, calling on those in government and positions of leadership to set up societies to develop such a moral movement in Britain.

One prominent leader, Lord Fitzwilliam, laughed in Wilberforce's face—of course there was much debauchery and very little religion, he said, but after all, this was inevitable in a rich nation. "The only way to reform morals," he concluded, "is to ruin purses."

Even so, in many areas, the proclamation was received seriously. Magistrates held meetings to determine how to enforce its guidelines, and long-ignored laws were dusted off and enforced.

Significantly, in his quest for reform, Wilberforce did not ignore the brutal and inequitable penal system of his day, which prescribed capital punishment for such heinous offenses as stealing hares or cutting down trees—applied toward men, women, and children alike. He urged reforms in the "barbarous custom of hanging" though Wilberforce well knew that "regulating the outward conduct did not change the hearts of men." Reforming the general "spirit of licentiousness" by turning men and women to Christ could provide the only cure to crime.

Wilberforce and his colleagues were sensitive to their critics' charge that the proclamation would be applied vigorously against the poor without affecting the rich. "To expect to reform the poor while the opulent are corrupt," wrote Hannah More, the Christian playwright, "is to throw odours on the stream, while the springs are poisoned." So Wilberforce and his companions focused much of their efforts on their own peers in the upper classes. It was to good effect, as increasing numbers began to crowd long-empty churches.

The aristocracy was also infiltrated by young servants and governesses who were converted in the campaign. One such governess took a special interest in young Anthony Cooper, who would later become the Earl of Shaftesbury, the crusading Christian politician who courageously pioneered the most sweeping social reforms of the nineteenth century.

The young Princess Victoria, later to lead her nation as one of history's best-known monarchs, was also affected, having an Evangelical clergyman as her tutor. Later Victoria's ladies-in-waiting would gather for prayer each morning before breakfast, lifting up the young queen in her leadership of what by mid-century would once again become a God-fearing nation.

In the campaign against the slave trade, Wilberforce had seen the enormous impact that small pamphlets had in shaping public opinion. So he set out to collect on paper his deepening convictions about holy living. Taking advantage of a six-week recess late in 1796, he finished work on a book he had been formulating for years. The title told the story: *A Practical View of the Prevailing Religious System of Professed Christians in the Higher and Middle Classes in this Country Contrasted with Real Christianity.*

He completed it in early 1797; his publisher, skeptical about the sales potential of such a narrow religious book on the market of the day, greeted him with less-than-encouraging words: "You mean to put your name on the work?" Assured that Wilberforce did, the printer agreed on a cautious first run of 500 copies.

In a few days it was sold out. Reprinted again and again, by 1826 fifteen editions had been published in England and twenty-five in America, with foreign editions in French, Italian, Spanish, Dutch, and German. Republished in 1982, it remains a classic today.*

Wilberforce's friends were well-pleased. John Newton wrote, "What a phenomenon has Mr. Wilberforce sent abroad. *Such* a book by *such* a man and at *such* a time! A book which must and will be read by persons in the higher circles, who are quite inaccessible to us little folk, who will neither hear what we can say, nor read what we may write."

In *A Practical View*, Wilberforce presented a clear biblical message of salvation and a call to holy living, as opposed to the insipid "religion" so commonly practiced.

Wilberforce minced no words: to enter the Kingdom of God one must be born again. He wanted to impress his readers that "all men must be regenerated by the grace of God before they are fit to be inhabitants of heaven, before they are possessed of that holiness without which no man shall see the Lord." The true Christian is distinguished not by his church attendance but by his likeness to the holy, righteous Christ.

One prominent reader who skeptically picked up *A Practical View* and ended up being converted by it said simply, "It led me to the scriptures." Countless thousands on two continents were similarly affected.

This book, written by a layman for laymen, revealed incredible theological insight and biblical understanding—evidence that Wilberforce had taken to heart the command to study, know, and trust the infallible word of God.

---

*Real Christianity, Multnomah Press, 1982. Edited by Dr. James Houston, foreword by Senator Mark Hatfield.

His growing spiritual maturity served him well in handling political pressures of his day. During the winter of 1797, when he differed with Pitt regarding the war with France, he wrote in his journal, "What conflicting passions yesterday in the House of Commons—mortification, anger, resentment—for such conduct in Pitt, though I ought to expect it from him and can well bear with his faults towards God—all these feelings working with anger at myself, from the consciousness that I was not what a Christian should be. . . . Yet even still I find my heart disposed to harbour angry thoughts. I have found the golden rule useful in quieting my mind putting myself in Pitt's place."

Wilberforce put into practice what he preached to others. Until his marriage in 1797, he regularly gave away a quarter of his income or more to the poor, Christian schools, and those in special need. He paid the bills of those in prison under the harsh debt laws of the day, releasing them to live productive lives; he helped with the pension for life given to Charles Wesley's widow. In 1801, when the war with France and bad harvests created widespread hunger, Wilberforce gave away £3,000 *more* than his income.

Since the group at Clapham were mostly political conservatives, it may seem ironic to some that they were constantly engaged in schemes to aid the oppressed. They organized the Society for the Education of Africans, the Society for Bettering the Condition of the Poor, the Society for the Relief of Debtors (which over a five-year period obtained the release of 14,000 people from debtors' prisons), to mention a few.

Various Clapham members were involved in prison reforms, hospitals for the blind, help for war widows, and distressed sailors. Zachary Macaulay, at one time worth £100,000, gave away all he had and died penniless.

That these two efforts—reforms of manners and abolition of the slave trade—remained linked through the years demonstrates the extraordinary spiritual insight of the Clapham sect. They understood the crucial interdependence of true spirituality and social reform: To attack social injustice while the heart of a nation remains corrupt is futile; to seek to reform the heart of a nation while injustice is tolerated ignores the lordship of Christ.

The years of battle had welded Wilberforce and the Clapham brothers into a tight working unit; with five of them serving as members of parliament, they exerted an increasingly strong moral pressure on the political arena of the day. Derisively labeled "the saints," they bore the name gladly, considering their persecution a welcome reminder of their commitment not to political popularity, but to biblical justice and righteousness. James Boswell's bit of snide verse shows the bitter abuse heaped on Wilberforce by his enemies.

Go, W— with narrow skull,
Go home and preach away at Hull.
No longer in the Senate cackle
In strains that suit the tabernacle;
I hate your little wittling sneer,
Your pert and self-sufficient leer.
Mischief to trade sits on your lip,
Insects will gnaw the noblest ship.
Go, W—, begone, for shame,
Thou dwarf with big resounding name.

Wilberforce and his friends were undaunted as they prepared for the fight in parliament in 1804. The climate had changed. The scare tactics of Jacobin association would no longer stick; and public sentiment for abolition was growing.

Thus the House of Commons voted for Wilberforce's bill by a decisive majority of 124 to 49—but victory was short-lived. The slave traders were better represented in the House of Lords, which adjourned the bill until the next session.

In 1805, the House of Commons reversed itself, voting against abolition, rejecting Wilberforce's bill by seven votes. A well-meaning clerk took him aside. "Mr. Wilberforce," he said kindly, "You ought not to expect to carry a measure of this kind—you and I have seen enough of life to know that people are not induced to act upon what affects their interests by any abstract arguments."

Wilberforce stared steely-eyed at the clerk. "Mr. Hatsell," he replied, "I *do* expect to carry it, and what is more, I feel assured I shall carry it speedily."

Wilberforce went home in dismay his heart torn by the notion of "abstract arguments" when thousands of men and brothers were suffering on the coasts of Africa. "I never felt so much on any parliamentary occasion," he wrote in his diary. "I could not sleep after first waking at night. The poor blacks rushed into my mind, and the guilt of our wicked land."

Wilberforce went to Pitt to press for the cause. Pitt seemed sluggish; Wilberforce pushed harder, reminding him of old promises. Pitt finally agreed to sign a formal document for the cause, then delayed it for months. It was finally issued in September 1805; four months later Pitt was dead.

Wilberforce felt his death keenly, longing that he might have seen the conversion of his dear friend. He said, "I have a thousand times . . . wished and hoped that he and I might confer freely on the most important of all subjects. But now the scene is closed—forever."

William Grenville became prime minister. He and Foreign Secretary Fox were both strong abolitionists; with their power behind it, the passing of Wilberforce's bill appeared now only a matter of time.

After discussing the issue with Wilberforce, Grenville reversed the pattern of the prior twenty years and introduced the bill into the House of Lords first, rather than the House of Commons. After a bitter and emotional month-long fight, at 4 A.M. on the morning of February 4, 1807, the bill passed.

It then went to the House of Commons. On the night of its second reading, February 22, a soft snow fell outside the crowded chambers. Candles threw flickering shadows on the cream-colored walls; the long room was filled to capacity but unusually quiet. There was a sense that a moment in history had arrived. A force more powerful than kings and parliaments and slavers' profits had triumphed; passions had been spent, and the moment was near that would mark the end of an epic twenty-year struggle.

Wilberforce, who had eaten supper earlier with Lord Howich, who was to introduce the bill, took his usual place quietly. He had written in his diary that morning with guarded confidence, "God *can* turn the hearts of men," but now, looking over the crowded room, he felt too aware of the defeats of the past to be certain of success.

Lord Howich, though an experienced speaker, opened the debate with a nervous, disjointed speech that reflected the tension in the chambers. Yet it did not matter; the opponents of abolition found they could do little to stem the decision about to be made.

One by one, members jumped to their feet to decry the evils of the slave trade and to praise the men who had worked so hard to end it. Speakers hailed Wilberforce and praised the abolitionists; Wilberforce, overcome, simply sat stunned. Waves of applause washed over him, and then as the debate came to its climax Sir Samuel Romilly gave a passionate tribute to Wilberforce and his decades of labor, concluding, "when he should retire into the bosom of his happy and delighted family, when he should lay himself down on his bed, reflecting on the innumerable voices that would be raised in every quarter of the world to bless him; how much more pure and perfect felicity must he enjoy in the consciousness of having preserved so many millions of his fellow-creatures."

Stirred by Romilly's words, the entire House rose, the members cheering and applauding Wilberforce. Realizing that his long battle had come to an end, Wilberforce sat bent in his chair, his head in his hands, unable to even acknowledge the deafening cheers, tears streaming down his face.

The battle was won. As one by one the members cast their votes for abolition, the motion was carried by the overwhelming majority of 283 to 16.

Late that night, as Wilberforce and his friends burst out of the stuffy chambers and onto the snow-covered street, they frolicked about like schoolboys, clapping one another on the back, their joy spilling over. Much later, at Wilberforce's house, they crowded into the library, remembering the weary years of battle, rejoicing for their brothers on the African coast. Wilberforce, the most joyous of all, turned to the lined face of his old friend Henry Thornton. They had worked through years of illness, defeat, and ridicule for this moment. "Well, Henry," Wilberforce said with joy in his bright eyes, "What do we abolish next?"

In the years that followed that night of triumph in 1807, a great spiritual movement swept across England like a fresh, cleansing breeze.

With the outlawing of the slave trade came an eighteen-year battle for the total emancipation of the slaves. Wilberforce continued as a leader of the cause in parliament as well as working for reforms in the prisons, among the poor, and in the workplace. In poor health much of the time, he watched many of his friends die as the years rolled by; others were raised up in their places. For though in the beginning of his crusade in 1787 he was one of only three members of parliament known as a committed Christian, by the end of his life more than 100 of his colleagues in the House of Commons and 100 members in the House of Lords shared that commitment.

Thus he could retire in 1825 knowing that God had raised up others to continue the fight. His health grew steadily worse; finally in late July, 1833, Wilberforce lay helpless on his bed.

On the night of July 26, the Bill for the Abolition of Slavery passed its second reading in the House of Commons, sounding the final death blow for slavery. Told the glad news, the old man raised himself on one boney elbow, then sank back, a quick smile crossing his lined face. "Thank God," he said, "that I should have lived to witness a day in which England is willing to give twenty millions sterling for the abolition of slavery!"

By the following Sunday he was in a final coma; and early Monday morning, William Wilberforce went to be with the God he had served so faithfully.

In the summer of 1978, my wife Patty and I were in London, where I was delivering a lecture series at All Souls Church. When I noticed a free evening in my schedule, I asked my hosts to arrange a visit to Clapham, the place where Wilberforce and the "saints" spent so much of their lives, praying, planning, and preparing for their glorious crusade.

Though I was a relatively new Christian, Wilberforce had already become a model for my life. Having experienced the lure of politics, power, and position, I well understood the kind of inner struggles he must have endured. When he anguished over his decision to follow Christ, he wrestled with the most fearsome dragon: "Pride is my great stumbling block," he wrote in his diary.

I wrestled with the same dragon that unforgettable night in August of 1973 when a friend shared with me how Christ, the living God, had changed his life. All at once, my achievements, success, and power seemed meaningless. For the first time in my forty years I realized that deep down in me was the most awful sin; I longed to be forgiven and cleansed. But the dragon of pride fought fiercely before it was slain in a flood of tears.

Wilberforce's life was also a magnificent inspiration for me in the ministry I had begun to prisoners. For his uncompromised commitment to Christ drove him all those years, one man taking his stand with a band of brothers for God's righteousness against the entire British Empire.

So I was anxious to visit the hallowed ground where Wilberforce and his friends had lived and worked.

A friend drove us through busy streets, heading south from the center of London. Clapham, in Wilberforce's time a peaceful village a few miles from the city, was long ago swallowed in the urban sprawl. We passed row after row of narrow, drab houses, and eventually came to the top of a small hill. "There it is," our friend exclaimed, pointing down a shabby street. "That's where Henry Thornton's house used to be!"

"Used to be?" I replied in disbelief. "Surely the Clapham sect's homes have been preserved as historic sites!"

"No," my friend shook his head. "Leveled long ago. People don't even know the exact location."

I was stunned and disappointed. In the States, one finds markers at the site of obscure battlefields, monuments to long-forgotten pioneers, the footprints of screen stars preserved in cement.

We drove several blocks to the Clapham green and stopped at an old soot-stained Anglican church. Our host had phoned ahead so the church rector was waiting to greet us.

"Wilberforce once preached in this pulpit," he announced proudly as he led me up a rickety flight of wooden steps to an ornately carved oak pulpit. For an instant I felt a twinge of excitement to stand where this slight, little man with his thundering voice had stood.

Painted in the center of a small stained glass window behind the altar was what the rector described as a "quite good likeness" of Wilberforce; I squinted but could barely make it out. "Is that all there is?" I asked, my disappointment deepening. "Oh, no!" the rector replied, leading me to a side wall where a small brass plaque was mounted in honor of the Clapham "saints." A pile of booklets about Wilberforce and his companions was stacked on a nearby table under a sign "50p apiece." That was it.

I'll never forget the scene, nor my emotions, as we left that little parish church. The cool, misty air sent chills through me. "After all those men accomplished," I mumbled, "surely more could have been done to honor their memory."

As we walked past the rows of dreary houses lining Clapham green, my host cautioned, "Not a good area to walk at night." It didn't matter; I felt I had already been robbed, somehow cheated.

Suddenly I stopped and stared across the green. In my mind's eye I began to see row upon row of black men and women walking right across the soft grass. I could hear the clanging of their chains as they fell from their arms and legs.

Of course, of course, I thought. Clapham is just what Wilberforce and his brothers would want. No spires of granite or marble rising into the sky. No cold statues or lifeless buildings in their honor. Rather the monument to Wilberforce and his friends is to be found in the freedom enjoyed by hundreds of millions of black people, liberated from bondage by a band of men who gave their all in following Christ.

Look at Africa today. It was Wilberforce and his friends who financed the first missionaries. Now Christianity, once the religion of the people's oppressors, is exploding across the continent, growing faster than anywhere else in the world.

The legacy of Wilberforce goes beyond even abolition and Africa. Taking a longer view of history, we can now see that he was a man standing in the gap at a crucial point in the history of Christendom—and the world. For in the late eighteenth century the age of reason dawned on the Continent. Humanist "enlightenment" was fast seizing the minds of the intelligentsia.

That is what sparked the bloody French Revolution. The revolution to end the unholy rule of divinely ordained tyrant kings would finally usher in man's utopia to reign on earth.

The main line of defense against the surging tides of enlightenment humanism had to be drawn in Britain. Where else? In the colonies, where a new nation was just taking root, fewer than 5 percent attended church. Rough frontiersmen had little time for religious niceties—and enlightenment writers like Thomas Paine were profoundly influencing America's founding fathers.

But Britain was, spiritually speaking, sinking sand. The church was apostate, the whole nation wallowing in self-indulgent decadence. But it was there that Wilberforce and his companions took their stand clinging to biblical truth, resisting barbaric injustice and striving to change the heart of a nation.

The eminent historian Will Durant once wrote that the great turning point of history was when "Christ met Caesar in the arena—and Christ won." Well might he have added that fifteen centuries later, Christ met vice and vested interests in Britan—and Christ won.

For out of Wilberforce's effort came a great spiritual movement in England. Social reforms swept beyond abolition to clean up child labor laws, poorhouses, prisons, to institute education and health care for the poor. Church attendance swelled. Evangelicalism flourished, and later in the century missionary movements sent Christians fanning across the globe. Christianity took such firm root in America as to convert a near-lawless frontier into a city upon a hill. The rising tides of enlightenment humanism were stemmed.

Monument to Wilberforce? Yes, the monument is a living legacy, found not only in the lives of millions of free men and women, but in the spiritual heritage of Christians everywhere.

Wilberforce has left a special legacy for today's Christians, caught up as so many are in the illusion that military might and political institutions are all-powerful. In the conclusion to his masterful book, *A Practical View*, Wilberforce wrote,

"I must confess equally boldly that my own solid hopes for the well-being of my country depend, not so much on her navies and armies, nor on the wisdom of her rulers, nor on the spirit of her people, as on the persuasion that she still contains many who love and obey the Gospel of Christ. I believe that their prayers may yet prevail."

FOURTEEN

Thomas Aquinas

by R.C. Sproul

RECENTLY I WAS ASKED to identify my favorite theologians of all time. I quickly named them: Augustine, Aquinas, Luther, Calvin, and Edwards. Then I was asked to rate them according to their brilliance. Being asked a question such as that is like being asked to compare Babe Ruth with Mickey Mantle, or Johnny Unitas with Dan Marino.

How does one rank the greatest minds of Christendom? Scholars tend to differ in style and scope. The magnitude of their brightness is as the stars in the Big Dipper. Luther was not systematic, yet he gave awesome flashes of insight, powerful vignettes of vision that changed the course of church history. Calvin possessed a systematic mind with the comprehensive grasp of theology that was unprecedented. Augustine was surely the greatest theologian of the first millenium of church history. Though his inconsistencies are well documented, he is distinguished by being one who didn't have the shoulders of giants to stand on. Rather, his shoulders bore the weight of later giants, and some dwarfs as well.

Though it is fashionable to contrast Aquinas and Augustine as following the disparate paths of Aristotle and Plato, it is vital to remember that Aquinas leaned heavily on Augustine. It is probable that Aquinas quoted Augustine more frequently than he quoted any other theologian. Which theologian did Calvin quote more often than Augustine? None. Luther was an Augustinian monk and Edwards is sometimes referred to as a neo-Augustinian.

The historic debt of all these men to Augustine is so evident that it guarantees a special place to the bishop of Hippo in the gallery of stellar theologians. But who, we ask, was the brightest? Whose mind was most acute, most keen, most penetrating? If the question is posed in this manner, then I am forced into a corner with a two-forked exit. I cannot choose between the two men whose intellects most intimidate me, Edwards and Aquinas. To choose between them is to choose between Plato and Aristotle, of whom it was said that in the realm of philosophy all subsequent work achieved by men like Descartes, Locke, Hume, Kant, Wittgenstein, and others, is but a succession of footnotes.

So who was the most brilliant ever? I don't know. I know the question cannot be raised without the name of Thomas Aquinas being brought to the fore. And I know that he deserves my salute.

Those individuals whom history honors tend to receive awards or titles never pursued or coveted. Such a man was Aquinas. Of the many titles lavished on him, the D.A. degree stands out in particular. We are familiar with degrees and titles of Doctor of Philosophy, Doctor of Laws, and Doctor of Literature. We have Ph.D.'s, D.D.'s, M.D.'s, and Th.D.'s. But Thomas Aquinas alone bears the title *Doctor Angelicus.*

That Thomas was to be the Doctor of the Angels was not readily apparent to his school chums. His physique was unlike that of the stereotype theologian. Scholars are supposed to fit the mold of the frail, diminutive recluse, with bodies underdeveloped because of a sedentary life. Not so Thomas Aquinas. He was a big man, portly, suntanned, with a large head. He towered over his companions, no less in his massive physical bulk than in his titanic intellect. His appearance was so ungainly as a youth that he was dubbed "The big dumb ox of Sicily."

The best estimates of historians set the date of Aquinas' birth early in the year 1225. He was born in a castle near Naples, of noble parentage. He was the seventh son of Count Landulf of Aquino and Theodora of Theate.

His early years show indications that the hand of Providence was on his life. His predilection for theology was marked in childhood. At the tender age of five, an age when the modern child would be glued to the television set watching "Sesame Street," Aquinas was placed as an oblate in the abbey of Monte Cassino. There he mused on the nascent questions of ontology that gripped his mind for his entire life.

Thomas' father had big plans for his precocious son. Deeply embroiled in the political machinations between the Emperor and the princes of the church, Count Landulf sought the title of abbot for his son. Thomas politely but steadfastly refused. He borrowed a page from the life of his Lord and said, "It is better to obey the Father of spirits, in order that we may live, than the parents of our flesh." Thomas was committed to the service of God through the pursuit of an intellectual life. He was driven by an almost monomaniacal passion to answer the question, "What is God?"

At age fourteen Aquinas left the Benedictine abbey at Monte Cassino and was sent to Naples to study at the Faculty of Arts. There he came under the influence of the Dominicans and entered their order in 1244. His parents were not pleased by this decision and were further agitated when the Dominican General sought to send him to the University of Paris. On the way, Thomas was kidnapped by his own brothers and forced to return home. He was held captive by his own family for a year, during which he refused to abandon his habit and diligently kept the observances of his order every day. His zeal was so contagious that his sister was converted and his mother so impressed that, like the biblical Rebekah, she assisted her son in escaping from a window.

Thomas made his way to Paris where he first came under the tutelage of Albert the Great. Albert (Albertus Magnus) was to Aquinas what Socrates was to Plato. Albert poured his own titanic knowledge into the head of his most able disciple and followed his career with fatherly love. At the death of Saint Thomas, Albert was deeply grieved. Thereafter when Thomas' name was mentioned in Albert's presence, Albert would exclaim, "He was the flower and the glory of the world."

After three years of study in Paris, Albert took Thomas with him to begin a house of studies in Cologne. In 1252 Thomas returned to Paris. In 1256 he received his licentiate to teach in the faculty of theology. In 1259 he went to Italy and taught theology at the *studium curiae*, attached to the papal court until 1268. In 1268 he returned to Paris to take up the mighty controversy of his day, the controversy with Arab philosophy. In 1274 Pope Gregory X summoned him to assist in the Council of Lyons. On the journey Thomas' mission was interrupted by the angels. They came to take their Doctor home. At age forty-nine the earthly ministry of the dumb ox of Aquino had ended.

The most familiar title given Thomas Aquinas is that of "Saint." Though Protestants are likely to use the word "saint" as a synonym for any believer, following the New Testament usage, there are times when the most zealous Protestant will make use of the term to refer to someone who has achieved an extra level of spiritual maturity. In Rome the title is conferred by the church to a highly select few who have achieved a godliness considered above and beyond the call of duty.

When we think of Aquinas, our first thoughts are usually of his extraordinary gifts of scholarship. His was indeed a prodigious intellect, but his greatness at this point should not overshadow the spiritual power of the man. We might conjecture that his canonization was prompted by his intellectual contributions alone, but the record belies such an idea. Thomas was as noteworthy as a spiritual leader as he was for his theological acumen.

Within fifty years of the death of Aquinas the church conducted careful investigations into his personal life and teachings. Strong opposition to Aquinas' teaching set in early, and insults were hurled against his memory. But on July 18, 1323, at Avignon, Pope John XXII proclaimed Thomas a saint. The Pope said of Aquinas, "Thomas, alone, has illumined the Church more than all the other doctors."

The modern theologian-philosopher, Jacques Maritain, was jealous to restore a high regard for Aquinas in the twentieth-century church. In his book titled simply *St. Thomas Aquinas,*

Maritain rehearses the traditions of Aquinas' spiritual power and provides several anecdotes of alleged miracles that surrounded the saint. It was said of Thomas that though he contended fiercely in theological debates, he was able to bear personal attacks with a tranquil humility. Maritain relates the following:

> One day a Friar in a jovial mood cries out: "Friar Thomas, come see the flying ox!" Friar Thomas goes over to the window. The other laughs. "It is better," the Saint says to him "to believe that an ox can fly than to think that a religious can lie."

Witnesses who were summoned to testify at the canonization process of Saint Thomas described him as "soft-spoken, affable, cheerful, and agreeable of countenance, good in soul, generous in his acts; very patient, very prudent; all radiant with charity and tender piety; marvelously compassionate towards the poor." If we examine these virtues carefully, we see in them a litany of what the New Testament calls the fruit of the Holy Spirit.

Saint Thomas was also a gifted preacher. He would sometimes become so moved during his own preaching that he was forced to pause while he wept. During a Lenten series that he preached in Naples, he had to stop in the middle of his sermon so that the congregation could have time to recover from their weeping.

It is the mystical life of Saint Thomas, however, that has sparked the interest of biographers. Immediately after Thomas' death, his disciple Reginald returned to Naples and declared:

> As long as he was living my Master prevented me from revealing the marvels that I witnessed. He owed his knowledge less to the effort of his mind than to the power of his prayer. Every time he wanted to study, discuss, teach, write or dictate, he first had recourse to the privacy of prayer, weeping before God in order to discover in the truth the divine secrets . . . he would go to the altar and would stay there weeping many tears and uttering great sobs, then return to his room and continue his writings.

A similar testimony comes from Tocco. He said of Aquinas, "His gift of prayer exceeded every measure; he elevated himself to God as freely as though no burden of flesh held him down. Hardly a day passed that he was not rapt out of his senses."

Being daily "rapt out one's senses" is hardly the routine we expect from abstract scholars and philosophers, particularly from someone like Aquinas who was given to the pursuit of logic.

The habit of passionate prayer is crowned by the extraordinary claims of miraculous visitations granted to Saint Thomas. Such incidents raise the eyebrows of Reformed theologians and we mention these accounts with the due reservations of our trade. Maritain recites the following episode as part of the Catholic record of Thomas' sainthood.

> Another time it was the saints who came to help him with his commentary on Isaias. An obscure passage stopped him; for a long time he fasted and prayed to obtain an understanding of it. And behold one night Reginald heard him speaking with someone in his room. When the sound of conversation had ceased, Friar Thomas called him, telling him to light the candle and take the manuscript *On Isaias.* Then he dictated for an hour, after which he sent Reginald back to bed. But Reginald fell upon his knees: "I will not rise from here until you have told me the name of him or of them with whom you have spoken for such a long time tonight." Finally Friar Thomas began to weep and, forbidding him in the name of God to reveal the thing during Thomas' life, confessed that the apostles Peter and Paul had come to instruct him.

Another event occurred in Paris when Thomas was lecturing on the Eucharist. As he went to the altar the brethren suddenly saw Christ standing before him and heard Him speak aloud: "You have written well of the Sacrament of My Body and you have well and truthfully resolved the question which was proposed to you, to the extent that it is possible to have an understanding of it on earth and to ascertain it humanly."

That sober philosophers like Jacques Maritain report such

incidences as simple historical fact is itself testimony to the extraordinary impact Aquinas' spiritual power had on his contemporaries as well as his future disciples.

One anecdote about St. Thomas is virtually beyond dispute. Toward the end of his life he had a powerful mystical experience that dramatically affected his work. Again we turn to Maritain for his account of it:

> Having returned to Italy after Easter of 1272, Friar Thomas took part in the General Chapter of the Order, at Florence, and then he went to Naples again to continue his teaching there. One day, December 6, 1273, while he was celebrating Mass in the chapel of Saint Nicholas, a great change came over him. From that moment he ceased writing and dictating. Was the *Summa* then, with its thirty-eight treatises, its three thousand articles and ten thousand objections, to remain unfinished? As Reginald was complaining about it, his master said to him, "I can do no more." But the other was insistent. "Reginald, I can do no more; such things have been revealed to me that all that I have written seems to me as so much straw. Now, I await the end of my life after that of my works."

After this experience Thomas Aquinas wrote no more. On his final journey he asked to be taken to the monastery of Santa Maria. As he was dying he asked for Viaticum. When he saw the consecrated Host, he threw himself on the floor and cried out:

> I receive Thee, Price of my redemption . . . Viaticum of my pilgrimage, for love of Whom I have studied and watched, toiled, preached, and taught. Never have I said anything against Thee; but if I have done so, it is through ignorance, and I do not persist in my opinions, and if I have done anything wrong, I leave all to the correction of the Roman Church. It is in this obedience to Her that I depart from this life.

There is a strange progression in the achievement of titles of honor and status in the theological world. A freshman student begins his pursuit of knowledge simply with his given name. When he graduates from college, some may now call him "Mister." When he graduates from seminary and passes his trials for ordination, he is granted the title "Reverend" or "Father." If he continues his education and achieves a doctorate, he is called "Doctor." If he is fortunate enough to secure a teaching position on a faculty, he must wait to progress to a full professorship. Then he can preface his name with the coveted title of "Professor." The irony is this: if he makes it really big and achieves a widespread reputation for his learning, he will achieve the highest honor, that of being known simply by his name. We do not usually speak of Professor Barth or of Doctor Calvin or Professor Kung. The leaders in the field of theology are known by their names. We speak of Barth, Bultmann, Brunner, Kung, Calvin, Luther, Edwards, and Rahner. A man doesn't seem to make it until his title returns to where he started, with his own name.

There is a special sense in which this strange progression reaches its acme with the titular honor paid to Aquinas. He is known not only by his famous last name, but in the world of theology and philosophy is recognized by his first name. No one speaks of Aquinasism. We talk about Calvinism, Lutheranism, Augustinianism, but with Aquinas it is Thomism. One need merely mention the name "Thomas" and every scholar of theology knows of whom we speak.

Think of all the Thomases there have been in the world. Think even of the Thomases who have been famous in Christendom. There is "Doubting Thomas," Thomas a Kempis, Sir Thomas More, and a host of others. But only one theological giant is recognized instantly by the simple mention of the name "Thomas."

In 1879 a papal encyclical was issued in Rome by Leo XIII that praised the contribution of Thomas Aquinas. Leo declared:

> Now far above all other Scholastic Doctors towers Thomas Aquinas, their master and prince. Cajetan says truly of him: "So great was his veneration for the ancient and sacred Doctors that he may be said to have gained a perfect understanding of them

all." Thomas gathered together their doctrines like the scattered limbs of a body, and moulded them into a whole. He arranged them in so wonderful an order, and increased them with such great additions, that rightly and deservedly he is reckoned a singular safeguard and glory of the Catholic Church. His intellect was docile and subtle; his memory was ready and tenacious; his life was most holy; and he loved the truth alone. Greatly enriched as he was with the science of God and the science of man, he is likened to the sun; for he warmed the whole earth with the fire of his holiness, and filled the whole earth with the splendor of his teaching. There is no part of philosophy which he did not handle with acuteness and solidity.

In the Code of Canon Law promulgated by Benedict XV, Catholic school teachers were ordered to "treat in every particular the studies of rational philosophy and theology, and the formation of students in these sciences, according to the method, the doctrine, and the principles of the Angelic Doctor, and to adhere religiously to them." Here Thomism is elevated to a supreme theological role in the church. Thomas moves beyond the scope of being *Doctor Angelicus* to the realm of being the Doctor of the Church *par excellence*, the Common Doctor of the faithful.

What then, is Thomism, the philosophy attached to the name of Aquinas? Is Thomism a philosophy or a theology? Was Thomas himself primarily an apologist or a theologian? Was he a biblical thinker or a speculative scholar who merely warmed over Aristotle and baptized his pagan philosophy? These are some of the questions that are evoked by the sound of Thomas' name.

The twentieth century has ushered in a revival of interest in Saint Thomas among Roman Catholic scholars. At the same time there has been a deepening cleavage between Roman Catholic Thomists and Evangelical Protestants. As Vatican Council I in 1870 looked to Protestantism as the fountain from which all modern heresies and distortions of truth flow, so modern Evangelicals have looked to the work of Thomas as being the poison that embittered the springs of truth.

The Protestant apologist, Norman Geisler (who at crucial points is pro-Thomas) is fond of quipping that "the new theme song of Evangelicalism is 'Should Old Aquinas Be Forgot, and Never Brought to Mind.'" On the other hand the late Francis Schaeffer was sharply critical of Saint Thomas, seeing in his work the foundations of secular humanism. He sees in Thomas' development of natural theology the magna charta of philosophy. With Thomas, philosophy was liberated from the controls of theology and became autonomous. Once philosophy became autonomous, separated and freed from revelation, it was free to take wings and fly off wherever it wished. Since Aquinas let the bird out of the trap, it has flown in the face of the faith. No longer is philosophy regarded as the handmaiden of Queen Theology but as her rival and possibly her destroyer.

Such an evaluation of Aquinas meets with resistance in some quarters of Protestantism. But the debate goes on. I, for one, am persuaded that the Protestant Church owes a profound debt to Saint Thomas and the benefit of a second glance at his contributions. I remind my Evangelical friends that when Saint Thomas defended the place of natural theology, he appealed primarily to the Apostle Paul and to Romans 1 for its classical foundation.

There is a sense in which every Christian owes a profound debt to Saint Thomas. To understand his contribution we must know something of the historical context in which he wrote. To gain a fair reading of any thinker, past or present, we must ask such questions as "What problems was he trying to solve? Why? What were the vibrant issues at stake in his day? What were the dominant controversies?" We know, for example, that throughout church history the development of theology has been prodded in large part by the threat of serious heresies. It was the heretic Marcion who made it necessary for the church to define the canon of sacred scripture. It was the heresy of Arius that provoked the council of Nicaea. It was the distortions of Nestorius and Eutyches that made the Council of Chalcedon necessary. The heat of controversy has been the crucible by which the truth of theology has been made more sharp, more lucid.

The threat to the church that awakened Saint Thomas from his own dogmatic slumber was one of the most serious challenges that Christendom has ever had to endure. Our present condition in the western world makes it a bit difficult to imagine the enormity of the threat. It was the rise and sweeping expansion of Islam that threatened Christianity in the thirteenth century. Our awareness of the threat tends to be limited to the more colorful and adventuresome element of it chronicled in the Crusades. Knights with crosses emblazoned on their chests riding out to free the Holy Land from infidels has a certain romance to it.

Saint Thomas also sought to rescue the Holy Land. Its walls were made of philosophical mortar. His lance was his pen and his coat of armor a monk's garb. For Thomas the war was a war of ideas, a battle of concepts.

Islamic philosophy had achieved a remarkable synthesis between Islamic religion and the philosophy of Aristotle. The powerful categories of Aristotelian thought became weapons in the arsenal of the two great Arab philosophers, Averroes and Avicenna.

The Islamic philosophers produced a system of thought called "integral Aristotelianism." One of the key points that flowed out of this was the concept of "double truths." The double truth theory allowed that certain ideas could, at the same time, be true in philosophy and false in theology. It was a remarkable achievement: the Arab philosophers were able to accomplish what no schoolboy could ever do despite the universal desire of schoolboys to do it—to have their cake and eat it too.

The problem with having one's cake and eating it too is obvious. If I save my cake, I cannot enjoy the taste of it while I am saving it. But if I eat it, then it is gone. I cannot save what is already gone. Seems simple enough. Philosophers, however, like lawyers, often have astonishing powers of making simple matters extremely complex, to the point that they think they can actually transcend the cake eating-saving dilemma. What's worse is they often have the rhetorical power to convince other people of their magic.

To translate the double truth notion into modern categories would look something like this: a Christian might try to believe on Sunday that he is a creature created in the image of God by the sovereign purposive act of a Divine Being. The rest of the week he believes that he is a cosmic accident, a grown-up germ that emerged fortuitously from the slime. On Wednesdays, however, he adopts a different standpoint. Wednesday is "Double-Truth Day." At prayer meeting on Wednesday, the Christian attempts to believe both viewpoints at the same time. One day a week he devotes himself to intellectual schizophrenia. He tries to believe and to live a contradiction. If he enjoys the game he might shoot for a long weekend of it until he gains the ultimate bliss and security of permanent residence in a lunatic asylum.

Aquinas was concerned not only to protect the Christian church from the attacks of Islam, but to protect mankind from intellectual suicide. He insisted that all truth is coherent. Reality is not ultimately chaotic. What is true in philosophy must also be true in theology. What is true in science must also be true in religion. Truth may be analyzed from different perspectives. Various disciplines may have specialized fields of inquiry, but Aquinas insisted that *all truth meets at the top.*

This cardinal principle of Aquinas presupposes some rather basic, though vitally important, axioms. It is based upon the prior conclusion that there is a God and that he is the creator of this world. The world is a universe. That is, the world is marked by diversity which finds its ultimate unity in God's sovereign creation and rule. The word "universe" as well as the term "university" comes from this mongrelized union of the two terms "unity" and "diversity."

The double truth theory destroys in principle the fundamental notion of a universe. The universe becomes a multiverse with no ultimate harmony or cohesion. Chaos is ultimate. Truth, as an objective commodity, becomes impossible. Here contradiction may be freely embraced at any time, and every day becomes Double-Truth Day.

One of Francis Schaeffer's most serious charges against Saint

Thomas is the allegation that Thomas *separated* philosophy and theology. The charge is heard from other quarters as well, that Thomas separated *nature* and *grace.* Schaeffer's lament is that, since the work of Aquinas, philosophy has been liberated from her role as handmaiden to the Queen of the Sciences (Theology) and has now become theology's chief antagonist.

It is the prerogative of the theologian to make fine distinctions. One of the most important distinctions a theologian can ever make is the distinction between a distinction and a separation. (This is the kind of distinction that yields Excedrin headaches.) There is a crucial difference between distinguishing things and separating them. We distinguish between our bodies and our souls. If we separate them, we die. We distinguish between the two natures of Christ. If we separate them, we fall into gross heresy.

To *separate* philosophy and theology, nature and grace, was the last thing Thomas Aquinas ever sought to do. It was precisely the issue he was combatting. The double-truth theory separates nature and grace. Such a separation was the dragon Aquinas set out to slay. Aquinas was concerned to *distinguish* philosophy and theology, nature and grace, not to *separate* them. He came to bury Averroes, not to praise him.

Aquinas maintained consistently that ultimately there is no conflict between nature and grace. His posture was that grace does not destroy nature but fulfills it. What God reveals in the Bible does not cancel out what he reveals in nature. To be sure it adds to the knowledge we can glean from a study of this world, but it does not contradict it.

Thomas taught that there are certain truths that can be discovered in nature that are not found in the Bible. To use a modern example, we cannot discover a blueprint for the circulatory system of the bloodstream in the Bible. Second Chronicles tells us very little about microchip computers. On the other hand, science can never teach us of the Trinity or of God's plan of redemption. The work of the Holy Spirit in the regeneration of a human soul cannot be detected with a microscope or x-ray machine.

Saint Thomas was simply stating what should be obvious, that we learn some things from nature that we can't learn from the Bible and we learn some things from the Bible that we cannot learn from nature. The two sources of information can never be ultimately contradictory. If they seem to contradict each other, then a warning buzzer should sound in our heads to alert us that we have made an error somewhere. Either we have misinterpreted nature, or misinterpreted the Bible, or perhaps we have misinterpreted both.

So far, so good. What has really raised the hackles of many modern Evangelicals is what Thomas said next. Thomas insisted that in addition to the specific information one can learn from nature and the information found only in the Bible, there is a field of knowledge that overlaps. There are truths that Saint Thomas called "mixed articles." The mixed articles refer to truths that can be learned either by nature or by grace.

The most controversial of the mixed articles is the issue of the existence of God. Clearly the Bible teaches that there is a God. Aquinas argues, however, that nature also teaches there is a God. There can be, therefore, a kind of *natural theology.* Natural theology means that nature yields a knowledge of God.

The question of natural theology and of proofs of God's existence drawn from nature has been a raging controversy in the twentieth century. We recall, for example, Karl Barth's rigorous rejection of natural theology in his debate with Emil Brunner. Theology in general and evangelical theology in particular has reacted severely to natural theology, seeing in it an intrusion of Greek philosophy into the household of faith. The dominant approach in our day is that of some variety of *fideism.* Fideism, which means literally "faithism," maintains that God can be known only by faith. God's existence cannot be established by philosophy. Nature yields no theology. The heavens may declare the glory of God, but such glory is never perceived except through the eyeglasses of faith.

Thomas appealed to the Bible for his defense of natural theology. He carefully reminded the Christians of his day that the Bible not only teaches us that there is a God, but that same Bible also teaches us that it is not the only source of that information. The Bible clearly and unambiguously teaches that men in fact not only can know, but *do know*, that God exists from his self-revelation in nature. Thomas simply reminded the church what the Apostle Paul labored to teach in the first chapter of the Epistle to the Romans.

When the modern Evangelical rejects natural theology in toto and adopts fideism as his standpoint, he becomes guilty of the very thing for which Aquinas is accused; he becomes guilty of separating nature and grace.

What is at stake here? Aquinas understood that fallen men and women will repeatedly seek to use the tools of philosophy and science against the truth of the Bible. However, he refused to surrender nature to the pagan. He refused to negotiate philosophy and science. Fideism is a policy of retreat. It hides behind a fortress of faith while surrendering reason to the pagan. It separates nature and grace in the worst possible way. The church becomes a cultural dropout; it seeks the sanctuary of the Christian ghetto. It seeks to reserve a safe place for the practice of worship, prayer, Bible study, and the like. In the meantime, art, music, literature, science, the university, and philosophy are surrendered to the pagan. If a Christian happens to be laboring in those endeavors, he is politely asked to live by a double-truth standard. Like the scientist who can't decide whether light is a wave or a particle, he is asked to believe that it is a "wavicle" or to believe that on Monday, Wednesday, and Friday light is a wave; on Tuesday, Thursday, and Saturday it is a particle. (Of course on Sunday it rests.)

We are acutely aware that the church in our day has staggered under the assault of philosophers and scientists. There are few philosophers who see their task as being servants to the truth of God. There are few scientists today who see their task as "thinking God's thoughts after Him." Secular universities are not known for their gentle nurturing of Christian faith. The popular music charts do little to promote the kingdom of God. Modern art and literature are not communicating the beauty of holiness. No wonder that the church seeks a safe place of solace far removed from the battleground of culture.

We need an Aquinas. We need a titanic thinker who will not abandon truth for safety. We need men and women who are willing to compete with secularists in defense of Christ and of his truth. In this regard, the dumb ox of Aquino was heroic.

FIFTEEN

Otto C. Keller

by W. Phillip Keller

DAD WAS ALWAYS, EVER, the Master's man. He saw himself clearly as the servant of the Most High. His intense loyalty to the living Lord Jesus Christ shaped his character. It directed his career. He was a man totally available to the purposes of God.

His unashamed love for Christ was the supreme secret of the remarkable impact of his rather brief life poured out for Africa. Though only an ordinary layman, he was incandescent, alight, bright, illuminating the pervading darkness of Africa early in this century.

He knew he was called to serve the sick and the suffering. He was a man sent to bind up the broken; to lift the downtrodden; to set free those enslaved by superstition, dark traditions, and grinding poverty.

No matter the cost of personal hardship, Dad never drew back from the call of duty. He was a man ready to comply at once with the Master's wishes. Because of such solid devotion to Christ, he was a formidable force in the rough and tumble frontier life of his times.

Not only was he a man dearly loved by God, but also a wonderful, warm human being beloved by his own family and claimed as a friend by untold thousands of Africans. Far and wide across the green hills and tawny plains of Kenya he was loved and esteemed as "The Beloved Bwana."

So engrossed was he in laying down his life for those to whom God called him, he seldom considered his own well-being. In twenty-eight years of tough service in the tropics, he took only two brief breaks. Little wonder most of the western world knew little of him.

He was a vital kernel of seed-grain planted by God in the stern soil of Africa that yielded a bountiful crop of remarkable results. He knew this. Nor did he ever seek for the applause and plaudits of his contemporaries in the civilized world. It was enough for him that he be a faithful servant for his beloved Master.

Just the smile of Christ's approval was all he desired.

Fame, recognition, human credentials were of little consequence. He had work to do for God and he would do it well. He had a life to be expended for others and he would live it gladly.

This brief biographical sketch is an honest attempt to portray the main features of this rather amazing person who was my earthly father. More than forty years have flowed down the stream of time since he passed on into the realm of rest in God. So it is possible to write with fairness, objectivity, and a certain degree of high regard that has not diminished across the intervening spans of time.

Dad was the eldest son in a family of nine children. Reared in the plain, austere environment of a rural pastor's home, he early learned what it meant to do without all the niceties of life.

Still there was instilled in him a quiet loyalty to God, a pressing need to serve others for fulfillment, a deep love for the land, and an intense determination to do one's very best for the Master, no matter how mundane the task.

He was the first to leave home to find work in the rough and tumble of middle America. Open honesty, total reliability, energetic work, and keen foresight soon assured him of success in the construction industry.

By his early twenties he was what they call a "self-made man," living in upper Michigan. But in his own soul Dad was wise enough to know that every ability he possessed to prosper was a direct gift from his Father in heaven.

He was not blinded by self-conceit or personal pride. His character was not tarnished with the self-importance of a self-centered individual. He recognized he was endowed with special aptitudes for service. These he was eager to put at the Master's disposal.

The direction in which he was to move came into clear, sharp focus through the death of his closest and dearest friend. This young man and his beautiful bride had gone out to German East Africa (now Tanzania) as simple lay missionaries. In calm faith they, along with another single man, had felt called to serve in this remote area.

The German authorities assigned them a tribe to work among in a drought-ridden region. For lack of surface water, the two young men dug a deep well. In ecstatic delight they struck a seep of water. But there was death in the seemingly precious liquid.

Within days the two young men were dead.

Only by a miracle of divine intervention, and her own sturdy constitution, did the young bride survive.

Strong, not only in her physical body, but also bouyantly brave in her confidence in Christ, she stayed on for another five years of full-hearted service in the bush.

When the shattering news finally drifted out of the African bush and back to Michigan, it simply galvanized the successful young businessman into action. If his friend could lay down his life for Africa, so would he. In a matter of weeks he disposed of his business, took his assets, and set sail. It was 1914.

To recount these events on paper, some seventy years later, is rather simple. But for Dad to take such bold steps without the support of any human agency or organization was an act of enormous courage.

Turning away from his family, his associates, his thriving business, his promising future, he set his will like a shaft of steel to do whatever God called him to do in serving Africa amid its agony.

It was a demonstration of formidable faith in his heavenly

Father, a quiet confidence in Christ, a sure trust that God's guiding Spirit would lead him.

On board ship, the young, eager bachelor was befriended by a Quaker doctor and his wife en route to open a hospital for the Friend's Society near the shining waters of Lake Victoria. It was the beginning of a profound companionship that would endure a lifetime.

As their slow ship moved along the hot, sultry coast of the great brooding continent, World War I erupted in Europe. As a consequence, fierce fighting also broke out in the African bush between the German and British colonial forces. By the time the steamer docked in Mombasa all passengers for East Africa were put ashore. None would be disembarking at Dar es Salaam in German territory.

Dad, in his usual decisive manner, immediately offered his services to the British authorities in Kenya. They promptly appointed him to serve in famine relief. For months the country had endured a formidable drought, similar to that now scourging the continent. Overnight he was plunged into the awesome anguish of forlorn people perishing all around him. He was to be cast into the crucible of a furnace of human suffering that would shape the contours of his entire life.

He was sent some 600 miles inland to a station near the shores of Lake Victoria. Happily this location was close to where the doctor and his wife would work. And there Dad literally buried himself amid the starving and dying natives that poured into the post from their devastated reserves.

In their agony he learned to love the tribe's people with a deep compassion and touching tenderness seldom matched among Europeans. He knew what it was to weep as they wept; to groan with hopeless agony as mothers groan who have no milk for their whimpering babes; to look with sun-seared eyes for some sign of rain that never came; to feel the utter hopelessness of a land and people perishing for lack of food and lack of loving care.

Standing there amid the surging masses of men and women with hands outstretched for a handful of cornmeal or a spoonful of beans, Dad became in truth a father to the fatherless, a friend to the forlorn, a tower of hope to those without hope.

Amid the chaos and despair he seldom heard a single word of English spoken. The sounds that came to him were a cacophony of various dialects. Yet in ways shaped by the trauma of his times his ears were attuned to the strange languages that engulfed him from dawn to dark. In a remarkably short span of time he became uniquely gifted in the local languages.

To the unbounded delight of the Africans he could converse with them fluently. He knew their colloquialisms. He understood the subtleties of their parable forms. He could even share the gentle mirth of their humor; his wit, like theirs, was a balm of refreshment to weary spirits.

But even more amazing were the bridges of love and bonds of affection built between this newcomer and his newfound friends. It was along these paths he brought them the love of God.

In the pain and pathos of the famine relief, God had given my father an open entrance into thousands of African hearts. There he shared unashamedly in the suffering of Christ. And so in the outpouring of his own life there was shed abroad the compassionate care of the living Lord. In one hand he brought maize meal, salt, beans and cups of cold water; in the other he bore the great good news of Christ's amazing love for these perishing people.

The famine dragged on month after month. The skies blazed with burning heat. The grass was gone. Trees withered and died. Streams and springs became desolate trenches filled with dust.

Then one day electrifying news ran along the human grapevine of the African community. Word had come that a remarkable, young, single, white woman had trekked across 256 miles of the Tanzania bush country. She was headed for the lake and hoped to return home to Canada by way of Kenya.

Dad wondered if it might possibly be the widowed young bride of his best friend. He went down to meet the next little lake steamer that came to shore. Sure enough on board he found the gallant girl, smitten by sunstroke, totally delirious, at the point of death.

He rushed her to the nearest mission hospital and there made arrangements for her long convalescence. She had been plucked from the edge of death as by a miracle of God's grace.

As time permitted Dad visited the young woman. Bit by bit her strength returned; so, too, did her vivacious charm, her joyous good humor, her shining spirit. She knew she had been spared to serve Africa.

Friendship flourished into warm affection. And so, by degrees, my father wooed and won her heart and love.

The engaged couple felt it was only fair that she should first return to her family for a brief visit before they were married. This called for great faith since the German U-boats, fierce marauders of the sea, had destroyed so many ships. Yet in spite of all the obstacles, my father's fiancée crossed the Indian and Pacific oceans to be reunited with her family again.

It was as though she had been resurrected from the dead. This quiet demonstration of God's care for her all through the war years was a means of moving the whole family to put their trust in Christ.

Soon she would return to East Africa where in the meantime Dad was making some long-range decisions. The famine years had ended. The rains had returned. There was grain in the bins and grass on the hills. Singing, laughter, and light-hearted banter filled the lives of those who had survived the scourge of the long drought.

For my father this respite from the famine relief set him free to move from station to station, serving as interim caretaker while the white workers went on leave. It gave him a profound insight into the methods used by various mission societies to establish a church in Africa.

He was convinced there were better ways to achieve great things for God than the stereotyped style of mission work common in those times. He was farsighted enough to see that a robust African church had to be built with people who were not only revitalized in spirit, but also sound in body, strong in mind, and socially stable. Only thus could the indigenous church flourish.

He was wise enough to know that the whole fabric of native life needed to be rewoven with vision and faith in God.

What he needed was a piece of land where such a work could be started. In his search he found a block of 110 acres of rocky ground on a height of land overlooking the lake seven miles away. It was a property abandoned by a would-be missionary who had turned hippo hunter. Yet it was a strategic site of God's arrangement.

Dad purchased it for a nominal price. On the surface it appeared a waste of scrub grass, brush, and rocks, haunted by hyenas, jackals, and wild game. Only one crude mud and wattle structure stood on the site.

But he could see beyond all of this. He could see down the long avenues of the years ahead when there would stand in this spot one of the most dynamic spiritual endeavors in all of East Africa. Here the life and power of the living Christ would outshine all the darkness around it.

Then one day, after a year of waiting, Dad took the rickety train down to the coast to welcome back his radiant fiancee. Without pomp or ceremony, the keen young pioneers were married in a magistrate's office. The two returned to set up their home in the mud house on the barren hill.

A year later I was born, delivered in the stygian darkness of the African night by the beloved Quaker doctor who had become Dad's dearest friend. A simple coal oil lantern supplied light. And warm water for washing was heated over an open wood fire in an empty kerosene tin. This was to begin life at rock bottom level.

Yet for my parents it was all an enormous and thrilling adventure in company with Christ. Their quiet, implicit confidence in his care for them was a legacy given to me as a small child that remains a timeless treasure. They simply trusted God their Father for every aspect of life. It was he who had brought them to this spot. He would keep them here. He would lead them on from here. All was well!

There never was a sense of drudgery or boredom or ennui about my parents. They were a couple intensely in love with one another, in love with the land of their adoption, in love with the Africans, in love with the Lord.

Dad was full of humor. It was one of his great saving graces, bestowed upon him by God to face the formidable challenges of his times. He was a master storyteller. His ability to recount some of the outrageous events of his colorful career would convulse his friends in mirth.

A typical tale involved the time when, as a bachelor, he went to the little kitchen unexpectedly to see what his young Marigoli cook was preparing for supper. To his utter astonishment and chagrin he found the lad straining the hot soup through one of his own socks.

When he remonstrated with the would-be chef that this simply was not done, the dear fellow, all embarrassed, blurted out: "Oh, but Bwana, please do not get angry, I did not use your clean socks!"

The constant impression that came to me as a small lad was that Dad, Mother, and God were all caught up in an exciting adventure together. Life was full of fresh advances. It abounded with new endeavors. New frontiers were being opened with faith and optimism.

These found form and substance in a dozen different ways against a background of primitive paganism steeped in animism and spirit worship. The blazing contrast between the crude and cruel culture of the natives around our home and the shining exhilaration of my parents was as clear-cut as night and day—death and life—despair and love.

Despite all the protestations of modern anthropologists, the fact remains that the Africans to whom Dad came as the Master's servant were sunk in debauchery and total degradation of the darkest hues. Witchcraft, superstition, and shrinking fear of evil spirits shackled the souls of the natives around our home. Most of the men and women were draped scantily in skins taken from their goats, sheep, or wild game. Their bodies were adorned with beads, massive coils of wire and fantastic arrays of feathers. To the uninitiated they appeared ferocious. But to Dad and Mother they were friends trapped in the tyranny of their own tribal traditions and grinding poverty.

Most of the men were notoriously indolent. Given to excessive debauchery they lolled in the shade of scrubby trees most of the day, then spent their nights in ribald revelry. They would stagger past our place shouting and chanting in the darkness, hoping to drive away the demons they dreaded.

Women were abused and maltreated as though of less value than even a dog or donkey. They not only bore the babies, most of whom perished in infancy, but also bore the entire work load of digging, planting, harvesting, gathering wood, and carrying water in clay pots on their heads.

It never ceased to astonish me how brutal was the behavior of the men in beating their wives and children. Throughout the nights the throb of the beer drums, the animal-like shouts of intoxicated men, all mingled with the screams of women and children beaten with clubs and whips.

The huts and villages built of mud and sticks, plastered with cow dung, were crude and filthy hovels in which human beings, goats, chickens, and a few scrub cattle lived together at a bestial level. With utter boldness and unflinching courage, Dad and Mother entered these places to bring help and healing. Their love and compassion was shed abroad so freely in their visits that many of the villagers were drawn from their despair to discover a new life in God.

The piece of land which Dad purchased held three remarkable assets which drew people to it from far and wide. First of all it had the only permanent water spring in that barren part of the hills. So women and children congregated there from miles around to fill their pots. These they bore away brimming full to huts scattered far and wide across the countryside. En route they passed our house.

Second, the property lay adjacent to the largest local native market. So tribe's people with every sort of produce gathered here to barter their corn and sweet potatoes for eggs, meat, or honey. Sitting on the ground, their goods spread around them, they would argue and haggle in the sun for a scrap of hide or handful of beads or a bleating goat. It was a noisy, colorful scene that drew hundreds of Africans to the environs of our home.

Third, this site to which Dad was sure he had been directed by his heavenly Father was like the hub of a wheel. For it was the center of conjunction at which the boundaries of four distinct tribal groups came together. To the west were the Luo people of Nilotic descent. To the north were the Marigoli of Bantu origin. To the east were the Kipsigis and Nandi of Hamitic stock. To the south was an enclave of Somalis with their Islamic traditions from the east coast.

All of these diverse people in their coming and going; in their intertribal trade; in their eternal search for wood, water, and food passed by our place. And what they saw and heard and touched there, astonished them. Before their own eyes they saw amazing changes taking place. Changes that became the main theme of the chatter in their village circles, changes that would touch and transform their own way of living, changes that would alter the appearance of the whole countryside.

From the outset Dad was regarded with a double sense of awe and affection. News of his long years of famine relief had reached these people along the grapevine of native gossip. They knew him as a friend of those in need. But beyond this his remarkable fluency in their own dialects, his sense of fun, his enormous energy, and his unbounded empathy for the Africans drew them to him.

One of his first achievements was to help protect them from predators. Leopards and hyenas were taking a heavy toll of sheep, goats, and calves. In the patchwork gardens, troops of baboons, monkeys, and warthogs devastated the meager crops. Dad was a superb marksman and formidable hunter in the finest frontier tradition. So the natives soon learned they could count on him to help save their stock and crops from total ruin whenever wildlife depredation was excessive.

As a small lad, I often heard the low growl of leopards on the prowl around our house. At dawn we often found the remains of a goat, a calf, or a wild buck lodged in the limbs of the great mussengeli tree in our front yard. The insane howl of hyenas and staccato yaps of jackals punctured the nights.

Very quickly Dad and Mother set up a small, sparkling medical dispensary back of the house. Word of this fanned out across the country. The region was notorious for its diseases. Malaria, intestinal dysentary, rickets, ugly ulcers, and other disorders were endemic. Most of the people were old by their forties, many dead by their fifties, because of malnutrition.

Dad was wise enough to know that the remedy for all of this was more, much more, than medicine and bandages and hospital beds. It would mean improved hygiene, better crops, proper soil management, upgrading of livestock, and the conservation of natural resources.

Poor soils make poor people the world over.

Nor can a virile, strong community of Christians be built upon a population with eternally empty stomachs and disease-ridden bodies. Dad was thirty years ahead of his times in seeing this.

Christ had come into the world to do the Father's work in ministering to the whole of man. So would he!

With almost terrifying single-mindedness of soul and spirit he and Mother flung themselves into the work of turning a rock-girt chunk of the African bush into a magnificent mission for the honor of God.

Using muscular teams of oxen hitched to plows and steel-wheeled wagons such as these people had never seen, he worked the wild land with care. Thousands of tons of stone and rock were removed from the soil to be used in erecting a sturdy stone house, granaries, workshops, and a magnificent building for worship and classes.

Dad taught the Africans how to cut stone, chisel rock, and lay up straight handsome walls resistant to termites. He instructed them in making brick from the rich clay anthills that dotted the country. The skills of building brick kilns, firing them, and using the end product were all skills shared with the Africans.

He set up workshops where apprentice lads could learn to be first-class carpenters. They became skilled in sawing logs, shaping timber, handling tools, building beds, benches, tables, doors, and windows for new homes and burgeoning buildings of all sorts.

The stirring, exciting, captivating changes on the hill drew a constant stream of people to our place. It was not a show. It was not a pantomime. It was a profound metamorphosis of life in which they took a personal part.

The transformation of the land itself was even more arresting for the natives than had been the buildings. Dad worked with the inspired fervor of a Luther Burbank. He knew that this soil beneath his bush boots was capable of prodigous production if only the proper crops, grasses, and trees suited to the tropics could be found.

He was hard-headed enough and spiritually sensitive enough to realize that his Father above was as concerned about corn in the field as a crop of spiritual fruit in the souls of his starving people.

With enormous energy and unflinching foresight Dad sent all over the world for improved plant material. He imported the first hybrid corn seed from America. He brought in improved vegetable varieties from Britain. He sent for stocks of exotic fruit trees from South Africa. He introduced scores of different species of eucalyptus trees from Australia. He planted new and superior strains of grass and legume cover crops to heal the eroded barren land.

The natives were taught new ways to till and improve the soil. They were shown how to terrace and contour their land. Dad shared the new seeds and cuttings and seedlings from the abundance of his own prodigious efforts. He wanted the Africans to share in the beautiful bounty of what their own land could produce.

He was utterly opposed to the concept of making "rice Christians" as had been done in the Orient, or "Kaffir-corn Christians" as had been the case in Africa. He had such incredible respect for the inherent intelligence of the natives that he refused to make them eternal recipients of Western charity. They needed, as we all do, a sense of self-esteem and personal achievement.

Dad was determined he would assist Africans to stand tall on their own territory. He would help them to help themselves.

In passing it should be stated that what Dad was doing in the fields and gardens and woodlots, Mother was doing in the homes of these astonished and awe-struck people. She had classes in child care, in simple hygiene, in improved nutrition, in sewing of fresh garments, in singing, reading, and writing.

It was as if a yeast of renewal and rejuvenation was at work in that desolate corner of the weary old world. She was a fearless frontier woman who with her hearty laughter and indomitable spirit brought light and life and love into the hearts of a hundred homes around us.

Dad had enormous respect for her. The two of them, like a tremendous team in harness together, were achieving extraordinary exploits in company with Christ.

In due course an improved road was built from the shores of the lake, inland to the cool highlands. An increasing influx of would-be settlers, gold miners, and traders hoping to make their fortunes in this frontier passed our home. Scores of strangers came through our place along this rocky African road.

They would stumble into the grounds astonished at the gorgeous beauty of the flowers and shrubs cascading over the gardens. They marveled at the splendid livestock grazing in the pastures. They were taken aback by the abundance of fruit and vegetables. They saw joyous Africans everywhere.

Not one stranger was ever turned away from our door. I recall again and again finding as many as a dozen guests seated at the great round table in our home. To all of them Dad and Mother gave and gave and gave of their strength, their love, and their compassion.

This in essence was the warp and woof of the fiber of their lives. They lived for others. They saw themselves as servants of the Most High. They were at Christ's command.

There was no pretext or pompous pride in Dad's makeup. He never behaved toward the Africans in a patronizing way. With their profound capacity to see clearly into and through human character, the natives recognized in this man qualities of loyalty, love, and esteem that they found in very few white people.

Dad never put himself on a pedestal. He did not pretend to be what he was not. He was simply "the Master's man." He never sought recognition or plaudits from his peers. He had an enormous job to do for God, and he got on with it. It was sufficient for him to please Christ and be a benefit to others around him.

This whole approach to life was the very heart of the way in which he spoke to others about God. He did not preach in that stilted and perfunctory manner so common to those of the cloth. He did not indulge in highbrow dissertations about abstract ideas. He was a lay person, chatting with lay people, about the character and conduct of his closest friend, the living Christ. It was this One whom he wished others to meet and know. It was this One whom he wanted them to trust and love. It was this One whom he desired above all else that they should learn to enjoy during their short years on earth.

Whenever he spoke to the Africans, he used parables just as Jesus did. He couched his remarks in vivid word pictures that were readily grasped and long remembered. He spoke much of water, grain, seed, soil, sheep, and cornmeal. These were the languages of the land but also the stepping stones that led the soul to lay hold of spiritual truth.

It was in the searching, seeking, thirsty souls of his hearers that such a sharing of God's amazing love took root. Africans by the hundreds came to hear the great good news of the compassion of Christ, of his forgiveness, of his freedom from their fears.

The church building which he first erected was no longer large enough to accommodate the crowds that came. A larger edifice had to be erected. Then in time people began to request that other churches and schools be started in their distant locations.

When I was a teenager it reminded me of a pebble dropped in a pond. The resulting ripples spread out wider and wider to move and touch the whole of society. The great good news was stirring spirits, changing lives, bringing hope and health and abundant goodwill wherever it went.

Africans were entering not only the family of God, but they were entering the twentieth century. They were keeping better livestock with surplus meat and milk to sell. They were planting groves of trees that sheltered the soil and supplied surplus wood for fuel and logs for lumber. They were building better homes, schools, shops, and storehouses of brick and stone. They had skilled services to offer as carpenters, bricklayers, stonemasons, and teamsters. They were growing superior crops of corn, fruit, vegetables, and grain to nourish their own flourishing families. This also encouraged a thriving trade with others.

On the sound basis of improved land management and enhanced human nutrition a whole new generation of keen and energetic young people began to emerge. They crowded into the classrooms. They built their own new schools, staffed with well-trained teachers. The same held true for the churches that sprang up swiftly, like mushrooms after the rains, one after another across the hills and plains.

It was all tremendously inspiring. I would come home on holidays from the wretched, boring boarding school I was obliged to attend, and find Dad ecstatic about the winds of change that were sweeping across the country under the impact of God's generous Spirit.

For a while there were sixteen churches, then fifty, then well over a hundred, and finally more than three hundred.

In his own sovereign generosity God saw fit to perform a mighty work of renewal among the Africans. In deep contrition and open confession they sought reconciliation with Christ and one another. Wrongs were put right and whole families flourished in their newfound freedom.

As the years went by Dad devoted more and more of his time and strength to instructing outstanding African youths to become the leaders of their own people. He was totally convinced that the African church was fully capable of being self-governing, self-supporting, self-perpetuating. And in fact subsequent events have proved him right. For in Kenya today there is perhaps the highest percentage of eager, enthusiastic Christians in the population to be found anywhere in the world.

He was not reluctant to relinquish leadership in the church to capable Africans. He was eager to see keen native leaders emerge. He was sure that God's grace, wisdom, courage, and guidance could be bestowed on a black man just as surely as on his white brother. This concept few in the United States today will concede, despite all the hypocritical talk of equal rights and equal opportunity in our society.

The net result was that God honored Dad's devotion to his duty as few men have been honored. First of all I give it as my own personal witness that never did I ever see such steady transformation in any person's life as his. The grace of God, the touch of the

Master's hand, the gentle influence of God's gracious Spirit were so apparent in his character and conduct that for me as a growing youth it was an ongoing miracle. He was my hero! No one ever moved me more to live only for God and the benediction of my generation.

His was a totally selfless life poured out for others. He gave and gave and gave that others might gain life. This in essence is the very life of God, the love of Christ, demonstrated in the brief, shining life of a common man.

When he died at the comparatively young age of fifty-four, it was the dear Quaker doctor who buried him in the warm soil of the land he loved so well. Dad left behind a legacy of over 500 African pastors and evangelists with uncounted thousands upon thousands of joyous Christians under their care. He had come to Kenya as a common layman in its hour of despair. He left with the honor and majesty of God's mighty presence sweeping across the country.

HE WAS THE MASTER'S MAN!

SIXTEEN

David Martyn Lloyd-Jones

by J.I. Packer

DAVID MARTYN LLOYD-JONES, the "Doctor" as he was called in public by all who knew him (even his wife!), resigned in 1968 after thirty years as pastor of London's Westminster Chapel. He died on St. David's Day, March 1, 1981. He was the greatest man I have ever known, and I am sure that there is more of him under my skin than there is of any other of my human teachers. I do not mean that I ever thought of myself as his pupil, nor did he ever see himself as my instructor; what I gained from him came by spiritual osmosis, if the work of the Holy Spirit can be so described. When we met and worked together, as we did fairly regularly for over twenty years, we were colleagues, senior and junior, linked in a brotherhood of endeavor that for the most part overrode a quarter of a century's difference in our ages.

It was a shared concern that first brought us together: I, who did not know him, went with a friend who did in order to ask if he as a Puritan-lover would host and chair a conference that we hoped to mount on Puritan theology. He did so, and the conference became an annual event. Other shared concerns—explaining evangelicalism to the British Council of Churches; the now-defunct

Evangelical Magazine; Reformed fellowships and preaching meetings; the quest for revival—these kept us together from 1949 to 1970. For me it was an incalculably enriching relationship. To be wholly forthcoming, genial, warmhearted, confidential, sympathetic, and supportive to ministerial colleagues of all ages was part of the Doctor's greatness. It was, I think, a combined expression of his Presbyterian clericalism, based on the parity of all clergy, plus his feeling as a physician for the common dignity of all who have charge of others' welfare, plus the expansive informality of the Welsh family head. It was an attitude that left countless ministers feeling like a million dollars—significant in their calling, purposeful about it, and invigorated for it. The Doctor's magnetic blend of clarity, certainty, common sense, and confidence in God made him a marvelous encourager, as well as a great molder of minds. He was a pastor of pastors *par excellence.* He would have hated to be called a bishop, but no one ever fulfilled towards clergy a more truly episcopal ministry. I know that much of my vision today is what it is because he was what he was, and his influence has no doubt gone deeper than I can trace.

To be sure, we did not always see eye to eye. Over questions of churchly responsibility we were never on the same wavelength, and this led eventually to a parting of the ways. Ironically, what made our head-on collision possible was the conviction we had in common, which for many years had bound us together and distinguished us from many if not most of England's evangelicals. What these convictions added up to was a consuming concern for the church as a product and expression of the gospel. We both saw the centrality of the church in God's plan of grace. Both of us believed in the crucial importance of the local congregation as the place of God's presence, the agent of his purposes, and the instrument of his praise. We both sought the church's spiritual unity, internal and external—that is, oneness of evangelical faith and life, appearing in a unanimous Bible-based confession and a challenging Spirit-wrought sanctity. Both of us sought the church's purity—the elimination of false doctrine, unworthy worship, and lax living. We both backed interdenominational evangelical activities, not as an ideal form of Christian unity, but as a regrettable necessity due to the inaction of the churches themselves, which made it certain that if parachurch bodies did not do this or that job it would never get done at all. Had these convictions not been so central to both our identities, we should not have clashed as we did.

The possibility of an explosion was there from the start. I was English and Anglican and the Doctor a Welsh chapel-man to his fingertips. He had little respect for Englishness, or for Anglicanism as a heritage or Anglicans as a tribe. (He saw the English as pragmatists, lacking principle, and Anglicans as formalists, lacking theology. When he told me that I was not a true Anglican he meant it as a compliment.) His world was that of seventeenth-century Puritans, the eighteenth-century Evangelicals, and nineteenth-century Welsh Calvinists. It was a world of bare chapel walls and extended extempore prayer; of preachers as prophets and community leaders; of spiritual conversions, conflicts, griefs and joys touching the deep heart's core; of the quest for power in preaching as God's ordinary means of enlivening his people; and of separation to start new assemblies if truth was being throttled in the old ones. In all of this the Doctor was a precise counterpart of the Baptist, C.H. Spurgeon, who himself fulfilled an awesome ministry of Puritan evangelical type in London nearly a century earlier. The only difference was that Spurgeon learned his nonconformity not in Wales but in East Anglia. I never heard the Doctor described as Spurgeon *redivivus,* but the description would have fitted. Like Spurgeon, he thought Anglicanism discredited and hopeless. To look for genuine, widespread evangelical renewal in the Church of England seemed to him "midsummer madness," (his phrase), and he was sure that in doing this that I was wasting my time. "They won't accept you," he used to tell me, and it was plain that he hoped eventually to see me leave the Anglican fold.

Denominationalism finally became the break-point. Officially a minister of the Presbyterian Church of Wales, the Doctor had become a convinced Independent, viewing each congregation as a wholly self-determining unit under Christ, in the Spirit, and before God. In the 1960s he began to voice a vision of a new fellowship of evangelical clergy and congregations in England that would have no links with "doctrinally-mixed" denominations, that is, the Church of England, the English Methodist Church, and the English Baptist Union. To winkle evangelicals out of these bodies he invoked the principle of secondary separation, maintaining that evangelicals not only were free to leave such denominations but must do so, for they were guilty by association of all the errors of those from whom they did not cut themselves off ecclesiastically. Opposing and repudiating those errors, so he urged, does not clear one of guilt unless one actually withdraws. Because my public actions showed that I disagreed with all this and remained a reforming Anglican despite it, our work together ceased in 1970.

The Doctor believed that his summons to separation was a call for evangelical unity as such, and that he was not a denominationalist in any sense. In continuing to combat error, commend truth, and strengthen evangelical ministry as best I could in the Church of England, he thought I was showing myself a denominationalist and obstructing evangelical unity, besides being caught in a hopelessly compromised position. By contrast, I believed that the claims of evangelical unity do not require ecclesiastical separation where the faith is not actually being denied and renewal remains possible; that the action for which the Doctor called would be, in effect, the founding of a new, loose-knit, professedly undenominational denomination; and that he, rather than I, was the denominationalist for insisting that evangelicals must all belong to this new grouping and no other. His claim that this was what the times and the truth required did not convince me. Was either of us right? History will judge, and to history I remit the matter.

Born and reared in South Wales, he was fourteen in 1914 when his family moved to London. He entered the medical school of St. Bartholomew's Hospital at the early age of sixteen, graduated brilliantly in 1921, and soon became chief clinical assistant to his former teacher, the Royal Physician, Sir Thomas (later, Lord) Horder, an outstanding diagnostician whose analytical habit of mind reinforced his own. But he soon found that medical practice did not satisfy him, since it centered on the body while the deepest problems are in the soul. Having found his own way to an assurance of God's pardoning mercy towards him, he became sure that God was calling him to preach the gospel to others. By "gospel" he meant the old-fashioned, Bible-based, life-transforming message of radical sin in every human heart and radical salvation through faith in Christ alone—a definite message quite distinct from the indefinite hints and euphoric vaguenesses that to his mind had usurped the gospel's place in most British pulpits. In 1927, having decided that seminary training was not for him, he became lay pastor of the Forward Movement Mission Church of the Presbyterian (Calvinistic Methodist) Church of Wales in Sandfields, Aberavon, not far from Swansea. On his first Sunday as pastor he called for spiritual reality in terms so characteristic of his subsequent ministry that it is worth quoting his words at length.

"Young men and women, my one great attempt here at Aberavon, as long as God gives me strength to do so, will be to try to prove to you not merely that Christianity is reasonable, but that ultimately, faced as we all are at some time or other with the stupendous fact of life and death, nothing else is reasonable. That is, as I see it, the challenge of the gospel of Christ to the modern world. My thesis will ever be, that, face to face with the deeper questions of life and death, all our knowledge and our culture will fail us, and that our only hope of peace is to be found in the crucified Christ. . . . My request is this: that we all be honest with one another in our conversation and discussions. . . . Do let us be honest with one another and never profess to believe more than is actually true to our experience. Let us always, with the help of the Holy Spirit, testify to our belief, *in full*, but never a word more. . . . I do not know what your experience is, my friends, but as for myself, I shall feel much more ashamed to all eternity for the occasions on which I said I believed in Christ when in fact I did not, than for the occasions when I said honestly that I could not truthfully say that I did believe. If the church of Christ on earth could but get rid of the parasites who only believe that they ought to believe in Christ, she would, I am certain, count once more in the world as she did in her early days, and as she has always done during times of spiritual awakening. I ask you therefore tonight, and shall go on asking you and myself, the same question: Do you know what you know about the gospel? Do you question yourself about your belief and make sure of yourself?" (Iain H. Murray, *David Martyn Lloyd Jones: The First Forty Years, 1899-1939*, Edinburgh: Banner of Truth Trust, 1982, pp. 135 ff.)

"Prove"—"reasonable"—"modern world"—"honest"—"the crucified Christ"—"the help of the Holy Spirit"—"experience"—"spiritual awakening"—"question yourself"—these were keynote terms and phrases in the Doctor's preaching, first to last. He started as he meant to go on, and as he did in fact go on, seeing himself as an evangelist first and foremost and seeking constantly the conversion and quickening of folk in the churches who thought they were Christians already.

Though the Sandfields ministry was directed to working-class people, the intellectual challenge was always at its forefront. Social activities were scrapped, and with intense seriousness the Doctor gave himself to preaching and teaching the word of God. Soon he was ordained; the congregation grew, many conversions occurred, the church was admired as a model, and its minister was the best-known preacher in Wales.

In 1938 the Doctor moved to London's Congregational cathedral, Westminster Chapel, as colleague to the veteran G. Campbell Morgan. There, after Morgan's retirement in 1943, he was sole pastor for a quarter of a century, preaching morning and evening every Sunday save for his annual vacations in July and August. As in Wales, he lived at full stretch. Guest preaching during the first part of the week and pastoral counseling by appointment were regular parts of his life. On each Friday night he taught publicly at the Chapel, for fifteen years or so by discussion, then by doctrinal lectures, and for the last twelve years by exposition of Paul's Letter to the Romans. At both Sunday services, and on the Friday nights when Romans was explored, attendance was regularly nearer two thousand than one. In addition to his steady converting and nurturing ministry there, he exercised much influence on English evangelicalism as a whole.

He did a great deal to guide, stabilize, and deepen the evangelical student work of the young Inter-Varsity Fellowship of Evangelical Unions (IVF). At first he hesitated to touch IVF, for he was Welsh, middle-class, church-oriented, and intellectually and theologically alert, whereas IVF was a loose inter-denominational grouping that had grown out of children's and teenagers' ministry and was characterized by what the Doctor saw as brainless English upper-class pietism. But in partnership with another ex-medical man, the quiet genius Douglas Johnson, he fulfilled a leadership role in I.VF for twenty years, and did more than anyone to give the movement its present temper of intellectual concern, confidence, and competence.

In due course the International Fellowship of Evangelical Students (IFES) was formed, an umbrella organization uniting student-led movements of IVF type all round the world. The Doctor drew up its basis, defined its platform, chaired its meetings for the first twelve years, and continued in association with it, first as president and then as vice-president, to the end of his life. In this, too, he was closely linked with the self-effacing Johnson, whose behind-the-scenes activity was a major factor in bringing IFES to birth.

Throughout his London years, the Doctor was also host and chairman of the Westminster Ministers' Fraternal (the Westminster Fellowship, as it was called), which met monthly at the Chapel for a day of discussion and mutual encouragement. Originally an idea of Johnson's, the Fraternal grew to a membership of 400 in the early 1960s. Through his masterful leadership of it, the Doctor focused its vision and shaped the ideals of many evangelical clergy in all denominations.

He campaigned steadily for the study of older evangelical literature, particularly the Puritans, Jonathan Edwards, and eighteenth- and nineteenth-century biography, from which he had himself profited enormously. Also, he gave much support to the Banner of Truth Trust, a publishing house specializing in reprints, which was formed and financed from within his congregation. It can safely be said that the current widespread appreciation in Britain of older evangelical literature owes more to him than to anyone.

What a fascinating human being he was! Slightly built, with a great domed cranium, head thrust forward, a fighter's chin and a grim line to his mouth, he radiated resolution, determination, and an unwillingness to wait for ever. A very strong man, you would say, and you would be right. You can sense this from any photograph of him, for he never smiled into the camera. There was a touch of the old-fashioned about him: he wore linen collars, three-piece suits, and boots in public, spoke on occasion of crossing-sweepers and washerwomen, and led worship as worship was led a hundred years before his time. In the pulpit he was a lion, fierce on matters of principle, austere in his gravity, able in his prime both to growl and to roar as his argument required. Informally, however, he was a delightfully relaxed person, superb company, twinkling and witty to the last degree. His wit was as astringent as it was quick and could leave you feeling you had been licked by a cow. His answer to the question, posed in a ministers' meeting, "Why are there so few men in our churches?" was: "Because there are so many old women in our pulpits!" (Americans, please note: that was no reference to female preachers! In Britain an "old woman" is any dithery man without grip.) In 1952 he complained to me of the presence at the Puritan conference of two young ladies from his congregation. "They're only here for the men!" said he. "Well, Doctor," I replied, "as a matter of fact I'm going to marry one of them." (I had proposed and been accepted the night before.) I thought that would throw him, but it didn't at all. Quick as a flash came the answer: "Well, you see I was right about one of them; now what about the other?" There's repartee for you!

He did not suffer fools gladly and had a hundred ways of deflating pomposity. Honest, diffident people, however, found in him a warmth and friendliness that amazed them.

For he was a saint, a holy man of God: a naturally proud person whom God made humble; a naturally quick-tempered person to whom God taught patience; a naturally contentious person to whom God gave restraint and wisdom; a natural egoist, conscious of his own great ability, whom God set free from self-seeking to serve the servants of God. In his natural blend of intelligence with arrogance, quickness with dogmatism, and geniality with egocentricity, he was like two other small men who also wanted to see things changed, and spent their mature years changing them. The first, John Wesley, another great leader and encourager, just as shrewd and determined as the Doctor though less well-focused theologically, shaped a new, passionate style of piety for over a hundred thousand Englishmen in his own lifetime. The second, Richard Wagner, not a Christian, but a magnetic, emotional, commanding personality, charming, ingenious, well aware of his own powers, and very articulate (though muddily; not like the Doctor!), changed the course of Western music. The Doctor might not have appreciated either of these comparisons, but I think they are both in point. It is fascinating to observe what sort of goodness it is that each good man exhibits, and to try to see where it has come from. The Doctor was an intellectual like John Calvin, and like him said little about his inward experiences with God, but as with Calvin the moral effects of grace in his life were plain to see. His goodness, like Calvin's, had been distilled out of the raw material of a temperament inclined to pride, sharpness, and passion. Under the power of gospel truth, those inclinations had been largely mortified and replaced by habits of humility, goodwill, and self-control. In public discussion he could be severe to the point of crushing, but always with transparent patience and good humor. I think he had a temper, but I never saw him lose it, though I saw stupid people "take him on" in discussion and provoke him in a manner almost beyond belief. His self-control was marvelous: only the grace of God suffices to explain it.

Beyond all question, the Doctor was brilliant: he had a mind like a razor, an almost infallible memory, staggering speed of thought, and total clarity and ease of speech, no matter what the subject or how new the notions he was voicing. His thinking always seemed to be far ahead of yours; he could run rings round anyone in debate; and it was hard not to treat him as an infallible oracle. However, a clever man only becomes a great one if two further qualities are added to his brilliance, namely, nobility of purpose and some real personal force in pursuing it. The Doctor manifested both these further qualities in an outstanding way.

He was essentially a preacher, and as a preacher primarily an evangelist. Some might question this since most of his twenty books (edited sermons, every one of them) have a nurturing thrust, and the quickening of Christians and churches was certainly the main burden of his final years of ministry. Also, his was supremely what Spurgeon called an "all-round" ministry, in practice as rich pastorally as it was evangelistically. But no one who ever heard him preach the gospel from the Gospels and show how it speaks to the aches and follies and nightmares of the modern heart will doubt that this was where his own focus was, and where as a communicator he was at his finest. He was bold enough to believe that because inspired preaching changes individuals it can change the church and thereby change the world, and the noble purpose of furthering such change was the whole of his life's agenda. As for force in pursuing his goal, the personal electricity of his pulpit communication was unique. All his energy went into his preaching: not only animal energy, of which he had a good deal, but also the God-given liveliness and authority that in past eras was called *unction.* He effectively proclaimed the greatness of God, and of Christ, and of the soul, and of eternity, and supremely of saving grace—the everlasting gospel, old yet ever new, familiar yet endlessly wonderful.

Unction is the anointing of God's Holy Spirit upon the preacher in and for his act of opening up God's written word. George Whitefield, who was in his own day the undisputed front-man of the evangelical awakening on both sides of the Atlantic, and whom the Doctor confessedly took as a role-model, once in conversation gave a printer *carte blanche* to transcribe and publish his sermons provided that he printed "the thunder and the lightning too"—but who could do that? In some way there was in the Doctor's preaching thunder and lightning that no tape or transcription ever did or could capture—power, I mean, to mediate a realization of God's presence (for when Whitefield spoke of thunder and lightning he was talking biblically, not histrionically, and so am I). Nearly forty years on, it still seems to me that all I have ever known about preaching was given me in the winter of 1948-49, when I worshiped at Westminster Chapel with some regularity. Through the thunder and lightning, I felt and saw as never before the glory of Christ and of his gospel as modern man's only lifeline and learned by experience why historic Protestantism looks on preaching as the supreme means of grace and of communion with God. Preaching, thus viewed and valued, was the center of the Doctor's life: into it he poured himself unstintingly; for it he pleaded untiringly. Rightly, he believed that preachers are born rather than made, and that preaching is caught more than it is taught, and that the best way to vindicate preaching is to preach. And preach he did, almost greedily, till the very end of his life—"this our short, uncertain life and earthly pilgrimage," as by constant repetition in his benedictions he had taught Christians to call it.

I mentioned thunder and lightning: that could give a wrong impression. Pulpit dramatics and rhetorical rhapsodies the Doctor despised and never indulged in; his concern was always with the flow of thought, and the emotion he expressed as he talked was simply the outward sign of passionate thinking. The style is the man, "the physiognomy of the mind," as Schopenhauer rather portentously said, and this was supremely true of the Doctor. He never put on any sort of act, but talked in exactly the same way from the pulpit, the lecture-desk, or the armchair, treating all without exception as fellow-enquirers after truth, who might or might not be behaving in character at just that moment. Always he spoke as a debater making a case (the Welsh are great debaters);

as a physician making a diagnosis; as a theologian blessed with what he once recognized in another as a "naturally theological mind," thinking things out from scripture in terms of God; and as a man who loved history and its characters and had thought his way into the minds and motives, the insights and the follies, of very many of them.

He had read widely, thought deeply, and observed a great deal of human life with a clear and clinical eye, and as he was endlessly interested in his fellow-men, so he was a fascinating well of wisdom whenever he talked. When he preached, he usually eschewed the humor which bubbled out of him so naturally at other times and concentrated on serious, down-to-earth, educational exposition. He planned and paced his discourses (three-quarters of an hour or more) with evident care, never letting the argument move too fast for the ordinary listener and sometimes, in fact, working so hard in his first few minutes to engage his hearers' minds that he had difficulty getting the argument under way at all. But his preaching always took the form of an argument, biblical, evangelical, doctrinal and spiritual, starting most usually with the foolishness of human self-sufficiency, as expressed in some commonly held opinions and policies, moving to what may be called the Isaianic inversion whereby man who thinks himself great is shown to be small and God whom he treats as small is shown to be great, and always closing within sight of Christ—his cross and his grace. In his prime, when he came to the Isaianic inversion and the awesome and magnificent thing that he had to declare at that point about our glorious, self-vindicating God, the Doctor would let loose the thunder and lightning with a spiritual impact that was simply stunning. I have never known anyone whose speech communicated such a sense of the reality of God as did the Doctor in those occasional moments of emphasis and doxology. Most of the time, however, it was clear, steady analysis, reflection, correction and instruction, based on simple thoughts culled from the text, set out in good order with the minimum of extraneous illustration or decoration. He knew that God's way to the heart is through the mind (he often insisted that the first thing the gospel does to a man is to make him think), and he preached in a way designed to help people think and thereby grasp truth—and in the process be grasped by it, and so be grasped by the God whose truth it is.

A Welshman who inspired Englishmen, as David Lloyd-George once did on the political front; an eighteenth-century man (so he called himself) with his finger firmly on mid-twentieth century pulses; a preacher who could make "the old, old story of Jesus and his love" sound so momentously new that you felt you had never heard it before; a magisterial pastor and theologian whose only degrees were his medical qualifications; an erudite intellectual who always talked the language of the common man; a "Bible Calvinist" (as distinct from a "system Calvinist": his phrase again) whose teaching all evangelicals could and did applaud; an evangelical who resolutely stood apart from the evangelical establishment, challenging its shallowness and short-sightedness constantly; a spiritual giant, just over five feet tall; throwback and prophet; loner and communicator; a compound of combative geniality, wisdom, and vision, plus a few endearing quirks—the Doctor was completely his own man, and quite unique.

On February 6, 1977, the fiftieth anniversary of the start of his ministry at Sandfields, the Doctor returned and preached. He announced as his text 1 Corinthians 2:2, "For I determined not to know any thing among you, save Jesus Christ, and him crucified." His sermon, printed in the *Evangelical Magazine of Wales,* in April 1981, the first issue following his death, began as follows:

"I have a number of reasons for calling your attention tonight to this particular statement. One of them—and I think you will forgive me for it—is that it was actually the text I preached on, on the first Sunday night I ever visited this Church . . .

"I call attention to it not merely for that reason, but rather because it is still my determination, it is still what I am endeavoring, as God helps me, to do. I preached on this text then—I have no idea what I said in detail, I have not got the notes—but I did so because it was an expression of my whole attitude towards life. It was what I felt was the commission that had been given to me. And I call attention to it again because it is still the same, and because I am profoundly convinced that this is what should control our every endeavour as Christian people and as members of the Christian Church at this present time."

There followed a very clear exposition of salvation through the atoning death of Jesus Christ, and then from the seventy-seven-year-old preacher came the application:

"Men and women, is Jesus Christ and him crucified everything to you? This is the question. It is a personal matter. Is he central? Does he come before anything and everything? Do you pin your faith in him and in him alone? Nothing else works. He works! I stand here because I can testify to the same thing. 'E'er since, by faith, I saw the stream / Thy flowing wounds supply, / Redeeming love has been my theme, / And shall be till I die.' 'God forbid that I should glory, save in the cross of our Lord Jesus Christ, by whom the world is crucified unto me, and I [crucified] unto the world'" (Gal 6:14).

"My dear friends, in the midst of life we are in death. This is not theory; this is personal, this is practical. How are you living? Are you happy? Are you satisfied? How do you face the future? Are you alarmed? Terrified? How do you face death? You have got to die.... What will you have when that end comes? You will have nothing, unless you have Jesus Christ and him crucified.... do you know him? Have you believed in him? Do you see that he alone can avail you in life, in death, and to all eternity? If not, make certain tonight. Fall at his feet. He will receive you, and he will make you a new man or a new woman. He will give you a new life. He will wash you. He will cleanse you. He will renovate you. He will regenerate you and you will become a saint, and you will follow after that glorious company of saints that have left this very place and are now basking in the sunshine of his face in the glory everlasting. Make certain of it, ere it be too late!"

Four years later, on the feast day of Wales' patron saint, the preacher himself was taken home. He died of cancer. He lies buried in the cemetery of the Phillips family, from which his wife came, in Newcastle Emlyn, near the farm which had belonged to his mother's people. The words, "For I determined not to know any thing among you, save Jesus Christ, and him crucified," are inscribed on his gravestone. Nothing more appropriate could be imagined.

"When nature removes a great man," said Emerson, "people explore the horizon for a successor, but none comes and none will. His class is extinguished with him." That is the case here. There is no one remotely resembling the Doctor around today, and we are the poorer as a result. To have known him was a supreme privilege, for which I shall always be thankful. His last message to his family, scribbled shakily on a notepad just before he died, when his voice had already gone, was: "Don't pray for healing; don't try to hold me back from the glory," and for me those last words, "the glory," point with precision to the significance that under God he had in my life. He embodied and expressed "the glory"—the glory of God, of Christ, of grace, of the gospel, of the Christian ministry, of humanness according to the new creation—more richly than any man I have ever known. No man can give another a greater gift than a vision of such glory as this. I am forever in his debt.

SEVENTEEN

Philip E. Howard, Jr.

by Thomas Howard

SOMEWHERE IN A SCRAPBOOK I have a snapshot of my father which I took with a box camera when I was a small boy. The picture shows him standing perhaps twenty feet away, wearing an old Stetson hat and a soft leather jacket, aiming a rifle.

His aim is at ninety degrees to the camera, off to stage-right, so to speak. He was very punctilious about guns, and would never allow us to aim so much as our index finger, let alone a toy pistol, at someone. He inherited this outlook from his father and grandfather. His grandfather had had experience with revolvers in Texas and New Mexico, in the days when that was serious business. An enormous long-barreled blue steel revolver lay in a bottom drawer of the highboy in my parents' bedroom, but there was never any ammunition, and I think my father had had the hammer welded shut. The pistol had belonged to his grandfather. I used to take it out and handle it from time to time. It seemed to conjure a whole world in which my father's origins lay, and which somehow constituted his native land.

I do not mean that he, or his fathers, had come from the Wild West. They were New Englanders. The rifle in my snapshot was actually a Daisy Red Rider air rifle which shot copper beebees by means of a spring mechanism. My father used to sting wandering dogs with these harmless rounds when they came onto the lawn with the clear intention of parking. He was kind to animals, but he did not want the lawn fouled.

These guns bespoke a world that was disappearing by the time I came along, and which is inaccessible and incomprehensible altogether to the generation now afoot. My son, for example, thinks of guns principally in connection with Viet Nam, the Mafia, 007 films, or drunken deer hunters in their pickup trucks.

My father's world was not a world of guns. But to see him settle the stock of that beebee rifle against his shoulder and squint through the sight was to see a man at home with certain suppositions about life. A good man and a gentleman may be trusted to know what firearms are for and to handle them with the skill and caution appropriate to such things. My father was justly proud of his marksmanship but had never fired a bullet at anything but a target. He was not a hunter. He took no pleasure in killing anything. But the notion that the way to prevent murder might be to enact laws banning all firearms would have struck him as insolent and maudlin. He and his generation would have objected that no murderer on earth will be deflected from his intentions for one moment by any such ban and that the people who plump for causes like this are themselves perhaps a threat to the sanity and continuity of civilization.

His was a world that counted on certain virtues and that saw these virtues as supporting the edifice of civility. Honor, courage, rectitude, courtesy: it was the responsibility of a good man and a gentleman to assist in protecting civility against all churlishness by embodying these things. My father was embarrassed and angered by any display, especially public, of churlishness. Indeed, it would not be going too far to say that any such display roused dread in him as well since, in the end, it will be churlishness that will bring down the edifice. Someone appearing in church or on a train dressed inappropriately; a couple nuzzling and billing in a public place; bad grammar, especially in print or from the podium; ducktail haircuts and diamond pinkie rings on middle-aged men; lucite stiletto heels and painted toenails on women: these looked like fissures in the wall to my father.

He loved fly-fishing. His long, whiplike, split-bamboo fly rods could be dismantled into three sections. I used to like pulling them apart, listening to the small pop as the metal-sheathed butt of one section came out of the hollow metal sleeve at the tip of the next. He would set his equipment out neatly at the edge of the wide porch of our summer house in the White Mountains: the basket with the square hole in the top, lined with wet grass fresh from the meadow next to the house; the fat leather envelope with the flannel pages in it holding the flies—Dolly Vardens, Parmachenee Belles, Silver Doctors; extra leader, coiled in its round, flat tin box (the leader he would fix for me had tiny split-lead shot pinched onto it at intervals, for my worm fishing); his reel; the net; and his olive-drab hip boots, standing upright side by side, with the upper part of them fallen over sideways from the knee, the rubber belt-straps trailing on the porch floor. He always pinned his fishing license to the band of his old Stetson hat.

If he were setting out to fish down one of the little brooks that come off the mountains up there, this was all he needed. If he were headed for a lake, he would put the canoe on the top of the car. He was a fine canoeist and had taught all of his children about the little flick you give to the stern paddle to keep the canoe from weaving back and forth in the water. To this day the first thing I look for when I see someone out in a canoe is whether they know how to do this or not. Almost no one does. My father felt that it is a great pity for people to have so little idea about what an exquisite thing a canoe is. They ought not to be out there, really. Let them flounder about in rowboats if they want to. Aluminum canoes, and Sponson canoes with the air chambers along the gunwales to keep them from tipping over, struck my father as betraying the grace that belongs to the idea of canoes. A canoe is made of canvas.

He would sometimes take me fishing with him. He taught all of his children as much about fishing as they wanted to learn. Two of my brothers became good fly fishermen. I never went beyond worms, but I learned very early that fly fishing is the finest sport there is.

My father would stand in the brook with the water rushing past his boots, just a little upstream from some nice hole under a big rock. He knew the habits and wisdom of trout and saw his fishing as a gentlemanly contest of wits with them. Native brook and rainbow trout were the most elegant fish in the world, in his view. Pickerel, pike, bass, perch, and the rest of them, lacked the grace of trout. Hatchery trout were becoming a melancholy necessity in a world where too many people were turning out to fish.

He would play out the line with his left hand, pulling it in length after length from the reel, which clicked quietly as it spun. His right hand waved the rod forward and back with the line sailing in a great S-shape in the air. You could not tell where the thin bamboo ended and the line began. When he was satisfied that he had exactly the right length of line out, he would let the fly alight on the surface of the pool, right above the nose of the trout that was lurking under the rock. He would show me how to do all of this without whipping the line. If you whipped it, you could snap the leader and flies right off and lose them.

When a trout would strike at the fly, all of my father's powers would gather and poise in the blissful, delicate, and taxing game of landing it. The tip of the rod would flicker, bob, then plunge sharply down in a deep arc. With a deft movement of his wrist he would snare the trout, then reel in the line, seeing to it that no slack allowed the trout room for maneuver. There was always a breathless moment while he reached gingerly forward with the net in his left hand and dipped down under the thrashing trout. Not until the fish lay curved in the bottom of the net were you sure you had it.

"It's a rainbow," or "It's a brook," he would call as he waded to the bank.

My father did not like to leave a fish gasping slowly to death in the basket, so he would show me how to grasp it, insert a thumb into one of the gills, and with a quick pressure snap the spine just back of the fish's eye. The struggle was over in an instant.

Back at the house at the end of the day he would lay the catch out to be cleaned, side by side along a board, arranging them by size. Most of them would be brook trout, about eight inches long, with rosy spots along their smooth black sides. If the array were crowned with a fat, ten-inch native rainbow with the faint pink stripe along its silvery side, this was the best prize. You knew the meat would be pink.

With his tiny bone-handled penknife he would cut off the heads of the trout and slit the belly from the tail to the gills. Sometimes there would be roe among the viscera, and he always felt bad about that. A mother. He would scrape the inside immaculately clean under the faucet which stood next to the porch, showing us how to get the last black bits of blood from along the spine. A good fisherman will leave no trace of blood here. There was always a hint of ceremony as he arranged the clean trout on a blue-rimmed, white enamelled tin plate and set it on top of the great blocks of ice in the wooden ice box on the back porch. The door to the ice compartment would shut with a thick click. Trout for breakfast tomorrow.

I would awake the next morning in my third-floor room to bright sunshine and the racket of crows in the white pines in the meadow across the road. Sometimes I could hear a crackling from downstairs: this meant that my father thought the morning was snappy enough to warrant a fire in the enormous fireplace. Through the open window I could hear my mother, in the kitchen-house below, getting breakfast.

My father had taught her how to cook trout. You dip them in egg and cornmeal before you fry them. He taught us all how to eat them. You lay the trout on its back (not its side) on the plate with the tail towards you, steadying it by placing the tip of your knife between the two fat sides, just touching the backbone. With the tines of your fork pressing gently on the meat, you gradually lay the left side of the trout flat, leaving the whole ladder of tiny, filament-like bones still attached to the backbone, separated now from the meat. You do the same with the right side. Now lift the backbone and tail away from the trout altogether. Brush the meat with a pat of butter and sprinkle it lightly with salt and pepper. This is how it is done. Very few people and no restaurants at all know about this. Once or twice in my adult life I have ventured to order trout from a menu, hoping that I might recapture some fugitive memory of those breakfasts. My hopes have been ill-placed: the best fish that the best restaurant can set out seems cardboard next to the light, custardy delicacy of the trout that my father caught for us.

He was a great ornithologist as well as a fly-fisherman. Once or twice a year he would take us for bird-hikes. His favorite birds were the ones that lived in the White Mountains: the hermit thrush, the olive-sided flycatcher, the veery, the winter wren, the white-throated sparrow, and the black-capped chickadee. He could imitate flawlessly the songs of dozens of species and would get them to come and flit from twig to twig over his head, answering his calls. It troubled me somewhat, since I thought they might be saddened when no mate showed up. He always carried his "Peterson" (*A Field Guide to the Birds*), a checklist, and a pair of six-power binoculars hung around his neck on a thong. He rarely needed to consult Peterson, but there are some warblers which always require looking up.

He taught us to walk along in the fields and woods quietly, mainly remembering not to make any sudden gesture with our hands. It was sudden movements more than noises that frightened the birds, he said. When he spotted a bird he would raise his binoculars very slowly to his eyes. This would push the front brim of his Stetson up, changing his appearance quite remarkably. Comedians wore their hats this way, but comedy was not at all the note being struck here.

To hear a bird, locate its whereabouts, call it, spot it, name it, and let us have a look through the binoculars: this was his pleasure. Vesper sparrow; chewink; pine siskin; Lapland longspur; yellow-breasted chat; snow bunting; dickcissel; prothonotary warbler; parula warbler; loggerhead shrike; blue-gray gnatcatcher; long-billed marshwren; brown creeper; wood pewee: the names arouse fathomless nostalgia in me. And all the hawks: duck hawks, marsh hawks, Cooper's, rough-legged, red-tailed, sharp-shinned, broad-winged, and ospreys. And the owls: long-eared, barred, barn, screech, saw-whet, Richardson's, burrowing.

In the winter he would take us to the marshes in southern New

Jersey, and to a sandy region known as the Pine Barrens, and to Barnegat Lighthouse on Long Beach Island, a thin, twenty-mile strip of sand off the coast. Here we hoped to see snowy owls, knots, sanderlings, curlews, ruddy turnstones, willets, godwits, semipalmated plovers, oystercatchers, stilts, clapper rails, black-crowned night herons, and all kinds of teals, shovelers, mergansers, oldsquaws, scaup ducks, buffleheads, and grebes.

After we had had a good look at a bird, or at a flock of them, he would take from his pocket the stiff card on which the checklist was printed and draw a small dash in the margin next to the name of the species. He used Autopoint pencils with very soft black lead, which he would buy at a shop called Pomerantz, on Chestnut Street in Philadelphia. As I type this manuscript I am using an Autopoint with soft black lead to make my corrections and changes with. It is the best pencil in the world, and along with trout and birds, forms part of my father's legacy to me.

He loved hiking. There were half a dozen trails in the mountains around Franconia to which he returned, year after year, for more than fifty years. The Greenleaf Trail and the Bridle path, up Lafayette; the Lonesome Lake Trail; the Jewell Trail up Washington; and the Kinsman Flume and Bridal Veil Falls trails: these were his favorites, and he never seemed to tire of repeating them. There was a cluster of peeled walking sticks under the stairs in our summer house, and he would get these out and distribute them to us according to our height. There were also three or four small, flat, square packs which he called haversacks, made of extremely heavy khaki canvas, which my mother would fill with sandwiches, little red boxes of Sun-Maid raisins, Hershey bars (for energy), and "hermits"—soft, cake-like, gingery cookies. On the day of a hike we would always be awakened earlier than usual so that we could have a hearty breakfast and an early start. Early starts were part of the fabric of my father's world.

My mother would drive us to the base of the mountain to be climbed. Here the ritual was always the same: shoelaces were checked, haversack straps adjusted and settled comfortably on your shoulders, windbreaker jackets tied around your waist by knotting the sleeves in front. You gave your walking stick a last few prods into the ground to make sure it was the right length. Even though it was August, you could see your breath, and the long grass and ferns at the opening of the trail were still silver with dew and cobwebs.

Usually the trail dipped down and crossed a brook before it started to climb. There were always black-capped chickadees flitting about in the birch and maple trees overhead, with their churring "chicka-dee-dee-dee" call or their fife-like two-note song. My father had a certain gait for mountain climbing—a slow, steady plod, with his hands clasped behind him. He told us that if you start out scampering you will soon run out of breath. This steady gait will serve you well, hour after hour. On the upper slopes above the timberline, when the sun is hot and you have been climbing for several hours, you will still be going at the same pace.

In the first half-hour or so, when you were still walking along under the hardwood trees, he would point out the bunch-berries, clintonia borealis (there seemed to be no English name for this plant with the long single stalk and one shiny, dark blue berry), and moose maple. He told us that the enormous moose maple leaves would always serve as a useful substitute if you had forgotten to bring along tissues in your pack.

Further up you began to see Labrador tea and creeping snowberry next to the trail, and the hardwoods gave way gradually to spruce trees. A few tall straight ones would appear among the birches and maples; then the hardwoods disappeared and on either side of the path there would be dense growth of scrubby, gnarled spruces, their immemorial roots grasping the moss-covered rocks like tough old fingers that had been holding on against winds and blizzards since the beginning of the world. My father would take out his penknife and cut off little deposits of spruce gum that had oozed through the lichen-covered bark and give them to us to chew. You felt that this was a much cleaner and healthier confection than Wrigley's or Dentyne. It was certainly more astringent and less sugary.

As the trail climbed higher the trees grew stubbier and stubbier, until suddenly you found yourself at the timber line. Often a single step would take you from the scrubby spruce growth out into the immense upland above the timber line, with the whole world spreading away from you.

Now you could see the trail itself, following the cairns in a zigzag track all the way to the summit, and hundreds of peaks stretching away into Vermont and Canada. The song of the white-throated sparrows came like a crystal echo up from the spruce forest below, and from the clumps of grass between the boulders scattered across the upper reaches of the mountainside. You could also hear a tiny, infinitely high "pink-pink" from some bird whose name I have forgotten. My father would call back and forth to the white-throats, and would stop every few minutes just to sniff the air and gaze, with his hands on his hips. On most trips he would observe at least once that the scene here was a very long way from Thirteenth and Wood, the dingy corner in Philadelphia where his office was.

On Mt. Washington, he did not mind the somewhat quaint chuffing of the Cog Railway, which looked for all the world like something out of a children's storybook. But it was very hard for him to conceal his dismay over the passengers who alighted at the summit, with their rope-soled shoes, Bermuda shorts, slant-eyed sunglasses, cameras, and Hawaiian sports shirts. They knew nothing about mountains, he felt. The summit was being wasted on this crowd who had no ears for the song of the white-throat. They came and pawed over the decals and ashtrays and bawdy farmyard postcards in the souvenir shop, then reboarded the train for the Base Station. To my father, their faces seemed jelled in expressions of ennui, surfeit, and confusion.

For most of the year, my father was a commuter. We lived in Moorestown, New Jersey, which had been settled by Philadelphia Quakers. When I was a small boy, the air of the town was still redolent of Quakerism: broad, quiet streets richly shaded by huge oaks, elms, and maples; large comfortable houses; and people greeting each other with nods, cheery smiles, and twinkly eyes that seemed full of old Philadelphia. "Good morning, Philip Howard, how is thee?" or "Good morning, Kathy dear, how's thee today?" I would hear them say to my parents. We were not Quakers, but my parents spoke the "plain language" with their Quaker friends.

Moorestown lay about ten miles from Philadelphia, across the Delaware River. A single track of the Pennsylvania Railroad came through the town, connecting Philadelphia with Atlantic City. There were steam engines in those days, and the passenger coaches were painted a dull brick-color. My father very much liked the ride into town (he always said "in town" when he referred to Philadelphia), since it gave him an unbroken thirty minutes or so to read. He would leave the house at 7:40 A.M. and walk the few blocks to the station, allowing himself the exact number of minutes to get there. There was never the smallest flurry. After breakfast and family prayers, which were timed so that none of us ever needed to race about hunting for school books and finishing up chores, he would go to the hall closet, put his maroon wool scarf around his neck, pinning it down with his chin as he put on his overcoat. Then his hat and gloves. He would pick up his briefcase, kiss my mother good-bye, tipping his hat back as he did so, and go out the door. His briefcase was a soft leather affair with straps that buckled. He had a certain way of flipping the straps back when he undid the buckles.

My father's professional life was familiar to all of his children, since we would often find ourselves in town for one reason or another, and this almost always included a visit to "the office." He was the editor of a weekly religious journal called *The Sunday School Times*, which had a very large readership all over the world. It was looked upon as an almost infallibly trustworthy court of appeal by hundreds of thousands of Protestants. The weight of responsibility which my father felt in this connection was almost insupportable to him and was made even more onerous by the fact that his uncle before him, and his grandfather before that, had been the only other editors in the century of the journal's existence. I grew up with the unconscious assumption that a man's adult responsibilities would doubtless crush him in the end. The "problems in the office" which we heard him talk about with my mother ranged from appalling ecclesiastical wars on which he was obliged, reluctantly, to adopt some official editorial point of view, to falling circulation, to quarreling and tears among "the girls in the office." This last problem contributed far more to the deep creases in his face and the gray in his hair than did the official matters.

The girls in the office were the secretaries, accountants, and proofreaders. Most of them were aging. Indeed, to my ten-year-old eyes, they all seemed to be very old women. They always greeted us with delighted shrieks and little favors when we came into the office; but we knew that they brought on our father's greatest agonies. He had neither the disposition nor the ability to cope with what would now be called "interpersonal relationships"—a phrase that would have given him worse pains than the quarrels themselves. But he felt that the whole atmosphere in the office depended on him personally. The sight of one of these women sniffing into her hanky and mopping reddened eyes filled him with more dread and vexation than almost anything else in the world.

The offices of this journal occupied the sixth floor of a factory building. Spaces had been created for the different departments by arranging dark-green metal bookcases into corridors and squares. A few paper-thin wooden partitions had been set up for the more important offices. My father had one of these. It was a small, cold, corner cubicle with enormous factory windows overlooking the morgue. I would prop open one of the metal-rimmed window sections and crane my head through it, fascinated with horror if a hearse drew up below. Once I saw them fling the stiffened, emaciated, stark-naked body of a man from the hearse onto the loading platform. Occasionally the air was heavy with a strange, sweet smoke.

I have, somewhere, another snapshot of my father at his desk in this office. He is sitting there, tall and straight, with his gold chain and Phi Beta Kappa key across the front of his vest. This key was the one concession that he made to anything that might at all be called vanity. My impression is that the question arose in his mind from time to time as to whether it might not, in fact, be vain for a man to display his Phi Beta Kappa key. But somehow or other he found room in his otherwise remorseless moral categories to go on wearing it. On one end of the chain there was some arrangement to keep the end in one of the vest pockets. On the other end, in the other pocket, was his gold Longines watch, thin as an after-dinner mint. This watch kept flawless time, decade after decade. He would check it once a week at a chronometer that sat in the window of a jeweler's on Walnut Street. He would show us this chronometer when he took us out to lunch on the days when we visited him in the office.

He usually ate lunch alone. If he had to entertain someone, he would arrange to meet them at the Whittier Hotel, which had a quiet dining room with starched white tablecloths. Otherwise he would leave the office and walk, with his very long strides, five or six blocks along Thirteenth Street to his favorite restaurant, a cafeteria called The Colonnade. It was in an arcade that opened off one of the small streets—Sansom or Juniper—near City Hall. You had to go down some stairs to get to this place. My memory of it is of a tiled floor, a great many mirrors and brass rails, and hundreds of small tables with bentwood chairs at them. The place was always crowded, but things moved so fast that there was never any trouble getting a table. Someone was always leaving.

My father liked The Colonnade because you could get plain, well-cooked food without wasting any time at all. He also liked the walk to and from his office. He rarely used the elevator on his comings and goings from the building. The trip up and down the six flights of stairs to his office was good for a man, he felt.

The desk where my father sits in my snapshot has no clutter on it. It never did. Any letter or manuscript on which he was not working at the moment lay in either the In or the Out box. There was a small marble rack on the desk with grooves, in which lay his pencils. He always carried a black Esterbrook fountain pen with an extra broad nib in his upper vest pocket. He used this to sign his name. Otherwise he worked with pencils.

He did all of his correspondence and writing on an Ediphone, which even in those days was an outdated model. It sat up on a little metal cart like a tea tray, with casters on the legs so that you could push it around. There were wax cylinders and a mouthpiece like a small horn at the end of a snakelike metal arm that had sections like little vertebrae to make it flexible. My father would tilt the upper edge of the mouthpiece against his upper lip and talk into it. He always included exact typing instructions in what he said. I would sometimes listen to him dictate and would hear "... Comma. Quote. Cap.," or "Paren. Point. Paragraph." He knew everything there was to know about editing, printing, proofreading, and prose. His own prose style was as flawless as the foundations of the City of God. It was without the smallest embellishment and perfect in its economy and integrity. He did not like polysyllables, elaborate metaphors, circumlocution, fustian, pyrotechnics, or any suggestion of self-display in prose (he would have drawn a single blue line through this sentence).

Every week he had to write an "Ed. Note." These were short essays, perhaps 300 words long, which appeared in a double column in the upper right-hand section of the front page. He enjoyed writing these pieces. The discipline of saying something helpful, clear, and substantial in such a short space kept his mind and his prose lean. He always had the simplest reader in mind as he wrote, and he usually drew some illustration of his point from ordinary life. Often his love for birds, fishing, and the mountains would appear, but only reticently and briefly, and never by way of displaying his personal hobbies or knowledge.

These editorial notes invariably had for their main burden some direct point from the Bible. He never pontificated about public issues. The world changes very little, in his view, from aeon to aeon. Hence very little is to be gained by raising the hue and cry about some new outrage, as though here were something that had caught us all off guard and about which we must become scandalized and take up arms. He had traditional political, economic, and social views, and hence it depressed him to watch

Franklin Roosevelt win election after election. But he spent very little time worrying over the enfeebling effect that liberalism has on civilization: he assumed that all civilizations are transitory and that most palaces and chancellories have been mare's nests of intrigue since the beginning of time. I never heard him puff and blow about corrupt political machinery, even though he was aware of it all, and it depressed him. By the same token, he rarely talked and never wrote, so far as I know, about Hitler, even though he, like all good men, was paralyzed with horror at the huge rallies in Nuremberg, and, later, at the revelations from Treblinka and Belsen.

We had an American flag leaning out from a bracket on the front porch railing at home during World War II, and, when my oldest brother went into the Army, we hung in a window the small red-bordered, white silk square with the blue star in the middle. My father was impressed and moved by military parades, not because the brisk, unison thud of martial heels roused a cheap jingoism in him, but because here came the flag, supported and attended by men who might die to preserve the gentlest kind of life ever offered to a people by a society.

The spectacle of military precision thrilled him. Strapping MPs with glistening boots, starched khakis, white gloves, and glossy helmet liners worn smartly forward almost touching the bridge of the nose; glittering jeeps and staff cars wheeling up with perfect timing and in perfect formation with little flags standing up stiffly from the front fenders; the long, harsh yell of sergeants-major snapping thousands of men from parade rest to attention without the slightest possibility of disorder, unrest, or protest. I think my father glimpsed in all of this the order that arches over things and that alone can shelter the gentility and civility that should mark human life. It all stood at a polar extreme from the slovenliness, egoism, truculence, and indulgence that deface life and make a ruin of it.

But public life and issues were not where my father's imagination dwelt. He believed that if a man studied the Bible sedulously, every day of his life, he would be in touch with the only finally enduring wisdom there is. Something like this seems to be very much the burden of the Book of Proverbs, and of Psalm 119, and, in some sense, of Christ's words about man not living by bread alone. My father had a very earnest, and very direct and personal, devotion to the Bible. This was apparent in the Ed. Notes that he wrote every week. He did his best in these short columns to lodge simple scriptural teachings in people's minds.

Certainly his favorite theme was trust. This was ironic, since he himself did not manage to reach anything like serenity until the last five years of his life. He was greatly burdened with life and its responsibilities. But he hung onto such texts as "Trust ye in the Lord forever, for in the Lord Jehovah is everlasting strength," and "What time I am afraid, I will trust in thee," and "Casting all your care upon him, for he careth for you." He wrote about this theme perpetually.

He himself studied the Bible most earnestly every day of his life, and in so far as he ever permitted himself to suppose that he might have any "ministry," I think he would have ventured to hope that he might be instrumental in pointing others straight to the pages of the Bible. He felt that Protestant modernism, arising as it did from the twin springs of nineteenth-century evolutionary optimism and of German biblical criticism, had perpetrated a monstrous and tragic fraud on people by robbing them of the Bible. Somehow the churchgoing public had been given to believe that Christianity was mainly a matter of everyone's endeavoring to cultivate amiable thoughts and support progressive social movements. Where was the miraculous? my father wondered. Where was sin? Where were the ancient doctrines of atonement, regeneration, sanctification, and judgment? Where, in this pallid and vitiated religion, was the individual Christian with his Bible and his daily fervent walk with God?

My father never attacked anyone in his writings. But he, along with the early Fundamentalists, tried to keep the ancient faith intact. He found himself, thus, in very odd company at times. Doctrinally he had cast his lot with these Fundamentalists; and the men who stood at the sources of the movement were congenial enough to him for the most part, since they shared not only his unabashedly traditional faith, but also his sensibilities. They, like him, had come from the old universities. Many of them were Presbyterians, as he was. Many were Philadelphians. As such, they were civilized men.

But the gospel, when it is preached in all of its apostolic simplicity, will not stay inside any such circle. It has a peculiar appeal to all sorts and conditions of men. My father found himself thrust into circles that he might not have picked had he been consulting only his own inclinations and frame of mind. But never once did I hear from him so much as a hint of anything that might at all be called condescension. He would not have known how to patronize. It certainly never occurred to him to reserve the smallest corner of his imagination as a kind of shrine where he could pay secret homage to his lineage, his breeding, his credentials, his education, or his sensibilities. He had neither the self-consciousness necessary for this sort of thing, nor any interest in it.

On the other hand, he reveled in his family. His mother's name was Trumbull, a name of some dignity in Hartford, and he had an array of Trumbull aunts, like duchesses from Trollope, who would come to our house for family gatherings. One of them actually did look something like the duchess in *Alice in Wonderland.* These aunts were not Fundamentalists, and I was never sure just where they might wish to locate themselves with respect to Christian notions. Their thin legs, pointy shoes with straps across the instep, complicated tangles of necklaces and pince-nez chains, soft-piled grey hair, freckled and blue-veined hands, and rings that slipped around under their fingers so that the stones were always underneath: this was what my father had come from, in my eyes. The Trumbulls were violent, imperial, and droll. They were all great raconteurs, exulting in scandalous exaggeration. My great-aunts had high, rich voices with that intermittent small, scrapy break in them that bespoke, I thought, a breeding fathomless in its impeccability and an aristocracy almost olympian in its serenity.

My father had inherited the drollery of these Trumbulls. It

made its appearance in him, not so much in wild exaggerations as in a wry, dry, understated wit that was at its best when he was telling of his own misfortunes. Once when he was bent over a small suitcase that had very tightly sprung clasps that flew up as you undid them, he exclaimed, with feigned vexation, "Say! Every time I open this thing I flay my thumb knuckles!" He knew that there was nothing in the world that made us all laugh more than the apt use of a word. Another time he moved away from a roaring fire in the fireplace with, "Say! This fire has nearly burned the nap off my suit!" Once, late at night, when my mother objected to a small pile of clothes that he had placed in a corner of their bedroom, to be put in the hamper next morning, he countered with, "Why? Do you think some lethal miasma will arise from them all night long?"

He was a pied piper with children. He had a small repertoire of tricks that he could do, and would often collect around himself a semicircle of rapt grandchildren or neighborhood tots, and regale them. He could "swallow" his penknife, for example, then pull it out of a child's ear. Or he would create an appalling little face using a handkerchief, his fist, and two matches for the eyes. He had worked up a miniature rhythmic tattoo by snapping his fingers and popping his open left hand against the hollow of his loosely clenched right hand. This always kept children mesmerized, and you would see them going away fiddling with their fingers, trying to get the effect. He had also composed a four-line tune which he named "The Burlington County March," which he would play on the piano for anyone's delectation. He would get any assembled children to march in a file around the pattern at the edge of our living room rug, in time to his tune.

But all the self-assuredness of the Trumbulls had been left out of his makeup. This is difficult to account for, if we are thinking of heredity alone, since his father, on the other side, was an immensely strong, serene, apparently uncomplicated man. I knew him only when he was an old man; but he seems to me to have been the most perfectly civilized man I have ever known. The whole world of New England and Philadelphia stood before you when you met him; and yet he was without the slightest trace of self-importance. His laugh was hearty without being the bore that so many hearty laughs are, and he was at home and delighted, apparently in almost any company. His attitude towards small children was completely natural. He did not try to gear himself down to some supposed children's level of things for you: he took you into his world, quite without affectation.

Next to this family heritage, I think it was my father's reading which often lay between him and the company of religious allies among whom he found himself. Besides the general fare of English literature which he had had to read as a young man at Haverford College and the University of Pennsylvania, there were a few minor writers whose prose seemed to appeal to him. I remember hearing him talk about Ambrose Bierce and Joseph C. Lincoln. He also liked James Whitcomb Riley, and would quote "When the frost is on the punkin" from time to time, and "The Raggedy Man," who "had two eyes like two fried eggs, and a nose like a Bartlett pear."

But his real home when it came to books was to be found among such works as Philip Doddridge's *The Rise and Progress of Religion in the Soul,* William Law's *A Serious Call to a Devout and Holy Life,* Jeremy Taylor's *The Rule and Exercises of Holy Living,* and Richard Baxter's *A Call to the Unconverted* and *The Saints' Everlasting Rest.* These, with Bunyan, Luther on Galatians, and John Wesley's *Journals,* were the works he mentioned, and read, most often. The Bible commentaries he used were Matthew Henry and Conybeare and Howsen.

Hence, he was very far from being at ease with the somewhat tatterdemalion set of sensibilities that eventually came to accompany Fundamentalist piety. Chattiness and rickety syntax in public prayers; pert or sentimental expressions of devotion in hymnody, or worse, rhapsodic protestations of self-consecration to God; flashy showmanship in evangelistic meetings; and the apparently *ad hoc* nature of a great deal of what went on in church services: these filled my father with anguished embarrassment.

He was looked to as a leader, however, and hence often found himself on the platform as a speaker. I can remember looking at him from the congregation at meetings and conferences, sitting on the platform as he was being introduced. He would endure the introduction, and, when the moment came, uncoil his lean, six-foot-three-inch frame and approach the podium. To my young eyes, he seemed almost paralyzed by awkwardness at these moments. But looking back now over the distance of almost fifty years, I would say that what one saw was the reticence and self-deprecation of a man who wished most earnestly to say something true, clear, and helpful to a miscellaneous gathering of people who represented all sorts of backgrounds.

It would be a great mistake to think of anything highbrow in connection with my father. Whatever his family and education and taste meant in shaping his approach to things, it had not made a highbrow of him. This will have been clear to readers already with my mention of James Whitcomb Riley. The only "classical" music which I ever heard him whistle was a piece called "Liebesfreude" which he knew from a recording of Fritz Kreisler.

His entirely unsophisticated simplicity showed itself in his taste in hymns. He loved, first of all, the hymns of Wesley, Cowper, and Newton. He would sing "When All Thy Mercies, O My God," while he was shaving at the mirror in the morning, and the hymn which he usually whistled was "There Is a Fountain Filled with Blood." He would often stop at the piano for a few minutes and play two or three hymns. Usually these were the Gospel hymns, "Praise Him, Praise Him, Jesus Our Blessed Redeemer," and "All the Way My Saviour Leads Me," and "I Will Sing the Wondrous Story," and "Sing Them Over Again to Me, Wonderful Words of Life." When we were small, he would sing to us "I Think When I Read That Sweet Story of Old," and "Jesus, Keep Me Near the Cross." Somewhere in mid-life he discovered, in a Plymouth Brethren hymnal, the Swedish hymn, "If I Gained the World but Lost the Saviour," and this immediately became a favorite of his, both its words and its tune.

His happiness and contentment at home with my mother and the six of us children was such that he really did not want anything else out of life at all. Once in a while he indulged patently fanciful notions of trout fishing in New Zealand "someday." But otherwise he wanted to be at home. He liked the idea that we were a well-traveled family, but he did not actually like traveling, especially if this meant going away alone for a speaking engagement. He was on the board of trustees of a college in Illinois, and he enjoyed his once- or twice-yearly trips from Philadelphia to Chicago in a roomette on the Broadway Limited. The isolation and quiet for reading, and the rocking of the train as it shot through Pennsylvania in the darkness, pleased him. He had very much loved the transatlantic crossings he had made on shipboard and was vastly impressed with his first flight, and even more so with his first jet flight. These feats of technology and power roused the same sort of admiration in him as did military parades. But he had no hankering for tourism and sightseeing.

His love for my mother was almost schoolboyish. I saw him vexed, impatient, or angry with many things over the years; but never once did I ever see him treat my mother, or speak to her, with anything other than tenderness and affection. He would come into the kitchen while she was standing at the stove or the sink and put his arms around her from behind. He admitted to us that he liked the songs "Roamin' in the Gloamin'" and "The Sunshine of Your Smile," because they took him back to the days of their courtship.

Next to the Bible, his love for my mother, and his delight in his children, his greatest consolation in life was an orderly schedule. He got up at 5:00 A.M. daily for forty-five years, as far as I know, and spent the first hour of the day in his study, reading his Bible and praying. In cold weather he always wore a heavy woolen wrapper, and if you saw him before he had come back upstairs to shave, wash, and dress, two things struck you. First, his hair, which he parted in the middle and kept very short, was ungroomed. He always massaged Wildroot into it and brushed it back with *two* hairbrushes. This gave him a whole different look from the dry, early-morning look. Second, he had not yet put in his glass eye for the day, so his left eye, which stayed shut when the eye was not in it, looked flat. It was not as odd as an outsider might think, and he never made anything of the rather bizarre business of taking out the eye at night and putting it in again in the morning. It was only the work of a few seconds, and his children, growing up with it, hardly thought about it either. He had lost the eye in a Fourth of July accident when he was twelve. The artificial eye was cup-shaped, not spherical, and he kept it in a small leather box lined with chamois. When it was in the socket you could not tell one eye from the other.

His daily schedule followed, without stress, from this early start, timed down to the minute. Like his clear prose, his clean desk top, his neatly arrayed fishing equipment, the military spectacles that thrilled him, the wholesome simplicity of The Colonnade, the safety of his roomette on The Broadway Limited, the well-laid-out streets of Moorestown, and his direct, biblical faith tutored by a moderate Philadelphia Presbyterianism, an exact daily routine bespoke a well-ordered world. Short of heaven itself, which he longed for quite unashamedly, this is what he prized more than anything else, as the setting for life—his own life and the lives of his wife, his children, his friends, and indeed of all men.

EIGHTEEN

Blaise Pascal

by Robert E. Coleman

IN THE YEAR OF GRACE, 1654,

On Monday, 23d of November, Feast of St. Clement, Pope and Martyr, and of others in the Martyrology,

Vigil of St. Chrysogonus, Martyr, and others, From about half past ten in the evening until about half past twelve,

FIRE

God of Abraham, God of Isaac, God of Jacob,
not of the philosophers and scholars.
Certitude. Certitude. Feeling. Joy. Peace.
God of Jesus Christ.
"Thy God shall be my God."
Forgetfulness of the world and of everything, except God.
He is to be found only by the ways taught in the Gospel.
Greatness of the Human Soul.
"Righteous Father, the world hath not known Thee, but I have known Thee."
Joy, joy, joy, tears of joy.

I have separated myself from Him.
"My God, wilt Thou leave me?"
Let me not be separated from Him eternally.
"This is the eternal life, that they might know Thee, the only true God, and the one whom Thou hast sent, Jesus Christ."
Jesus Christ.

JESUS CHRIST

I have separated myself from Him: I have fled from Him, denied Him, crucified Him.
Let me never be separated from Him.
We keep hold of Him only by the ways taught in the Gospel.
Renunciation, total and sweet.
Total submission to Jesus Christ and to my director.
Eternally in joy for a day's training on earth. Amen.*

Seldom has one expressed with such precision and feeling his confrontation with Jesus Christ. The terse stenographic account was written on a parchment, at the top of which was etched a cross surrounded by rays. As a constant reminder of this experience, the paper was sewed by the author inside the lining of his coat. One can imagine him during times of temptation and suffering slipping his hand over the hidden treasure and pressing its hallowed message to his heart. Not until after his death was the document discovered. The reality which it describes changed the life of Blaise Pascal, universally acclaimed scientist, inventor, psychologist, philosopher, and Christian apologist; by any comparison one of the greatest thinkers of all time.

I was introduced to him while a graduate student at Princeton Theological Seminary. Dr. Emile Cailliet, a professor whose academic renown had not diminished his fervency of spirit, spoke so endearingly of Pascal that I was constrained to look into his life

---

* Blaise Pascal "Memorial" in *Great Shorter Works of Pascal*, translated by Emile Cailliet and John C. Blankenage (Philadelphia: Westminster Press, 1948), p. 117.

and work. The more I read, and the more deeply I read, the more I was captivated and challenged by his thought.

What insight to the reality of God! Here was a man without rival in intellectual attainment, yet possessing childlike simplicity of faith. I realized that I could learn a great deal from him. During these intervening years, the writings of Pascal have been close by my side.

He was born in Clermont-Ferrand in France, June 19, 1623. His mother, a godly woman, died when he was three, leaving his father to care for Blaise and his two sisters. The elder Pascal, Etienne, was a man of genuine devotion and ability, and he eagerly sought to stimulate the minds of his children. In order to improve their educational opportunities, he gave up his post as magistrate, and moved with his family to Paris in 1631.

The extraordinary gifts of the son began to appear very early. By the time he was twelve, having mastered Greek and Latin, his compulsive desire to find things out for himself led him to work through, on his own, the thirty-two geometric theorems of Euclid's *First Book*. When this almost unbelievable feat became known, he was invited to accompany his father to the weekly meetings of the Academy of Science, where he mingled freely with the greatest intellectuals of his day. Before he was sixteen, the young genius had unraveled the mystery of conic sections, composing a treatise which anticipated projective geometry. Thereafter, he discovered the famous lemma in mathematics which came to be called the Pascal theorem. Just as an aside, while still in his teens, he invented and constructed the first calculating machine, showing himself as skilled in applied science as in pure thought.

The Pascal household observed a nominal Catholic religious practice until 1646 when they came into contact with Jansenism. This group within the Roman Church, somewhat comparable to Protestant Puritans, stressed divine grace and election in redemption. Blaise embraced their teaching, and soon won over to his new faith the other members of his family. From this time on, he became a diligent student of the Bible and generally tried to follow a life of personal piety.

His resolution to "live only for God" did not keep him from continuing his scientific research. In the course of his experiments, he demonstrated the fact of atmospheric pressure, the vacuum, and the weight of air. These findings, published in 1647, led to his investigation of the equilibrium of liquids, establishing the principle of hydrodynamics. From these discoveries came the barometer, the vacuum pump, the air compressor, the syringe, and the hydraulic press. Not stopping with these practical applications of his thinking, he later explored the concept of universal, physical relativity and developed the theory of probability, from which emerged infinitesimal calculus. During this time, he advanced the axiom which was to become the guiding dictum of modern science—"that experiments are the true masters to follow in physics."

Interestingly, this passion for objective proof comes through in his treatment of theology, not in the sense that religious truth can be demonstrated through the human sciences or metaphysical reasoning, for it is of a supernatural order. But in its own order of knowledge, spiritual reality can be validated through the testimony of scripture, which Pascal believed to be "the Word of God infallible in the facts which it records." In this position, he came to reject the speculative approach of scholasticism and maintained that the Bible alone is our basis for the Christian faith. He recognized the importance of church councils and tradition in defining the proper interpretation, but insisted that no authoritative view can be contrary to the Bible. For, as he said, "He who will give the meaning of Scripture, and does not take it from Scripture, is an enemy of Scripture."

Pascal's father died in 1651, and soon afterward, his younger sister, Jacqueline, entered the Jansenist convent at Port-Royal (his older sister had married earlier). Bereft of family companionship, Blaise unwisely turned to some of his aristocratic friends to fill the void, and with them sought diversion in the pleasures of fashionable society. After a year or more of this attachment to the "world," he was left disillusioned and became more convinced than ever of the vanity of man. Neither the delight of idle amusement nor the renown of great achievement could satisfy his yearning soul. He was brought to the point of despair.

It was in this state that he was reading the scripture on that eventful evening in 1654 when God appeared to him in Fire. He had opened to the seventeenth chapter of John's Gospel where Jesus is seen in prayer before giving himself over to be crucified. As he read, suddenly the room was filled with the flaming Presence of him who is perfect holiness and love. The Word written in the Book was confirmed by the Word present in the Son. Here was certitude. Before such experiential Truth he could only bow in "total submission to Jesus Christ."

After this experience, called his "second conversion," the broken and penitent scholar saw even more clearly the futility of living for self. He renounced every resource of the fleshly nature and gave himself completely to the message of scripture. All his worldly endeavors were abandoned. He sold his coach and horses, his fine furniture and silverware, and gave the money to the poor. Even his extensive library was discarded, keeping only a few devotional books and his Bible. The glory of his Savior became his only concern. Never again would he ever sign his name to his own writings, nor let his name be mentioned in praise. Taking the guise of Monsieur de Mons, he left Paris, and went to live among the Jansenist "solitaries" of Port-Royal.

The views of this holiness sect were not popular in the more easy-going establishment of the Sorbonne and among the Jesuits. Eventually the pope was persuaded to condemn them. Amid the controversy, Pascal came forth to defend their cause. His vindication, appearing as *The Provincial Letters,* began in 1656 and established him as the most articulate polemist of his generation. The dialogues cast the whole dispute in simple logic, showing by withering irony and wit that the real issue was one of morality, not dogma. He did not deprecate official church doctrine, but decried the way clever maneuvering with words was being used to subvert the intent of scripture. Such casuistry he saw as a form of self-esteem, which therefore leads to concupiscence or creature love. To Pascal, the love of God alone motivates the body of Christ, and this love is evidenced by obedience to his word.

His *Letters* suddenly broke off in 1657, for his attention had focused on the larger task of constructing an *Apology for the Christian Religion.* It was designed to be a demonstration of Christianity, setting forth reasons which would convince the unbeliever. He planned to spend ten years on the work, but as it turned out, due to his early death there was time only to prepare his notes for the final draft. Ranging from a few cryptic words to short essays, the "thoughts" were collected by the Port-Royalists and published as the *Pensees* eight years after his death. The more than seven hundred fragments have come to be regarded as his greatest masterpiece.

Beginning with the human dilemma, he draws a picture of natural man's misery on the one hand and his glory on the other. There would be no meaning nor purpose in life apart from God's disclosure of his word. Indifference of the skeptic is overcome by means of a "wager," based on his law of probability, whereby everyone is confronted with an all-encompassing choice. God is or is not. One who responds in the affirmative has everything to gain and nothing to lose; whereas the person who denies God has nothing permanently to gain and everything to lose. Though it is self-interest which provokes the reasonable decision, still it causes one to move from a habit of disbelief and invites a new direction toward truth.

God's saving revelation, however, comes only through divine illumination in the believer's soul. "It is the heart which experiences God, and not the reason. This, then, is faith: God felt by the heart." By this Pascal does not mean mystical emotion, but rather, an intuitive love for God himself. Those awakened by grace will have this perception. Moreover, God has so constructed the universe that he will be found by those who search for him with all their heart.

The focus is Jesus Christ, the object of all scripture, for he alone incarnated the Infinite Word in our human estate. In his Person is revealed both the Truth of God and the truth of man. Yet only persons who renounce self-love will know what this means.

Herein is exposed the error of those who do not find the Truth. A genuine Christian does not squabble over signs; he humbly bows in adoration before his majestic Lord.

A hurried reader, sitting in a cushioned rocker, with a box of chocolates at hand, probably will not derive much from the writings of Pascal. But the serious reader who pauses for reflection will be rewarded in mind and spirit. The following gems of thought, excerpted from the *Pensees*, signal the strata of riches to be discovered:

> *The Mystery of Jesus*—Jesus suffers in His passions the torments which men inflict upon Him, but in His agony He suffers the torments which He inflicts upon Himself. This is a suffering from no human, but an almighty hand, for He must be almighty to bear it.
>
> Jesus seeks some comfort at least in His three dearest friends, and they are asleep. He prays them to bear with Him for a little, and they leave Him with entire indifference, having so little compassion that it could not prevent their sleeping even for a moment. And thus Jesus was left alone to the wrath of God.
>
> Jesus is alone on the earth, without any one not only to feel and share His suffering, but even to know of it; He and Heaven were alone in that knowledge.
>
> Jesus is in a garden, not of delight as the first Adam, where he lost himself and the whole human race, but in one of agony, where He saved Himself and the whole human race.
>
> He suffers this affliction and this desertion in the horror of night.
>
> I believe that Jesus never complained but on this single occasion; but then He complained as if he could no longer bear His extreme suffering. "My soul is sorrowful, even unto death."
>
> Jesus seeks companionship and comfort from men. This is the sole occasion in all His life, as it seems to me. But He receives it not, for His disciples are asleep.
>
> Jesus will be in agony even to the end of the world. We must not sleep during that time. (Article 552)

> Do little things as though they were great, because of the majesty of Jesus Christ who does them in us, and who lives our life; and do the greatest things as though they were little and easy, because of His omnipotence. (Article 552)
>
> It seems to me that Jesus Christ only allowed His wounds to be touched after His resurrection. We must unite ourselves only to His sufferings.
>
> At the Last Supper He gave Himself in communion as about to die; to the disciples at Emmaus as risen from the dead; to the whole Church as ascended into Heaven. (Article 553)
>
> Jesus Christ came to blind those who saw clearly, and to give sight to the blind; to heal the sick, and leave the healthy to die; to call to repentance, and to justify sinners, and to leave the righteous in their sins; to fill the needy, and leave the rich empty. (Article 770)
>
> So I hold out my arms to my *Redeemer*, who, having been foretold for four thousand years, has come to suffer and to die for me on earth, at the time and under all the circumstances foretold. By His grace, I await death in peace, in the hope of being eternally united to Him. Yet I live with joy, whether in the prosperity which it pleases Him to bestow upon me, or in the adversity which He sends for my good, and which He has taught me to bear by His example. (Article 736)

He was still working on his *Pensees* when urged by some friends to solve a geometric problem which had baffled mathematicians for centuries. Thinking that it would give his Christian apology a greater hearing, and also to distract his mind from an incessant headache, he analyzed the nature of cycloid curves. His findings, published in 1658, laid the foundations for differential and integral calculus. In another moment of inventive genius, noticing the numbers of people walking long distances in Paris, he designed an omnibus carriage for public transport, which brought into being the world's first bus service. However, such scientific exploits were mere pastimes. His attention now was fixed on something far more profound. So engrossed was he in thought on spiritual things that he wrote in 1660, "I would not take two steps for geometry . . . I am engaged in studies so remote from such preoccupations that I can scarcely remember that they actually exist."

But the terrible pain which had punished him through most of his life grew worse, and finally he was unable to continue any mental exercise. One of the last things he wrote was "A Prayer Asking God to Use His Illness for a Good End." The following excerpt beautifully reflects his trust in the perfect will of God.

> Lord, whose Spirit is so good and so gentle, and who is so compassionate that not only all prosperity but even all afflictions that come to thine elect are the results of Thy compassion . . .
>
> Grant that I may conform to Thy will, just as I am, that, being sick as I am, I may glorify Thee in my sufferings. Without them I cannot attain to glory; without them, my Saviour, even Thou wouldst not have risen to glory. By the marks of Thy sufferings Thou dost recognize those who are Thy disciples. Therefore recognize me as Thy disciple by the ills that I endure, in my body and in my spirit, for the offenses which I have committed. And since nothing is pleasing to God unless it be offered to Him by Thee, unite my will with Thine and my sufferings with those that Thou hast suffered; grant that mine may become Thine. Unite me with Thee; fill me with Thee and Thy Holy Spirit. Enter into my heart and into my soul, there to bear my sufferings and to continue in me that part of the suffering of Thy passion which yet remains to be endured, which Thou art yet completing in Thy members until the perfect consummation of Thy Body, so that it shall no longer be I who live and suffer but that it shall be Thou who dost live and suffer in me, O my Saviour. And thus, having some small part in Thy suffering, I shall be filled wholly by Thee with the glory which it has brought to Thee, the glory in which Thou dost dwell with the

Father and the Holy Spirit, forever and ever. Amen. (*Great Shorter Works of Pascal,* pp. 220-28)

On August 19, 1662, his intense bodily suffering ended. The awe-inspiring saint, with faith "simple as a child," died at the home of his brother-in-law, having turned his house over to an impoverished family. He was thirty-nine years old.

Few men have ever lived who thought more deeply upon the nature of reality. "At an age when others have hardly begun to see the light, he had completed the cycle of human knowledge," and seeing its emptiness, directed his remaining energies to know him in whom is hidden all the wisdom and the glory of God. Here Pascal found the answer to his heart's desire, and in that assurance, he discovered the Truth that sets men free—the Truth that every man can know by faith in Jesus Christ.

NINETEEN

T. Stanley Soltau

by Charles Turner

SPRING, 1914. PRINCETON THEOLOGICAL SEMINARY. Two young men are walking toward Miller Chapel. The taller—the red-haired one—is Stanley Soltau, who will be graduating soon. His companion is Arch Campbell, his future brother-in-law, a junior. They are late for the Tuesday night meeting, but their pace is unhurried as they round the stately privet hedge near the entrance. The days are noticeably longer now, and it's as though the lingering sunlight has beguiled them into thinking they have plenty of time.

Actually, the season has little to do with it except in a cumulative way. Neither student has missed a Tuesday night meeting since the beginning of the academic year, and Stanley is wondering what harm it would do if they were to sit this one out.

Before they reach the steps, he slows to a halt. He turns to the other and says, "What say, Arch, let's skip the meeting tonight and go to my room and talk."

"It's all right by me," Arch replies.

Stanley gives the matter a second thought. He knows that he should set a good example for the younger student. Besides, it would be a shame to mar their record at this point. He says, "Perhaps we ought to go on, after all, but let's sit in the back row so we can skip out if we like."

The Tuesday night meetings are, as the Princeton Seminary Bulletin states, "for devotion and for instruction in general lines of Christian activity." These assemblies are in addition to the regular evening prayers, which every student is expected to attend. Because this is the first Tuesday in the month, the program will be under the direction of professors rather than students, and there will be a speaker on missions and a "concert of prayer" for missions around the world.

Although Stanley's interest on this occasion is less than stalwart, he is not indifferent to the subject of missions. He was born into a missionary family and for most of his life he has believed that God will give him the same vocation. Indeed, it is for this kind of endeavor that he has been preparing himself during these years at seminary. A mission field is out there waiting for him—of that he feels certain. Which mission field? Well, Stanley is curious about the geography of his future, but he has stopped sniffing around in every direction trying to precede the Lord. He is confident that he will know the appointed region at the right time. If there is a question that nags him about any aspect of missionary life ahead, it is this: is it fair to ask Molly, his fiancee, to abandon her family and all the familiar furnishings of her culture to follow him into a strange realm where circumstances are uncertain and the outlook promises one strenuous adjustment after another? This, it occurs to him as he and her brother enter the chapel, is what he subconsciously has been wanting to talk about.

The meeting has begun. The crowd is thicker than usual. With everyone standing for the hymn, it is difficult to tell exactly where the empty seats are. The back row is full, they discover, and so is the next row. By the time they find two seats near the aisle, they are deep in the tide of male voices and closer to the front than they are to the doors. Professor B.B. Warfield, who is to introduce the speaker, sends a nod, almost a smile, to absolve their tardiness.

Stanley realizes that he and Arch are speared to the pew. There will be no vanishing act tonight.

What he does not realize—not at first—is that the perspectives of his life are lined up and he now has moved into a position where, captive, he will see his past and his future come together with precision, to a focus that will define each more distinctly than ever before.

The speaker is Dr. George Shannon McCune.

The mission of concern is Korea, where Dr. McCune is headmaster of a Christian academy.

At least two listeners *hear*, and one of them is Stanley Soltau.

He was to look back on that evening as an example of man's footsteps and determinations being swallowed up in the mystery of God's sovereignty, for it was then and there that "the land of the morning calm" reached out and claimed him.

In those days, thirty-five years before the resounding Korean conflict of the mid-century, that country was little known in the Western world except as Japan's booty from the Russo-Japanese War of 1904-5. Stanley Soltau knew its location on the globe, could put his finger to it, even knew of the Presbyterian mission there, and yet he usually thought of Korea in vague and subtractive terms: it was neither China nor Japan, it somehow was "neither this nor that." Certainly, before that evening, he had never felt a pull in its direction. Perhaps that was because it was an established field and he had longed for the challenge and romance of uncharted territory. But on the other hand, perhaps it was due to the fact that Korea, as a ministry, had not received the wide journalistic coverage that some countries had, and he simply had overlooked its invitation. Whatever the reason for his delayed interest, it was of the past and did not lessen his enthusiasm for the call. His recognition of divine guidance was so strong that he knew, even before Molly responded to his letter about it, that she would perceive it too, and that she would be at his side when he journeyed to the Orient. His reservations about subjecting her to hardships lost out to his acknowledged need of a helpmeet and his vision of her as the best missionary wife ever.

Stanley Soltau was born in 1890, on the island of Tasmania, forty minutes after the arrival of his brother, David Livingston

Soltau. Their parents, who had not suspected that twins were in store, had hoped for a boy and already had chosen the name of the famous missionary-explorer. When the surprising gift of the second boy (their eighth child and sixth son) was delivered, they named him Theodore Stanley—Theodore for its meaning ("gift of God") and, appropriately enough, Stanley for the newspaper correspondent who followed Livingston to Africa. David was called David, but Theodore was known by his middle name throughout his life.

Another historic name linked with the Soltau twins is that of J. Hudson Taylor, founder of the China Inland Mission, who, on a visit to Tasmania when they were small, laid his hands upon them in a dedication service. His life intersected theirs again when they were ten years old and living in England, on which occasion he offered his hands once again, this time in a firm and memorable clasp as he inquired about their Christian growth and bequeathed to them as much of himself as he could.

The Soltau family came from a Plymouth Brethren tradition. The twins' paternal grandfather, Henry William Soltau, born in Plymouth in 1805, gave up his law practice to devote himself to the study of scripture. Both his scholarship and his spirituality are reflected in his writings, which are considered classics and are in print today: *The Holy Vessels and Furniture of the Tabernacle* and *The Tabernacle, the Priesthood and the Offerings* (Kregel Publications). Adding to that heritage was the visible ministry and example of their parents, George and Grace. It would seem merely a thematic progression that the Soltau twins, each in his own time, each in his own calling, became servants of the Word.

After accompanying their parents to the United States on a speaking tour in 1904, they stayed on and received schooling at Morningside Academy in Sioux City and at Northwestern University. Summers and long holidays were spent in Seattle, their family's "headquarters" in the States. Not the least of the attractions in that city of hills overlooking Puget Sound was a girl named Mary Campbell. David and Stanley became close friends of her brothers and were welcomed on a regular basis into the

Presbyterian household of her parents. The hospitality of Joseph and Anna Campbell was so unfeigned and easygoing that they had sanctioned a veritable dorm in the upper reaches of their weathered gray manor on 88th Street.

Mary—who was to be Molly in Stanley's life—was brown-haired and hazel-eyed, as statuesque as a Gibson Girl, with the clean planes of bone structure that cinematographers look for. She was, in the flesh, the fair and winsome heroine of the romantic novels of the era. Her own love story began one day when, in the flurry of a girlish emotion, she sailed into the arms of the nearest male, whom she took to be her brother. The house being rampant with males, and the blur of her tears having misdirected her, she found herself in the appreciative embrace of Stanley. In years to come, when her daughters were old enough to delight in hearing of it, she would relate the incident many times, never remembering exactly what had caused the tears, but always remembering the warmth and the special stillness she had drawn from her comforter.

Stanley was rather shy with girls, according to his own reports, and he feared that Mary's eyes were only for his twin: David was an extravert and a charmer. But her pleasant mistake emboldened Stanley to court her outright. And her seemingly chance gravitation toward the shy one was prophetic. It was to him that her heart turned later, sure of its compass and with promises to last a lifetime.

As the younger twin prevailed in that situation, so must he prevail in this narrative. David Soltau's life was interesting in its own right (he went to Korea too, taught physics there, and after returning to the States, became an Episcopal priest and taught physics at Redlands University), but his story is for someone else to tell. David Soltau I did not know. Stanley Soltau I knew and respected and liked. He was my pastor in his later years. He himself was the inspiration for this portrait I'm attempting, and he himself was the basic source of my research.

I advanced many questions in the hope of gathering material for a full biography. He had kept no journals, no copies of his correspondence, and even though his memory was a large and colorful canvas, I was not able to extract from its richness the kind of order and detail necessary for the comprehensive treatment I had in mind. But I did glean enough to encourage me to put him on paper in one shorter form or another, someday. Now is someday, and it has occurred to me that perhaps I can capture Stanley Soltau's likeness and tell of his life faithfully in a sequence of brief glimpses, compressing his years for their essence, while I might have lost him—or, worse, misrepresented him—in a longer work.

Through the influence of the Campbell family, Stanley adopted a Presbyterian view of scripture, especially in regard to its emphasis on God's covenant promises. Perhaps his personality also played a part in the shift, his natural reserve tending toward a more precise approach to worship than the one in which he had grown up. A result of this development was his choice of Princeton Theological Seminary for further education. He financed his tuition himself by summer work as a surveyor in the State of Washington.

After graduation in May 1914, he was ordained to the ministry and commissioned by the Board of Foreign Missions of the Presbyterian Church in the U.S.A. He and Molly married in August, and in October they set out on the long voyage toward their first Korean winter. On the horizon, knowable even before the days were fulfilled, was the bleakness of Christmas in a strange land. Stanley was surprised to find that he suffered as keenly as Molly the loss of all that was familiar. Despite a warm welcome from fellow missionaries and Korean Christians, the loneliness for family and friends was like a tunnel through which they had to pass, and in which they had to reaffirm their belief that God truly had called them to this remote post.

The sense of strangeness, common to aliens in every culture, persisted after the doubts had lifted. It was intensified of course by the realization that *they*, Stanley and Molly, were the curiosities. Westerners seldom were seen in rural districts, and often the couple found that paper doors and windows had been perforated neatly by wet fingers for the convenience of inquisitive eyes.

Sometimes the discovery was immediate: they would think they were enjoying the privacy of a closed shelter, and then, hearing themselves discussed in detail just beyond the thin barrier, they would know they were being observed with amusement.

Even more disconcerting was the laughter which surfaced from time to time when he was preaching. An early incident involved a boy who broke into snickering when Stanley happened to glance at him in the middle of a sermon. Stanley supposed that an incorrect verb ending had prompted the glee. His next glance brought forth the same effect. I am making one blunder after another, he thought. He concluded the sermon quickly and went on to the thoroughly practiced grammar of the Lord's Supper. But his language teacher was present and informed him that mistakes had been fewer than usual, that the eruptions had been caused by matters more difficult to remedy. The teacher was Korean and two years his junior, and it was an awkward moment as Oriental courtesy gave way to brotherly candor. "You see, Pastor, you are too tall and your hair is such a strange color and your nose is so big and your eyes are so deeply set in your head. This boy is a country boy, not used to seeing foreigners. He could not keep from laughing."

Bouts of homesickness prepared Stanley for counseling prospective missionaries later on. They would feel disconnected at times, he would warn them. They would, in a small measure, enter into the loneliness of Christ, whose ministry on earth he saw as the basic foreign mission experience. It was always a case of having been amputated from one's natural environment. "But," he would tell them, "it is in this loneliness that the companionship of the Lord becomes a blessed reality."

He spent three years in Syenchun, in the north, a railroad town of mud-walled houses thatched with rice straw. Nestled against hills known as the Dragon's Back, and entrenched in ancient superstition deeply enough to claim the dragon as the town guardian, Syenchun was nonetheless a Christian center boasting two churches, two academies (one for girls, one for boys) and a well-staffed hospital. Stanley's main assignment there was language study, but his duties included teaching English and Bible to some of the classes in the boys' academy. He enjoyed playing tennis with the boys, and since none of them spoke English, the activity with them helped him to learn their language and to get to know them.

Among the students was pleasant-faced Chinsoo Kim, who was working his way through school. Chinsoo's parents, like many other poor Korean farmers, had moved into Manchuria to escape the increasingly severe Japanese taxation. When he learned that the Soltaus would be taking the gospel to the settlements in Manchuria, he felt that he had something in common with them—an interest above the border. His father and mother, both Christians, had placed great importance upon his attending the academy. Only for the sake of his Christian education had he remained in Syenchun. Now that he was separated from them, he turned to Stanley and Molly for the warmth of a family, visiting often in their home, bringing his problems there, seeking advice about his future. He was quite serious about his own faith in Christ, and they grew to love him like a son.

In the years to come, Chinsoo would attend college and seminary and be ordained as a minister himself. During those years of further study, he would continue to visit in their home at every opportunity, wherever that home happened to be. (After Syenchun, they were stationed for a while in other towns in the north, and then for seventeen years in Chungju, in the south.) The Soltau children, as they came along, regarded Chinsoo as an elder brother who was always good for play. He manifested his devotion to the family by leading their newly purchased milk cow the three hundred miles to Chungju when they moved. Later, when he was pastor of the third congregation in Syenchun, he and Stanley would see each other at meetings of the General Assembly. Stanley could count on Chinsoo to be absolutely honest with him when there was friction between the Korean pastors and some of the missionaries. Their "father and son" relationship allowed a communication which helped to solve problems when the Korean pastors rightly insisted that they were grown and could think for themselves.

The mission had been in Korea almost thirty years when Stanley arrived. Its policy from the beginning had been to establish national churches that were self-supporting, self-governing, and self-propagating. In this the pioneers had followed the example of Dr. J.L. Nevious, a Presbyterian missionary in Shantung, China. Most mission boards in that day considered the practice a radical innovation, but Stanley embraced the principle as his personal philosophy of mission, seeing it as apostolic in heritage and therefore the most workable and promising method of planting the gospel in every land. His own observations proved to him that it was the one way to ensure natural, sturdy church growth. It was the opposite of colonialism. The dignity of the nationals remained intact, for essential in the process was a point beyond which the "foreign" missionaries could not lord it over them as benefactors and decision-makers.

While the Soltaus were stationed in the north, Stanley made numerous journeys into Manchuria. These mission projects required that he be separated from Molly and the little ones for weeks at a stretch. Molly's brother Arch, who had accompanied Stanley to that Tuesday night meeting at Princeton Seminary, was now serving under the same mission. He and his family were also stationed in the north, so Molly did not feel quite so alone when Stanley was away. The two families lived together for a while in a house in Kangkai. They called the house Camelot. The Arthurian connotation seemed to fit the mood of the residence, and it was a wonderful place for little cousins to romp.

Often the travel in Manchuria was crude and sluggish. Stanley tackled the mountainous distances by various means—pony, bicycle, sled, raft, dugout, bean boat—and he covered many a mile on foot. Against typhoid, and against the diminutive fish swimming in the pots of cool drinking water at the inns, he was armed with chlorine. Against the powers of darkness, he was armed with the Word. The name of Jesus, so far as Stanley knew, had never been spoken in many of the villages he entered. It was an awesome experience to approach a community like that and think about his privilege and his responsibility. It was also extremely humbling. In those moments he felt an acute kinship with missionaries Paul and Patrick and Brainerd and Livingston and Taylor, and with all of those messengers who before him had announced the gospel in localities where it had never been heard. One of his goals was to help establish churches among the expatriate Korean Christians, but he was always conscious of his duty to evangelize, and he saw the life of Christ take hold and grow in areas where there had been no former witness.

Frequent absences from home continued as a way of life after his move to Chungju. He was in charge of a circuit of churches in the province and had to visit all of them regularly. His itinerary took him through rice fields and pine forests and valleys showered with persimmons and walnuts. The persimmons were giant, dusted with natural sugar after the first frost, and the walnuts were a white variety, paper-shelled and delicious. On homeward jaunts, in season, Stanley would lade himself with selections for the family larder. By the fifth year in Chungju, there were four children: Eleanor, Mary, George, and Addison. The girls were born in the north, the boys in the south. (A third daughter, Theodora, born during a furlough in Seattle, had died of diphtheria at the age of two.) Molly never had to wonder what to do with her time when Stanley was away. In addition to the usual business of motherhood, she undertook the schooling of her brood, and, with the professional guidance of Calvert correspondence courses, saw each of them through the sixth grade at home.

The year 1936 brought difficult times for the Korean church. The Japanese government, attempting to unify the empire in preparation for the war it was planning, decreed that students and faculty of every school in the domain must attend ceremonies at the State Shinto shrines. It was not simply a matter of being present and accounted for: obeisance was to be done before the sun goddess, Amaterasu-Omi-Kami, patron saint of the Japanese army and mythical ancestress of the imperial household. A profound bow was required of all. Mission schools were not exempt—they were in fact a major target. The church was the one institution over which the Japanese had not been able to gain control, and for that reason it was continually an object of suspicion. Shrines were erected near every school, and one by one they sprang up in every village of any size throughout the land. The day was foreseen—and it did come—when all churches and the entire population of Korea were included in the order.

Although the main purpose behind the order might have been to inculcate a spirit of patriotism among the Koreans, who were regarded as Japanese subjects, the move did violence to the religious freedom promised in the constitution. It did especial violence to the hearts of those individuals whose God had said, "Thou shalt have no other gods. . . . Thou shalt not bow down to them." Many Christians were loyal to that first commandment and resolved to suffer persecution rather than comply with the ruling. Others wondered if perhaps they should consider attendance at the shrines a civic duty and the compulsory bow merely a patriotic gesture.

Stanley, as Chairman of the Executive Committee of the Mission, stood against compromise. After his meetings with high officials in the government availed no leniency for Christians, he took the position that it would be better to close the mission schools than to go along with Shinto worship. Worship was what it was, he believed. The separation of State Shinto from Sectarian Shinto had been effected for the appearance of insuring religious freedom, but it actually had cleared the way for forced participation in the State Shinto ceremonies, which now were promoted as nonreligious even though prayers and oblations were essential. The misrepresentations confused very few people who took their Christianity—or their Buddhism, or their Shinto—seriously. Dr. Kato Genchi, of the Imperial University of Tokyo, had stated in his 1935 treatise on Shinto, "I regard National Shinto, embracing both Kokutai Shinto and Jinja Shinto, as a variety of religion—a religion with aspects differing from those of Buddhism and Christianity, but nevertheless always a religion."

Most of the missionaries supported Stanley and voted to close the schools if demands were pressed. This was not an easy policy to adopt. Every session of the mission and every committee meeting was haunted by a member of the police who was present to kill discussion of the shrines. The government, next to its insistence on school participation, was determined that those schools not close, for such action would place a burden on its own education system.

Demands *were* pressed.

A number of schools *did* close.

Persecution began.

The mission board back in the United States approved the mission's decision at first, but later, treating the question primarily as an administrative matter, resorted to a formal silence on the basic issue of idolatry. Among their concerns was the fact that mission properties were at stake. The silence served to uphold the minority who believed that the schools should remain open at any price. Stanley saw the board's attitude, in principle, as a bow toward Amaterasu-Omi-Kami.

The arguments for acquiesence seemed to boil down to these points: God knew the circumstances, knew the hearts of the students and faculty, knew the difference between an act of patriotism and an act of reverence. Surely a token bow to a nonexistent deity in a toylike shrine would not offend the true and reasonable God. Would it not be preferable to snuffing out the means of Christian education which had operated so successfully in the past? The bending would be physical, not spiritual.

Stanley had never thought of himself as holding a full-fledged sacramental view, but he realized that at this juncture he could not divorce that which was physical and visible from that which was spiritual and invisible.

"Not so much as a nod of the head should be offered," he said at the beginning of the troubles, and he never slackened his advice. In his opinion it was no more possible to associate the worship of the sun goddess with the worship of Jesus Christ than it was in the days of Elijah to associate the worship of Baal with the worship of Jehovah.

Within a few years, according to figures released by the police, sixty thousand Korean Christians were arrested and thrown into jail.

In the summer of 1937, in the thick of the controversy and before the tyranny had reached its peak, the Soltaus' furlough came due. The girls were in college in the United States, having finished their high school education at a boarding academy in Pyeng Yang. Stanley and Molly and the boys, traveling north toward Vladivostok, where they would board the Trans-Siberian Express to journey home by way of England, passed through Syenchun, Stanley's first post, the town where Chinsoo Kim was now pastor of a new and growing church. Stanley had sent word to Chinsoo. He knew that the young man would be at the train station to say good-bye. He looked forward to seeing him and wished that they could have a long talk instead of the brief chat the scheduled stop would permit. The shadows under which they were living caused a man to treasure his friendships.

As the train approached the Dragon's Back and the thatched roofs of Syenchun began to multiply, Stanley gave himself to thoughts of those earlier days. It seemed natural at this point to summarize the years since then. It was not so much a matter of taking stock as it was of letting his memories and his previous summations come upon him freely.

One hut in particular caught his attention. It reminded him of the hut to which he had been called on his first itinerating trip. His main duties—the duties for which he had been prepared—were preaching and administering the sacraments of baptism and the Lord's Supper. But when he arrived at the last church on the circuit, he was asked to visit a demon-possessed woman. With trepidation he had followed the concerned Christians who led the way. They explained to him that the woman had watched an exorcist driving evil spirits out of another house, and that while she was standing there, a demon had taken residence in her! Stanley entered the hut and found a shambles. The woman lay on the floor, a revolting sight, muttering unintelligibly. The husband and three small boys stood by helpless. She was bound hand and foot to restrain her from tearing off her clothes and doing further damage to the dwelling. Stanley read portions of scripture. She would quiet only when he spoke the name of Jesus. After prayer, he commanded the demon to come out of her. He had never received ecclesiastical instruction in the procedure, but he did the best he could.

He suggested that she be brought to the mission hospital in Syenchun if there was no improvement. This was done. But little was accomplished except for the benefits of soap and water and the forcing of nourishment. After her release from the hospital, he arranged for a Bible woman to take her in for a while. Other Bible women were asked to come and pray over her. Stanley had a profound respect for the work of those mature women disciplined in scripture and prayer. Confrontation with demons was almost a specialty with them, so often had they seen deliverance. This time the women applied themselves for weeks in an unceasing circle of attendance and supplication, and they all agreed that it was a very stubborn case. Their prayers were finally answered when the woman was taken to church at their insistence. "Where am I?" she had asked during the service, and from then on she was normal. The demon had left silently, without the usual climactic display, its violence defeated at last by the gift of peace. Stanley remembered that the woman and all of her family became believers in Jesus Christ.

It occurred to him that she might have become a Bible woman herself in the years he had been gone from that circuit. It was impossible for him to keep up with every convert on an individual basis. The Korean church was too large for that. One thing was sure: there had been opportunity for her to become a Bible *student*, at least. The reason for the rapid growth of the Korean church, he felt, was the importance placed on Bible study. With week-long Bible conferences held in every district once a year, and with attendance seldom dropping below the total baptized membership, Korean Christians as a whole could be called "Bible people." Although Stanley was pleased to have had a part in that emphasis, he realized that a strong factor in the success of the conferences was the average Korean's studious temperament and desire for knowledge. He knew Korean farmers who walked for more than two hundred miles round-trip to attend the conferences, their daily rice on their backs.

But all the lay scholars and Bible women and delivered personalities receded when he thought about Chinsoo Kim. In Stanley's personal mosaic of Korean Christianity, Chinsoo was always there, prominent, an excellent image to represent all of the national pastors. The fact that he was like family was beside the point, Stanley tried to tell himself. Yet he knew that "a father's heart" was involved.

The train lurched to stillness.

There Chinsoo was now, outside the window, waiting on the platform as Stanley had known he would be. Nearby stood three other Korean pastors of the area, and in a separate cluster stood their wives. Chinsoo had moved out from under the roof and was shielding his eyes. His white cotton took the sun cleanly, telling of a woman's care. He had married, but Stanley and Molly had never met his wife. Stanley matched the other pastors with their wives, and he was disappointed to find that Chinsoo's had not come to the station.

George and Addison, aged thirteen and eleven, disembarked on their own and made straight for Chinsoo. He boxed them warmly, then directed his attention to Stanley and Molly as they stepped down from the train. He placed his hands before him in the attitude of ceremonial courtesy. He bent slightly.

Stanley's right hand went to Chinsoo's shoulder, not disrespectful of the formality but ending it nevertheless. After an exchange of greetings with Chinsoo, Molly turned toward the women who waited for their visit. Stanley talked with the other pastors for a minute or so. Chinsoo, at the first opportunity, pulled him aside for a few words in private. They walked along the platform.

"How is your wife?" Stanley asked. "I'm sorry she didn't come with you."

"She is well. She honors us with her absence, knowing my desire to speak alone with you as long as possible. She is a person small of body, but she has a very large mind."

"Does she make good squash soup?" It seemed to Stanley that good squash soup could accomplish in Syenchun the same wonders that a winning cherry pie could accomplish in Seattle.

Chinsoo said, "Yes—and she makes good kimchee."

Stanley said, "I am relieved to hear that!"

They laughed. The turnip pickle dear to the Korean palate was dear to Stanley's palate too. His love of kimchee was almost a matter of pride with him. It was a food that most missionaries had learned to swallow but not to enjoy.

Time was short. Chinsoo grew serious as they started back. "Father, I fear that hard times are ahead for us in this country. We cannot tell what will happen. We cannot tell what we shall be called upon to face. I shall miss your leadership while you are gone, but your past counsel will sustain us."

"It is the Lord who will sustain you."

"It is you who have spoken his word to me. Pray that I shall be strong in that word when the time comes."

"I shall indeed."

"The stand we are taking against shrine worship—tell me again that we are doing the right thing. Some people are likely to suffer dire consequences. It must not be for less than the honor of Christ. This *is* the issue, is it not?"

Stanley gave it thought once more. He wished he could say something that would alleviate the situation and prevent further suffering. Still, he knew that a weaker position would never be acceptable to Chinsoo or to himself.

"There is no question about it," he said.

The train shook. Departure was imminent. Chinsoo took from his pocket a folded piece of paper and pressed it into Stanley's hand. A chorus of good-byes lifted, but Chinsoo's was the voice that lingered in the ear as Stanley followed Molly and the boys into the car.

When the waving was over and the assemblage at the station had dispersed, one figure remained. Chinsoo was visible until the station itself was lost behind a curve.

Stanley settled against the ungiving seat. He opened the paper. *My dear Father,* the note began, *May the peace of God accompany you and Mother and the boys on your long journey and take you to your home in safety. As for us, I fear that hard days are ahead . . .* Here was repeated most of what Chinsoo had spoken in person. Evidently he had written the thoughts down in case he did not find a chance to express them face to face, yet the tone of the note was stronger, more positive . . . *Of one thing I am certain, you will never feel ashamed of your son. Whatever comes, I am looking to the Lord for his enabling power, so that in all things I shall be faithful to him and shall never deny him or bring disgrace to his name. Your loving son, Chinsoo.*

The Soltaus were unable to return to Korea. Toward the end of their furlough, Stanley was felled by intense pain that turned out to be a large kidney stone. Surgery was required. By the time he had recuperated, the mission horizon was darkening with World War II. The terminology "postponement of plans" had to be dropped, finally, for the more realistic "cancellation of plans." (Arch Campbell and his wife, still in Korea when the Japanese attacked Pearl Harbor, remained on duty for the duration of the war. Stanley's brother David had left Korea years earlier.) Unwelcome though the situation was, the closing of the door simplified the step that soon was necessary for Stanley—necessary if he was to live up to his conscience. His strong convictions against the mission board's continuing laxity of principle regarding Shinto shrine worship led him into ministry outside the denomination.

From 1942 until 1968 he was pastor of First Evangelical Church in Memphis, Tennessee. The congregation was, and is, a mix of believers from various denominations, a flock desirous of biblical preaching. Founded in 1935, the church was in many ways typical of the independent drift which marked that decade and has widened since. And yet, while severed from historic liturgy, Stanley Soltau with his inborn dignity kept the services from wandering off into too surprising informality, the brambles of which seemed to snag and impair any sense of worship in some of the breakaway "fundamental" Bible churches. His stress on the preaching of the Word was balanced by his concern that the service preceding the sermon be objective preparation and not subjective entertainment. His view of Christ as friend and mediator did not lower his view of Christ as the Majestic and Holy One. He did not approach the wonders of Word and sacrament in a casual or cheeky manner. I was a member of that church during his years there, and to me it was as though Stanley Soltau, like the prophet Isaiah, had seen the Lord "high and lifted up."

On Sundays from October to June he appeared in morning dress, evoking the formalities of an era gone, a civilization swept from the earth by two world wars and the inflow of windy new ideas about what was important and what was not. From that previous civilization—let's say, from the world of Princeton Theological Seminary, 1912-14—he had let nothing slide that he could hold stationary. He had held to worthwhile custom as tenaciously as he had held to sound Christian doctrine, although he never would have confused their imports. To those individuals who remembered the vanished proprieties, the figure he cut was nostalgic, no doubt. To those of us who were younger, of a more slipshod generation, he appeared merely *interesting*—and something of a show, which was the last thing he would have wished. But I would take nothing for that show as I screen it in my memory, and I thank him for it. I see the tails of his black cutaway lifting in the November gust as he rounds the back of his Oldsmobile to open the door for his wife. Beneath his homburg he is mostly bald now, but a glint of red is visible in the cropped gray remainder near his ears. I see Molly, coiffed and hatted, come forth serenely at his arm to be spirited up the church steps. Even that brief "film clip" somehow reminds me that *every* Sunday is Easter, and that a meeting with the Risen One is an affair to perk up about.

He spoke an English that was very close to the king's. He said he had learned to speak several languages, but "southern" wasn't one of them. It was true. After twenty-five years in Memphis, his a's, while not as broad as they once had been, held their own to the degree that they still had to be dealt with by the southern ear. Perhaps this added, not fairly, to the unease with which some people viewed him as an authority figure. He *was* an authority figure, and I believe that such an image is the fleshing out of a scriptural principle. I found that some people disliked Stanley Soltau for the very reasons that I liked him. In this day of clamorous individualism, which has touched churches as well as every area of our culture, I still like an authority figure—one who doesn't abuse the image, of course. I still want to hear a servant of the Word say, "Thus saith the Lord," and not "My idea is this, what's yours?"

He preached from the Old Testament often, and deeply, but even there his themes were so Christocentric that the gospel grew richer and richer. His sermons were too long by today's standards and I agree that most of them could have been improved by a tightening of five or ten minutes, but ears that listened all the way received immeasurable content, all of it applicable in a life of faith. His pastoral prayers were lengthy too, never less than ten minutes, but those individuals who stayed awake were carried to the throne of God with confession and praise and an orderly raising of supplications, the list of which encompassed the world. A major theme of his preaching was *Possessing the possessions that are yours in Christ*—and he wasn't talking about Cadillacs and swimming pools. Another recurring theme was *God's presence with his covenant people.* I thank him for unfolding this truth, which for me contains a wealth of New Testament realities, especially when viewed in connection with the Eucharist.

Doctor Soltau, he was called. I sometimes called him Pastor Soltau, or simply Pastor, for I like the meaning *and* the sound of that word, but usually for everyone it was "Doctor Soltau." He was known—and known by that handle—in evangelical circles well beyond the Memphis area. He identified with the conservative Presbyterian movement and, while still with the independent church in Memphis, joined the denomination which became Reformed Presbyterian Church, Evangelical Synod (which, ten years after his death, would lose its name in union with the Presbyterian Church in America). From 1958 until 1972 he was President of World Presbyterian Missions. Other boards on which he served were North Africa Mission, Greater Europe Mission, and Covenant Theological Seminary. He imparted to his congregation a concern for missionary work, and under his ministry the church designated 51 percent of its income to missions. After his retirement from pastoral duties, he renewed his own foreign missionary endeavor by making himself available to various boards. He traveled extensively for three years, on this or that assignment. He had lived to see the jet age and he was very much a part of it. He was "on the go" at eighty, for missions were still on his mind.

The freedom to pack up and leave and trace the curve of the earth again and again was not without its sadness. His Molly, whose regal posture had been destroyed over the years by rheumatoid arthritis, whose hands had frozen into an awkwardness that expressed the pain in which she was imprisoned, died in an automobile accident in 1969. Until his retirement, she had kept up certain appearances and made it a point to stand at his side at the church door after every sermon, but during the next year—her last—she became totally crippled and was dependent on him to assist her every move. He cared for her hour by hour. Had she not been taken from him, he would have been unavailable elsewhere. But he knew that her release was far more blessed than his. He was driving when the accident occurred, and although not at fault, he at first was tormented by the thought that he should have been more cautious at the intersection. On the other hand, when the young man who ran the stop light visited the Soltau house on the day after the death, begging forgiveness, he was met by a Stanley Soltau who was able to console him and pray for him and openly thank God for the fact that Mary Soltau, his own dear Molly, would suffer no more.

He told me that on one of his trips, on a jet to Brazil, he happened to be seated next to a girl of ten or eleven, of Spanish descent and obviously from a Roman Catholic background, who spoke delightful English. Being the Protestant Evangelical missionary that he was, he asked her, after they had chatted for a while, if she knew Jesus Christ as her Lord and Savior. He said that she looked up at him with steady eyes and said, "Indeed I do. I pray to him every day to make me a better servant of his." With that, he said, they settled back and enjoyed fellowship the rest of the flight. This man who would make an issue when the issue involved loyalty to Christ was happy to overlook differences on a personal level if basic Christian oneness was evident. His dividing line and his grounds of communion were clear. He would not have thought of himself as an ecumenist, and surely he wasn't in a loose or compromising way, but perhaps he was an example of the ideal one. His denominator was not low. It was always as high as the position to which Christ had ascended.

Serious as he was about foreign missions, he never made the person who was not a foreign missionary feel that he or she was involved in the lesser glory of God. He was truly gracious to me in this respect. A writer of fiction, in the estimation of some Christians, is not exactly "about his father's business." But Stanley Soltau read my stories and seemed to enjoy them. Now and then he would ask me, "What are you working on?" and I would say something like "Oh, a little trash." His comment would be on this order: "Good trash, I hope." He told me that as he browsed in airport newsstands in search of reading material to pass the miles away he seldom saw anything "fit to read" or that he would wish to "be seen with." He believed there was a definite need for good short stories and novels, and his sanction was a freeing influence in my own work.

His interest in "the indigenous church" as a mission ideal had not waned when his work in Korea ended. He had continued to support the concept at every opportunity. His book on the subject, *Missions at the Crossroads* (Van Kampen Press, 1954), found a receptive readership and its wake spilled over denominational boundaries, contributing to the swell of changing views that would have an impact on post-World War II missions. He was firm in his statement that Christian outreach would never be at the crossroads in regard to message (the gospel would always be "the power of God unto salvation to everyone that believeth"), but he felt that history was pressing down, that it was necessary for boards in general to determine and adopt the best method of completing the task of world evangelization.

I began to comprehend the book's influence one afternoon in 1970 as I talked with Pastor Paul Martens in his study at Trinity Lutheran Church in downtown Memphis. *Missions at the Crossroads* stood shoulder to shoulder with other mission books on a crowded shelf behind his desk. Martens had served from 1939 until 1949 as a missionary in China, and was in his fourteenth year on the mission board of Lutheran Church-Missouri Synod. He told me that Soltau, not long after the book's publication, had been invited to lecture at Concordia Seminary in St. Louis, where his missions perspective had gained esteem. Martens, who had heard him there, said that his appreciation of Soltau's viewpoint was grounded in his own experience in China. "We had been moving along the same lines," he said, "and I fully agreed with his conclusions." Because Martens had been forced out of China by Communist oppression, he saw that a major advantage of autonomous national churches was the fact that, no matter what political surge might evict the foreign missionary, a Christian constituency would remain in the land, active cells in the body of Christ. Those churches which had been allowed to mature on their own would survive and grow, even if underground.

Soltau's post-retirement responsibilities directed him to various corners of the earth, but not back to Korea. He returned there only once—in 1952, while the Communist conflict was still raging. It was not a journey into the past, for the past was no longer there, a new oppression having replaced the former one. But it was good to renew old friendships and learn of Christ's presence in the continuing tumult.

He had not heard from Chinsoo Kim since the day they talked at the station in Syenchun. Now he learned what had transpired. A few weeks after they had said good-bye, Chinsoo was arrested by the Japanese police because of his refusal to do obeisance to the sun goddess. He was sent to Pyongyong and imprisoned there with many other Christians. After a year or two, his wife was permitted to visit him, but he had been tortured so effectively that he failed to recognize her. She never saw him again. A friend of his, passing the jail one winter day, saw a pile of corpses, frozen, stacked like cordwood. He perused them and his gaze fell upon the icy husk of Chinsoo.

I believe that Soltau, from the moment he heard of Chinsoo's sacrifice, carried that death around with him just as he carried the death of Christ around with him. He understood that Chinsoo's death was a part of that greater and salutary death. The one obedience was in union with the other obedience. Chinsoo was Soltau's closest "family connection" to have been called to enter bodily into the drama of redemption and the fellowship of Christ's sufferings. Soltau did not speak of Chinsoo often. When he did tell the story, it was clear that he was not able to tell it as matter-of-factly as he would have liked.

His own death was gentle and quiet, in 1972, only three months after the death of his twin brother. There was no warning. He was at home in Memphis, in his comfortable chair at the end of a summer day. His hands passed from stillness to stillness without dropping the book he was reading.

Were he alive today as I write this, I think I might ask him, "Does it ever burden you that Chinsoo Kim and many other Korean Christians gave up their lives following your counsel when you yourself were freed from the dire situation and from experiencing or even viewing the consequences of your endorsed stand?" No disrespect would edge the question. I would be going for character, sure of the character to be revealed.

I of course do not know what he would answer—what he *would have answered.* I suspect, though, he would have offered a simple and undertoned "yes" and then gone on to explain that the burden was mitigated by the knowledge that Chinsoo and his sacrificed brethren were among the noble army of martyrs, victorious, resident in Light. I suspect he would have implied that the Communion of the Saints was richer because of Chinsoo's witness, although he probably would not have expressed it in those terms. He might have referred me to verses like these: "For as the sufferings of Christ abound in us, so our consolation also aboundeth by Christ" (2 Cor 1:5, KJV). "As ye are partakers of the sufferings of Christ, so shall ye be also of the consolation" (2 Cor 1:7, KJV).

His stand against idolatry never weakened, and he knew that the most dangerous idolatry was in everyday territories of the human heart, far removed from the question of Shinto shrines. Were he alive today, I am confident that once again he would challenge all Christians to identify with Chinsoo Kim and not bow down to a false god, no matter what form that false god might take, no matter what the seeming advantages, whether the worship be coerced from without or enticed from within.

But it's somewhat misleading for me to keep saying, "Were he alive today . . ."

The benefit I continue to draw from his ministry is not purely of remembrance. When in worship I am brought "to the souls of just men made perfect" ("With angels and archangels, and with all the company of heaven, we laud and magnify thy glorious Name, evermore praising thee and saying, Holy, Holy, Holy, Lord God of Hosts"), I sometimes call a silent roll of my strongest connections in that Church Triumphant. High on the list is Stanley Soltau.

His faith remains active in the lives of his offspring: Eleanor is a medical doctor serving the Lord in the Kingdom of Jordan; Mary recently retired from a ministry in food service in a center for the handicapped; George is involved in prison ministries on a full-time basis; Addison is Professor of Missions at Covenant Theological Seminary.

I rejoice with them in their heritage.

I still detect their father's voice in the reading of the Word. He sounds especially close in the doxologies of Saint Paul. I can hear him now:

"Now unto the king eternal, immortal, invisible, the only wise God, be honor and glory, for ever and ever. Amen."

Amen.

TWENTY

Alexander Solzhenitsyn

by Malcolm Muggeridge

I HAD THE GREAT PRIVILEGE of interviewing Alexander Solzhenitsyn in May 1983, when he was in London to receive the annual Templeton Award. The interview took place in a private house, not in a TV studio, which in my experience always gives a flavor of unreality to words uttered and thoughts expounded. Solzhenitsyn and I sat at ease in armchairs, and soon became unconscious of the cameras and other TV gear. Our interpreter, a Russian lady from Cambridge University, was wonderfully skillful, to the point that I soon had a sense of talking directly with Solzhenitsyn, without any intermediary. Of the interview itself I can only say that in a lifetime of journalism involving many interviews the one with Solzhenitsyn impressed me more than any of the others with the exception of Mother Teresa and General de Gaulle.

After Khrushchev took over in the Kremlin and abolished every trace of Stalin, he amazed everyone by authorizing the publication

---

Note: Malcolm Muggeridge's interview with Alexander Solzhenitsyn was originally a BBC broadcast; an edited version of the interview was also published in the *Listener* in July 1983.

of Solzhenitsyn's novel *One Day in the Life of Ivan Denisovich,* which gave a devastating account of life in the labor camps, or "Gulag Archipelago" as Solzhenitsyn called them. The book's enormous success opened the way for Solzhenitsyn, had he so wished, to follow the example of Maxim Gorky, and make his peace with the Soviet regime and enjoy its favors—in Gorky's case, among other things, it was a villa in Italy and the freedom to come and go. I have a vivid memory of Gorky in 1932, when I was the *Manchester Guardian* correspondent in Moscow, seeming to sleepwalk on and off platforms on public occasions, looking for all the world like a performing seal—which is precisely what he was.

In the circumstances Solzhenitsyn could scarcely be sent back to the labor camps, nor, after *One Day in the Life of Ivan Denisovich,* was he likely to produce books suitable for publication in the USSR. So the authorities, to his great distress, forcibly exiled him, and he settled in America, in Vermont, to undertake the task he had set himself—to stand by his fellow prisoners, the *zeks,* and to, as he puts it, restore Russia's history, which, ever since the revolution of 1917, has had a great hole in it.

Here too, had he so wished, he could have established himself as the leading anti-Soviet exile. Instead, he lambasted the USA almost as severely as the USSR; for instance in his much-abused Harvard speech, and, more loftily, in his warning of what may befall the Western World as a consequence of the feebleness and moral confusion of those who shape its policies and direct its purposes. In a BBC broadcast he says: "We have become hopelessly enmeshed in our slavish worship of all that is pleasant, all that is comfortable, all that is material—we worship things, we worship products." Our conversation likewise conveys his wisdom and his prescience. The script follows. . . .

MALCOLM MUGGERIDGE: *When your three books about the Gulag were published they had a terrific impact. But I have the impression that with the passage of time people think that the prison camps are a thing of the past. Whereas, in actual fact, they are still very much in operation.*

ALEXANDER SOLZHENITSYN: There was a moment in our history when it seemed as though the Gulag Archipelago was indeed becoming something of the past. But this was a very brief moment and a deceptive one. The Gulag is still alive. In terms of cruelty it has not changed. It simply employs other forms of cruelty, making use of certain technical innovations. But in terms of its actual dimension, the Gulag Archipelago is indeed now smaller. In the past, it encompassed fifteen or twenty million people at one time. Now, the US State Department conservatively estimates that it consists of over four million people. According to emigré organizations which actually count the number of camps in existence, the Gulag now encompasses about six to seven million people. What has reduced the population? Not the kindness of the Soviet leaders. The reduction is due to the fact that Stalin, in his day, made an enormous advance in terms of horror and cruelty. He annihilated people far beyond the numbers that he needed to annihilate. And that created an inertia of horror. Now, only very little pressure is required in order to produce the desired result.

Would it be true to say that the free labor which the Gulag provides is an essential element in the Soviet economy?

This free labor has always been and still is essential. It is particularly used to accomplish jobs that no one else is willing to do, such as working with radioactive material where no protection is provided. Gulag labor is used to obtain radioactive material and to clean radioactive parts on submarines. These people, of course, die within a few months.

Do you think it possible that the Gulag apparatus could be removed from the Soviet regime without some violent upheaval in the USSR?

Violence is inherent in the communist system. The Gulag is an extreme manifestation of this violence. But there is a whole gradation of violence; so really your question should be turned round in this way: is communist totalitarianism possible without violence? The answer is no, not for one single day.

That makes it absolutely clear. In the US and the USSR there have been vast build-ups of nuclear weapons. Is it possible to imagine, given this situation, that we shall avoid nuclear war?

For some reason, I am convinced that there will be no nuclear war. There can be various explanations of why this conflict will not take place. If only, after 1945, the West had not disarmed itself, had not let all its armed forces disband but had retained conventional forces, then today there would be no danger of a nuclear confrontation. I won't go through all the possibilities, but I will consider one, and it is a very, very pessimistic variant. It is a possibility that arises as a result of ten years of concessions and capitulation. One of the reasons why there will not be a nuclear conflict is that the West has given in on the nuclear balance and has lost any kind of initiative in a balance of conventional forces. It is, therefore, very unprepared for subversion from within. Even without recourse to nuclear confrontation, there are all sorts of possibilities for the communist leaders.

I am a very old journalist, and people often ask me what I consider to be the most interesting or significant thing that has happened in the last fifty years. I tell them that the most important event is the revival of the Christian faith in the one place in the world where I would have expected it to have no chance of reviving. Would it be true to say that the efforts of the Soviet authorities to prevent any faith in Christianity or practice of the Christian religion has been a failure?

What you have said has a profound significance. For the last five or six decades all we have seen in many places in the world is the victory of communism. True, these are victories which don't really bring much good to people. They are not economic victories; they are not good, positive victories. They are really victories of power. In our country, the communist powers took military steps against the Christian faith. The signal for an attack against Christianity was given right at the very beginning by Lenin and Trotsky. The secret political police were mobilized against the faith. Millions of peasants were slaughtered in order to eradicate faith from the very roots of the people. Millions of hours of propaganda time were used in order to burn out faith from the hearts of the children. Yet, despite all that, we can say that after all these years communism has not destroyed the Christian faith. Christianity went through a period of decline, but now it is growing and reviving. That is the most hopeful sign that one can see anywhere, not only in my country, but anywhere in the world.

For the moment I see no end to the military victories of communism. It looks as though the shadow of communism is covering the earth more and more deeply. It is like an eclipse of the sun. But in an eclipse only a small portion of the earth is darkened, whereas with communism, it is half the earth which is in darkness, maybe even three-quarters. But because communism has already shown its weakness, its inability to destroy Christianity, we may hope that its shadow will gradually pass across and clear the earth. It will perhaps clear precisely those countries which have been in the deepest shadow until now.

It is amazing that Dostoevsky saw all this at least 100 years ago. Not only that, but he saw in The Devils *that the demon that would bring it all about was the demon of liberalism. I always think that you are rather like Dostoevsky.*

I never stop wondering, never stop marveling at the prophetic power, the prophetic vision of Dostoevsky. We already see happening what he foresaw in many parts of the world. But it is amazing that he saw the very first beginnings and sometimes even perceived things that had not yet begun in his time. When we think about our own times, it is amazing how often we return to Dostoevsky and can only marvel at how accurately he foresaw everything.

Dostoevsky wasn't supposed to be read in the Soviet Union. But now they've revived him. The fascinating thing to me, the most amazing ideological acrobatics that I've ever seen, is that they're trying to persuade us that Dostoevsky was a hangover from Karl Marx and that even Lenin, though he spoke severely about him, admired him.

There is no end to Marxist acrobatics. It's not only Dostoevsky who communists have, so to speak, colonized as an ally, but while attacking Christianity, they are ready to colonize our Lord Jesus Christ as well. The political atheist literature, in fact, maintains that Marxism continues what Christianity began, that it makes possible what Christianity failed to achieve. If this were only limited to the communist countries.... But this trick, this sleight of hand, we find throughout the world, because socialists everywhere constantly ascribe Christian virtues to themselves. Socialism is, in fact, absolutely opposed to Christianity. Christianity is founded on good will; whereas socialism is founded on violence or, if you like, on pressure. Nonetheless, socialism constantly tries to appear in a Christian guise, attempting to exploit what is, in fact, Christian.

Do you ever expect to go back to Russia?

In a strange way, I am inwardly absolutely convinced that I shall go back. I live with this simple conviction: I shall go back. I mean my own personal physical return, not just a return through my books. Now that contradicts any rational assumption. I am not so young and I can't point to any actual facts which make me say this. History is so full of unexpected things that some of the simplest facts in our lives we cannot foretell in advance.

You have lived in the West for several years. Do you think that we are fated to be swallowed up in this thing—that there will be a complete disintegration of our Christian civilization?

The threat is very much alive, very much present. If one were to speak merely of the simple advance, the push of communism, yes, it is very possible that communism may come to obscure the West. But, by the same law of the eclipse of the sun, the shadow shall pass. The West may escape this destiny, this fate. Maybe the West still has several decades of development before it. But if the West does not find in itself the spiritual forces, the spiritual strength to rise again, to find itself again, then, yes, Christian civilization will disintegrate. We use the same words to describe the same phenomenon: democracy. Democracy was originally developed before the face of God. And the foundation of its concept of equality was equality before God. But then the image of God receded, was pushed away by man. And this same democracy changed and acquired a very strange character. What is now demanded is an equality that favors mediocrity. The responsibility that each person had before God, this concept of responsibility has been lost. Whereas the so-called democratic institutions cannot exercise any force, any pressure. And so, having lost any concept of true responsibility, we are, so to speak, free to destroy our institutions and ourselves.

Do you think that the situation, then, is hopeless?

Thank God, and I mean thank God, the situation is never hopeless. In the USSR, you might say that we have lost everything and yet our position is not hopeless. I do not consider that human history has reached its ultimate point. The measures that we use are far too small, too short to really measure. The history of the decline of Christian civilization, the history of communism which has come into the world—all this will be measured in sections, but history will continue. The lesson that we—mankind, humanity—have to learn takes many centuries to learn.

I've thought about it a lot, and I've thought this: when we say Western civilization, we mean Christendom. And therefore we could say that Christendom is finished, but not Christ.

No, I would not like to take it upon myself to say that the social form of Christian life has gone forever. It may be that there are possibilities of change or development which we simply don't know about. And indeed, if it were not still present, then Christianity would be something that would be removed from us. It would, so to speak, ascend to the heavens. I think we shall see many forms of Christianity on earth.

I have heard that you feel it a duty to give Russia back its history.

As a writer it is my duty to speak in the name, not only of those who are in the Gulag and who died in the Gulag, but also in the name of those who died in the revolution. Yes, it is my aim to return to Russia the memory of its past. I have been working on this for forty-seven years. And in my work I have discovered that the year 1917 offers an extraordinarily compressed summary of the whole history of the twentieth century. The eight months from February to October 1917 in Russia are like an accelerated film. Now the film is being replayed in slow-motion throughout the whole world. I did not set out with the intention of explaining that to the world. My original aim was simply to return to Russia its own memory. But in the last few years, now that I have completed a number of volumes, I see that I have been writing something of the history of the whole twentieth century.

I was first in Russia as a young journalist in 1932-33. At that time everybody adulated Stalin in an utterly extravagant way, including many distinguished Western authors. Then came Khrushchev's speech at the Twentieth Party Congress. Suddenly all the busts of Stalin were removed, the statues were taken away. It was time to abolish Stalin. Do you think that they'll ever put him back?

There isn't really a need for this any more. It's enough simply to have the two models, Lenin and Marx. If there are too many in between, then the significance, the importance of the originals is diminished.

What about the ordinary Russian people? They are given this extraordinary idea of Stalin, this great man. Then they wake up one morning and hear he is not a great man after all. Do they start to think that perhaps his successor is not a great man either? Does it destroy their confidence?

Here, I think, for the Western mind, history has been written inaccurately. Even in the thirties, I knew scores of people who had absolutely no respect for Stalin. In the villages, it was the most uneducated, the simplest people. So really, the sort of dethronement of Stalin was no event and no surprise to them. It was a shock at the highest levels of the Soviet intelligentsia, for the communist elite, and for the so-called progressive western circles who actually believed in Stalin. Khrushchev's speech at the Twentieth Party Congress only opened the eyes of those who had willfully deceived themselves. In the camps we all shouted hooray when we heard that Stalin had died. Those who wept were the young fourteen- and fifteen-year-old girls in the communist youth movement.

I've always been very interested in underground publishing in the USSR, what is called the samizdat. *Are your books coming out through the* samizdat?

In the Soviet Union, *samizdat* is the dissemination of texts by the person, or by the people who have actually written them. To this day various sort of declarations and statements are made through *samizdat* and distributed through *samizdat.* Serious works of research in religion and in philosophy, for example, are also distributed through *samizdat.* When I was still living in the Soviet Union, there was quite a lively distribution of literary work through *samizdat.* Two of my novels, *The First Circle* and *Cancer Ward,* were very widely distributed and read precisely through *samizdat.* But when I began being widely published in the West, people preferred to try and get one of those editions. Yes, my books do penetrate into the Soviet Union, though not in enormous numbers, but they certainly do penetrate. Every book is read by perhaps fifty to sixty people. For example, whenever someone's flat is searched, among the objects found will be a book of mine. It means an enormous amount to me to know that my books do get to Russian readers and that they are available there.

You've been living in America. Have you been dreaming the American dream?

In America I was able to realize that which I had always dreamed about—that all my life should be a life of work. In the Soviet Union I could never devote myself entirely to literature. I had to earn my livelihood by some other means. Also, I could never keep all my books or all that I had written in my own flat, in my own house. At any moment, whether day or night, I had to expect a search by the KGB. So every evening I had to think, now where shall I hide this? I kept so few manuscripts within reach that sometimes when I had to compare two sections, say two texts of the *Gulag Archipelago*, I couldn't do so, because one or the other of them wasn't there. And I had hardly any access to a library. And, of course, emigré editions were totally inaccessible. Whereas now, I have five or six tables full of manuscripts and books. My life from early morning till late at night consists of working on my writing. No exception is made for any holidays or journeys anywhere. And I really do feel that at last I am doing that for which I was born. But all this is, so to speak, illumined by the sun, the light that is my hope of returning to my country.

Solzhenitsyn and the Consensus

It has fascinated me to see how the media have decided to go after Solzhenitsyn because he has not played the Emigre Game as they consider it should be played. Instead of gratefully finding himself in what we still call the Free World and being duly thankful, he has ventured to point out that the Free World is not really a Free World at all, and that freedom is not what it purports to be in our so-called Free World.

What has given the consensus people the feeling that

Solzhenitsyn was not after all their particular hero has been his insistence that what he is concerned about much more than ideologies is Christianity. Furthermore, he has stated that the only way in which Russia can find its way back to a real existence is through Christ, and that his answer to the Gulag Archipelago is Christianity, not liberalism. This goes dead against consensus considerations—a man brought up in the USSR, and coming from a labor camp, stands up and says that the answer to it all has nothing to do with "One Man, One Vote!"; it has everything to do with Christ.

All kinds of criticisms have been developed. For instance, articles are written suggesting that Solzhenitsyn wants to re-establish Tsarism, which is nonsensical. What he does say is that men are not made free by being allowed, and having the means, to do what they like. In the second Gulag book, in a chapter called "The Ascent," he says that it was in the prison camp that he learnt what freedom is, and that the line between Good and Evil runs, not between countries, not between classes, not between political parties, but down each separate individual heart. And he adds: "Thank you, camps, for teaching me this truth." Then there are the subversives who want to believe that there is a possible compromise between the so-called Free World and the communist world—as it might be vegetarians and the Worshipful Company of Butchers seated together on the same platform.

To me Solzhenitsyn is like a projection of Dostoevsky, whom he even somewhat resembles. Some years ago, on the occasion of the centenary of Dostoevsky's death, I went to the USSR to do the commentary for a TV program on him. It came as a surprise that anything of the kind should be permitted; ever since the Revolution he had been anathema and his works suppressed, but now the ban has been lifted, and he is once again a popular and greatly admired author, despite his anti-Marxist and anti-revolutionary attitudes. To bring about this change, the most amazing dialectical acrobatics were required. Almost the last thing Dostoevsky did was to deliver an extraordinary address at the unveiling of a Pushkin Memorial in 1880, which delighted all the so-called reactionary elements in Tsarist Russia. When we were recording our program and came to Dostoevsky's great oration, I found myself walking about the streets where the Pushkin Memorial stood, and echoing the English translation of Dostoevsky's speech. Somehow, although no one could understand them, they boded good.

More clearly than any other commentator in the world today Solzhenitsyn sees the dangers that encompass us all. In a murky time he represents what is noble and wonderful in human life. A very great man.